WITHDRAWN

D1504432

In Praise of *Citizen So*

THE BOSTON HERALD'S Laura Raposa writes..."Stories of Howie Winter and his lieutenants are legendary in Boston, but 'Citizen Somerville' brings them back to life with a bonus: the stories behind the stories. The underworld dramas in the Boston burg have made headlines for decades, but we've never heard from the supporting cast, namely the women and children. Their tales make for an eye-opening, fascinating read."

NEW REVIEW: "Bobby Martini and Elayne Keratsis have written a truly magnificent work. A gripping account of the Winter Hill Gang and other remarkable events that occurred in and around Boston over a span of many decades. It's one of the best books that I've read in a long time. Get it today!"
—— Ed Begley, Jr., actor and activist

NEW REVIEW: "An instant classic....written by a true insider. Bobby Martini's account of Boston's legendary Winter Hill gang will have you turning pages late into the night. The stories are dripping with authenticity, and the rough-and-tumble characters within are alternately harrowing and hilarious. A great read!"
—— writer/director Bobby Farrelly

CITIZEN SOMERVILLE

Growing Up With The Winter Hill Gang

CITIZEN SOMERVILLE

Growing Up With The Winter Hill Gang

BOBBY MARTINI
&
ELAYNE KERATSIS

Powder House Press
North Reading, Massachusetts

CITIZEN SOMERVILLE
Growing Up With The Winter Hill Gang

Published by
Powder House Press
North Reading, MA
USA

For information, contact:
citsomemail@gmail.com

ISBN: 9780982991503

First Edition: October 2010

www.citizensomerville.com

Front Cover Photograph
Photographer: Philip Wages
Designer: Barbara Peterson-Malesci
Art Director: Danny Davilla

Print-Ready Cover and Text Preparation:
John A. Oberteuffer

WGA Registered #1267967

For Rob Martini
Beloved son

"Everything happens for a reason."

~ Robert Vincent Martini

How To Write A Book

THREE YEARS AGO I decided to write down a few stories, events in my life that, quite frankly, I had forgotten over the years. Memories that resurfaced with age as I had hit the half-century mark and almost overnight my life changed. When I was younger, I'd been a street brawler, an amateur fighter and a backyard athlete, when suddenly I was in a hospital bed looking at the ceiling after extensive neck surgery and wondering what the hell I was going to do with my body for the second half of my life.

My partner, EK (Elayne Keratsis), and I met on a movie set in Miami and after listening to some of the old stories she encouraged me to write them down. I did and she turned them into a pretty amazing film script. It was my life and all of the past that inhabited it. A year later I was recovering from surgery and housebound. Stir crazy, I picked up EK's screenplay again. Then I truly knew that she was the one I could trust to help me write the story of all citizens Somerville.

I wasn't a writer. The extent of my reading revolved around the sports pages, but back when I was a cop I was a hell of a typist and they say you never lose it. So I hunkered down in front of the computer and started banging the keys. It wasn't the same as hitting the bag, but it helped break the monotony of healing. Writing was slow and painful at first. With thousands of words, how do you go about the daunting task of isolating the best ones and putting them in correct order to make sense? Then you have to string those sentences together into a paragraph that tells a story with impact without switching ideas until you complete a thought. How the hell anyone from New England ever manages to complete a manuscript is beyond me. Rapid-fire changing of subjects is our birthright! I've never been a Stephen King fan but I have a whole new respect for him now. All of those words – unbelievable!

I typed in all caps so I didn't have to be bothered with which words were the important ones. Since I'd never written before, they *all* seemed pretty important to me, until it was brought to my attention that caps are the equivalent of screaming. Punctuation seemed a waste of time and that stemmed from the staccato delivery of Massachusetts dialogue. Since we seldom stop talking, run-on sentences were my specialty.

If you're not from Massachusetts, you'll probably think you're seeing a great deal of typos, but we pretty much dispense with words "at" and "in." If you're down in your cellar, you simply say, "I'm down the cellar." So if Howie Winter wants you "up" Marshall Motors, you shouldn't worry too much about the "at" part, you should just go. Quickly.

We also like to add the word "the" for other purposes. For example, if I want you to come over for a few beers and to watch the ball game on TV, I'll say "Come ovah, we're gonna watch **the** football." Maybe it just elevates a subject to a level of greater importance. More on that later.

Tense was and still is a big problem. I was constantly correcting myself, trying to figure out the differences between "I went down the prison," "I'm going to the prison," and "I will go to the prison." Hopefully, I'm close. Not to prison, though.

EK and I agonized over dialogue. Until you start writing, you don't realize how it sounds to an outsider. I worried we should correct grammar – especially my own. There was a real concern readers would scrutinize quotes like "I come down the bar" instead of wondering why the hell the speaker went to a bar where there was sure to be trouble. Should we correct it to protect people who had given their time (and secrets) to us in good faith?

And when anyone asked what I was doing for hours at the computer, I'd reply, "I'm typing."

Eventually all of that fell away. We wrote the words we heard; the local vernacular, mine included. You cannot tell a story like this without allowing the citizens to speak for themselves. Not one of them has reason to be embarrassed or the need for my protection. The citizens of Somerville can take quite good care of themselves, as I am sure you will discover.

I learned to punctuate by reading the pages back and forth with my partner for hours, looking for natural pauses, stops and starts. I still like a long sentence. Now I try to split the difference so you don't require a bathroom break in the middle of any of them. Semicolons are still a mystery to me.

Content evolved. I hate to admit it, but in the beginning much of it was "cop talk", the dry reporting verbiage so often spoofed. I wrote story after story about fistfights and bar brawls. Once I got the hang of it, I had pages of anecdotes but it wasn't very satisfying. Yet I wasn't just typing any more. If the guys called me up for a few beers, I found myself saying, "I can't right now, *I'm writing.*"

Then I surprised myself and did something I never guessed I'd enjoy - reading for pleasure. I'm not illiterate, it's simply that reading for fun or escape was never part of my adolescence. I had no desire to escape the fun I was *already* having by burying my nose in a book. My Teamster job already required tremendous amounts of reading; scripts, schedules, memos. But I wanted to see what, if anything, I'd savor about reading solely to enjoy a story.

I read quite a few. From historical non-fiction to Jim Thompson's crime noir (and I learned what "noir" meant), I staggered and reeled with Bukowski and roamed the streets of Boston with Lehane's detectives. I walked the beat with Ken Bruen's Irish Guards and understood as I once was police, ran with Scissors and struggled with a Dunce from a distant Confederacy. Holden Caulfield became a close friend even though he was stuck at seventeen and I was well into my fifth decade. I was shocked to discover Fredo Corleone was gay and shed an acceptable guy tear as I shared Tom Hagen's last few moments. I was amazed at how easy it was to fall effortlessly into a book and become lost in the story.

What I enjoyed most was seeing how other writers chose their words and arranged them perfectly to make me feel as if I were in the same room with the characters, how conflicts were resolved and how to restrain myself from flipping to the last page because I couldn't wait to see what happened. As months went by, I realized I didn't just want to write – I wanted to write a real story about real people. The ones I knew were from Somerville. And the story that inspired me most – the life of Howie Winter and the fact he lived long enough to tell it, if he chose to do so.

Howie has been reluctant to have his life spread across the printed page. As the decades since his time on The Hill rolled by, he's been quite happy to rest his past in the shadows of those who came after him. A succession of writers pitched scenarios for a biography. He always politely declined.

"I don't mind telling it," he said. "But I do mind having my words twisted. I've been misquoted so many times I've lost count. I'll tell the truth and where you can dig up the facts to back it up, but if writers aren't interested in the truth, I'm not interested in talking to them."

From the start we wanted the truth. Howie, EK and I agreed on very few rules. He asked we not write about his children, except for my own close relationship with his late son Gary. His family life was private. We were free to ask any questions we cared to but he could choose not to answer those he felt would hurt the families of his old friends. "You can ask me anything you'd like. I won't lie to you," he promised, "But I'll tell you if I don't want to answer. Other than that, have at it. It might be fun."

Three years and hundreds of interview hours later, I don't know how much fun it was for any of the interviewees. It was very painful for me at times, but we got through it. Despite the fact I am getting better at choosing words, in this instance I cannot find the right ones. I can only thank all of the citizens Somerville for allowing me complete access to their lives, patience and dignity as we traveled that very long road. I'm forever grateful for the gift of words and privilege of friendships. And to the city of Somerville.

"This is a very unique city – Somerville. The best way to illustrate it is to tell you about every St. Paddy's Day."

What the rest of the country refers to as "St. Patrick's Day."

Originally, the term "Paddy" was used by the British to refer to any Irishman. It was a terrible slur. It evolved into the Irish equivalent of the "N" word; acceptable for Irish guys to call each other Paddy, but heaven help any Italian who used it. Now it's a generally accepted nickname and the short form of Patrick. So here, in the most Irish part of the U.S. we celebrate St. *Paddy's* Day.

Tom Leahy has had sixty-one of them. Trim and rangy, he looks like an ex-jock of the swimmer or soccer variety, most comfortable in sweats and sneakers. He's a lifelong resident of Somerville.

"I'm still here, unlike some other people."

He smiles, at the same time casting a sidelong glance at me. An expatriate, I don't live in Somerville anymore and I know he feels it's his duty to remind me.

But even though my address is not Somerville, I'm still here in my heart. I couldn't escape if I tried.

"The city of Somerville is probably the greatest city in the world. Everybody is like family, even those who don't like each other. On St. Paddy's Day we'd all make our rounds. We'd start at one end of Broadway and go all the way to Teele Square."

In a unique sort of parade, residents traveled through the streets stopping at every watering hole pretending to commemorate the death of St. Patrick or insisting they were paying respect to the saint who drove the snakes out of Ireland (they never really had any). In reality, it was *the* traditional communal drinking holiday in a predominantly Irish burg. The biggest one anyway, we also had Christmas, Thanksgiving, New Years, Bunker Hill Day, you get the idea.

"Everyone knew each other. Seldom were there strangers in sight. Not everybody got along, but God forbid an interloper tried mixing it up with one of the locals. That local might be your worst enemy, but if an outsider went after him, the whole city rallied to his defense."

The translation? We might have had a few assholes in Somerville, but they were our assholes and nobody was going to fuck with them.

During our childhoods many residents were steeped in poverty. Yet out of that impoverishment, we grew athletes, politicians, college graduates, artists, writers and yes, some criminals. We had families who stuck together and who took care of each other and their neighbors.

Tom Leahy sprung from a medium-sized Irish family.

"I'm the oldest of seven children."

Yeah, me too. He settles back in his chair, as do I. There are no short stories in Somerville.

His father worked for the phone company, a job that paid well in the sixties. Although the Irish Gang Wars were unfolding in the streets, Tom's father was careful to stay out of the turmoil, even as his close friends divided up between the two bloody sides. But there was still a Leahy funeral on the horizon.

"I was sixteen years old when my father was killed in a car accident on New Year's Eve. My God, it was tough. One of the first people who showed up at our house after my father's death was Howie Winters."

Tom uses the locally accepted version of Howie's last name. As a teenager steeped in deep shock, he was aware of who Howie was but didn't know him personally.

"Yet he seemed to have genuine concern for us, that I still remember. Just after the funeral, bags and bags of food began showing up."

It was a godsend to Tom's mother, now faced with the dilemma of how to feed seven children. Relatives with good intentions wanted to split the kids up and parcel them out to different households to lessen the burden, but Tom fought them and won. The kids stayed together. So Howie began to keep an eye on the Leahys, Tom surmises, now that there was no father to ride over the herd.

"As time went on, we just accepted that he'd always be there. Howie gave us a sense of security. There was someone who was there for us if we needed it. He was generous, loyal and always there."

Gradually Howie became part of the Leahy family, an Irish Godfather of sorts. He was at weddings, graduations, sporting events and the funeral of Mrs. Leahy.

When Tom graduated from high school, he was accepted at several colleges but there were the younger children to consider. He didn't want to leave them alone. Tom got a job with the phone company and installed all of Howie's telephones.

"I wouldn't take money. I was happy to do anything to pay him back in some small way."

Tom was also offered other sorts of opportunities, as many of the young guys were, to engage in darker activities within Somerville but he tried hard to stay on a straight path.

"It's not that I was better than anyone else, I just had the other kids to look out for. Howie had a good deal to do with us staying close and on the straight and narrow. We are still very close to this day."

And the Somerville standby to drinking and fighting – athletics – was there for Tom. "I played everything, full baseball games before school in the mornings and basketball after school."

When Howie was sent to prison, it was confusing to the Leahys. "We not only missed the security of knowing he was there, we didn't understand how they [the government] could have taken him away from the entire neighborhood."

Now that Tom is older, he finds it sad on an even larger scale. "I think that the very organization we thought was there to protect us, the FBI, turned out to be a bunch of guys that sank so low."

He is referring to the decade-long FBI scandal in which the Boston Bureau had agents courting informants and cozying up to certain gangsters under the guise of attempting to convict others. The plan deteriorated into a scandalous mess when it became evident that the same agents eventually become tools of the crime lords themselves; cover for their various charges and essentially becoming accomplices to mob murders. One result of this state-sanctioned crime spree was the downfall of Howie Winter at the hands of two of his closest associates – and their friends at the Federal Bureau of Investigation.

"Bobby, this isn't the first time I've said these things, just for your interview I mean," Tom says, with a touch of anger. "I've said this before and will say it again, Howie never did anything to or for my family that wasn't completely above board and with concern. I've heard all the stories but I talk about things I *know*, not things I've *heard*."

The things people say about Somerville. And all of us.

Then he smiles. "That's why I'm glad you're doing this, Bobby. The story of Howie and this unique city. People used to call us 'Slumerville.' First when the Italians moved in, then the Brazilians, African Americans, whoever was different. 'What's happening to Somerville?' I'd hear it all the time."

Boston and the surrounding cities have never been known for tolerance of anyone who is different – which is another way of saying "not Irish."

"What happened to Somerville? I'll tell you. It made it better! People outside don't realize that as different kinds of folks moved in, they didn't change Somerville. They *became* Somerville. They became part of us. Somerville was and it still is a great city. I hope it always stays the same – keeps that feeling of family. You're doing a good thing."

I have a twinge of regret, guilt even, when I leave Tom. I love Somerville as well, but I know that not every story I will tell shows our city in its best light at first glance.

My hope is that the violent stories, descriptions of the pain and loss that are also Somerville, along with the memories of those of us who lived to tell the tales, will help to underscore that despite those very events, we always took care of our own. Or at least most of us did.

I lived in Somerville most of my life and half of it I've spent reading about us - the collective Citizens Somerville - in newspapers from The Boston Globe to The LA Times and all papers in between.

Tom thinks of us as a family but we are also known, in media circles, as the burg that spawned the seed of the Irish Mob in the United States – the Winter Hill Gang - and the home of the infamous Irish Gang Wars that spanned years and resulted in the murders of over sixty men on our streets.

The Winter Hill Gang is, in essence, Our Gang.

We are also the focal point in the country's largest FBI scandal as dozens of agents got into bed with some of the most vicious organized crime figures of the twentieth century.

What we are not known for is being a city of one hundred thousand crammed into four square miles. Four squares of fights and families, crime and compromise, murder, mayhem, death and dignity, and yes, approximately two hundred barrooms.

Some of these stories readers may have heard before. But I am telling them truthfully - by using the words of the individuals who experienced them. Many of them run contrary to newspaper stories and previously published books.

Before anyone jumps up and down, screaming that this book is going to be a whitewash, another "I Didn't Do Nothin', It Was All Someone Else's Fault!" book, let me put that to rest right away. It's not. In fact, this isn't a Mob tale at all. It's a story about a bunch of guys with wives and girlfriends and children who lived in the same city I grew up in.

You've read about them before. But somewhere in between all the articles, books and documentaries, the half-truths mixed up with the lies, exists the city of Somerville, Massachusetts and what really happened in and around a small neighborhood called Winter Hill.

And it's a story about me - Bobby Martini - and my old man.

I have an idea there'll be a few people plenty pissed off by the time we get to the last page, but try and remember this; I won't tell you anything about anyone that I wouldn't admit to doing myself. I might have my regrets about some of the things I've done, but fifty-six years into it, I'm not ashamed. What I did over the years – good and bad - made me the man I am today.

The most important thing in life to me is how it all plays out in the end, and - if it were all worth it, would I do it all over the same way? I'm still here, so I guess I have to say yes, it was worth it.

And I'd do it all again, *but I wouldn't do any more of it now.*

So if anyone takes offense at my version, what else can I say other than my own family was right in the middle of it all and I heard it from the horse's mouth?

We are the sum total of our crazy, painful history. At least that's true of all of us, the Citizens Somerville. Maybe you too.

So, until we reach the end of this book together,

Bobby Martini & Elayne Keratsis 2008

A New England Winter

WE BURIED HOWIE Winter's son Gary on a cold February morning, just days after his fiftieth birthday.

The cemetery was stark, the trees stripped by the harsh winter. As I tried to concentrate on the priest's cadence, my mind wandered across the large crowd of mourners who had braved the chill to see Gary to his final rest.

His girlfriend Marlene stood by the grave, expressionless. I was sure she was still in shock. Although his health had been deteriorating, Gary's sudden passing still ripped the rug out from under all of us.

Ellen Brogna, Gary's stepmother and dear friend, was there alone; the Bureau of Prisons had denied her husband's request to attend his own son's funeral.

Gary's brother Young Howie supported his three sisters. The girls were crying. They'd recently reconciled with their brother only days before his death.

My sister Patty made it despite worsening physical problems. As she wiped her eyes with a tissue, I wondered if she was thinking of her husband's funeral eighteen years ago. He'd been gunned down in cold blood at the Boston pier.

Annemarie Sperlinga and her husband Bobby McCarthy also attended. She and Gary had known each other from childhood. Annemarie was the daughter of Howie's former partner, Sal Sperlinga, the bookmaker shot to death by a drug dealer as he played cards at a social club one afternoon in 1980.

And so many more. Sal and Howie's old friend Willy Cellata, my brother Leo, our friends John Baino and Vinny Champa, Willy Medeiros who drove the legally blind Gary up to visit his father in prison, Linda and Kenny Swift; his friends and de facto caretakers, the faces blended into each other. Scores of people I'd known my whole life were huddled together against one New England winter in order to pay their respects to another.

I could also feel the ghosts of the past hovering around us. Buddy McLean, Sal, my father, my brothers Eddie and Joey, Brian Halloran, all of them gone on ahead but somehow still here in Somerville.

There had been a time in my life when I never even considered the possibility I'd someday spend a great deal of time at wakes and funerals, but that time had past. And here I was again.

Instead of bitching about being hung-over after what was supposed to be a spectacular celebration of Gary's half century, I was standing in the cemetery watching him being lowered into the ground and thinking about, of all things, Roberta Woods' breasts.

Gary had been diagnosed with diabetes ten years prior and soon after had gone blind. A bus accident only added to his debilitated condition. But Gary was always strong in spirit, and even though he had lost his sight, he retained his soul. And a wicked sense of humor. One night he and I were at a party at the Irish American Club in Malden and I took Gary into the bathroom.

While I was at the urinal, he asked me where he could wash his hands. I looked over at him and then down at my privates, pointed and said, "Right over here, Gary."

Gary started to make his way over to the urinal when another patron in the bathroom looked over at me. "That's not very nice," he scolded. Gary heard him and started laughing like hell.

"Listen pal," I said to the guy, "If it was me that was the blind one, he would have already had my head in the urinal."

As we left the bathroom, we ran into a girl neither of us had seen since high school. Roberta Woods. *The* Roberta Woods. Roberta had the biggest set of breasts in Somerville High School. The fact that she could open the double doors in the school hallways with those puppies before her hands could reach them was always a source of our undying admiration. She was still hot and she was happy to see us. Roberta immediately started talking, bringing us up to date with local gossip, but Gary didn't recognize her voice. He leaned over to me.

"Bobby, who is it? Who are ya talking to?"

I reached over and grabbed his hands in mine and placed one on each of Roberta's huge breasts.

"Gary, guess who?"

A big grin spilt Gary's face. "Roberta!" Gary exclaimed. "How the hell are you?"

Roberta smiled back at Gary and shook her head at us. But she didn't push Gary's hands away. Instead she looked right into my face.

"Bobby, you are one sick bastard."

That was probably true. There were quite a few of us in Somerville that had all been called worse on occasion. But on that cold day in February, watching them lower Gary Winter into the ground, I was also one very sad bastard.

CHAPTER ONE

The Last Stand-Up Guy
An Introduction to Howie Winter

1962. MY FATHER, Bob Martini Sr., was playing cards with a few Somerville cronies in a second floor apartment located at the Mystic Ave projects. The air was rich with cigarette smoke and cigar fumes although the game stakes were very low. Most of the players were older and ex-military, the projects at that time almost strictly affordable housing for veterans and their families. Bob liked the old guys, they were full of stories about days past and it was a brief respite from his small cramped apartment filled with a wife and seven kids. One old marine tossed out some coins, opened his mouth to proclaim his bet and was reduced to a fit of phlegm-filled coughing.

"Oh for Chrissakes!" Bob threw his cards down in disgust.

"I keep sayin' if somebody don't open a window, we're never gonna get through this game."

He shoved his chair away from the table.

"Fine by me," grumbled the grunt, "I'm losing so bad I might as well stay here until I die."

The man to his left mumbled, "What you should do is try and win so you can get on an iron lung!"

Another old-timer leaned his cards protectively into his chest as Bob rounded his corner of the table. He was a retired sailor with a drawer full of medals and a brutal sense of humor.

"Ya, you're losin', Bob. Don't think I don't see ya, comin' around and readin' our cards!"

"Uh oh..." murmured someone else. Even in jest, intimating that a Somerville guy was a cheat was one small step above calling him a rat – and everyone knew what kind of response you'd get back for that comment.

But Bob just laughed good-naturedly as he maneuvered his way around the wooden chairs, pretending to grab at the cards.

"Ya, that's right we worked it all out before we got here. I told him to wait until I'm finally winnin' for a change and then to pretend he's coughin' up a lung just so I can get up and try to take a look at your...."

The deafening sound of a massive blast reverberated up the side of the building. Bob felt the sturdy floor shudder under his feet, he watched, uncomprehendingly, as a huge sheet of metal and flame shot upward past the window. He reached out to the table to grab hold. Cards and coins jumped up, beers spilled dark across the tablecloth.

"Get down!" Bob yelled. The men hit the floor instinctively. One elderly (and remarkably spry) fellow dove under the table. In any another town in America, a bunch of army guys would have been flooded with Pearl Harbor memories, but not here in Somerville.

In this town, a small civil war was waging. As the men lay on the floor covering their heads, they were all thinking the same thing.

"The fuckin' Irish are at it again!"

They themselves were all Irish, at least in part, but a different generation. They weren't fighting in this local war. They waited together as if in a foxhole. A moment. Then another. No machine gun fire, no car tires screeching a getaway. Slowly my father started to get to his feet.

"Stay away from the window, Bob!" The phlegmy marine whispered loudly.

"Yeah, yeah," my old man muttered as he ape-walked across the room until he was at an angle to see down to the street. A small

cloud of smoke hung in the air over a car and he could hear neighbors beginning to venture out.

"What was it?"

"How many dead?"

"Is anyone down there alive?"

Bob motioned for them to get up. "It's OK, it's not the building. It's just a car bomb."

"Oh Christ!" The sailor grumbled as his bones creaked upright. "I hope it didn't hit mine by mistake, the old lady will kill me."

If the bombers who would eventually claim responsibility for the blast were the ones Bob figured they were, it was a group notorious for fucking up their murder attempts.

Bob craned his neck closer to the window. "I dunno, can't see." But his stomach rolled. He might know but if he did not say, maybe it wouldn't be true.

The men slowly pulled themselves up off the floor. They filed out the door and joined the small cadre of residents headed down the stairs.

In the street, what was left of a formerly full-sized automobile was still smoking. Bob took a deep breath and cautiously stepped forward with a sense of death-dread. He knew the owner of this car very well. The vehicle belonged to Howie Winter, the reputed head, along with childhood friend Buddy McLean, of Somerville's Irish mob, the Winter Hill Gang.

Members of the rival McLaughlin Gang from neighboring Charlestown were stepping up efforts to wipe out their Somerville counterparts and car bombings, although unsuccessful to date, seemed to be their favorite manner of execution.

As the smoke cleared and police sirens grew louder, Bob's lungs released, air rushing out. Howie was not in the car, nor was anyone else. The front seat was just a mass of melted plastic and mangled steel. "Jesus," coughed the Marine behind him. "Howie was fuckin' lucky." The others agreed, that luck of the semi-Irish still held occasionally.

Bob shook his head, his fear gone and replaced with his usual bravado.

"Fuckin' McLaughlins, I swear to Christ, they couldn't blow a trike to bits with an atom bomb!"

His friends laughed. From a distance, they saw flashing lights. "Might as well go play some cards," the sailor said. "There's as much smoke down here as there was up there."

The guys headed back to the card game. The cops would round the corner any second. They hadn't seen anything and of course they'd report they had no idea who the car belonged to nor why anyone would destroy it, so best not to be questioned. The warriors knew without saying that as soon as the debris was cleared, the wreck's skeleton towed and cops gone, the card game would end. Then, despite the fact they were not directly involved, the card players would have other business to address.

As they mounted the steps, Bob turned and took one more look at his friend's car. A photo of Howie removing what few unsinged belongings survived would dominate the next day's front pages in the local papers.

Goddamn, he thought. You were fuckin' lucky, Howie. Maybe that's the last time you'll have to dodge a bullet. Maybe now it'll all be over.

But really, it was just the beginning.

Let me introduce you to Howard T. "Howie" Winter. Howie Winter, at seventy-eight, is still dapper and meticulous in dress and appearance and gentlemanly in his manner. Somerville's most famous — or infamous — retiree, depending on who you ask or what you may have read, is a man I've known my whole life. He was a dear friend of my father's and is now one of mine. On this, our first in a series of semi-formal-not-just-shooting-the-shit interviews, he's dressed in a perfectly ironed shirt and dress pants, short gray hair trimmed, wire rimmed glasses in place.

The newspapers called Howie, in his days on the streets, the head of the Irish Mob; the Winter Hill Gang that ran certain parts of Boston, most notably the Somerville area called Winter Hill.

Despite local legend, it is simply coincidence that Winter Hill and Howie Winter share the name of the loneliest season. Somerville's Winter Hill community was named for the large hill that rests in the neighborhood and not for the infamous The Winter Hill Gang.

The Irish Mob, the Irish Mafia, and Howie - the Irish Gangster.

"Am I Irish or am I the Irish Gangster?" Howie repeats the question with a twinkle in his blue eyes. "Which question do you want me to answer?"

I defer to Howie that which he chooses to answer. He ticks off the points on his fingers.

"Well, let's see. My mother was Irish and English. My great-great grandmother came over from County Cork – and by the way, when she came over she had a letter with her, attesting to the fact that she was a good girl. That's the way they did it in those days. I was born on St. Paddy's Day in 1929. So yes, I guess you could say I am Irish."

"Your father?" I want to hear some more about Howie's roots.

"A little bit Irish," he smiles, because as every Irishman insists, there's no such thing. You are or you aren't, there's no escaping it by trying to dilute it, even with English beer or an Italian last name.

"Dad was from Jersey. He was of German descent, part Irish and some Sicilian that slipped into the family somehow."

Howie's Sicilian background is a little known fact. Things are different now in our city than they were years ago. No Irishman wanted to admit he was part Italian and vice versa. Guys like me, with an Italian last name and an Irish face, couldn't couch the cross breeding, but everyone else usually rode their last name and hung with that group. I can remember what a real shock it was to my Italian buddies that hung down the local corner when they finally discovered that actor Robert DeNiro was actually part Irish. For me it was an ethnic godsend.

Howie laughs. He's always moved easily between local descendants of the two countries. "No one ever asked me if I had any Italy in me, but I'm proud of both my parents' backgrounds. My dad was a Boston cop and rode a Harley Davidson, if you can believe that. We called him the original biker."

Sure I can, my old man rode a Harley.

Howie grew up within the four square miles that encompass Somerville, Massachusetts, the most densely populated city in New England and the fifth densest municipality under 100,000 in the United States. So did I. Somerville is just north of Boston, but decades ago it may has well been across the country. It's a town so stubborn and set in its ways that in 1842, it separated from neighboring Charlestown and became its own entity. The rivalry between the two cities survives even today but not nearly as deadly as it was in the 1960s during which a gang war blossomed and left over sixty families fatherless.

Somerville was a city built and inhabited by the blue-collar working class and due to the amount of poor, coupled with the rising crime rates, it was for many years referred to by uppity Bostonians as "Slumerville." Despite the fact that in the early twentieth century, some real estate offices posted signs on rental properties that read "Irish Catholics need not apply", the city has always been predominantly Irish and Italian and it has just been over the past few decades that varying ethnicities have moved in.

Gentrification of Somerville has been an ongoing project but although reducing the crime rate and renovating buildings makes for higher real estate values, there are some things about the city that will never change no matter how many condos they build. That's the history of us, who we are, and how we came to be.

Boston is full of famous genealogy from politicians and a president, to actors, writers, painters and, yes, Whitey Bulger. But Somerville is a different country. Our whole world was in that four square miles and this is the story of all of us Citizens Somerville. We've also had some famous residents who dropped stakes in the city for a time, including a Harvard Law student who racked up seventeen parking tickets and $400 in fines by the name of Barack Obama, but the most recognizable of our own spawn is Howard T. "Howie" Winter.

Somerville is also, by the way, the birthplace of Marshmallow "Fluff", that thick white crème spread. A decades-old routine for any Massachusetts mother worth her salt is packing a "Fluff-N-Nutter" sandwich in her kid's lunch box – white bread, peanut butter and Fluff. Or at least it was in the days before trans fat and the South Beach Diet. Invented in 1917 and sold door to door by resident Archibald Query, it is never ever to be confused with any other brand of marshmallow crème. That's a big deal up here, not that it has a damn thing to do with this story.

"I was actually born in West Roxbury," Howie likes the facts to be correct. "Which is not to be taken as Roxbury, it's a bigger town out by the Dedham line and it was an upscale community. I was born in 1929, and unfortunately, my family went broke before I had the chance to enjoy any of those privileges. When he lost his police job, my father and mother also lost the house. But her family was from Somerville so we migrated back."

By 1937 Somerville, along with the rest of the country, was in complete financial disarray as the Great Depression deepened.

Howie's father became a machinist. His mother went to work in the Charlestown Navy shipyard, one of only six yards established during the American Revolution to build warships for the country. Way after we dumped all that tea into Boston Harbor, New Englanders were still committed to keeping the British at bay. The Civil War came along and brought in more business as the North went balls to the wall, blocking every Southern port and harbor with ships. In an interesting turn of events, during World War II, the Charlestown yard was kept busy repairing British warships damaged by the Germans.

At the time Howie's mother was employed, the facility was open twenty-hour hours a day and over 45,000 workers toiled for the war effort.

"Horrible to say," Howie admits, "but that war put everyone back to work in 1939 who suffered so badly during the Depression."

There was also the start of the WPA, the Works Progress Administration in 1935 that provided jobs and food for those suffering the effects of poverty.

"We started to do a little bit better, but it wasn't enough. My brothers Bill and Norman went to live with my aunts who helped out. My brother Bob and I stayed with my parents. We just didn't have enough money."

Being poor was one thing, being dirt poor was something else. Like just about everyone in Somerville, Howie lived in a coldwater flat. Summer or winter, no hot water. In New England that was painful. Some days before school he, along with some of his buddies, stopped by the Somerville Vocational School ("You could take a hot shower for three cents!" he informs me, and it was much quicker than boiling water on the stove and trying to fill the bathtub before the chill set in.) After school and before work, they scoured the railroad tracks for coal that might have fallen off the trains going by for the small stoves that heated their homes.

"It didn't matter how young or old you were, you were expected to try and help out," Howie muses, "and you were proud to contribute something to the family."

Existing in the neighborhood without ending up in trouble was just as difficult as trying to keep the family afloat. With so many men out of work, crime was rife, more out of desperation than anything else. "Generally, you were either part of one gang or someone who was ratting them out to another or worse yet – the police. It was the times and the poverty that drove so many to such desperate behavior."

The cops weren't above giving a good beating to kids they caught or merely suspected of petty theft. "It was easy to join up but I wasn't interested," and yet he is quick to point out, "I also kept to myself, didn't get into any beefs with guys or allow myself to get put in the position of being questioned about anyone else's business."

Howie's close friends were of the same mind. The small group functioned as their own smaller family unit as each of them had siblings spread out across the homes of relatives.

"That had to have been very hard," I say, as I think of going to sleep with four brothers and two sisters stacked up in two rooms. At least we were always together, even though we didn't appreciate then what a privilege it was.

"We were still lucky," he insists. "We didn't have to go to Shirley."

Shirley is a prison in Shirley, Massachusetts, but apparently prior to becoming a prison in 1970 it was a facility where overflow children were sent during the war.

"It used to be a place where kids were sent, kids that weren't bad or in trouble, but their families couldn't take care of them."

There were other places children would go to if their families could not afford them, it was a common practice. "What did they call it? The CCCs, was it? Catholic Children's Charity, I believe. My friend Tony Bilara, he came from a big family and his parents had to put him in the CCCs because there just was not enough food to go around. Everyone was starving to death in those days. So the fact that my brothers at least had relatives to live with was a terrific thing."

Howie's father assured him that the troubles were temporary and his parents would find a way to bring everyone back under the same roof. He was not to worry. "Care about the family, rely on the family," his father said over and over, "and you'll always have strong ties. Stick together even if you aren't together."

It didn't ease his anxiety. "I was always trying to come up with another angle, another way to help out, maybe get my brothers back home. When you're a kid, you just think you can do anything, you can make everything all right." Howie looks at me. "Then you get older, and things are never as simple as you thought they would be when you were that kid. So I started looking for a real job when I was about ten or so."

He wasn't alone. Everybody worked anywhere they could. The days of being able to pick and choose a profession were decades away.

"All of my brothers worked. My oldest brother William was artistic. He used to design the windows at Jordan Marsh; he trained himself so he could get the job. Norman worked at Welsh's Candy and used to bring by as much candy as he could carry. I was the only kid in the neighborhood with holes in his pants and shoes but a pocketful of goodies! My brother Bob was always working at a gas station or something. Everyone was trying to pick up a job."

Howie was not about to sit back while everyone else was employed. He got one job selling newspapers before school and a second one shining shoes in the afternoons.

"I worked both jobs and went to school. It sounds like one of those old Depression stories, but most of us had to wear the same clothes days in a row. You had to scrub 'em out every night to at least look clean."

"The clothes don't make the man," his father assured him. "The man makes the man." And so Howie learned to carry himself with an air of dignity that gives him the meticulous appearance that he still has today.

Even though his brothers would not return home again except to visit, Howie kept working. "If my brothers weren't coming back, I could still help out. I wanted to buy my mother a hot water heater." He eventually managed to buy a hose and pipe device that heated the water as it ran through the tube so it spat out hot.

He grins like a little kid. "It was pretty cool."

Howie began to work fulltime as soon as he was able. "I was twelve when I moved up in the employment world, working for Fay Strapping Company with my friend Buddy McLean. We were pretty proud of ourselves."

Just like the other families, the Winters survived.

"It wasn't so terrible all of the time," Howie assures me, "you know how old people will tell you those horrible stories, walking two miles to school barefoot in the middle of a snowstorm."

We both start laughing. There isn't a guy in New England who hasn't heard that one at least once in his lifetime; it must be in the Yankee Parenting Manual.

"When things started to ease up a little, we were still poor - but we had some fun. We had something almost no one else had - a piano. It was my mother's and when they were forced to move, they couldn't find a buyer so it came along with us. So if someone could be convinced to play the piano, that was the entertainment. And of course, everyone listened to the radio. Bill played the trumpet – even played for a time with Harry James. He used to take me down to see whatever band was in town. He could have stayed with James permanently but he eventually got married and didn't want to go on the road."

Bill's world changed when the war broke out. "He went into the service." By the time Howie was fourteen, World War II was in full swing. "Finally, they all went in."

The Winter brothers scattered, one with General Patton, one with the Air Corps, and another in the Marine Air Corps. Howie was sure it was his turn even though he wasn't even close to being of age.

"My buddy Jimmy Ryan and myself, we were about 13 or 14, when we went down to the courthouse and registered for the draft. Buddy stayed home."

I've heard of guys joining up early, I did it myself at sixteen, but fourteen?

Howie reminds me that it wasn't about age; it was about the country. "I think that was the thing to do for everybody. The war effort was everywhere. I had three brothers in so I felt that I should be there with them."

I also wonder if it wasn't somewhat about the feeling of belonging to the family, even if they still would not actually be together.

"Did they let you guys in?"

I'm thinking of two baby-faced Somerville guys trying to sign up to be soldiers.

Howie laughs, "Well, not at first. The recruiter looked us up and down and said, 'You boys don't look old enough!' So we acted like big, tough guys, shrugged him off. 'OK,' I told him. 'But remember, we were here to register and you turned us down.' Then we turned and tried to kind of saunter away. We didn't even make it to the door when he said 'All right! Come back!' So he ended up in the Army and I ended up in the Marine Corps."

"Howie," I say, "wasn't there some kind of regulation about multiple siblings enlisting?"

"I don't know about any rules, we got in, but I do remember I got a strong letter from my brother Norman, who was with Patton in Europe and he told me, 'What are you doing? You should be home with Mom and Dad!' He reamed me good for joining up. But I did. I planned my whole life from that point on. Then I got out when I was seventeen and the war was over. I was lucky. I came back to Somerville, a lot of other guys didn't."

There were more than a few of Howie's friends who didn't survive the service and I ask about them, but he shakes his head quickly. "Too painful."

When Howie got home, Buddy was waiting. Despite the loss of friends, they were still triumphant, high on the victory.

"We had made it. America and all of the rest of us were on the upswing. We had absolutely no fears about the future. So we went into the trucking business."

Their plan was simple. They'd become successful businessmen, guys everyone would respect. But they'd never forget what it took their families to make it through. As soon as he and Buddy made it big, he would never turn his back on anyone who needed help. Support, money, a job, food, if he had it, he'd give it, no questions asked.

"That was our plan."

He pauses and the silence lengthens. He clears his throat.

"And then what came after, what happened was...well, you know the rest, Bobby." He sits back in his chair and folds his hands.

I do, but maybe the readers don't.

When Howie was seventeen years old, he thought the hard times were over and suffering was behind him and his beloved family. He survived the war, but didn't realize the pain was just beginning.

He had no hint of the different twists and turns his life would take at the hands of interfering factions, both in the street and at the hands of the federal government.

If a gypsy fortuneteller forecast the teenager's future, he would have questioned just how lucky he had been to return safely home from the war.

You will, she might say, grow to be a man that scores of people outside your own family will depend on. Dozens more who will not even know you will fear you.

You will be betrayed by your own kind, your so-called allies will turn on you.

Your closest friends will be slaughtered; your trusted compatriots will disappear.

You'll gain wealth and power, and lose a beloved child.

Politicians will run entire campaigns based on putting you behind bars, but you'll gladly serve the time rather than name the names. You will be rewarded with physical abuse.

You will work to keep your own family together only to stand by helplessly and watch them fragment into broken pieces.

Once you have finally made enough money to take care of your beloved mother in the way you'd always hoped you could, you'll find her dead and alone in her apartment one afternoon when you drop by for a visit.

Your face will become a front-page favorite, and you will retire into relative obscurity. That, my friend, is your future.

And she'd be right.

Almost overnight, Howie Winter swiftly rose from a simple trucker to the top of the underworld in the Boston area like none before him. His name was in all of the newspapers, whether the stories were fact or fiction made no difference – he sold them out off the stands.

Here's where I come in.

My name is Bobby Martini, just like my father's. My old man was a close friend of Howie's and worked for him for years. Bobby Senior - Big Bob - was a fixture in Somerville, but Howie was legend and during the time I was growing up, to be a friend of Howie's or to even be associated with him drew you into a respected, tightly protected circle.

Guys used his name in general conversation just to feel more important than the person they were talking to. Many a night at the after hours eateries you could hear some drunken ass bragging about the brutal and lurid adventures he'd shared with the legendary Howie Winter roaming the wild streets of Somerville.

I heard it all. And it's always pissed me off.

There is more to Howie than newspaper fodder and informants' fiction.

If I were within earshot of this bullshit, I'd be sure to pass by the talker on my way out, lean into his conversation and ask if there were anything else he'd like Mr. Winter to know. I was his son's roommate, after all, so I could pass along any message he'd like to the old man. Conversation always stopped dead and eventually the big mouth choked out a garbled apology.

Shit, man, if you're going to tell a story, at least tell it right – the bad *and* the good.

There's been a lot written and a lot said about Howie Winter since I was kid.

Some of it's true; some is pure bullshit.

Here's the first true story and then you can, if you want, keep reading.

My father worked for Howie at the Marshall Street garage, his base of operations. One afternoon I was heading in to see my old man when he called me over to the bay door.

"Hey, Bobby, c'mere." He gestured inside.

"What's up?"

He gave me the "Ssh!" gesture as if I should have known to shut my mouth and pulled me over. "Look," he pointed down the street.

Howie was coming up Winter Hill dressed in a freshly cleaned sweat suit – matching jacket and pants – a combination that was all the rage in the seventies for the non-disco crowd. In fact, we wore them out of style and kept on wearing them until the young hip hop guys brought them back into fashion. So never let it be said that we in Somerville can't keep up with the times – even if we never let go of them.

"See the kid on the curb?" my old man asked. Across the street there was a young boy sitting on the concrete. "You know him?"

The boy was only eight or nine. At nineteen, not only did I not know him, I had no interest in whatever was rolling around in the old man's mind.

"Naw." I shook my head.

My father pulled me closer to him and angled me into his view of the street. "See his shoes?"

Even from my vantage point, I could see the holes in the boy's shoes, the scruffy leather separating from the worn soles. Inwardly I groaned. This would probably be the lecture about walking two miles to school barefoot in the middle of a snowstorm.

"Yeah, yeah. I see. Old shoes. Better than no shoes, right?" I shot back.

He cuffed me on the back of the head so hard I bit my tongue.

"Watch your mouth, smart guy! Just look, I'll bet you ten bucks Howie don't make it past the kid, but don't let him see ya."

We stepped back into the shadow cloak of the garage door.

As Howie approached the boy, he suddenly stopped. The older man leaned down and spoke quietly to the child and then led him across the street to a store. Big Bob slapped his knee triumphantly.

"See? What did I tell ya? Huh? You owe me ten bucks!"

I was so curious I forget to argue that I'd never agreed to any bet. I sat on a wooden auto parts crate by the door and waited.

My mind wandered in the warmth of the afternoon and I was reminded of another story about shoes. Brian Leahy is Tom's younger brother. Brian had six siblings and despite the assistance their mother received from Howie after their father was killed, all the kids went to work in order to insure they weren't separated and farmed out to relatives. Brian shined shoes and one day he was working on an especially important customer, local bookmaker Billy O'Neill.

As Brian finished the buff on the bookie's leather, he stood up. The holes in the knees of his pants didn't get past the older man. Billy grunted and carelessly tossed a few extra bucks at the boy.

"Get some decent clothes, kid," O'Neill snapped, "You oughtta be ashamed lookin' like that."

Brian's face grew hot with shame. He knew he was going to start bawling.

I understand why it hurt so much. I shined shoes as a kid to make a buck and it's a hard job. The heavy shine box consisted of as many decent rags as you could manage to finagle and a brush to buff out the shoes. The creamy polish could repair cracked up shoes and make them look brand new but you had to really put your back into the process.

I can still smell the aroma of the polish as I write this – it was like the leather smell inside of a brand new car. I loved the sensation as I dipped my fingers into the small can and scooped the cream out. At the end of the night my hands would be solid black because the best way to apply the polish was with your fingers. It's a tip driven business and the patron always appreciated the extra effort. It was a dirty job but truly somebody had to do it.

Brian was crying when he burst through the front door. After getting the short version of the story, an incensed Mrs. Leahy made a call to Howie. The man who was once a shoe shiner himself made sure that not only did O'Neill show at up the Leahy's to apologize to the kid in person, he spent the rest of his life repeating it each time he and Brian Leahy crossed paths throughout the years.

I'd almost fallen asleep by the time Howie exited out the front door of the store and continued on his route toward the garage. A few moments later, the kid also pushed his way out to the street. He was wearing a brand new pair of sneakers and he strolled down the street as if he were also wearing a brand new sweat suit, and the requisite heavy gold chains. This boy was strutting.

"Hey, what the hell are you doin' over there? Sleeping?" my father called out to me, yanking me out of the memory.

I jumped up off the crate and sprinted to the back bay of the garage, immediately feigning interest in whatever mundane repair he was doing. Howie was steps away; I didn't want to embarrass him for his deed or myself for basically spying on him. But I thought about it for a long time afterward and still do.

Howie did what he had to do and sent the kid on his way. He didn't toss a few bucks at him or humiliate him. He didn't make a tough guy joke. He didn't look the other way. He wanted no thanks or any favors. I think he just wanted that boy, who probably reminded him of himself, to have a pair of decent shoes.

My point is that there's always more to the story. That I can tell you. I can tell you a few other things too.

CHAPTER TWO

Paddy Public Enemy Number One
Buddy McLean

"DO YOU STILL have that picture of Buddy?" Howie asks me as we settle down in his modest living room and begin the interview. "That picture your father had on the wall at your old house?"

1964. Somerville Massachusetts. I was living with my parents and six brothers and sisters on George Street on the border of Charlestown and Somerville. We had three bedrooms for nine people. My father, Big Bob, worked somewhere doing...well, I don't really know what he did. As a kid, your old man just went "to work" and mine was no different that anyone else's. He eventually did that work at the garage where a bunch of guys like Howie Winter and, later on, Whitey Bulger and Stevie "The Rifleman" Flemmi worked. Maybe as a kid I thought they were all mechanics or car salesmen. Now I know differently.

One night my father came home early. I was eleven years old. As he walked through the door, a big guy followed him. Huge and imposing, I could tell from the way my old man sort of deferred to him that the guy was someone important. Apparently they were going to do some kind of car salesmen work. As my father led him through the parlor into the kitchen, the man stopped where I was on the floor, Indian style, reading a comic, and looked down. I had to crane my neck back to get a full look at him. When I did, I recognized James "Buddy" McLean.

Although I didn't know it then, Buddy was taking a chance coming to our house. The Irish Gang Wars were in full swing and none of the Irish guys wanted to be seen anywhere for fear of immediate execution.

"Whattya doin', kid?" Buddy looked down at me.

I couldn't think of one word to say. I was paralyzed with the awe kids get when they see someone that, in their dreams, is what they see for themselves in the future. This wasn't the first time I'd seen Buddy. The McLeans were regulars at our neighborhood cookouts and get-togethers and all of us kids played together, but I had never really paid him much attention. In those circumstances, he was just another father drinking a beer and joking with the other men as we struggled to stay out of their eyelines, as we ran and wrestled through various backyards.

But here, without a pack of kids to herd, he was something completely different. A big good-looking guy, broad shoulders and better yet, my father trailing behind ushering him through the house, he was practically a demigod. My father never followed anyone and he was treating this guy like a visiting dignitary. That in itself was something of a miracle.

I pointed in the general direction of my comic to indicate my high level of reading skills.

Buddy nodded thoughtfully.

"Readin's good, you know. You're not just lookin' at the pictures, are ya?" he asked, mock stern.

*I was. But I vehemently shook my head. This was not the backyard Buddy. If **this** Buddy said "readin'" was good and I was successfully giving off the appearance of reading, well, I was halfway there.*

He nodded again. "Good. 'Cos that's cheatin'. You never want to cheat nobody and you never wanna rat on nobody. Got it?"

No cheating, no ratting. Got it. And as I got older, I'd remember at least the rat part.

He reached a huge hand into his pocket and pulled out a quarter. This was 1964. A quarter went a long way. He squatted down and held out the coin. Behind him, my father nodded. That meant it was OK for me to take the quarter, it was a gift and not charity, which would get you a swift beating because only poor people accepted charity. It wasn't someone else's, which was stealing, and for which I had suffered such a thrashing after helping myself to a handful of my father's coins that I was in bed for three days. This was a gift I could take without fear of having to pay for it, one way or the other, later.

"Go ahead, Bobby. Take it."

Buddy pressed the quarter into my hand. I closed my fist around it and Buddy stretched back up.

"Thank you," I managed. My father nodded his approval. Buddy smiled again.

"Get yourself another book." Then just as quickly as he had entered the house, Buddy McLean was gone, off with my father to do some car salesman business.

Buddy McLean grew up with Howie in the Winter Hill neighborhood. They became friends the minute Howie moved to Somerville.

"I was in the seventh grade then," Howie thinks back over the decades. "Buddy was a bit younger than all of us. I think we kinda looked after him because Buddy grew up with a different family [that had taken him in]. Mrs. Reposa brought him up and he always loved her. She was a real nice lady."

Buddy's mother was not in evidence and he was cared for as a kid by Mrs. Reposa, a neighborhood woman. This was the subject of much speculation amongst the other kids as to who Mrs. Reposa actually was and what had happened to Buddy's mother. It was particularly strange that Buddy's father

William, a clerk on the Boston waterfront, was still around and yet parent and child lived apart.

"We never mentioned it to Buddy, we didn't want to embarrass him. Later on we found out that Buddy's father had gotten a girl pregnant. A short time after Buddy was born, she took off, leaving him with the baby. Bill paid Mrs. Reposa to take care of Buddy. But it didn't make any difference, the money. She treated him like her own and the money just helped feed him."

In 1941, the two industrious twelve year olds were always looking for new ways to turn a buck. Howie had given up wasting his daylight hours in the ninth grade and had moved fulltime into the adult workforce. The two managed to land jobs at the Fay Strapping Company in Boston. "We would strap up the boxes that were being shipped," Howie remembers. Soon they began to look around for more lucrative jobs. At the loading docks, the Teamsters were getting fifteen dollars a day for an eight-hour shift.

Vinny Murphy was the mechanic at the Fay Transportation Company, "He was older and we all looked up to him." With good paying jobs in short supply, anyone looking to make decent money had to know someone to be hired on for the few coveted positions. Vinny managed to get the younger guys on.

Vinny got the boys invited into yet another exclusive "club" – the International Brotherhood of Teamsters, Local 25. At the tender ages of fourteen and fifteen, the former newspaper boys and shoe shiners joined the union.

At Fay, Howie and Buddy loaded and unloaded trucks at fifteen dollars a pop, often as many as six full loads a day elevating their pay scale to more than the average adult Teamster. They also found occasional work on the docks as longshoremen. Inseparable, the guys did anything that came along to keep the flow of money coming into their respective families.

As his friends went off to war, Buddy stayed at home. Having a father at the waterfront did have its perks. As was the system, a father usually passed his "book" down to his son – it meant Buddy was able to secure one of the revered and much sought after union cards.

Years later, Buddy's son Michael would be passed the book after his father's death. He is still there today doing very well for himself.

Howie was in the Marines for just over two years, and when he returned, he and Buddy took up right where they had left off. They were back at Fay from dawn until dark every day for the next six years. When they both hit twenty-two Buddy and Howie decided they'd had enough of working for someone else and opened their own trucking outfit, Travelers Transportation. As the business got off the ground, the new owners still worked as longshoreman, as well as for other trucking companies. Soon they started to hire their own workers.

To expand the company, they hired gypsy drivers to haul their loads to upstate New York and further. Gypsy is trucker slang for a non-union driver that owns his own rig and travels all over the country delivering goods. Paid by the load, gypsy drivers are constantly dropping and picking up.

Travelers Transportation was hired to run to upstate New York every day to deliver hundreds of fabric bolts, cotton, or anything required by the garment district. The Big Apple was always hungry so both guys made the daily trek, tag teaming with two men driving while two men rested for the next shift. Howie and another guy drove the front tractor-trailer, while Buddy and his partner followed in a second rig. There wasn't as much rest as there should have been. Buddy made sure of that. Quickly bored with the long hauls, he preferred to keep things exciting and became popular amongst the drivers for his antics.

"When I say popular," Howie laughs, "I mean he was popular with other drivers, but occasionally we had a hard time getting guys to partner up with us!"

Buddy would climb out the passenger window of his truck while it was moving sixty miles an hour. His driver was instructed to get right up against the ass end of Howie's rig. In one swift leap, he'd jump on the back of the trailer and creep across the top of the load. As soon as he reached the cab, he'd slide down and plant his feet firmly on the hood.

"It...scared...the...living shit out of us! I can't count how many close calls we had. It was the main reason we could only hire young guys – no heart conditions!" Howie howls. "You never knew what Buddy was going to do."

A truck driving legend in his day, Buddy was fearless and, according to his drivers, more than a bit crazy. His "stunts" weren't restricted to trucking. He managed to either entertain or horrify local residents (depending on who was on the street) with his car driving as well.

"If I'd had enough money back in the old days," Howie laughs, "I would've financed Buddy in the race car business or sent him off to become a Hollywood stuntman. That guy could drive like you see in the movies. He'd go around a corner, put the car on two wheels and drive that way for as long as he wanted. There wasn't much he couldn't do with a car."

Buddy married a local girl and had four children he adored. Every chance he got between his three jobs, he'd take his family to the beach or to the theatre, or out for an ice cream run.

Even with the new company and all of the Teamster and longshoreman work, there were still financial down times, especially when kids started coming. So, as industrious as they had been a decade ago, Howie and his friend began to do the occasional bookmaking to supplement their incomes.

By this time, Buddy had become quite a street fighter and kept himself in top physical condition. With a reputation that he "could fight forever", long steady brawls entertaining to the spectators, challengers came in from neighboring cities for the chance to best him. Brawling has always been one of the favored leisure pastimes in Somerville, second only to drinking and screwing. If Buddy were in the mood, he'd fight any comer just for the hell of it.

But eventually the strain of the endless stream of competitors cut down on his limited free time. He was also becoming unpopular with barkeeps due to the smashed glass and busted furniture he left in his wake. When he wanted nothing more than a few beers, he'd park at the end of his pal Joe Donahue's Capitol bar on Winter Hill. If some punk strutted in, chest puffed out and loudly demanded, "Where's Buddy McLean?" Buddy snuck out the back to avoid the confrontation out of respect for his pal Donahue.

"Buddy," Joe pled on more than one occasion. "You keep tossing guys against these walls, I ain't gonna have a bar left. I can't afford for you to drink here much longer!"

He was the perfect compliment to a partnership with Howie "The Gentleman" Winter and they had no problems launching the bookmaking endeavor or collecting their due.

Both guys became respected fixtures in Somerville, but Buddy was also a character in his own movie. While Howie trained both of them in the bookmaking business, Buddy trained his dogs, two German Shepherds. My father loved to tell us about seeing Buddy and his kids with the dogs at the Tufts running track. "Buddy loved to run," my old man would start off, as if he were amazed.

That must have been impressive to Big Bob. The one time in my life I ever saw him run was just after he was shot during a barroom brawl that escalated into deadly gunplay. According to my father, Buddy also taught the dogs to do a form of babysitting.

"Buddy trained the dogs to stand outside the movie theater when he took his kids to the show. He'd drop the kids off and slip into the bar for a few drinks with his buddies. But them dogs were always there outside, in case any of 'em came wandering out before Daddy got back. The shepherds sat there for hours, just waitin'."

As the bookmaking business grew, the partners found themselves in the middle of a series of events that no dogs could protect them from - it made them famous and made Boston's bloody history infamous. It also killed one of them.

1961. Labor Day. The most coveted of all New England holidays, the last official weekend of summer and traditionally the time to throw one hell of a party. Like the ones we also throw on Memorial Day, Fourth of July, Bunker Hill Day ... you get the picture. We like holidays and love parties. This particular weekend would also go down in Massachusetts's history for another reason.

The opening salvo of the Irish Gang Wars was fired at Salisbury Beach where a few Somerville and Charlestown guys were partying with their women at a rented cottage. There are multiple versions of this story – who did what, who was actually there – but the true story came directly out of Howie Winter's mouth.

Georgie McLaughlin and his brothers ran the gambling and loan shark operations in Charlestown as well as other areas in New England. In the days following The Depression, loan sharking was a booming business nationally and economically depressed areas of the Bay State were no exception.

Loan sharking strapped a monkey on a borrower's back in the following way: you borrowed money from "the office" and paid them back a weekly vig (from the Russian word for "winnings"). Say you borrowed five hundred dollars and the vig was 5 per cent. You'd pay the office twenty-five dollars every week. That was only the interest. You still owed the original five hundred to be paid in separate increments. McLaughlin customers knew what would happen if they missed a payment. Just a minor insult to any of the brothers, real or imagined, could result in an ice pick embedded into the eye of the offender.

Years earlier, the sharking McLaughlins were contracted out by the Genovese Family to take care of a renegade group who had broken loose from the operation and upset the New York financial apple cart by opening their own office. The brothers were flown in to shut down the offenders permanently. They assumed this assignment gave them carte blanche around Boston.

Back in Salisbury, Georgie was staggering drunk. His buddies, Somerville guys Bill Hickey, a grocery store employee, and roofer Red Lloyd, were also in attendance. Bill brought along his wife Ann, who happened to have the biggest breasts you ever laid your eyes on; the kind that most guys couldn't help but stare at.

I guess you've figured out by now that the female breast was pretty much revered in Somerville.

Bill himself was on-again off-again with Ann, but he never could end it completely, such was the awesome power of Ann's cleavage. Georgie was eyeing those mounds throughout the afternoon and finally temptation overcame him. He crossed the line of admiration and decided to reach out and touch. Bill was bullshit mad, he blocked Georgie's advances but on the advice of Red, let it go.

After the girls retired to bed, the men continued imbibing. The earlier incident resurfaced when Georgie mouthed off again about Ann's amazing breasts. Bill reared back and cracked Georgie dead in the face. That should have ended it – you run your mouth to one guy, he closes it for you. But a woman's honor was at stake, so Bill decided to give Georgie a few more for good measure.

Georgie was ranting and raving; but couldn't seem to land one back, angering him even more. Across the room, Red sighed. He better break it up before they busted up the cottage.

He poured a glass of booze. Motioning for Bill to back off, he offered the drink to the breast admirer.

"Georgie, that's enough now."

It was too late. Georgie's fuse was already lit. He grabbed the glass out of Red's hand and smashed it right back into his face. Red was a big guy, much more than either of the combatants and when he pulled his fist back, Bill stepped aside. McLaughlin went down again for good.

Georgie's face was bleeding profusely. "Now what are we gonna do?" Bill looked over at Red.

Red decided the hospital was the best option. But as they drove it seemed apparent that Georgie, who was making gurgling noises, might not survive. So in an effort to save their victim's life, they compromised and dropped him on the lawn in front of the emergency room. McLaughlin survived with just a badly broken nose.

"That's all it really came down to that night," Howie says, "a broken nose and a lady's breasts." But it was much more to the McLaughlin clan. Georgie had been disrespected, as had the whole gang and their status as a sort-of crime family. In their collective minds, someone had to die and that decision brought down a hail of hell to Charlestown and Somerville.

The McLaughlins laid low for a week until brother Bernie went up to Buddy's house. Buddy was to Somerville as the McLaughlins were to Charlestown and beefs were normally settled by the higher ups. Bernie wanted Hickey and Lloyd set up so he could unload the McLaughlin revenge on them.

"I want 'em dead, Buddy!" Bernie was one decibel below screaming as Buddy opened the door.

Buddy gave his visitor a long look, but did not ask him in. "Is that so?"

Bernie was fuming, red faced. "They gotta go, Buddy, those fuckin' bastards! This ain't right."

He stood shaking, waiting for Buddy's certain handshake. But he didn't get it.

"Bernie," Buddy drawled as he leaned against the doorway, "your brother was way out of line. This is one I suggest you let go of, it's not worth it." Then Buddy shut the door.

Getting no satisfaction was not something McLaughlin was used to, so Bernie immediately sought out Howie to try and talk some sense into his partner.

Bernie, his older brother Edward (known as "Punchy") and another thug pulled up alongside Howie as he was walking down the street and "invited" him into their car for a chat.

"I got in," Howie recalls, "but I had a feeling there was a good chance I'd never get out."

As Howie slid into the backseat, Punchy got right to the heart of the matter. What did Howie think about the incident in Salisbury? Howie demurred; he wasn't privy to the details.

"We need your help to do this thing." Bernie growled. "You with us?"

Howie paused for a long second. Finally, he asked, "What did Buddy say?"

"What do you mean, what did Buddy say? I'm askin' *you* now."

Howie carefully replied, "However Buddy feels is the way that it is and I'm not going to go against what he's already told you." There was another moment of tense silence in the car. Howie sat completely still, waiting for what would come next. He silently counted off the seconds passing.

"I could feel the sweat soaking my shirt. They'd shoot me, I was sure. The last thought I'd ever have would be the number I counted up to before someone pulled the trigger."

After what seemed like hours, Bernie leaned across Howie and opened the door.

"Get out." Bernie turned Howie loose. Howie watched as the Charlestown boys roared away.

"I knew that would never be the end of it. But I felt lucky I had gotten out of the car without a hole in me. I don't think they really knew at that point what they were going to do next. But one thing was for sure; they wanted to kill Lloyd and Hickey. By the next day, Buddy agreed with me."

The next evening Jean McLean was watching television and heard their two dogs barking. She looked out the window and saw movement in the shadows. There were men in the driveway.

"Buddy!" Jean screamed. "Buddy, there's someone out in the yard!" Buddy yelled for her to get into the back bedroom. He grabbed his Luger from the closet and burst out of the house. The shadows scattered as Buddy began shooting. He sailed into the nearby bushes for cover, firing as the men ran for their lives. Buddy recognized Bernie rounding the corner and jumping into a car.

The next morning, Buddy's neighbor Tony from across the street, knocked on the door and ushered Buddy outside.

"C'mere," Tony said quietly. "Take a look at this." He pointed under Buddy's car. Both men saw the telltale wires underneath the carriage of the vehicle. Buddy walked carefully around to the partially opened hood and lifted it slowly.

He took a deep breath. Nestled next to the engine was dynamite rigged to the ignition. Tony galloped back to his house to call the bomb squad. As he waited for the law to arrive, Buddy walked up to his porch, shaking. He'd had no plans to use the car that morning. Jean had been getting ready to take the kids out. His children would have been in the car when she turned that key had Tony not crossed the street to investigate. It was nauseating and it was unacceptable.

Buddy McLean was a Somerville street guy, brought up to mind his own business until someone else's interfered. Now that someone, in the form of the McLaughlin tribe, had done just that. Buddy McLean's days of juggling jobs, jumping on cabs and fighting for fun had ended forever.

A few days later, on Halloween, Buddy and pal Alex "Bobo" Petricone were due in court to answer a charge of disturbing the peace after an altercation at the notorious White Tower.

Tom Leahy has a keen memory when it comes to the old days.

"The White Tower was a hamburger joint on the corner of McGrath Highway and Broadway. There was always something going on up there, and it wasn't always good."

The Tower was pure Somerville and the main hangout of guys too young to hit the bars. It was also a magnet for the hoods from Charlestown to pass by when they were in the mood to mix it up. The war between the older guys in both cities didn't affect the White Tower at all, the place maintained the even steady flow of testosterone trouble it always had.

"It got so bad that eventually the White Tower Corporation erected a pole above the restaurant with a blue light so when a fight broke out, one of the waitresses hit a switch."

Like Batman's logo projected high above Gotham City, the cop cruisers would immediately swoop in to round up the troublemakers.

Buddy and Bobo had to answer for their own White Tower blue light special the day they headed downtown. Fellow Winter Hill regular (and Metropolitan District Commission police officer) Russ Nicholson drove them. When the court went to recess, Buddy and his friends made their way over to Charlestown.

My father was the local barroom historian of the Irish Gang Wars. Big Bob prided himself on getting the details right and on his sons being taught the lessons so history never repeated itself. This is his account of that morning.

"Bernie was a creature of habit. Every day he'd head over to the Morning Glory Lounge at around noon to collect the loan money he'd lent out in the streets. Everyone knew his route."

Buddy left the house that morning without even bothering to bring along a disguise (no Whitey Bulger, Buddy preferred the old fashioned method of revenge – plain street clothes), along with his two close friends. They were in Charlestown just before the noontime whistle.

The car screeched to a halt next to a parked tractor-trailer as Bernie exited the lounge. Buddy jumped out and emptied his gun into Bernie, killing him on the spot. Then Buddy ran back toward the tractor, slipped underneath and emerged to hop into the waiting car. The trio sped back across the city line to the Capitol bar. They parked out back and that's where MDC cop Joe McCain felt the hood and discovered the engine was still warm. The cop was ecstatic; sure he had fingered the killers. Buddy would be implicated in the murder partially because of that warm hood.

Bernie McLaughlin was gunned down in front of the liquor store near the police station in Charlestown. Dozens of witnesses had to have seen the executioner, yet none made a positive ID.

"It all happened too fast," was a common witness statement.

One man was even reported to have strolled up to bleeding Bernie, leaned over him and said, "Bernie you poor bastard, you're dying and the guy who did this should get a medal."

Buddy called Howie and the trusted Somerville crew together; he carefully laid out the details of what had happened. Howie didn't want to believe it, things had been perfect and now it was all about to come crashing down on them.

"Nobody wanted it, but there wasn't a choice. The McLaughlins weren't going to back down and now it wasn't just the two guys from the beach weekend they wanted dead. It was all of us."

The men agreed that the sides would be chosen fast and from here on out, everybody was a target. Anyone who ever hung out with Buddy or Howie would be in danger. Their operation immediately ground to a halt. The popular bookmakers couldn't be out in the street doing business, nor risk being pinpointed by the enemy at the office, there was no way to continue without some help.

Former Marine sergeant Salvatore "Sal" Sperlinga was a bookmaker on the lower rung in town who did pretty well for himself. He took action at the Terminal Bar in West Somerville. Sal knew Howie, Buddy and my father from the Somerville pool halls where they all hung out as teenagers.

"Sal was a man we trusted. I won't say he didn't have any beef with the McLaughlins because he was a loyal Somerville guy, but he wasn't directly connected to this situation so he wasn't a..."

Howie thinks for a moment. "What do they call it now? He wasn't a 'person of interest' to them."

Howie and Buddy decided to keep it that way. By distancing themselves from Sal, the independent bookie could keep their action afloat by servicing their customers and all three could continue to make money.

"It was a good thing too. The war cost money, guys had to rent different places to live, constantly stay on the move, change cars. It was very expensive."

It was more than just financially costly. The rules of engagement were clear; if you went home to your family, you'd be putting their lives in danger also. Some listened and some didn't. At first.

"When that trouble started, guys were yanked off the streets and never seen again, not in one piece anyway. Nobody connected to either group was safe." Howie explains. "I didn't figure I was gonna live too long."

It wasn't just Howie's paranoia. The local bookies began taking bets on the survival of the bookmakers. "They gave us a week. Then a couple of weeks and then...we were still alive."

The Irish guys did their equivalent of "going to the mattresses." Households on both sides of the Somerville-Charlestown border began to empty of men. Within a few weeks, all of the little row houses, the double and triple-deckers and the apartments were void of adult male residents, Howie's included.

"Back then you never exposed your family to business. It was an unwritten rule. No matter what the man did, his family was never involved. So you had to go away and you had to stay away."

Being alone and out of touch was torture on the wives and girlfriends. "They were constantly weighing their options," my own mother told me years later. "Which was better – not knowing or knowing what could really happen?"

I remember in my early adolescence I was packed up and sent off to stay with my grandmother in Wilmington, Mass. My siblings were farmed out to other relatives. My father did not want to have to disappear for a time while leaving my mother in sole command of seven rambunctious kids.

Messages were passed along, from party to party, until they finally reached home, but no woman could be sure the information she was getting was still current upon receipt.

"The time from one message to the next was eternity," my mother said. "He was still alive at the time he passed the message, but for all I knew, he was dead the next moment. And what do you tell the kids when they ask, 'Where's Daddy?'"

You can bet a lot of those kids figured their dads were just off somewhere selling cars.

Yet despite the fear of assassination, Howie continued to attend every Sunday Mass at East Somerville's St. Benedict's Catholic Church, much to the chagrin of his buddies. "They were always asking me if I had a death wish," Howie says, smiling. "But my feeling was that no Irishman, no matter how crazy, would kill another on his way to or from Mass." The two camps may have been thirsty for blood, but it was the shared opinion that too many gallons of it had already been spilt in Ireland trying to keep the Catholics from their Church. No one ever bothered Howie on those Sundays.

Rumors were as thick as smoke and the paranoia gripping Winter Hill was palpable. By no means do I want to imply that every single man in Somerville or Charlestown was embroiled in the fray. The guys I've been writing about belonged to a certain faction of our society. I suppose I could write more about the men whose only involvement was reading the daily headlines; men who worked regular jobs and never walked that fine line between crime and compromise– there are many of them in both towns. I just don't know them very well.

That being said, the Gang Wars did indeed affect people on the outside of the direct circle. There was gunplay in the streets; neighbors became afraid they'd accidentally be caught in community crossfire. If you were not directly involved, you knew someone who was, a friend, a cousin, a brother-in-law. You became reticent to take your car into the mechanic if there was a possibility that a guy who had ties to either gang also got his car serviced at the same place. Businesses began to suffer, just on rumor alone.

The Winter Hill boys heard talk about men on the periphery. Guys who lived in Somerville but were perhaps considering throwing their loyalty in another direction due to Charlestown connections; they had one foot on each side of the line.

Howie remembers it vividly. "You'd hear a guy was thinking about joining the other side. Maybe his wife was related, family connections." He sighs and shakes his head. "The pressure was brutal."

Buddy devised a plan to minimize the gang's own exposure. He assigned guys the job of clocking anyone in danger of changing loyalties.

"A guy – the clocker - sat outside of a subject's house and followed him like a private investigator. The clocker took notes on his subject's activities in his daily life."

If the subject left home at a certain time every day, the clocker put it down. If he went to the same coffee shop at a regular hour, it would be dutifully documented. His license plate, address, wife's name, kids, even the family dog was noted. In just a few days, the clocker had his subject's routine down.

"Buddy would visit the man in question. After a little small talk, he'd pull out the notebook, tear off the piece of paper and hand it to the guy."

The response was always the same; the man's mouth went slack as he read a schedule of his own daily activities. He wasn't threatened, it was just made clear his life wasn't a secret and should he be influenced to cross over to the other side, well, it might not be such a safe decision.

Buddy told Howie that his new system was called "Preventative Maintenance."

"This way," Buddy reasoned, "he's got an excuse to get out. He ain't pressured to join any side. Usually, these were guys who didn't want in on this beef – but were getting pushed just the same."

There would be no recruiting of new soldiers. The veterans would fight this war.

The subject always took the Preventative Maintenance to heart. Bodies had already started to fall and these "subjects" had no intention of joining that group either. Within days, the family moved out of the way and into safety in another neighborhood.

And as the weeks dragged into months, everyone paid a price in one way or another.

The cops arrested Buddy and Bobo for the murder of Bernie. The case seemed like a slam-dunk; there were literally a hundred witnesses that day but back then the rules were different. You kept your mouth shut and minded your business. Not like today where the government pays you to tell on your friends.

The day after their arrest, a young Boston attorney named F. Lee Bailey got them sprung for lack of evidence. Bailey went on to a hugely successful career and defended such clients as Joe "The Animal" Barboza as well as an infamous running back while Bobo caught a plane to Los Angeles, changed his name to Alex Rocco and eventually became a successful Hollywood character actor. In his best-known role as racketeer Moe Green in "The Godfather", Rocco gets one in the eye as he reclines on a Vegas massage table. How ironic that he would play a part in a movie that could have been a real life incident if he stayed in Boston.

Buddy's old friend Russ Nicholson, a cop once cited for a heroic rescue and lauded for his investigative successes, was fired from the force soon after Bernie's murder. Law enforcement was quoted as saying Russ had gone from a good cop to "a real leg breaker."

The fact is that some of law enforcement had already been digging deep to find something, anything, to get Russ off the force. Howie remembers a night when Buddy and Russ got into a brawl with a couple other guys. "Finally, it was just what the cops needed. Russ was tossed for 'consorting with a known criminal element.' That was the best they could do and it broke Russ's heart. But he wouldn't turn his back on his friendships." If hanging with Buddy cost him his cop job, so be it.

The feeling on Winter Hill was that it was fellow cop Joe McCain who wanted Russ off the force, and for a different reason.

Howie says, "Russ was a good friend of McCain. McCain was friendly with Buddy and I as well, and in fact McCain and I both attended the same police school way back when."

I am intrigued. The last we spoke of his education, Howie quit formal schooling in the ninth grade.

He laughs. "Didn't I tell you? I went back and got my G.E.D. and finally graduated from the University of Kansas." He grins, "I get around."

"Howie, you wanted to become a cop?"

Howie smiles and shakes his head. "I found out the pay was for shit. Anyway, Russ and Joe used to take their wives out together, visit at each other's homes. They were very close. Joe wanted to be a cop in the worst way and Russ was already on the force. There had been two openings but they had been filled. Russ actually went to see the Governor at that time and insisted that McCain be given a spot. He got McCain his job. Russ was very excited to be working with his buddy. That's a true story."

After McCain joined the force, the old friends drifted apart.

"We didn't see too much of McCain after that, although I can remember one incident very clearly," Howie says. "McCain was on the corner one day and a few guys were bothering him." It seems McCain's mouth had gotten him in over his head and he was outnumbered. "Buddy and I went down as soon as we heard there was trouble and we took care of it. On that day McCain was only too glad to remember we were all friends."

Howie sits back in his chair and folds his arms across his chest. "But, of course, no one ever bothers to print those kind of stories, do they, Bobby?"

I do find it interesting that with all the books and articles written about the Winter Hill guys by outsiders, you seldom read that any authors bothered to contact the subjects for a quote. I can attest to that personally.

Tom Leahy also remembers Russ well.

At six foot four and two hundred and ten pounds, "Russ was a helluva guy to me when I was a kid after we lost our dad. He used to come over and play football in the yard for hours. He was never anything but kind." Tom's loss is painted across his face.

He's given me many great stories for this book, but this is one neither of us enjoyed. "It was an awful time [the Gang Wars] and good men got caught up in it. I was very sad when I heard he had died."

In 1964 Russ was found dead in a wooded side road in Wilmington, a bullet in his head. He'd been yanked off the street in broad daylight, a victim of the McLaughlins.

McCain was sorely disappointed his discovery of the warm car hood did not lead to the conviction of his old pal and defender McLean, as well as Bobo Petricone who McCain accused of making threatening phone calls to McCain's home during the days before they all had to testify in court. "McCain always thought he was Super Cop," says a retired detective, "and erroneously so."

Howie is philosophical. "It's every lawman's job to carry out his job. And at the same time, it is every man's job to protect his family. The day that Buddy's family was not blown sky high as expected was when Buddy decided he had a job to do."

He sighs and chooses his words. "Each man has to make his own decisions and live with them."

My father was not so philosophical. I heard him say over and over, "What the hell would McCain have done if he saw Bernie McLaughlin running away from a bomb he had planted in McCain's car?" He hated McCain and refused to allow his name to be mentioned in his presence.

After Bernie's killing, there was a never-ending supply of murder and mayhem to keep newspapers turning a profit. Bookmakers continued to raise the odds of the life spans of Buddy, Howie and the crew from Somerville. But the childhood pals slowly began to realize that they did have some advantages over the seasoned Charlestown thugs. True, the Charlestown crew was feared. But they were absolutely insane, knee-jerk reactionaries who responded instantly to violence with yet more violence, most of the time without any planning.

The Somerville guys had carefully planned out their lives since age twelve. Smart and resourceful, they had set themselves up financially in a variety of businesses without using guns or intimidation. Even the bookmaking operation was considered a tough, yet "gentleman's office" where the use of deadly force was not the order of the day. Their crew was respected. All they had to do, Buddy reasoned, was to stay one step ahead of the

McLaughlins until the opportunity arose to finish the war, and the two remaining brothers, off.

Buddy's plan never came to fruition. Neither of the two McLaughlins were ever together, nor were Howie and Buddy.

No one knew how long the war would continue to rage on, nor did anyone, including the national press and local law enforcement, anticipate the eventual final body count.

And nobody could have foreseen that one of those four remaining gang leaders would seal his own fate with a split second decision.

CHAPTER THREE

If I Should Fall from Grace with God
The End of The War

THE COPS DID what the McLaughlins couldn't. They caught up with the Somerville brawler. While Buddy was not prosecuted for Bernie's murder, he was sent away for two years on an illegal gun possession charge, leaving Howie and a small crew to contend with the vicious battle.

When Buddy was away, he told my father that his cellmate was an avid reader of sorts and squirreled away piles of true detective magazines. He gave Buddy one with an article about body disposal by a professional hitman. "Bob," Buddy was shocked, "it said when you put someone in the water you're supposed to cut the body from the stomach to the neck. Then there's no possibility of the body bloatin' and floatin' to the top. Also you're supposed to wrap the body in chain link so it can't come loose."

"Ya," my old man agreed. "That makes sense."

"But Bobby, these fucking guys do this to people they don't even know, just for the money!"

Buddy said the article made him sick; he knew he could never have made it as a professional killer. He didn't have the stomach for it.

My father made it crystal clear to me that amongst the Somerville men there was another unwritten creed. To use deadly violence to settle personal scores was perfectly acceptable. To take money from strangers for murder for hire was verboten. Just another lesson from the Somerville rulebook.

During his stint in jail, Buddy met Tony "Blue" D'Agostino and they became good friends. When they got out, Tony became a very valuable ally as well as Buddy's personal bodyguard. He was the car man for the Hill. He had boilers all over the city; cars loaded with guns, ammunition, masks, and whatever else required for the successful crime – especially murder.

Good looking and always surrounded by beautiful chicks, Tony was a mystery. Every man wondered how he kept a flock of girls with his particular brand of romantic prose - " I get more ass than a restroom full of guys with diarrhea."

While in jail, Buddy also met Rhode Island Patriarca Family enforcer Joe "The Animal" Barboza. Barboza took a liking to the brawling Buddy. Barboza may have been a crazed murderer – actually he *was* a crazed murderer, but he was no fool. As it was rumored the McLaughlins were muscling in on Patriarca's own Boston loan sharking operation, the Somerville boys automatically became "the good guys" in the eyes of the Italians.

Mob boss Raymond Patriarca also knew he wasn't going to get anything from the McLaughlin clan except for trouble. The wily old Italian entered the fray and appeared to be siding with the Somerville men by sanctioning hits on enemies (and men he himself deemed enemies) of the Hill.

Some of the casualty corpses of the Gang Wars were actually victims of Patriarca's hand. He dispatched a couple of assassins to kill Paul Colicci, an ex-boxer once close to Patriarca who had written the boss a series of threatening letters when Colicci was incarcerated. According to Vincent Teresa (*My Life in the Mafia*), the fighter sealed his fate when he publicly called Patriarca "a fag."

Patriarca knew that with bodies dropping all over Boston, another hit would be chalked up to the Irish. And even though he genuinely liked Buddy, the Don saw himself taking over the Boston rackets as soon as the warring Micks pummeled each other out of existence. In the meantime, he seized the opportunity to knock off a major pain in his ass.

In July of 1964, Colicci was hustling televisions with fellow thief Vincent Bisesi. On the steamy afternoon of the 23rd, a dog walker outside of a Quincy motel was dragged towards a parked car by the excited canines. There was a thick gooey substance dripping from underneath. When the trunk was sprung, the bloated buddies popped up, bullets in the back of their heads. Colicci's days of questioning anyone's manhood were over.

The Irishman Buddy McLean made it clear to an eleven-year-old kid that to be fingered as a rat was one of the ugliest things a man could ever be called. Apparently, in the world of Italian guys, there was actually one worse moniker you could have thrown at you. And they took that one very seriously.

In the meantime, Somerville was also stepping up their attacks on the neighboring enemies and as soon as Buddy was back on the street, he implemented a few upgrades to technique.

He had all the keys to the local waterfront fish houses and used them to his advantage. Early one morning, an owner opened up his restaurant and checking the lobster tanks, he found one very unusual catch – a man's watch. The man couldn't believe his luck; the expensive timepiece was still ticking.

Its owner, however, was not. Like others, the would-be assassin was apprehended, taken to one of the fish houses after hours and drowned in the tanks. These bodies were disposed of in a variety of ways. The worn out cliché of noir fiction, the cement shoes, were employed to sink one non-swimmer into a local lake. Other enemies weren't so lucky as to merely sleep with the lobsters. The "Sicilian Necktie" was occasionally employed to show the opposite crew that they meant business. Although the Irish as a rule give wide berth to all things Italiano, the necktie, they grudgingly admitted, was sheer genius.

It involved wrapping a wire around the neck of the victim and then connecting it to the hands behind the back of the soon-to-be dead enemy. The wire was then connected to his feet, and whenever the victim moved, the wire tightened around his neck in a strangle death grip. Then they'd drop the squirming bundle into the nearby harbor and allow the currents to take the body away.

In August of 1964, McLaughlin associates Harold Hannon and Wilfred Delaney were two of these sea goers. Hannon was a vicious and adroit killer, Delaney his young subordinate. Both were acquaintances of a woman named Dorchester Dottie, sort of a Massachusetts Mata Hari. Dottie had one foot (and one boyfriend) on each side of the Gang Wars. Their story made the rounds of Winter Hill for years. I can't swear to it – but I've included it because the end result is documented fact.

Hannon and Delaney were visiting Dottie when she announced she had to leave.

"I've go to run an errand," she supposedly said, "make yourselves at home." Dottie then departed. In a few moments, there was a knock at her door. Buddy and another guy were on the other side. Dottie evidently called Buddy and told him Hannon was at her apartment. Delaney's presence was just an unfortunate accident.

On Buddy's face was a deadly grin, in his hand - a gun. Out of respect for Dottie, instead of shooting the men on the spot they were forced to swallow a quantity of sleeping pills pinched from Dottie's bathroom. Delaney readily agreed, but Hannon had to be convinced with a beating.

Buddy confiscated a large trunk and a heavy rug from the bedroom. Delaney went into the trunk while Hannon was rolled up in the rug. Rug rolling was a popular disposal method for the Italians but the Irish guys seldom utilized it – their wives would be bullshit to find a bare parlor floor.

"This rug thing works pretty good," Buddy groaned as they hauled Hannon to the station wagon.

The other man agreed. "The guineas use 'em all the time."

"If this war lasts much longer, maybe we should think about gettin' into the rug business," Buddy mused.

The plan was Sicilian neckties and a toss into the ocean. It was dark by the time the boys headed toward Boston Harbor. As they drove, the driver realized one of the headlights was flickering out.

"Shit!" Buddy exclaimed. "We better pull off and fix it or we're gonna get stopped."

The wagon pulled into the next gas station and the guys waited patiently while the young attendant replaced the bulb and made small talk.

"You guys goin' on a trip?" the kid asked as he peered at the trunk inside the vehicle.

"Yeah," Buddy smoothly replied. "A cruise. You don't have any wire layin' around, do you?"

What is undisputed fact is that on August 20th, Dottie's visitors were fished out of the harbor. The newspaper reported that Hannon was dead when he went in but Delaney actually drowned. Apparently they couldn't wait for Delaney to strangle himself. We the Irish can be a bit squeamish, and don't care to hang around watching a slow death (we have our own to think about), which was a source of many laughs for the Italian mob.

The McLaughlins, however, preferred the cowardly yet effective (if they could just get the damn things to work right!) car bomb method. They tried again but never really perfected their technique. Howie's car was blown up in 1962. The device, set to explode when the key was turned in the ignition, initially didn't. *For a whole day.*

After the incident, it was discovered (via a more aggressive session of Preventative Maintenance) that the McLaughlin bomb man wired the dynamite a day prior to the actual explosion. Howie tooled around town for twenty-four hours, unaware of impending death under his hood until the next day when my old man was playing cards in that smoke filled Mystic Ave apartment. The Charlestown guys had to cringe in secret humiliation each time they heard that Howie was seen driving down the street and I wonder what happened to the bomb specialist after his installation failed.

Earlier that morning, Howie had lent his Oldsmobile to a female friend to run some errands. As the woman pulled up in front of the building the device suddenly went off, destroying the hood and its contents, but no human targets. It was divine intervention that no children were hurt as the final resting place of the hood was the nearby playground.

This was a double dose of embarrassment to Charlestown. Not only did they fail at execution once again; their carefully crafted missile and its projectile dysfunction merely resulted in everyone in town laughing at them.

The Somerville guys, however, were bullshit mad and planned a swift retaliation. Not only was their attempt also unsuccessful, it resulted in another of the few moments of cruel comedy during the sixties slaughter.

They set up an ambush for Punchy McLaughlin. He was one of the two surviving Charlestown ringleaders that Somerville referred to as "the dumb fucks." They'd tried to kill Buddy and almost blow up Howie. There was no question that they had murdered Russ Nicholson. Punchy had to go.

But Punchy had already survived several assassination attempts including one outside Beth Israel Hospital in which Catholic boys Stevie Flemmi and "Cadillac" Frank Salemme were dressed as rabbis.

He was also a veteran of wild goose chases. It pissed him off that the cops were constantly following to bust his balls and he busted right back. Punchy actually drove the one hundred and ten miles to Provincetown at under thirty miles an hour just to make a telephone call and turn right around, knowing his tail had no choice but to stay right behind him.

This particular group of Winter Hill-ers knew *they* would get it right. Fuck the disguises and tailing, it was all about careful military planning. The word was out that Punchy was hiding up in Weston and made a daily trek down the hill for supplies. Once arrested for walking out of Sears with just ten dollars worth of goods he neglected to pay for, Punchy was notoriously cheap and bought just what he needed at the moment. It was a matter of time before he emerged. The boys lined the hill and waited for the hapless ex-boxer Punchy to wander into their line of fire.

He did. As soon as his car rounded the bend, the shooters opened up. Hundreds of bullets missed his vital body parts. The hail of ammo only managed to blow off his waving hand as he jauntily drove off.

The boys slunk embarrassingly back to Somerville to pray Punchy pulled off to the side of some road and bled to death so they could claim success.

The next day they were all down at a local club plotting when Somerville cop Younger MacDonald strolled in. He carried a bunch of fresh carrots; the green leafy tops still attached and topped off with a huge bow.

"Gentlemen," he tipped his hat as he bellied up to the bar and ordered a dose of whisky, oblivious to the stares of the patrons. He downed the shot and carefully smoothed the ribbon on his vegetation.

Finally bewilderment got the best of the bar. One of the guys yelled out, "Young, what the fuck's with the carrots? The old lady got ya grocery shopping or didja get a pet rabbit?"

Then the gloves were off.

"Hey Younger, better not be giving that to your girlfriend! The last thing you want is to improve her eyesight!"

"Figures a cop needs to carry around a bunch of carrots – they're all half blind!"

The bar exploded in laughter as Younger smiled and slowly turned to men.

"Why, fellas, these," he pointed at his vegetables, "ain't for me. They're for you, the gang that, so I hear, can't shoot even a little bit straight." With that, he raised one hand up, palm flat and waved, a brilliant impersonation of the Queen of England.

He had them, but he also knew that no one was going to file a charge, even if the complainant had to sign it with a different hand. Younger didn't have to pay for a drink for a week.

The dark humor was welcomed as a welcome respite from the lonely routine of kill or get killed.

The penultimate attempt on Buddy's life worth mentioning came in the form of a request from a pining lover to the dirty cupid Georgie McLaughlin in September of 1964.

Ron Dermody was a Winter Hill bank robber and son of Joe, an old time gangster residing in prison. Ron was head over heels in love with a woman named Dorothy Barchard – Dorchester Dottie.

But Dottie belonged to McLaughlin ex-con James "Spike" O'Toole. Ron didn't care, he had to have her, but he needed some help. He crossed the city line and went to Georgie. Ron made him an offer that was – well - just not to be ignored. "I'll kill Buddy if you kill Spike."

The future executioner had been robbing banks with Bulger since the mid-1950's and also counted Buddy as a friend. But now those ties didn't matter, neither Buddy nor Whitey would keep him warm at night like the curvaceous Dorchester Dot.

In sort of a Hitchcockian crisscross, Ron figured Buddy wouldn't see it coming from him nor Spike from Georgie. It was a perfect murder. He proved to be a stranger without a brain.

"Dermody," Georgie demanded, "you gotta shoot Buddy first as a act of good faith."

Ron was so desperate for Dottie that he readily agreed to kill the man who'd been his friend. Ron knew where to find Buddy the next day. Sliding his pistol from his pants, he pushed through the door of the Capitol bar, took a bead on Buddy and pulled the trigger. Buddy hit the ground. Except for one small detail.

Buddy turned out to be a local thief named Charlie Robinson. Buddy wasn't even in the bar. And when he heard the news, he didn't waste time wondering about friendship. Ron Dermody was found in a parked car with three bullets in his head.

Dottie made a quick recovery and sued Spike for child support in 1965, claiming he was the father of her two illegitimate children, although the charge was filed by default. After applying for government aid to assist her in the children's upkeep, she was required to name their father in order for her check to be released. Whether or not Spike ever paid any child support is unknown, but if he did, it wasn't for long. Spike got drunk in 1973 and was gunned down when he came rolling out of a Savin Hill Ave bar. The neighborhood whispered it had been the work of the Winter Hill Gang.

Howie admits he is clueless about Spike's death. "He was a tough guy, but a decade later? I was out of the loop. I knew nothing about them making a move on O'Toole until it was all over."

I want to know if "them" means Whitey and Stevie Flemmi. Howie just smiles and shakes his head. "Not my deal."

Dottie eventually snagged a husband but not before her name surfaced during an unrelated court proceeding in 1973. Two attorneys representing co-defendants had an off-the-record conversation while awaiting their verdict. After a few drinks, they began discussing an item in the local paper concerning an alleged affair between a local woman and an unnamed attorney. Each lawyer accused the other of being the man in question.

The woman was Dottie. The attorneys were F. Lee Bailey and John Fitzgerald. Fitzgerald once represented O'Toole, knew Dottie and was concerned he may have to shoot first, in which case he would need Bailey to represent him. Fitzy never did get into a quick draw and went on to represent Joe Barboza. The attorney lost a leg in a car bombing orchestrated by Frank Salemme and eventually migrated to the gentler climate of a South Dakota judgeship.

In 1968 Stevie Flemmi and Frank Salemme were engrossed in fine-tuning the best way to plant a bomb. My father didn't think it was at all unusual.

"You gotta remember," the old man said, "the Wars were over but every guy was still paranoid and nobody wanted to be disrespected."

Flemmi announced, '"If there's ever another war, we aren't gonna get caught like the McLaughlins – planting bombs that never go off.'"

So Big Bob didn't find it unusual when the two steered an Oldsmobile into Howie's garage, popped the hood and began tinkering. "They put a thick slice of rubber snug against the firewall of the car and practiced putting a dynamite cap on the ignition."

When both were satisfied, they'd stare down at their watches until Flemmi yelled, "GO!"

"Frankie jumped in the Olds and turned the key. The cap went off every other time. The first time they did it, all the men in the garage hit the deck until they realized it was a half-assed dry run. The actual dynamite wasn't attached so the explosion was minimal. But the guys were getting frustrated."

"Hmm," Flemmi grunted after the third misfire. "It's not as easy as I thought it was."

My old man shook his head. "They practiced putting those caps on the ignition for hours until they got it right. Then look what happened. It wasn't insurance for 'just in case.' They blew the leg off that lawyer."

Dottie's new man, South Boston bank robber David Glennon, was a known associate of Flemmi. Glennon disappeared toward the end of the war and Dottie called Howie. She was desperate and asked if he would meet her.

"So we met at Brigham's for coffee," Howie recalls.

"Howie," she sobbed, "David's gone and I don't think he's coming back."

Howie was sympathetic. "Now Dot, he's around, you two have a fight?"

Deep down Howie knew Glennon was probably dead. Back in the early sixties, the New York Mob bosses feared their enemies attempting to kidnap their children for a ransom. Glennon and a fellow Irish thug had been overheard talking about kidnapping Gerry Anguilo's son. In fact, one of them had broken an arm attempting to clock the Anguilo waterfront compound from the sea wall. Howie sternly warned Glennon after hearing the rumors. This was not the way to try and make a living.

The woman was inconsolable. "Howie, I know he's dead! Some sonofabitch killed him!"

As Dottie bawled, Howie sighed. It could be true, bodies turned up almost every day. This was not the first wife he'd been called upon to console.

"Dottie, honey, what can I do? How can I help you?"

She stopped crying mid-sob and cleared her throat. Dottie was immediately all business.

"Here's the deal, Howie. I need you to make some calls for me. All I need is a finger."

Howie stared at the now composed Dottie. "I'm sorry, I thought you just said you needed..."

"A goddamn finger, Howie! That dumb fuck is buried somewhere and I don't give a damn who killed him – all I need is one finger with a print so I can take to the insurance company, let them run it against his record and get the policy paid! Can you help me or not?"

Howie and I burst into laughter.

"Howie what the hell did you say after that?"

He smiles. "I told her that I was very sorry but I wasn't in the finger recovery business. And that is true. I have no idea what happened to Glennon. I never did hear from Dottie again."

After Dermody's attempt on his life, Buddy was constantly devising new ways to sneak up on his enemies.

"I ever tell you about Buddy and the potato?" my father asks me one night over beers. What he actually said was, "Buddy and the puddada," but if I write it the way we say it, you'll never figure it out.

"It was during the war," my old man starts it off like any bedtime story, but with a Somerville twist. Other sons may have heard quite a bit about WWII, but for my father the Gang War was "The Big One."

"We were drinking at Pal Joey's. Buddy says he heard if you put a potato on the front of a gun it suppressed the noise." Sort of like an organic silencer, I muse (but to myself as I was also an organic silencer when it came to interrupting my father in the middle of an oration).

"Buddy was packing a .38 with a six inch barrel. It was a pretty big gun to carry but," the old man shrugs, "who was I to question anyone?"

Except me, I think.

"Buddy wouldn't use an automatic because they have a tendency to jam when you fire too fast. He liked the old fashioned six shooter that wouldn't fail in the middle of a firefight."

Good to know, just in case.

"So I go across the street and come back with two potatoes. Me and Buddy go down the cellar to the walk-in cooler. The cooler walls and floor are a foot thick. The floor can take a bullet easy. Buddy put

the potato on the muzzle, pointed at the floor and fired. Even with the buffer it was fucking deafening!"

"The fucking potato blew all over everything. Buddy had this puzzled look on his face. 'Hey, Bob, gimme another, willya? That was loud, maybe I did it wrong.'"

The cooler was only about ten feet wide so any noise would reverberate.

"This potato shatters all over and covers me and him with pulp. I look at Buddy, who has gunk all over his face and I say, 'Ya want me to get a turnip or should we just go upstairs and get a drink?'"

Buddy swiped a huge paw across his face, removing a portion of the gunk, threw back his head and laughed. "Fuck it, let's go get a cocktail. It's cleaner and a helluva lot quieter."

Buddy's cocktailing days were soon to come to an abrupt end. On October 30th 1965, Buddy McLean was thirty-six years old. Still strapping and handsome, despite a bad left eye and multiple facial scars from his incessant brawling, he was at the top of his game. The feud with Charlestown was in full swing and he was the uncontested leader of Somerville. He had the support of Patriarca and looked forward to settling all scores so his boys could return home, and business for himself and Howie would be once again be as usual. (In 1987, the FBI released transcripts of wiretaps from Patriarca's vending machine company in which the Mafia kingpin denied favoring either side but assured his men that if the killings didn't stop, he himself would declare "martial law" in Boston).

Buddy was with friends and bodyguards Tony Blue and an ex-fighter Rico Sacramone in the back room of Pal Joey's on Marshall Street. Buddy's Buick Electra was parked in front of the boarded up Capitol Theatre.

The three guys exited the bar and crossed Broadway to Buddy's car. As Tony and Rico started around to the passenger side, a thunderous crack accompanied by a flash came from the theatre doorway. Tony immediately raised his left arm and got a bullet into his elbow. Three other slugs from the same shotgun blast ended up in his lungs. Rico was hit with four rounds in the top of the head. He fell to the ground and appeared to be dead. From behind, Buddy saw it all and made his last decision. He opted not to leave his guys behind.

The Somerville boss dropped into a crouch behind his Buick and slid alongside of the car trying to pull Tony, who was closer to him, to safety. The shooter, McLaughlin associate and pal Stevie Hughes, was blasting away and as Buddy reached Tony, one of Hughes' shots hit him directly in the temple. Big brawler Buddy McLean, former daredevil truck driver, husband, father, bookmaker and local legend was instantly relegated to just another Somerville casualty. Hughes knew better than to stick around.

A few doors down was old man Grande's pizza shop. A Winter Hill sympathizer, Grande had fearlessly continued tossing pies in the plate glass window of his store during the Gang Wars, never caring he was an easy target if an example was to be made by McLaughlin minions. The boys from Somerville actually used his cellar for storing guns and taking action for the bookmakers. He was seemingly immune to the bloodshed occurring almost daily around the neighborhood. On this day, he was serving up a slice to a local cop when the violence began.

The vantage point from Grande's was a front row seat to the brutal shooting unfolding in the street and yet the cop never ventured outside. Howie is a man who even now as a retiree, chooses his words carefully.

"Yeah," he says with a small, ironic smile. "I heard that. Maybe if the cop came out blasting, things would have been different. But he didn't."

If he had, three may have survived instead of two, but the door to the pizza joint never opened as the men lay bleeding on the ground and the shooter disappeared.

"Do you remember that cop's name?" I ask Howie. He looks me straight in the eye and says tightly, "Red Bavin." He even spells the name for me. Howie holds my gaze for a moment and then shrugs. "I believe that was his name anyway."

Howie is a careful, cagey old guy. That *is* the name of the police officer always repeated when the story of Buddy's killing is told.

Howie Winter still remembers the call informing him of the ambush.

"I was sleeping when the phone rang. 'Buddy just got shot up Winter Hill!' And that he was with Rico and Tony Blue, and guys at the pizza stand saw it happen."

I asked Howie what he did after hanging up the phone.

"We always kept cars around, you know, loaded for bear. So I jumped into one and come flying up Temple Street, took a left and when I saw all of the squad cars and lights, I knew. I didn't stop, I knew Buddy was already gone."

Howie pauses, sits back in his chair and stares out the window for a moment. "From what I could gather, he was on the safe side of the car when the boys got hit. He could've gotten away but the shooter waited. He knew what kind of guy he was, knew Buddy wouldn't leave the others. He was the target. If he'd just ducked down he'd probably be here with us today. But when he reached around help, he caught one in the side of the head. He died a day or two later."

Howie is silent. I try to be quiet and not fidget, as a sign of respect but Howie knows I'm not famous for periods of silence, so he waves me on.

I recalled an old newspaper photo my father had years ago with Howie near the aftermath of the shooting but neither of us is able to locate the photo now.

Howie shrugs. "I might have driven around. I probably did, but couldn't get close. The cops knew us pretty well and for the most part, we got along. So I didn't have anything to be afraid of. "

What about the rumor of an accident on the way to the hospital? Was it staged by the cops to keep Buddy from medical attention?

Buddy's old partner shakes his head.

"I never heard that but it would have been a genuine accident, Bobby. We rarely had a beef with the cops. They liked Buddy so much that one of them, Officer John Canty, directed the wagon [carrying Buddy] right to Mass General, which was and still is one of the best hospitals around. Canty told me, 'Howie, I knew Buddy was hurt bad. I thought he'd have a chance at the best hospital.' They tried to save his life. But it was too late."

They couldn't have saved him. The doctor's report stated that had "Mr. McLean survived, he would have been a vegetable" due to the massive head wounds.

My last question is a sensitive subject. Frank Salemme is an alleged former Winter Hill Gang member, friend of Stevie Flemmi and now-convict who eventually pled guilty to eight gangland murders. He was a free man living under the crowded umbrella of the Federal Witness Protection Program until 2003, when his old pal and fellow rabbi Flemmi implicated him in yet another murder and that landed him back in the slammer.

During Salemme's first round of indictments, he swore under oath Buddy was an informant for later disgraced FBI agent H. Paul Rico and it was that relationship that assisted Buddy in finding (and killing) Ron Dermody so easily.

Howie Winter sits back. "Let me think of how I want to word this, Bobby."

I've just asked the man who chose prison over turning in his friends if he thought his childhood pal and partner could have been partnered instead with the law. I'm also wondering how much credence can one give to a Catholic boy who dresses up like a rabbi in order to execute an Irish gangster.

It's early in the interview process. I'm trying to follow the rules I studied in volumes of books on how to write books. I already broke the first. " Don't put yourself in the story." Fuck that, it's too late. Now I'm breaking another, "Don't assume the subject's emotion during the interview – ask him." Fuck that too. I'd be a complete idiot if I didn't realize my question has saddened my subject.

Finally Howie exhales and shakes his head.

"I don't know what happened to Frankie. When he was young, I really liked him. Then he and Stevie got into some problems and he went away. Just prior to that he had gone to the North End."

He's talking about Boston's own Little Italy; the north end of town that is a magnet for tourists and fans of architecture, great Italian restaurants and wonderfully authentic bakeries – there are about one hundred places to get a bite in the one-third square mile area. The city's oldest residential neighborhood, it was predominantly Irish until the late 1800's. Now it has become a melting pot of residents, but back in the sixties and seventies, the North End was almost exclusively Italian and the territory of the Angiulos under Patriarca. Salemme, like so many of us, is half Italian and half Irish, and moved easily between Winter Hill and the North End.

"He was with those guys and even though [the Angiulos] were friends, I didn't get involved in their business. But I don't know why he'd say such a thing. It's very painful. Buddy had no dealings with the FBI, nor did he need help in doing what he felt he had to do."

He's familiar with Rico, the FBI agent turned mob groupie, and his partner Dennis Condon. He dismisses them with a wave. "Those were always up the Hill, sniffing around. Buddy and I used to laugh and say to each other, "the pickin's must be slim if we're the biggest fish those two wanna bait!"

Howie leans in close to me. "If it were true, if Buddy had been involved with the Feds – which he was not, make no mistake about that – he never would have been murdered."

I have to agree. Stevie Flemmi, who had already been tapped by the Bureau to "assist" them by providing information in the mid-1960's, survived the gang wars without a scratch. Later on, Rico filed a report with J. Edgar Hoover stating, in part, that Flemmi "appears to be emotionally stable, and if he survives the gang war, he would be a very influential individual in the Boston criminal element." A rather slobbering bit of gangster worship, but Flemmi did indeed survive.

"They [the FBI] never would have taken the chance of allowing the McLaughlins to control the city. If Buddy had been with them, they would have protected him. As it was," Howie concludes, "the only protection we ever had or needed was what we gave each other."

In the world of organized crime, the McLaughlins caused the Feds a much bigger headache with their unbridled violence and New York ties than a couple of bookmakers from Somerville.

"That's all," Howie says, and then, "Will you be sure to put that in your book? I'd like people to know it."

Throughout the next year, Howie and I will have hours of conversations. Not once will he ever ask me to include, or eliminate, any other story, even those about himself.

"Yes," I reply. "I will."

One more thing about Cadillac Frank. In 1989, Frank got into bed with a Hollywood company looking to shoot in New England without hiring union workers. In exchange for thousands of dollars, Frank promised to make the deal. The company turned out to be a bunch of FBI guys pretending to be producers. Matthew Broderick starred in the fictionalized account of the sting in a real Hollywood movie called *The Last Shot*. He did not play Salemme.

The urban legends continue to flourish, but in the end, Buddy McLean, a man who grew up hard and wasn't afraid of anything, died along with over sixty men because some vicious drunk couldn't keep his hands to himself.

In what can only be described as bizarre juxtaposition, the three men who helped start the war survived. After dumping Georgie on the hospital lawn the two hapless partiers, Bill Hickey and Red Lloyd, wisely packed and blew town, leaving years to come of death, destruction and scores of widows in their unintentional wake. Hickey headed for the relatively huge hiding space of Texas. Lloyd disappeared.

"Never saw or heard from them for decades," Howie says. "I finally bumped into Lloyd years later down the Cape and invited me to his house. He'd moved and started a business. He always was a capable kid."

Americo "Rico" Sacramone survived, the bullets only grazed his head. He was sent back to jail for his remaining sentence for armed bank robbery. He was killed February 3, 1975 and his body dumped in the marshes near the abandoned Saugus racetrack on Route 107.

In one of the last ambushes attributed to the Irish Gang Wars, hitman Stevie Hughes was driving with his new boss, aging Charlestown loan shark and abortionist Sammy Lindenbaum, when a car pulled up along side them and sprayed the moving vehicle with machine gun fire.

Poor Sammy was warned he shouldn't be riding around with Hughes. Stevie was first and next on the Winter Hill guys' hit parade. They had already blasted at him with five shots a few months earlier and succeeded in killing his brother Connie but to date, Stevie was still breathing.

"Sammy," one guy warned, "you keep ridin' with him, all I can promise that we'll try not to hit you in the crossfire, but he's goin'. You gotta decide if you want him to drive you there."

The Irish Gang Wars ended but the grudges survived well into the coming decades.

Tony Blue, paroled from prison in 1964, was put into the hospital under protective custody with his shattered arm in a cast. Once he recovered he was sent back to jail to serve the rest of his four to seven for assault and battery. Howie and Tony remained close friends until Tony's death in 2010.

The third survivor, eighty-year-old George "Georgie" McLaughlin, is spending his retirement at Walpole State Prison in Massachusetts, convicted of the 1964 murder of a bank teller – the one murder unrelated to the war he had started. His brothers Bernie and Punchy are long buried. Punchy (sans that one hand) was obliterated by Bulger cohort Flemmi at the behest of crooked FBI agent Rico. Punchy made the fatal error of insulting Rico on an FBI wire with the same epitaph that the unfortunate Paul Colicci slung at Raymond Patriarca.

Georgie's road buddies and enemies are all gone, and the elderly murderer is left alone to face the ghosts of the lives he destroyed.

In the years that followed the incident in Salisbury, entire communities of decades-long loyalties were called into question. This time has been dubbed "The Irish Gang Wars" and depicted historically as an organized crime free-for-all in which thugs and gangsters blew each other away with reckless abandon, but in fact, it was much more than that.

In Somerville, an Irish American burg less than four square miles with almost 100,000 residents, the grainy fabric of loyalty within the community was what held it together during a time in which the state and the nation as a whole were changing, fueled by fear and anger.

Boston and its surrounding areas had already been in the death grip of terror from 1962 to '64 as an unknown serial killer was going house to house, strangling women.

The confusion and anger after the assassination of President Kennedy spread across the country like the opening of an ugly seeping sore and nowhere was that more evident than in the predominantly Irish cities and towns that felt as if they had lost one of their own.

A drunken argument between three men did not just set off a war between two factions of thugs; it clearly drew the line between two side-by-side communities. The boys from Somerville, as well as the guys from Charlestown were locals and it became nearly impossible for their respective communities not to begin to feel as if a civil war was being fought in their very streets, leaving innocent men, women and children at risk of being caught in the crossfire. Life in the city of Somerville changed almost overnight and we still carry the scars of that terrible time.

As for Buddy McLean?

In life, Buddy was as large a persona as one could imagine and even over forty years after his demise, his name is still spoken in those rare hushed New England tones reserved for the Red Sox or a local legend. That legend and the history leading up to it left deep scars on his own family.

Buddy's son Jimmy suffered the pain of losing his father. Jimmy was brilliant and a top student at Northeastern University in Boston. But he had his own demons he fought inside.

I knew Jimmy pretty well. We used to cruise around town together and he drove like a madman. We'd had a few near misses until one afternoon he took me down Huntington Avenue in Boston doing a hundred and forty miles an hour, gliding from lane to lane without so much as a glance in his mirrors. If another car had been in our path, so be it. Not much scares me, but I was sure this kid was trying to fulfill a death wish. I was not. I jumped out at a light and never got back into a car with him again. He scared the shit out of me.

Jimmy overdosed in his apartment on Revere Beach. His father's death had a great impact on him. He never got over it.

Buddy McLean had an impact on my own life, even though I was only twelve when he died.

My father kept Buddy's picture on our wall for over ten years after his murder. He loved Buddy McLean and was profoundly affected by his murder.

One afternoon, as the two of them headed down the street toward the corner bar, Buddy suddenly turned to my old man and said, "Bobby, walk on the other side of the street, willya? I'll meet ya."

My old man asked why the hell should he walk on the opposite sidewalk. Buddy didn't miss a beat as he replied "You got seven kids and I know you're with me, but those bastards really want me dead bad, and I don't want you to go when I go."

With that, he pulled ahead of my father and whistled his way down the block and into the bar, the two German Shepherds at his heels.

Buddy was a smart guy, he knew the life he'd chosen and he also knew, deep down, what would eventually befall him. He didn't want any of his friends to get it along with him. My father told that story until the day he died. "That was the way it was," he would say, "in Somerville."

I never bought another comic book or anything else with that quarter Buddy McLean gave me. He left such a profound impression on me that I saved it for months, hidden deep in a bureau drawer until eventually one of my brothers found it, stole it, and I beat the living daylights out of him. First, because he stole from me and second, because Buddy McLean was dead by then, one shot to the head and facedown in the street, his long legs casually crossed as if he were napping in the afternoon sun.

I had wanted to save that coin forever. That was the magnitude of the impression Buddy made on one eleven-year-old guy.

"Bobby," Howie asks me a second time. "Do you still have that picture of Buddy that your father had hanging on the wall in your old house?"

I don't have the photograph anymore, but I wish I did.

CHAPTER FOUR

Pinball Wizards, Leg Breakers and the Salesmen of Fear

IN THE EARLY 70's, there were two illegal poker machines at the VFW Pointer Post my old man ran. In fact, there were illegal poker and pinball machines all over the city. The DAVs, Moose Club, all of the private clubs had them. Gambling in Massachusetts was illegal, as were coin operated vending games, but like so many things, the legality and morality of a variety of different activities was predicated more by community acceptance than actual laws on the books. Survival in Somerville was already a gamble day-to-day, so stuffing a few coins into a machine was a risk that at least had a potential payoff.

There was always somebody on the machines. Always. My old man had a closet where he kept his tucked away from the general bar population. Occasionally he'd get a call in the middle of the night from one of the local cops. He was tight with them and he also had five "rambunctious" sons, so an officer on the line wasn't unusual.

"Bob, how you doin'?" The cop would invariably start off the conversation as if it were noon instead of one in the morning.

Immediately, my father tallied the names of "possible suspects" to himself, Bobby, Bobby (better count him twice) Leo, Eddie – count him three times, Joey, Jimmy....

"How's the family?" Not the boys. Good.

"Oh ya, good," my father would respond, already reaching for his battered notebook of phone numbers. If this were about one of his boys he'd have known by now. He also knew it wasn't a social call. He responded in kind, "And you, the kids, wife?" as he patiently waited for the information.

"Ya, good too." The conversation would speed up. "Listen Bob, something I was just thinkin'. If I was runnin' a private club, I'd make sure I didn't have any illegal machines there in the next, oh I dunno, say two hours from now?"

My father would agree, perhaps this evening was not the time for customers to be lined up in front of the closet, especially himself.

"OK, then," the cop would say. "Take care."

"You too. Thanks," my old man would say even as he was dialing.

The cops were planning another raid on the local clubs and time was of the essence.

When the phone on the other end of my father's was picked up with a sleepy grunt, he simply said, "Come and get 'em!"

"On the way."

The machines were gone before the law arrived. Every time. It was a little thing Big Bob thought of as reducing the odds. Then he'd go back to his business of working through a pile of scratch off lottery tickets.

In 1974, Massachusetts became the first state to legalize and offer the scratch off ticket lottery and it changed the face of my father's entire life. He bought them by the fistful, convinced he would be the one to cause the Bay State to go broke paying out his winnings. And there was always a winner, but it wasn't Big Bob. It was an even split between the State and the huge green trash barrel that filled up daily with losing tickets.

Howie and I are seated in his dining room in the late afternoon. I ask how many times he'd been arrested.

"Bobby, I was never arrested until I was forty-nine. In September of 1977 all the local bar owners were complaining about illegal pinball machines in the clubs," Howie tells me. The clubs he's talking about are private clubs like the DAV (Disabled American Veterans) and the American Legion.

The town of Somerville had refused to issue licenses for coin-operated amusement machines since 1954.

Invented in 1895 by Charles Fey of San Francisco, the slot machine, the early model for the pinball and subsequent video gambling revolution, soon became a cherished commodity and the scourge of the working class. For a nickel, a patron could take his chances on a big win. It wasn't long before somebody said, "Hey, I can make loads off these suckers." And so, another gambling avenue was born for law enforcement to try and shut down.

In the 70's, Howie and Sal's bookmaking business was booming. But even with the advent of racetracks, sports betting, scratch tickets and the country clamoring for legalized gambling, the Joe Average Income Or Belows were still looking for a new way to pay their money and take their chances. In Somerville, it was the private clubs with vending machines. And although amusement machines were not something Howie and Sal were interested in, public bar owners were, as they watched their profits begin to drain away.

Howie explains, "Suddenly bar patrons were sparse and the bar owners lonely. Former customers were at the private clubs, playing the one armed bandits. Then their wives started bitching about the men blowing their pay. Bars were losing those profits to little places that didn't pay near the overhead."

Truth be told, the bar owners wanted not just their customers back, but a piece of the action as well. They couldn't compete due to the lack of legality in machines that paid off. A private club had control of their members, a sort of secret society of patrons. Barrooms were public; the lure of the machines did not outweigh the potential loss of license.

And the wives didn't restrict their complaining to their spouses.

"Neither Howie or Sal could walk across the street without hearing about the machines from neighborhood women," Sal's son-in-law Bobby McCarthy says, shaking his head.

The local aldermen began to get a hint of something more than the usual problems between husbands and wives, and it did seem that tavern owners were hurting. If the men weren't spending hours in local watering holes, what was left to fight about? In a loyal drinking town like Somerville, that was certainly unusual.

Howie called Sal and told him what he had been hearing and Sal related the same story back.

"Howie, all of the clubs have 'em, the family machines."

The "family" Howie is referring to is the well-circulated community awareness that the vending machines - pinball, poker - were operated, in part, by the member of a well known political family close to the heart of Somerville.

No, it wasn't the Kennedys. Haven't you been paying attention? Somerville ain't Hyannisport.

"I found that all out later," Howie says, and I figure that I will too.

"Anyway, the bar owners got together to try and make the machines legitimate so they would be allowed to have them."

This would not only level the playing field in the game of winning customers, but would also dilute the thrill of illegitimacy enough so that business would be steady.

"Sal and I supported all local politicians. We always bought out the tables at fundraising events for anyone running for office, we never said no."

Back in the day before Internet campaigns, free YouTube videos and email blasts, tables were the sole mainstay of local small town politics. Fundraisers ran constantly and the costs of reserving a table at any given event brought in the needed cash to keep the political machine running smoothly.

Howie and Sal, along with bar owners felt it was time to put it to the test; to see if the games could be legitimized. Scratch lottery was mainstream and sanctioned by the state, why not amusements? Someone had to get the ball rolling.

"I felt comfortable enough to approach the politicians and say 'Look, the bars are losing business due to something that is out of control. Eventually the ordinance was passed to allow coin-operated amusements."

Confused? What made some of the amusements legal after Somerville's ordinance passed and others not? Simple. A coin-operated game was now allowed for entertainment purposes. A slot machine that paid back in cash was not. On July 28, 1977, Somerville did indeed enact an ordinance allowing coin-operated amusement devices. It did not legalize one-armed bandits, or any gambling at all.

Jimmy Ardizzoni worked for Melo-Tone Vending in Somerville for over thirty years. Jimmy's knowledge of all things vending is vast and he helped me to figure out exactly how the pinball payouts worked.

A pinball machine could only grant the winner a free game. There was no way to pay out directly from the unit, but each machine used for gambling was rigged to a button behind the bar. The player was paid his winnings in cash by the barman who then reset the machine.

"At the top were the most holes and the lowest odds and scores. As the field went down, there were fewer holes and the odds went up. You could win upwards of a hundred dollars a hit."

That makes it clear to me. A player could win a helluva lot of money if he knew what he was doing, and the only way to do that was practice. Rolls and rolls of quarters of practice.

Jimmy knows Howie well. "He was a frequent visitor to Melo-Tone."

I ask him about rumors that Howie was laundering money through Melo-Tone.

"I can't say that I ever saw anything like that at all." Jimmy is a little embarrassed, "Bobby, I don't even know how money laundering works."

I'm glad to return the favor and give Jimmy the Cliff Notes version of laundering. You hand a guy a thousand bucks to move and he gives you back eight hundred for his trouble and the risk of sliding the money into legal channels.

Jimmy shrugs and shakes his head. "Nope, never saw that. But I did see Whitey come around a lot."

"Whitey Bulger? What was he doing there?"

Jimmy thinks for a second. "Actually, I have no idea. But if it were office business, I wouldn't know anyway."

Jimmy tells me that Melo-Tone would not solicit accounts for any vending whatsoever in Somerville even after the ordinance had passed. "There was always an unwritten rule in vending of not stepping on anyone else's territory. We didn't solicit Charlestown either. We didn't want to step on anyone's toes."

He will not say whose toes would have been bruised, though. "I don't know, my boss just said we were to stay out of both places."

With all of the noise being created by the wives and the bar owners, why didn't the cops just sweep in and shut it all down? Except for the occasional phone call to the Pointer Post or another club, the illegal machines were allowed to stay in their places. The profits kept rolling in.

This is a subject Howie is passionate about, and with good reason as it set into motion a downhill snowball for both himself and Sal.

"We decided to look into it. Just to see what the deal was."

They were surprised, it was no wonder the taprooms were going belly up. The vending was bringing in anywhere *from six to nine thousand dollars a week* for the private clubs! They also discovered the bulk of machines were provided by a guy named Arthur Agostinelli who ran the Somerset Vending Company.

Howie and Sal decided to pay a visit to one of the clubs still supporting the illegal machines. By the next month, Howie, Sal Sperlinga, and a guy by the name of Herbie Foster had been arrested on charges of attempted extortion and conspiracy.

A five week trial, a sort of legal Cirque du Soleil, ensued and when it was all over, the motions numbered in the hundreds, transcript pages into the thousands. Some guys were locked up, some walked, some ran and Howie Winter was left shaking his head, wondering what the hell had really happened.

It started with a visit.

The DAV Post Chapter 27 in Somerville was run by Austin Griffin who served as the post's adjutant and service officer. This location was one of the major complaints.

"We rang the bell like you do at those clubs and introduced ourselves. Well, I did. Sal was just looking around. We saw the machines. They looked exactly like Vegas one-armed bandits."

Griffin claimed Howie and Sal threatened him. During trial, he stated, "Winter said 'I just spent a bundle of money making those machines legal and I'm going to get it back. Those machines are going out and mine are coming in. . . . I'll give you to Friday.'"

Not true, according to Howie. "We hadn't even been in his club or seen the machines. We were still trying to find out what it was all about. What I did say was that if his machines were illegal machines, they'd have to be replaced."

Howie says, "Griffin got aggressive, raised his voice right off the bat. 'We [the DAV] own the machines and the club spent a lot of money on them.' I raised my voice too, I have to admit, but told him we'd just come to talk and didn't appreciate being yelled at. That guy was way too defensive. I should have known something was up."

There was and it had to do with getting Howie out of the way.

After everyone calmed down, Griffin deferred to the Club's board; at their next scheduled meeting, he'd bring it up.

"I knew he was just trying to get rid of us. I knew how the boards worked from your father. They could meet anytime. I did say, 'Look, we'll come back on Friday.'"

Griffin told the court he was "scared blue."

Howie shrugs. "He shook hands when we came in and again when we left. He was the one who started yelling. No one ever threatened him."

In the meantime, Griffin called one of the financial officers of his post and that gentleman called ATF investigator Maurice DelVendo.

"That wasn't a cold call, like they made it appear. As if they called the law immediately. DelVendo was a member and knew Griffin well, as he also knew me. He used to follow me around, always looking for something on us."

DelVendo also knew Sal and finally reached out to him on the phone and asked him about two guys showing up at the DAV inquiring about pinball machines. According to DelVendo, Sal said, "I'll look into it."

The agent testified he ran into Sal two days later at Magoun Square and Sal told him that he had looked into the matter and that the DAV club was "clean." DelVendo recalled he then told Sal that he and Howie were "foolish to be doing their own strong-arm work."

Sal shook his head and smiled. There wasn't any strong-arming going on. But maybe there was something else lurking in the wings. He replied, "Maury, are you wired?"

"Sure Sal said that," my father agreed. "He and Maury were friends. He didn't mean Maury must have heard some threats. You gotta remember, Sal was a very smart, very shrewd guy. He was ribbing Maury back because both he and Maury knew that neither Sal nor Howie was in the strong-arm business. And," said the old man, rather shrewdly himself, I must say, "If they was as big of organized crime dons as the DA made 'em out to be, Howie and Sal would have had guys for that. You know, buffers."

Howie and Sal continued on their route. They went to see the man who provided the DAV with their machine, Arthur Agostinelli at the Somerset Vending Company.

"I told Agostinelli we'd been to the DAV and his machines appeared to be one-armed bandits. The whole purpose of the law was to let everyone have a chance at a profit. Agostinelli got hot right away."

The pinball owner testified that "Winters and Sal" informed him he had two days to pull his machines out of the city or he'd be sorry.

"You're all done. This is my city and I own it," he insisted Howie announced.

"Bullshit," Howie laughs. "He said to *me*, 'who the hell do you think YOU are? Do you think you own this city? You're going to tell me what to do with my machines?'"

"I don't own this city," Howie replied, "but neither do you. Then Sal, who'd said nothing up to this point, jumped in," Howie remembers. "He said, "Wait, we came to talk business, not to argue. Let's cool down and we'll come back in a couple of days."

Agostinelli swore under oath, "Winter said I could put a reasonable price on the machines and Winter would buy them or just take them out and…install his own machines."

And, in an out-of-court statement, Agostinelli told a co-worker that Howie, "says if we don't get out of the business, they're going to break my legs, they're going to do other things."

I sometimes work out of town and on one occasion I walked into a bar where, coincidentally, a famous Boston mob attorney was having a drink with a companion also from the Bay State. The companion whispered under her breath as I approached them to say hello, "I can't believe it! Look who just walked in! That's Bobby Martini, the leg breaker from Southie!"

A leg breaker is someone who breaks another's leg for money (as opposed to a psycho who does it for pleasure); an enforcer for a certain entity usually attached to organized crime.

It was doubly offensive because as many fights as I've had, I've never broken anyone's leg and certainly wouldn't for money, which was the connotation, but even more painful was the Southie part.

I'm from Somerville. People think all of Boston is Southie from the movies, but trust me; there isn't one guy in either city that wants to be mistaken for the other.

The point of my story? Leg breaker, breaking legs, all of that stereotypical Mafia bullshit is just that; bullshit, so when someone says it, I just think of myself, a guy who's never broken anyone's legs but can't shake the stereotype. I also have to throw in with my father on this one. If some big time gangsters stroll into your place to personally threaten you with something, I believe it wouldn't be just breaking your legs.

Howie sighs. "It wasn't even part of the testimony. It was something one of Agostinelli's employees *said* Gus told him. I've never been known as a leg breaker."

There's one of us at least.

But it sure made for great newspaper sales.

Enter vending salesmen Gerard "Bud" Robinson and Herbert "Herbie" Foster, soon to be Howie and Sal's co-defendants.

"Herbie was an associate of Sal's, I didn't really have anything to do with him business-wise," Howie says. Foster owned a company called Ball Square Air Hockey, also amusements. For a city that didn't allow coin-operated amusements, we sure had an overflow of companies to supply them.

"I did know him, though. He was a good guy. He owned the bowling alley down Ball Square and I think he had some machines, legal ones. No big deal. Sal wanted to get some legit machines in the bars and he asked me to come and talk to Foster with him."

"What would your take have been?" I ask.

The sides of Howie's mouth turn down. "Nothing. I wasn't interested. Look, Bobby, it's no secret that Sal and I were bookmaking. That was my business. I wasn't interested in amusements, but Sal was – it was an avenue for a legitimate venture. But the fact remains that when guys kept saying we were going to bring in our own machines – we simply didn't have any."

In the meantime, another Boston guy was quietly procuring his own under the noses of everyone else.

Bud Robinson worked for International Products of America, the company who manufactured the machines offered by Somerset Vending. Robinson testified that in August of 1977, he received a call from a guy he didn't know, a Herbie Foster, for a meeting.

Robinson contends that Foster told him "Howie was taking over all the [vending] locations in the city immediately." He testified he attended a meeting at a Chelsea motel where Howie and Sal demanded he back out of all the clubs. They would buy Robinson's machines for a fair price or put their own in.

"I didn't have any machines," Howie reminds me as we go over the trial transcripts.

And then, of course, Howie supposedly said again, "You're all done. I own this city."

Robinson swears he laughed in Howie's face.

"Geez, Howie," I say. "There were quite a few allegations of who said they owned Somerville and who accused others of owning it in this trial. We are very territorial, I guess."

He stares at me and I wonder for a second if, as often happens, my mouth got ahead of me. But then he bursts out laughing.

"It would seem to be the case, Robert."

"So who was Robinson?" I ask.

Now Howie is pissed.

"Bobby, I never went to Chelsea to meet anyone. I never laid eyes on this guy until he appeared at the trial. In fact, they called him as a witness and then couldn't find him for something like six days. We had no idea who he was. And why the hell would I have gone to a manufacturer if I were in the business of, as they said, 'taking over the city' anyway? What the hell were they trying to intimate, that Sal and I bought a manual and were building our own pinball machines in the garage? I never met with or even was introduced to Robinson."

The First Assistant District Attorney said Robinson "felt very real fear as a result of being threatened," thus the reason for his disappearance to the Virgin Islands. Robinson returned voluntarily after he made a phone call to the DA's office and complained he was "being followed." The DA called the chief of police on the island of St. Thomas; Robinson was taken into custody and subsequently returned to Massachusetts.

The DA. He's a big name. Not a Kennedy either.

The whole disappearance was "well orchestrated" according to Howie's attorney Ralph Champa Jr., and very convenient. It certainly peaked the interest of the media.

Robinson testified he had subsequent meetings with Foster.

"That I don't know," Howie says. "I had no idea Herbie even knew the guy."

Then things started to go, as they say in 50's noir novels, hinky, for Robinson. He admitted that in 1973 he'd been found guilty on three separate occasions of possessing and selling illegal slots. He also testified that his machines were either a direct sale or a lease-purchase in which the clubs paid a flat $25 a week fee. Then the defense introduced evidence that not only were Robinson employees making collections from the club machines, but that Robinson and the clubs were actually splitting the profits.

The trial itself brought the circus to Somerville with so much innuendo as to the reputation of Howie Winter that the trial judge was prompted to admonish "Howard Winter is on trial for certain offenses, but he is not on trial as Howard Winter," meaning that the state could not mount a case on Howie's reputation as an organized crime figure.

There were delays and motions, arguments and objections all day long in the five-week trial. The defense saw the other side try repeatedly to interject the taint of organized crime into the proceedings ("How did you feel when you knew it was Howie Winter who came to see you?").

The prosecution asked Robinson if he was receiving protection.

"I sure am!" he replied happily, even as the judge ruled the defense's objection sustained. No evidence was ever presented that Robinson was threatened, yet the prosecution slipped in the question of protection so quickly, the witness answered.

Prosecutor J. William Codhina tried to word the question of "Do you live with your wife?" to Howie *seven* different times on the stand until the judge became exasperated. Howie was still married to his first wife but they did not live together - he lived with his girlfriend. The prosecutors wanted to get some of the more salacious details of his life out for the jury.

They made numerous references to James "Jimmy" Martorano, even though he was not connected to the case in any way, just to keep that Mob connection in everyone's mind. The crowning glory in the prosecution's rather sick cap was asking

Howie if he'd burned down Chandler's Restaurant because his tenant had stopped paying rent. It didn't matter that the question was inappropriate and the judge shot it down. It was out there, the suspicion of the Boogeyman.

"Salesmen of fear...leg breakers [there's that word again!] ...contemplating murders...against the little people who don't carry guns," the prosecution pulled out every worn out euphemism and it worked. Codhina coined the "salesmen of fear" title in his closing and the connotation was, if you think about it, chilling. Big bad gangsters leaned on a small American charitable club and in the process had done the Mob equivalent of burning the flag and slapping the Pope.

It was a confusing carnival of theories and rumors that one needed a scorecard to follow.

The defense team, Albert "Albie" Cullen Jr., Ralph Champa Jr. and Daniel O'Connell Jr. planned from the beginning to show that Robinson, Agostinelli and Griffin were engaged in a counter-conspiracy as they were "involved with illegal gambling machines" and didn't want legal revenues undercutting their profit margin. But even Judge Paul Garrity had his doubts that the jury could follow this case. There were just too many one-on-one accusations and weird sidebar issues.

The three juniors did a valiant job defending their clients, filing one hundred and forty pre-trial motions in attempts to delay the trial long enough to wade through possible evidence, probable rumors, and definite lies. Part of the evidence against Sal was a piece of paper wrapped around a bundle of fundraiser tickets for a Somerville alderman candidate that was seized, seemingly illegally, from his car glove box and the defense fought hard to have it thrown out.

"They arrested Sal outside his apartment," Howie tells me. "The officer testified that he saw Sal's glove compartment open and a list with names written on it."

Somerville cop Lt. Raymond Peck did say he saw, through the passenger-side window, that the glove box was open and based on what he saw hanging out of it, he got a warrant and searched the car. This list was allegedly the names of fifty Somerville bars with numbers written next to them.

But when Judge Garrity and the lawyers for both sides sat in the car during the trial, the light was burned out in the glove box and even Peck had to admit that he couldn't read anything. It was his assertion he could decipher names and figures on the paper that convinced a judge to issue the search warrant in the first place.

The name of the alderman for whom the event tickets had been purchased by Sal was never disclosed. It was a trial, but it was also Somerville, after all.

The court asked for a handwriting sample and when all three defendants declined to comply, they were promptly deemed in contempt and sent to the Billerica House of Corrections to think about it. They thought about it and still refused.

"We weren't giving a handwriting sample for evidence that had been seized illegally to begin with," Howie says flatly. "And Peck? He came to us on more than one occasion for help with thugs selling angel dust! We got hold of the dealers and told them they couldn't sell in this town. We'd solve the problem for him and we were only too glad to do it."

Judge Garrity eventually threw the list out – after the jury heard it and the defendants were already cited for contempt.

Cullen asked Agostinelli on the stand if he had changed the settings on his machines so that the "payout" would be larger. Agostinelli never denied the accusation, instead he said he couldn't remember, leaving open the possibility that indeed the machines were tampered with in order to up an ante *that was already prohibited by law.*

During his closing, Champa stated his case simply. His clients were guilty of one thing, "being stupid enough to believe that normal, flipper pinball machines could replace illegal gambling devices bringing in thousands of dollars a week."

Champa called the prosecution witnesses "reprehensible liars" who "raped these [private] clubs, lined their own pockets at the expense of the clubs." Robinson had admitted to it during his own testimony.

As the testimony continued, it became front-page local news and the community responded in strong support of Howie and Sal.

In the end, it was too late. On February 1st 1978, Howie Winter and Sal Sperlinga were convicted of conspiracy to commit extortion. The eight men and four women on the jury voted to let Foster skate. The DA promised the sentences for the two "reputed organized crime figures" would be "close to the maximum."

Judge Garrity immediately revoked bail and remanded Howie and Sal back to Billerica, while Foster hit the streets and the prosecution celebrated their "victory for the little people." But that wasn't the end of the drama surrounding the free for all.

"As we were indicted, a very interesting thing happened. The vending machine guys had state police escorts to each of their locations."

"To finally take the machines out?" I ask.

Howie laughs and slaps his knee. "No, no, Bobby. Not to remove them. The state police were escorting them to collect their money *out* of the machines."

"You mean the illegal machines kept operating in these places even after you guys were indicted for allegedly threatening the owners?"

He winks at me. "And guess who was supervising it all? Remember the Assistant District Attorney from the trial?"

I do. You know him if you're from Massachusetts, but if you aren't, you might recall his name – he ran for president last time around.

"John Kerry."

The future Senator and future almost "second-President-of-The-United-States from Boston"?

"His office was sending state police around to help collect profits from machines that were installed against local, state and federal laws."

While Howie and Sal mounted a defense, the vending owners got their money, the customers got their pulls, the illegal machines kept spinning and the profits kept rolling in, protected by the cops.

Howie raises both of his hands. "You saw it," he says matter-of-factly. "You saw it, everyone saw it happening."

More than a few old friends of my father agree, they saw it with their own eyes. Cops entering the club, one on each side of Agostinelli's guy. Maybe it was a jangle of keys, the turn of a tumbler, and coins clanging out into bags.

"Ya, we saw it every other day or so, but we never put it together," one old friend confides.

"Somerset Vending. That was the family company," Howie says, "Agostinelli's partner was married to one of the O'Neills."

Tip O'Neill was and is, even in the afterlife, a Massachusetts icon. The famously liberal longtime Speaker of The House and congressman was a hometown boy and hero who worked for traditional Democratic causes, as well as peace and aid for Northern Ireland. Rather than give a history lesson, I'll quote Bill Clinton who said, "Tip O'Neill was the nation's most prominent, powerful and loyal champion of working people ... . He loved politics and government because he saw politics and government could make a difference in people's lives. And he loved people most of all."

Massachusetts loved Tip O'Neill. Somerville loved Tip O'Neill.

"And their machines, they were all over the state. No one was going to go up against that," Howie explains. "It was common knowledge his relatives were in vending and certainly the law wasn't going to blow that out of the water, even if ol' Tipper wasn't involved directly."

It appeared that with Howie and Sal out on bail and the business of the secret society of vending now the worst kept secret in town, vending owners sought the protection of law enforcement to insure no one walked away with the profits – which was their goal from the start. It was billed as protection from "organized crime."

The afternoon sun has given way to the blanket of night but I have one more question. John Kerry eventually ran for higher office on a platform that included putting away a dangerous mobster – Howie Winter. He got quite a bit of leverage out of that and ran full-page ads bragging about the win for years.

"And," Howie shrugs, "as anyone that knows him will say, John Kerry doesn't do anything unless there's something in it for John Kerry."

"Howie, Kerry called you 'the number two organized crime boss in New England'. What do you call him?"

The edges of Howie's mouth struggle not to turn into a full-fledged grin. "What do I call him? The number one publicity hound."

I wonder if Howie took offense to Kerry's statement. In another community, perhaps, one would be offended to see their name linked with that infamous phrase "organized crime" but up here? Here in Massachusetts we pride ourselves on being number one at everything we do, even if it does happen to be on the other side of the law. If Kerry was going to go to all of that trouble to put on such a show, you think the least he could have done was given Howie the higher billing.

Howie began to serve his pinball sentence, but more trouble was just around the corner. His name would become forever linked with a guy known as "the greatest horse fixer of them all" and Howie's partnership with Sal was about to come to an abrupt end.

Arthur Agostinelli convinced a jury in 1978 that he wasn't involved in any shady gambling deals but in 1995 both Agostinelli and his son were sentenced to two years probation and ten grand in fines for running an illegal video poker machine business. Assistant U.S. Attorney Kevin J. Cloherty released the information that the Agostinellis leased video poker gambling machines to social clubs in Somerville, *"all the while having the knowledge that the games were being used as illegal gambling devices."*

Howie leans back and shakes his head. "Well, he serviced every illegal machine in the city. He was one of them involved in a conspiracy to keep illegal machines in the clubs, but I was convicted. It was conspiracy all right, but it wasn't Sal and I. I was a political football. And all of the prosecutors, especially John Kerry went along with it."

"And Kerry, he was rarely in the courtroom, but he made sure he took all the credit for it after the convictions," he concludes. Howie remains convinced of the conspiracy.

"Austin Griffin's brother was the head of the General Services Administration during the Carter Administration until he was forced out. Guess who appointed him?"

I don't even need to venture a guess.

"Tip O'Neill," Howie affirms. "You can see how it all ties together.

In 2004, John Kerry lost his bid for the Presidency to the reigning occupant of the White House, George W. Bush. Kerry remains the other Senator from Massachusetts – the one who is not Teddy Kennedy. The joke, I guess, was on Kerry the entire time and I wonder if he's bothered to catch up on all of that old Somerville Irish Mob news over the years. Unfortunately, it was also on Howie.

Sometime between the end of 1977 and the beginning of '78, the owners of National Melo-Tone Vending complained to the FBI that they had received threats from a couple of well-known Boston guys. Guys with the reputation of real leg breakers, Whitey Bulger and Stevie Flemmi. The boys had *their* own vending company – National Vending – and they wanted Melo-Tone out of wherever *they* had machines. If Melo-Tone didn't comply, they would be, they were told, very, very sorry.

That's pretty much an Irish offer you cannot refuse, unless you want to get real closer to what we call The Final Misery.

The Melo-Tone men called the FBI and unfortunately were forwarded to agent John Connolly. Connolly and fellow agents Tom Daly and Peter Kennedy already had a laundry list of complaints about Bulger from a variety of individuals.

Whitey's childhood friend Connolly did not give Melo-Tone that warm and fuzzy feeling one expects when seeking protection from bad guys. In fact, he intimated that the owners and families would be in extreme danger if they pursued a case against Bulger. Connolly's warnings completely dissuaded the executives from filing their complaint.

So, it seems, while Howie and Sal were pushing for the passing of an ordinance for legal machines, Bulger and Flemmi were pursuing their way in — with the knowledge of the FBI and under the rather pompous nose of John Kerry. I'd like to think Kerry knew about it as well, but that seems doubtful at best. The Boston FBI was pretty crafty for a while.

Howie Winter went off to jail, but FBI agent Daly didn't forget about him in the coming years.

Born on the 4th of July, Austin Griffin passed away in 2006 at the age of 91, hailed as a war hero and the man who "stared the mobster down."

Born on St. Patty's Day, Howie Winter rolls his eyes.

"He had plenty to say about me, because he knew he could get away with it. He played on his war hero status and made himself into a victim, but let me tell you, that DAV club was his own private domain. God knows how much he robbed out of there over the years — not gave to the members, just stuffed in his kick. Too bad the IRS didn't investigate him."

I'd been trying to confirm stories about Austin Griffin I'd heard over the months. I ask Howie about Griffin's demeanor.

"Bobby, if I said I spoke to the guy for more than two minutes on that one occasion, I'd be lying. I don't know anything about him except that he started screaming right off."

In his obituary, Griffin's daughter wrote "There are a lot of people who aren't proud to be from Somerville, but he's not one of them, I have an uncle who said, 'If you're going to write something about Austy, make sure it begins, 'Born in Somerville.' He'll haunt you if you don't.'"

With all respect due, I don't know what the hell she meant by the Somerville slam, but I do know it pisses me off. I'm *proud* to be from Somerville and so is everyone I grew up with. There's something about letting us know that you're proud of our hometown *in spite* of us that is more than offensive.

As far as starting writing with where Griffin was from?

I'm from Somerville and if you're gonna haunt ME, pal, all I can say is — get in line...behind my old man, my brothers and all the rest of the boys that ran the streets and are now rattling their chains in the hereafter. You don't scare me.

Much more terrifying ghosts of Somerville past are already snapping at my heels.

CHAPTER FIVE

The Phony Gangster:
Sal Sperlinga

I WAS BORN in '53 so by the early 1970's I was in prime smart-ass form. Good with my hands in the way you want to be in the streets, I was gaining a reputation as a guy who not only wouldn't back down from any fistfight, but also never lost.

By then there weren't many things my father and I did together peacefully, but we had an occasional pastime that served as sort of a truce between battles. We went down to Somerville's Trum Field where softball was a fairly safe way for us to spend time together. We'd occasionally meet up with Sal Sperlinga and his son Ricky and swing a few.

Sal was the kind of guy that even if you were doing something for fun, he expected you to do it seriously and perfectly. This was especially true of his passion – softball. He'd send us out into the field and hit balls to us for hours, barking encouragement and hurling criticism.

I wasn't an impressive football player. I got by in basketball because I knew how to hustle, but softball was my game. I could catch almost anything. Sal whacked and I rarely missed. Gentleman that he was, he never failed to praise me afterward, "You looked damn good out there, kid." And I did.

*I'm sure I believed I looked even better and knew I was cooler. So under the watchful eye — but out of earshot - of my old man, I always swaggered and said thanks, but my attempts at coolness came off in typical twenty-something wiseguy backsnap, something that New Englanders refer to as "being fresh." My mouth threw the words out like a challenge; the translation -"My catching **is** great and I'm younger, stronger and faster than you."*

Sal was actually the cool one. He had a standard reply I've never forgotten and eventually came to adopt as I headed through my forties and use frequently now into my fifties whenever some young guy is getting fresh.

"Kid, you're in a 'no win' situation. Say you beat me up. I'm an old man and all of your friends would laugh at you."

He'd laugh and mimic a younger guy's taunting tone. "Ha! Ha! Ha! Bobby beat up an old man!" Then he'd shrug.

*"But let's say for a minute I get lucky and end up breaking your nose, or a couple of ribs. Maybe even an arm. Then, my friend, you'll look even worse because an old man beat **you** up. Your friends will always make fun of you."*

Sal knew nothing took the wind out of the sails of a street brawler's reputation quicker than being laughed at by the very guys who's ass you had already kicked on more than one occasion.

"So, Bobby," Sal would finish up, "Just remember, always respect your elders."

Looking back, I'm sure Big Bob probably heard me being fresh to Sal. But he wasn't stupid either. He figured that a quiet friendly reprimand to his grown son from Sal Sperlinga — the man who never carried a gun because he didn't have to, was much more powerful than even the occasional pounding he still administered. He was right.

"I found them," Howie says to me as he opens his front door. Immediately a small flurry of snow slips past his feet, disappearing as soon as it hits the warmth.

"Come in, Bobby! You'll freeze out there!"

The New England wind is blowing frozen shards and my hands are so cold, they're stuck to the handle of my camera bag. I shut the door behind me and pull off the layers of clothing required to survive the short distance from the truck to the house.

Howie is already in his kitchen; I can smell the hot of coffee. This time of year everything smells only hot or cold to me, actual aromas are an afterthought that will return when we thaw out in the spring.

"I found them, the old pictures." Howie gestures for me to sit at the large mahogany table. One side is lined with neat stacks of letters, documents, and clippings. At the end closest to me sit several vintage cardboard cigar boxes filled with photographs.

"What's with all the papers, Howie?"

Howie's wife Ellen breezes through. She rolls her eyes in greeting and laughs. "Oh God, that's his filing system! Don't touch anything, he's got it all in some special order!"

Howie brings the coffee to the table. "There's nothing wrong with being organized." He pushes a mug toward me. "Are you warm enough, Bobby?"

Through the kitchen window, I catch a glimpse of the frozen lake and am glad to be inside. I'm fine, I assure him.

"Good," he nods approvingly. "This time of year you have to stay bundled up, you get that flu, you'll die, you know."

The cigar boxes wait in front of us. The old, heavy-duty cardboard with the hinged covers still attached. Dutch Masters. Rembrandt's five clothiers stare back at us, their faces questioning.

Not realizing I'm talking out loud, I exclaim, "Hey, the Dutch boys!"

They are old friends of mine.

When my brother Joey was a little kid, my old man told him that the painting on the cigar box was a famous one and that the reason the guys in it looked so shocked was that someone in the unseen audience had just accused them of a crime.

We were down Howie's garage, Marshall Motors, watching the old man work. Well, Joey was anyway. I was fourteen and bored stiff but the kid hounded me for hours to walk him down so I finally caved.

"See, Joe? See how they all look guilty? Like they're about to confess somethin'?"

My little brother was completely enthralled. From a distance, even I squinted my eyes and seriously studied their faces. The men did look sort of pissed.

My father had the box balanced on the bumper of a Buick. He traced the painting with a thick mechanic's finger.

"Some guy just yelled out something to them, 'Hey you bums did such and such!' and they can't believe it! You can't see the man who yelled it out at 'em, he ain't important so the painter just painted him out."

"Yeah?" I interrupted from a safe distance from the old man's paws, "how'd you know what they said?"

My father cut his eyes over to me without turning his head. "You want some of this?" I did not need to be told what some of that was. I shut up.

Joey's six-year old mind knew about getting in trouble. "What'd they do?"

The old man slapped a hand down on top of the box, making Joey jump.

"It don't matter what they did! You never mind about that part. I wanna tell you why they look so shocked. One of their friends here in the paintin' ratted the other guys out and deep down they know it. They don't know which one but they're pissed because they were all real good friends. They trusted each other. Now you tell me which one is the rat."

In sort of a pre-Sesame Street game of "which one of these things is not like the other" my smart little brother pointed to the obvious, the sole man who was not wearing a hat.

My old man nodded sagely and for once he made the kid feel like one of the big guys, like he was in on a secret, even if he had no idea what the hell it was.

"That's right. That's good. You can tell he's with them, but not really with them."

Even if Joey had trouble following our father's artistic interpretation, he recognized a valuable compliment. Dad may have been full of creative reviews but he was low on kind words. He leaned closer to the kid, speaking out of one side of his mouth.

"You can always tell which one is the rat. He ain't wearing a hat. Don't you forget it! Now go on, get outta here, I'm busy."

He shoved a cigarette between his lips, sparked up his lighter and sat back, satisfied with his cigar box lesson. Joey was practically beaming with adult knowledge. As we left the garage, I pushed Joey gently ahead of me toward the sidewalk so I could ask a question.

"That has to be the fifth version of that painting I've heard you tell, c'mon Dad, what is it really?"

He stared at me. "The story always ends the same way, don't it? Take it for what's its worth. Now go get your brother before someone runs him over and I really get pissed."

I seriously doubt that the Dutch painter wanted to send out a warning about how to spot a traitor in the midst, but I realize the lesson itself is actually my father's version of Rembrandt's masterpiece. He saw honor and betrayal battling each other everywhere, even on a cardboard box top.

"Your father," Howie says as he pulls the scary old Dutch boys closer, "was a character. And you know, maybe he wasn't far off with his art lesson."

If he were, you wouldn't have been able to tell him.

Trying to work sequentially through Howie's life, he and I have had to segue from the murder of one dear friend straight into the life and death of a second. He wanted to show me a picture of Buddy the last time I was here, but he couldn't find these boxes.

He'd grumbled, "We've got albums all over the place, more in boxes and in the closets. I got to get all of them together someday."

I think he's putting off the start of today's interview as he rummages through the box. He finally upends it so he can shift through the pictures easily; then the next, and finally a third. His fingers touch friends and family that have spilled across the table; the sepia of the last century – stiff grim faces frozen suspiciously for the camera, the old black and whites – the kind with the fancy serrated edges, small children frolicking in Kodachrome, Polaroids that Howie and his friends posed for from federal prison. Decades fan out over the table.

"Ah," Howie pulls a black and white away from the rest. "Here he is, here's Buddy."

I expect a tough guy pose, pleated slacks and white t-shirt, leaning up against a new car, cigarette hanging precariously cool from his lips but I am surprised. A teenager with a crew cut is sitting on a floral patterned sofa. His face split into a gloriously proud grin, his eyes appear almost closed as he looks down at the diapered infant he's displaying. Buddy's huge hands secure the baby around his middle as he lifts him up. The baby's hands grasp Buddy's, little chubby fingers hanging on. It is a stark comparison to the one Irish thugshot that makes the rounds of the Internet.

"God, he was a good kid." Howie takes the photo back and gently puts it away. His gesture tells me we're done with Buddy and have to let him go. He pulls another from the pile.

This photo is of a muscular guy, posing upside down, feet pointed toward the ceiling and suspended in the air. He's holding himself up between two chairs, biceps taut, fingers balancing his body.

"That's Sal," Howie grins. "He had his own stunts. Just like Superman. Sal was just the best."

In late 1966 Buddy McLean was gone. His executioners, the savage siblings from Charlestown were also dead. The

McLaughlin brothers, the only real threat to the Winter Hill crew, were either buried or incarcerated. It was time for the boys from the Hill to return to the business of making big money with Howie at the helm. The operation had done well under the watchful eye of Sal.

"I knew it would. I'd known Sal since we were kids. He was very diligent. His parents were born in Sicily. His family was really close, hardworking people."

Like many of the others, Sal went off to war – WWII – not the one at home. "He was a Sergeant in the Marines and when he come home after the war...." Howie smiles.

"He became a very successful bookmaker. But anytime anyone was down and out or needed the rent money, Sal was right there. It seemed natural we should become partners."

Howie and Sal built an empire from inside their gambling "office" at a local auto body shop, Marshall Motors.

"We took horses, dogs, and the numbers but we couldn't seem to make money. Then we took on the bigger sports, which is the main thing in booking today and we made a decent living doing it."

Loan sharking was another profit avenue, lending out bucks just as Howie and Buddy had before the battle with Charlestown. Football season proved to be their major moneymaker. Bettors placed bet after bet on the games and the football cards the bookmakers created sold like hot dogs at Fenway.

The football cards were preprinted with the games to be played over the next few days. There was a point-spread option for each and the buyers chose the winning teams and spreads. But gamblers had to pick all of the winners in order to hit that ever-elusive big payday. It was truly a bookies' game with outrageous odds but that fact never affected their popularity, especially if Sal were the salesman. He made sure that not only were his football cards plentiful, they were also pleasing to the eye.

He designed the cards and logo himself, calling them LAS Football Cards.

"LAS, Sal spelled backwards," Howie laughs. "They were the best looking cards on the street."

Howie pauses and smiles wryly when I ask him how much money did they make a year.

"Well, I dunno, maybe we were losin' money, come to think of it."

I can't believe that. "The biggest bookmakers in town were losing money? Come on, Howie!"

He laughs and raises a finger to correct me. "Excuse me, the biggest bookmakers in all of New England, but..." he spreads his arms and sighs. "The baseball was killing us."

Oh yes. The baseball thing.

Baseball is the fuel that runs Massachusetts. We live it, breathe it, curse it and swear by it. You've probably even heard of our team. For New England, baseball season is the essential renewal of life. Each year is the same as the last; everything that happened prior to that first pitch falls away. The pain, the loss, all momentous defeats are as if they never happened. Baseball season is a new beginning and all things are possible.

Of course by the fall, it was back to shit. It never did dampen the hope that surfaced each spring when it started all over again – for over eighty years. You know the story.

It was just the opposite for bookmakers. Baseball was their *worst* time of the year. In baseball, the gamblers would bet on the pitcher and after a while, the bookies started adding runs along with odds if certain high profile pitchers were playing. When, for instance, Roger Clemens was in his prime, it was a guaranteed twenty plus winning season for the gambler. They would put a two run spread on the game just to scare the average bettor away.

"Baseball killed us. The pitchers were slaughtering us. Nobody wants a baseball customer," Howie confides. "But we still kept them; mostly as a courtesy."

Gamblers are superstitious, vengeful and fickle. "If you turn them away during baseball, they won't return in the fall. We laid off bets when we had to."

Laying off meant that when their own office couldn't take the bet, the bookmakers would pass the wager on to another "friendly" office in the area that agreed to accept the wager. This way the large bettors could be split up while the boys of summer cost them all money.

Somerville had quite a few one-man offices. Bringing them into the fold or wiping them out would create a financial monopoly. In other neighborhoods, the big offices worked hard (and violently) to shut down the small guys. But in Somerville these offices were allowed to continue without interference.

"We didn't buy them out, we didn't pressure them. Some of these guys were quite a bit older than us, had been in the same spot for decades – even since we were kids. Somerville was their city too. Call it..." he winks at me, "honor among thieves. We really were 'live and let live' guys."

Not all of Howie's guys agreed with his decision.

"Some of my guys wanted to muscle these places. 'Why is this one or that one allowed to operate without turning [a fee] in to you?' I used to say 'How long is the guy gonna still be around? Leave him alone.' I'd protect him if I heard something, keep him going. It just wasn't something we did."

When asked which guys he was referring to, Howie grimaces and shuffles through his photographs. After a beat of hesitation, he mentions the two most infamous of his former employees. Whitey Bulger and Stevie Flemmi. At that time they were fledgling underlings.

"Whitey demanded we take over all the offices and shut down independents. He was pretty adamant. Even back then he always had something to say about everything. I told him 'no way' and for him to stay out of our business."

There was another reason to allow the smaller offices to stay alive.

"Where were Sal and I going to bet? What no one realized was that – yes - even though we did have the biggest bookmaking business, we were also gamblers ourselves and as bettors - we were just like every other guy – we *loved* baseball."

Howie readily admits they both loved a good wager, but Sal? "He bet constantly and won some very hefty sums. He hated to lose. If he bet seven games a day and only lost one, he'd be bullshit."

There are major setbacks attached to gambling professionally just as there are in bookmaking. "If we claimed taxes we'd have made a pretty good living, but since we couldn't, it was difficult to use all of that cash."

He gives me an example. "One day Sal says 'Howie, I don't know what to do with all the money I got. The attic is filled to the ceiling. It's stacked up all over the place!' I just laughed, because I knew that no matter how much was in the attic today, by tomorrow he could be broke. He was soft when it came to people who needed help. Yet he was actually a tough guy."

"One night we were out drinking when another buddy tapped me on the shoulder. 'Howie, I think Sal's in trouble.' I looked over and saw three guys surrounding him. I shook my head, 'I don't think so.' All of a sudden, there were three very loud cracks! The men were flying in different directions."

Sal was quick and powerful, always in great shape. He also indulged his first passion and sponsored softball teams throughout the city and the community loved him for it.

His favorite print shop was Piro's Printing owned by his friend local Alderman Pete Piro. Sal had his football cards produced at Piro's and the two had much in common – including the devotion to Somerville sports. Pete sponsored teams, never missing a game. His 5'8" rotund frame parading up and down the field was topped off with a ten-gallon cowboy hat and his presence at the events was as entertaining to the fans as the action on the field. Peter's wife Penny was just as entertaining. From her permanent seat on the sidelines, there wasn't anything she wouldn't say and no words she wouldn't use.

A little note about the women of Somerville.

Penny was not the exception; she was the rule. These were tough women who had endured loss, suffered through the wars - WWII, and the Irish Gangs - alone. As the community slowly began to move toward healing, the women kept an eagle eye out to make sure none of it ever happened again. Perhaps there wasn't much they could do about events unfolding on foreign soil, but they'd be damned if the local guys were going to devastate their lives again. They didn't take any shit and were never shy about doling it out if they felt it would keep everybody in line.

It was about this time that drugs began to make the scene in Somerville. Almost overnight, junkies began littering the streets. The hard drinking community was used to seeing men stumbling out of bars at the end of each night, but the junkies brought a new, skeletal horror to the streets.

"Drugs were a big problem for our business as well." Dave Deveney is a second-generation donut maker; his family owned the Big Dipper Donut Shops during the early seventies. The store in Magoun Square was open twenty-four hours and was suddenly transformed from a lively coffee shop to a defenseless outpost inundated with junkies nodding off at the tables. It was akin to a zombie invasion.

"We had so many junkies in our place that regulars wouldn't come in anymore." Dave's older sibling Dennis was a boxer who suddenly found himself in the position of having to work the store all night to make sure no one got out of line.

"Basically, we had to have a bouncer for a donut shop. My father had enough. He knew Sal for many years and he went to speak to him."

Sal didn't blink an eye. He picked up a two by four and went directly to the Magoun shop. "He handed the wood to

Dennis and told him to stand at the window where he could be seen," says Dave. Sal pushed his way back outside into a crew of thirty or so kids hanging around and made an announcement.

"From now on, you guys get your coffee, drink it and leave," he gestured in the direction of the big brawler to punctuate his words. The next day the shop was junkie free.

About the same time, Dave's younger brother found himself in trouble with some North End bookmakers - fifty thousand dollars worth. He was allowed to incur such a huge debt as he assured the bookies he owned the Big Dippers and had plenty of means to pay it back.

The bookies retaliated by paying a visit to the senior Deveney at the shop. "My mom and I were working the front when two very big Italian dudes came in."

It sounds like a stereotype, I know and forgive me, but the guys from Winter Hill were predominantly Irish, the North End Italian. Hard to believe now, but in that time period that's how each neighborhood recognized strangers in their midst.

Dave watched the men saunter in. "Right away I know they didn't come for donuts," Dave recalls. "They asked for my father. Then they informed him they were our new partners. My dad just stood there, confused."

"New partners in what?" The old man had no idea what the men were talking about.

"The donut shops."

"Our jaws dropped. The guys explained my brother owed them fifty grand and he'd skipped town. Furthermore, he told his North End friends that he was the owner of the family business."

"My son doesn't own these shops," the elder Deveney said, "I do."

That seemed to satisfy the visitors. It made their jobs that much easier.

"'OK, so now *you* owe us fifty thousand bucks and we are *your* new partners.'"

Deveney Senior told the men that he needed a couple of days to think about it.

"Don't take too long," one admonished, "Business will suffer."

After they left, he immediately called Sal. "Sal was calm and matter-of-fact. He told my father to set a meeting at another one of our businesses – a grave monument company in Medford. On the day of the meet, Sal came early and stood in the backroom. I was with my parents up front."

When the two big fellows from the North End entered, Sal was listening.

"We gave ya a few days, so we should be all square. Here's how it goes, " the larger of the two said. "We're your partners. We're buyin' into your business. So first thing - you give us ten grand."

The old man nodded. "That's a lot for me to pay you to buy into my business."

The thug hunched his shoulders and spread his palms in a "whattya gonna do" gesture. "Cost of doin' business, inflation and all that shit. Now if you feel that price is too much and you don't pay, something else is gonna happen."

The donut maker nodded again. "What kind of thing?"

"It isn't gonna be a nice thing is all I can really say."

The thug crossed his arms and waited. The Deveneys were silent.

Then Mrs. Deveney began to cry. "I was sixteen," Dave says. "And I was terrified. Almost immediately, Sal came strolling up from behind the curtain. He put my mom's hand in his."

Sal wagged a finger at the two thugs.

"That was real smooth what you just did. You made a lady cry and you scared a kid. I'm sure your boss would be impressed. So here's the deal. First off, these folks don't owe you money, their son does. Second, this is Somerville, not the North End."

The men stood quietly. Sal was known in all parts of the city, yet his appearance at this negotiation was never anticipated.

Sal continued, "I think you should tell this woman you're very sorry for scaring her family and then you should be on your way. Their son is in Florida and when he comes back we'll see if we can't settle this reasonably."

It was also the perfect opportunity to provide a lecture about the rules of bookmaking.

"You never should've let the kid get in that deep. You thought you were getting a donut empire out of it and you thought wrong. Next time you have customers from Somerville, you come and see *me*."

Dave laughs loudly. "The two thugs just stood there with their mouths wide open. They couldn't apologize enough as they backed out of the door. We never heard from them again."

For the Deveney family, it was a lifesaver. For Sal, it was just a favor to some friends.

Dave eventually started his own monument company. As his business grew, he never forgot that favor. He employed Howie when Howie was on work release after his second stint in jail and was required to be gainfully employed per the terms of his parole.

"I got to help someone out and it was a thrill for me. Howie and Sal helped out so many people, I was glad to have my chance. I never did feel as if I adequately paid Sal back, though. When his father died, he came to see me about a headstone but absolutely refused to allow us to donate it. 'No way,' he said. 'I'll pay.' Sal didn't want nothing for nothing."

Sal was all for the working man, but in some instances he was mystified about how it worked. Tom Leahy was having coffee one morning before work at Dawn's Donuts. "Remember Dawn's?" he asks me.

I do. We both stop for a moment of reverence. Dawn's had a series of owners over the years from an elderly lady to a lesbian couple but the taste of the baked wheels never changed. Tom smiles as the aroma of fresh donuts and coffee wafts up to us from memory.

"Dawn's was the *real* place where everybody knew your name. I was sitting drinking coffee when Sal walked in and sat down."

"Hey Tom, what are you up to?" Sal announced as he slid into a seat and waved the waitress over. Tom told the older man he just dropped in for a cup before hitting the arduous job of repairing the telephone lines around the city.

"Let me ask you something before you go," Sal was seriously studying a group of people chatting across the street. "Every morning I see the same bunch of people standing on that side of the street at the exact same time. You with me so far?"

Tom nodded, wondering what Sal could be getting at.

"Then around five o'clock, I see them on *this* side of the street. Where do you think they all went?"

He must be pulling my leg, Tom thought. But Sal's face was intent as he waited for the young man's answer.

"Sal," Tom explained, "they're waiting for the bus. In morning it picks them up, and at night it drops them off."

Sal shook his head uncomprehendingly. "Sal, they're probably going to work."

The older man was incredulous. "What for?" he exclaimed.

For a man who made his business strolling up and down the boulevards, it seemed like quite a sacrifice to have to live from bus to bus with only regimented mundane duties in between. Sal respected them, those bus riders, but he felt sympathy for them. He loved *his* job.

And he took it seriously. Tom has another story about Sal and his work.

"Let me start off by saying that Sal could have been pulling my leg," Tom's eyes twinkle as he delivers his self-imposed disclaimer. "I was there when Marshall Hall, the huge brick building on the corner of Marshall and Broadway, burnt down. It was a grand edifice – a beautiful old building."

"Anyway, it went up in flames and a crowd gathered while we waited for the fire department. I was standing next to Sal. I turned to him and said, 'Geez Sal, that's an awful big fire.'"

Sal agreed the fire was quite a spectacle. Together they watched the flames grow higher in silence. Finally Tom, a fan of architecture, shook his head sadly, "It's too bad, isn't it Sal?"

Sal looked at his watch and back at Tom. "It sure is! That fire wasn't supposed to start until ten!"

We both roar, laughing until tears run down our cheeks.

"That's just another great Winter Hill Gang story," Tom chokes out as he mops his face.

Willy Cellata is another close friend who remembers those men in the Winter Hill Gang as friends that span his entire life. "You hung out on the corner after school. That's what you did. You met and kept nearly all of your friends that way. I'll be sixty-five this year and I still have friends that I met sixty years ago." He counts Sal and Howie among that number.

"My mother used to cook for Howie and Buddy and later for Sal. He was her favorite. We all played softball with Sal. He was terrible but he played like he was terrific. And, of course, we gambled with him."

Unlike Howie, Willy remembers Sal as one of the worst gamblers he ever met. "Sal couldn't win a bet with tomorrow's newspaper." The sure way to win was to "bet on the opposite team that Sal was betting," Willy insists. "It didn't matter what the odds were, he never won a bet when I was around."

I ask Willy about Sal.

"I can only tell what I saw, a guy who'd have a few thousand in his pocket in the morning and go down to the oil company in the afternoon and clear the bills for families that couldn't make it through the month."

Willy leans over his desk. "He didn't ask to be repaid and didn't want the owner to tell the families who paid their bills."

I understand his inference. A gangster doesn't do anything for nothing. He expects something in return eventually. So was he a gangster?

"No." Willy is adamant. He refers to Sal as "the phony gangster" and dismisses the media referring to Sal as Howie's lieutenant.

"Give me a break, Bobby. People can say what they want, but Sal was a bookmaker. Pure and simple. He didn't even carry a gun. This lieutenant stuff is for the Italians. Not a bunch of friends that decided to take action. He'd defend himself in a fight and if you threatened one of his friends, but he'd never hurt anyone over money."

*There are still many in Somerville that take great offense at the use of the words "mobsters" and "gangsters" when used in the same sentence as the names Winter and Sperlinga. My father used to say "If you need money and you borrow it from a guy because the bank won't give it to ya, why shouldn't the guy you get it from expect ya to pay it back with interest? If you're gonna gamble, you know you're taking a chance you're gonna lose your money. Then you gotta pay it back. It's a business, and they were businessmen just like any other. If you think other businesses don't work the same way, try not payin' the IRS what they say you owe and see what happens to ya when **their lieutenants** come knockin'."*

CHAPTER SIX

The End of Superman

SAL MET HIS future wife, Pat Campbell, at a church dance. Pat loved to dance and she was another Somerville character. Known for her hats, she had a different one for every day and occasion and if she needed a reason to wear a new one, she manufactured an event.

Pat was close to Buddy McLean's wife Jean and they went out with their friends every week, usually to a local club to dance. Grown women with families, they were still girls who'd married young. It was the norm instead of the exception in our town, my own mother had given birth to me at sixteen. Escaping the responsibilities of family and the pressure of the lives their husbands led was a special treat. And although their spouses frequented the bars in the city almost daily, the men would never have condoned the girls dancing in clubs – despite the fact they only danced with each other.

Pat had an ingenious way of planning their outings. She and her friends took turns sending each other invitations to fake showers so they could sneak out to the Boston clubs. In such a vast Irish-Italian Catholic community, no husband ever questioned a round of bridal and baby showers every single week.

Even my mom, Claire, occasionally threw up her hands at the prospect of another evening managing seven unruly kids while my father was already out and joined them. She never failed to have a good time, and for a woman with that many children, I think the good times were few and far between. No one bothered them when they were out on the town. Certainly their husband's reputations preceded them, but also because they held their own. The girls of Somerville had grown up learning how to take care of themselves.

The Sperlingas had three children, Annemarie, Ricky, and Billy.

Annemarie Sperlinga McCarthy is a grown woman in her fifties, attractive and poised, with her own family. Smiling and laughing, she's open about her parents and their history, and quick to tell funny stories. But there is an underlying fragile sadness about her she works hard to keep in check.

When I arrive, Annemarie and her husband Bobby usher me into a comfortable living room lined with framed photographs. Friends, family, so many faces I recognize. We've all known each other since we were kids but with expectations on all sides we're still nervous.

"Annemarie," I start off slow. "Didn't we go to high school together?"

She grins. "No, Bobby, but we did go on a date once!"

Uh oh. I am well known for my poor memory. I don't remember.

Her husband gives me a mock-growl and I throw my hands up in feigned defense. "Hold on, I took her home early and that was all!"

Annemarie laughs, "As a matter of fact you did. You were a perfect gentleman."

I smile right back. "Ok, good, chalk up one for me."

Now we're laughing and any ice that had formed out of nervousness puddles away. I ask Annemarie to tell me about her parents. She smiles at the mention of her parents' rocky relationship.

"They were a little crazy. He adored us kids, but he was a real womanizer. They divorced when I was three and married again when I was five. My brothers were born after that. Mom called them her reconciliation babies." Her memories of her father are still crystal clear.

Her brother Ricky was next in line. "He was The Messiah, the first boy in an Italian family – that was a big deal."

When asked about her relationship with Sal, she rolls her eyes and grins. "Oh my God, he was the best. I was on a pedestal, I could never do anything wrong. He called me Queenie. If I cried, he'd melt."

The young girl's favorite day of the week was Sunday, the day football patrons paid off their debts in whatever they had in their pockets. "I didn't know whatever he did, but on Sunday that was the big day for it. Dad would bring home a Crown Royal bag - I got to keep all of the coins every week."

Sunday was also her mom's night out – with the growing number of showers to attend, Pat needed someone to sit with the kids. "Dad would be in charge of dinner and babysitting – it was very special, always Chinese food. Then we would watch 'Candid Camera' and eat hot fudge sundaes."

Annemarie became aware of what her father actually did for a living when she was about eight years old. "My parents always said that he was a bouncer at the Kenmore Club in Boston. Dad actually went away for booking in 1960. They lied and said he'd gone to Florida for six months. But I knew."

Sal really was the bouncer at the Kenmore, but it is common knowledge that he actually owned a piece of that club as well as several others.

Despite Sal's success as a father, he did not prove to be any better husband the second time around. By the time

Annemarie was fourteen, her parents split up for good. Following yet another Somerville custom, they never bothered with another divorce.

"He was legally married to my mother until the day he died. They just didn't live together any more. But he was always there for me."

My own parents never divorced when they split up. My father moved in with his girlfriend and lived with her until he died, but he stayed married to my mother. In Somerville, if you had a family, you may not live under the same roof, but it was your bound duty to take care of them. The women - the wives and even subsequent girlfriends - accepted the terms. The wives preferred it rather than go through the humiliation of divorce and the girlfriends knew better than to try and push. I think the bonds of where we come from and the history of what we've been through is just too strong to sever completely. A man moves in with someone new, or a couple goes through a long divorce process only to head home and go to bed. The point gets made, but to cut it off completely – it's too hard. So we don't bother to even try.

Howie Winter was a friend of the family. Buddy and Jean McLean were also frequent visitors. In a strange Somerville twist of fate, the teenage Annemarie also crossed paths with Red Bavin, the cop who took no action during the gunfight that killed Buddy.

"As a child, I actually contemplated becoming a nun and I used to go to church almost every day. Everyone teased me, especially my dad. One afternoon I was on the way to pick up my girlfriend in the projects so we could say our novenas and there was a gang of kids hanging out in the hallway. As I was going up a floor a man grabbed me by the neck and dragged me down the entire flight of stairs."

Most people hear "housing project" and think of crumbling low income slums run by an errant government landlord in violence ridden neighborhoods, the isolating of the poor in accommodations so denigrating that inhabitants have no choice but to deteriorate along with the buildings.

The subject of housing projects and our government's refusal to address the dignity of those who may need assistance at a certain point in life is an argument for another day and those who can grasp and accept the concept of warehousing people better than I can.

Tom Leahy best describes the Somerville projects back during the days when we ran safe and free through the streets.

"They were built around 1949 with the intention of housing veterans and their families in clean, affordable apartments with a feel of camaraderie. We lived there until the mid fifties. It worked on a sliding scale, you paid twenty five per cent of your monthly pay as rent."

This enabled vets to mainstream back into society in an environment that was a growing community. "It was great," Tom recalls. "We hated leaving. My father had to because as his pay rose, that twenty-five percent also rose and finally he decided it was time to buy a house."

The guy who yanked Annemarie down the stairs turned out to be Red Bavin, doing a sweep of the hallways. Apparently, from behind she was a dead ringer for another girl who had been raising hell.

Annemarie ran home crying and Pat immediately called Sal. Bavin had always been under a cloud over his perceived inaction the day of Buddy's murder and coupled with the fact that he had put his hands on Sal's daughter, he was lucky that all he received was a brutal beating.

"My father went after him and threw him up against the car. Red was yelling 'Sal, I'm in uniform!' and Dad said, 'That's no problem.' He tore Bavin's shirt off and pounded him. All the while Bavin kept screaming 'I didn't know she was your daughter, Sal!' My father replied, 'Next time you'll think twice.'"

As the story goes, Sal received a standing ovation the next time he went through the projects. There is no doubt that Sal acted as any father would if his thirteen-year-old daughter was accosted by a grown man — cop or not — but there was also a remarkable sense of control on Sal's part that he didn't go further. Buddy had been his close friend.

Bavin never filed charges. He also has never been accused of participating in Buddy's murder nor am I implying it here; it was just generally thought that his failure to get involved had been an act of cowardice, fear of retribution from the McLaughlins. Perhaps he took Sal's punishing beating without complaint as it somehow assuaged his guilt.

Annemarie is married to a successful plumber, Bobby McCarthy. Blond-tan and freckled, he's an Irish Somerville kid. Affable and personable, he's a regular guy. And he is very protective of his wife. Annemarie says that as of this writing they have been married thirty-five years.

"Thirty-six years, honey," Bobby interrupts.

"Thirty-six? Really?" She laughs and shrugs in agreement. "We met playing cards – well, he was playing cards. That gambling must run through all of us! Anyway, he stole me away from another boyfriend thirty-six years ago and here we are. And now we're grandparents."

Sal didn't like the Irish Bobby at first. During the end of the nineteenth century, the communities of Boston had been divided squarely by nationality. As the century drew to a close, unions between the Irish and Italians became more prevalent – my own family a prime example. But although Sal's closest friends were of a variety of backgrounds, an Italian father looks forward to an Italian son-in-law. That was the perfect excuse for Sal to bluster, but in reality, it was the age-old gripe of any father; no man was good enough for his only daughter.

Bobby tells the story of their quick courtship. "We found out Annemarie was pregnant. We told Pat right away because my intentions were always to marry her."

No one, however, told Sal immediately. The father discovered the news in another way and didn't wait to have a family discussion. He went right to the McCarthy's.

"Sal pulled up with an ex-boxer friend in his white caddy. He told me to get in. I wasn't a big guy and had gotten this man's daughter pregnant, so I thought I'd lighten things up."

"Will I be coming back?" the teenager quipped.

Sal didn't appreciate the humor and took Bobby for a ride. After an excruciating silence, Sal finally spoke. "I know Scoli [his pet name for Annemarie] is pregnant and you can leave right now and we'll still be friends. But if you marry her and hurt her, I *will* kill you."

The humor, and the breath were sucked out of the shivering kid.

"I said, 'I love your daughter and intend to marry and respect her for the rest of my life.'"

Sal nodded, turned the car around and dropped the shaken Bobby back at his house. "I heard he told his friend later, 'that kid's got balls. I never would've gotten into this car.'" Bobby knew he had at least earned his future father-in-law's respect.

The young married couple found themselves with a different car to drive every other week. Sal took possession of any car from a wiseguy who owed him money until the man's unpaid debt was settled.

"He never took the cars of the working stiffs, he knew guys needed wheels to get to work, pick up their kids, whatever. But wiseguys? Sal made them hand over their keys."

It took a while but Bobby did finally prove himself to Sal and the bond was finally forged in Disneyworld of all places.

"One of the best times we ever had," Annemarie says, "was back in 1976 when he took us on vacation along with the kids, my brothers and some friends.

Sal covered the group's airfare, hotels and meals. Bobby wanted to contribute to his father-in-law's generosity so he snuck out and bought the whole party Disney hats as a surprise. "Sal was bullshit. It was definitely the wrong move. He told me to never do it again and trust me, I didn't. He didn't want anyone to spend his own money."

Despite the Mickey Mouse ears, Bobby knew he had finally arrived on that trip. He brought along a Kodak movie camera Sal had given him. The Winter Hill crew had hijacked a truck and part of the shipment was one of the newest innovations on the market. "It took four more months before the actual film came out for the camera. I got the assignment of shooting the family video for the weekend. After that, I knew I was in. Even if that meant I was only the video man, I was the *family* video man."

Having arrived also had its own cross to bear. "He had me giving money to people down on their luck but demanding they didn't know where it came from. How could they not know? I was married to Sal's daughter! But he insisted I do it his way."

Bobby began to be integrated into the *other* family business, especially when Sal was away. And he also had to interact with less popular individuals on the periphery of Sal's work. At the mention of some alleged members of the Winter Hill Gang, Bobby waves his hand mid-air, indicating disgust.

"Sal hung with Howie, he had little dealings with Whitey or Stevie. He didn't like them, didn't respect 'em and most of the time he didn't even speak to them." Sal avoided the couple at Marshall Motors, most of the time completely ignoring the men.

When Howie and Sal went to jail on the pinball charge, Bobby oversaw some of the day-to-day operations of the business. "It was right after they went away, like the next week. I was working on the end of the week — can I say this? — receipts. And Whitey and Stevie showed up. 'We just come by,' Whitey says, 'to see if you need any help.' I told them right away I was fine, didn't need anything."

Bobby related the incident the next time he visited Sal in jail. "Tell them to stay the fuck out of there," his father-in-law ordered, his voice rising. "They didn't come back after that."

The message was clear. Whitey and Stevie may have physically been on Winter Hill, but they were most decidedly *not* part of Howie and Sal's Winter Hill Gang.

Although no one realized, it was a foreshadowing of things to come in the management of the Winter Hill Gang, the loose collection of men from the Hill that the press dubbed "Boston's Irish Mafia."

Willy Cellata has scores of Sal stories he wants told, too many to include. Funerals Sal paid for, families he helped, beefs he settled. He shakes his head. "Sal gave thousands of dollars away and he always drove the worst cars in the neighborhood. Garbage cars, isn't that funny? He didn't care about things like that."

It is clear to Willy at least, the impact on Somerville with the loss of his friend.

"When Sal Sperlinga died, it was like they took a quarter of the city away with him."

Annemarie visibly changes when asked at what age did she lose her father. Her cheerful animation is gone. One can see her crumble inward as she replies with one of her only clipped responses of the entire interview. "Twenty-seven."

She nods as if affirming the answer to herself and her eyes fill up immediately. She sits still as if waiting for what is to come next. After a beat, she continues without prompting.

"Our third child was only three and a half weeks old. I just got off the phone with my dad. He had called to check up on me. I'd had blood pressure problems toward the end of my pregnancy. I'd just lost my grandmother. My husband hadn't slept."

"My dad was worried. He rang and asked to speak to his first grandson. 'Put the baby on the phone, Scoli,' was what he said. So I did."

Annemarie's brother Ricky had borrowed her car. "It was a few hours later and a priest came to my door. My mind went immediately to my brother. I thought Ricky had been in an accident."

"No, no, no," the priest said. "A shooting. Your mother will be up in a minute."

"My father?" Annemarie asked tentatively. The priest didn't answer.

"I never asked another question until my mother came through the door. My whole world was crushed. I thought he was Superman and that bullets would just bounce off him."

Annemarie's analogy brings to mind Howie's story of Sal balancing himself between the two chairs, hanging in air, flying like Superman. But just as the superhero, one of Sal's enemies found his vulnerability point.

And there had indeed been a shooting but truly it was drugs that killed Sal Sperlinga.

The increasing drug trade in Boston was a major concern to both Howie and Sal. They knew that while the scene was prevalent everywhere, it could blossom at a faster rate in economically depressed areas and with it came increased crimes of violence and the eventual destruction of lives.

In December of 1979, Sal had been involved in an altercation with Dan Moran, a local drug—dealer. Sal had approached Moran and ordered him to stop peddling angel dust and heroin in Magoun Square. Moran underestimated the older man and mouthed off to him. His senior rewarded the dealer with an embarrassing beating.

On the morning of January 4, 1980, Sal Sperlinga underestimated Dan Moran. "I was with him," says Willy, "but I had to go over to my mother's. Sal was wearing a speckled suit and carrying a lot of money. He was off to play cards and we were gonna meet over at Mom's late in the day. I remember I asked him if he wanted me to hold the package [money] until later – something I did for him when he didn't want to walk around with too much cash, but Sal said, "Naw, I'm fine."

Sal was in good spirits. He was a healthy fifty-two year old man, free on bail pending an appeal on his 1978 conviction in the 1977 pinball case. He planned out his day; play some cards, have lunch with Pete Piro, and meet up with Willy Cellata for dinner.

The Medford Street location had no actual name and was rumored to be the latest stop in a moving gambling operation the Somerville Police couldn't seem to catch up with. The club was really nothing more than a small storefront with blacked out windows, a worn black and white checkered linoleum floor and tables and chairs for the players.

Sal was playing cards with friends Bobby D'Onofrio, Tony Cangiamila and a few others when Moran entered. He looked around and demanded, "Has anyone seen Sal Sperlinga?" Moran's initial view of Sal was blocked by another player but as Sal leaned forward, the drug dealer raised a .22 caliber handgun, aimed at Sal and pulled the trigger.

For one excruciating second, there was silence and then a loud click as the gun's empty chamber moved. Misfire. Sal grabbed the opportunity and moved quickly. With D'Onofrio at his side, he sped to the back of the club. Moran's gun clicked again and he began firing, hitting Bobby in the right wrist. Sal and Bobby knew a second later they were in deeper trouble. The two-room storefront had no rear exit. They were trapped. As they turned, Sal pushed Bobby away and grabbed a board that was on the floor, Moran was almost on top of them.

Sal turned to face the gunman and took one in the belly. Moran's next shot missed completely. Sal raised the board over his head as blood poured out of his stomach. Moran held the gun just below Sal's left eye. Face to face, the two men stared at each other and then the few remaining witnesses heard Sal speak his last words.

"No. Don't."

Moran pulled the trigger. The gun did not misfire.

"What was Sperlinga doing at that point?" the Assistant Middlesex County District Attorney later asked Bobby D'Onofrio.

"He was dying."

Peter Piro was on his way to meet Sal for lunch when he ran into a frantic Ricky Sperlinga on the street. "My father's been shot!" Ricky blurted out to anyone who would listen.

"No one knew what had really happened yet, or who had done it. We feared for Ricky's life as well," Willy says. Friends grabbed Ricky and hustled him into Christie's Lunch, adjacent to the club, and locked the doors in an effort to protect him from whatever may be coming next.

But nothing did, except the sad news.

Sal Sperlinga died on the worn black and white checkered linoleum floor of a private social club. In the end, it didn't much matter. What did was that Sal was gone.

"That was it," Willy says sadly.

Moran was picked up the same day. A career criminal, Moran had previously been acquitted of the 1965 murder of a Charlestown butcher killed during a robbery attempt. After his arrest for Sal's murder, Moran was committed to Bridgewater State Hospital for psychiatric evaluation and deemed competent to stand trial.

He was eventually sentenced to life for the killing of the Somerville Robin Hood. Sal had tried to control the flow of drugs coming into the city and had lost his last bet in life, doing what he had always done. Trying to help out.

The days after the murder were brutal for Annemarie. The mother of three little kids, she – like the families of all victims of violence – had to keep moving. She found herself sleepwalking through the surreal days.

"I remember waking up and hearing cartoons on TV. I couldn't believe it, how could cartoons be playing when my father was dead?"

Pat Sperlinga was devastated. She had just suffered the loss of her own mother the month prior and although she no longer lived with Sal, he was still her husband. Ricky and Billy were also immobilized by the shock. In the end, it fell to Bobby McCarthy, the one-time Irish interloper, to take charge of the family and the arrangements. He had a wealth of support from the Somerville community.

Annemarie recalls little about the funeral. "I'd been diagnosed with depression. I do remember that there were lines and lines of people at the wake, and it was freezing cold in January."

Bobby adds, "The mourners were just continuous, non stop."

The wake at Cataldo's Funeral Home had to be extended an additional day to accommodate the over fifteen hundred people that attended. The local newspaper reported that over four hundred people crammed into the church for Sal Sperlinga's funeral. After seven flower cars arrived, additional ones had to be turned away for lack of space.

On the way to the cemetery, the limo passed a nursing home whose residents had regularly been the recipients of free spaghetti dinners sent by Sal. The elderly came out into the cold and waved as the procession went by. They would miss the man who had provided when everyone else had forgotten them.

I remember I was down my cellar with Bobby and Dave Racicot when we heard the news. If you live in any part of the country that doesn't afford you that extra level of living space, you've missed a lot. The cellar is everything from a laundry/storage area to playroom, sports room or additional living room with an extra TV. Mine was a little bit of everything – a hangout. After the call about the shooting came, Bobby and Dave bolted up the stairs to see their sister Yvonne. Yvonne had been seeing Sal, well...more than seeing Sal. Yvonne was pregnant with Sal's baby.

In what has to be one of the most selfless acts of kindness, the kind that only women seem to understand and implement, Pat

Sperlinga allowed Yvonne to say her goodbyes to Sal at the wake after the family departed. It was a heart-wrenching scene and added to the suffering we all felt. Yvonne named her son Sal, and that's how we all know how long Sal has been dead. Her kid is our benchmark. Yvonne eventually married Mark Nicholson, the son of Russ, the former MDC cop killed during the McLean and McLaughlin war. How ironic that two of Buddy McLean's best friends would be interwoven in such a complicated way into the tight web that is Somerville.

"I remember parts of the eulogy," Annemarie thinks back. "They called him the Robin Hood of Magoun Square." And Reverend Mullaney closed the homily in typical Somerville style. "God have mercy on Sal, and on all of us for our weaknesses." Then he shrugged and admonished the mourners to remember, "We all have our good points and bad points." The casket was draped with an American flag signifying Sal's service to his country in the Marine Corps.

Howie Winter told the press years later, "Sal Sperlinga was my partner and my friend for years. He got killed because he tried to keep the drugs out of Somerville. We'd kicked them out of the city. He didn't keep his guard up with this one punk, and he got killed over it."

Friends were in shock; everyone I knew was devastated. And even people I didn't know. The day after the murder and the local cops weighed in.

"The uniforms lining the street shook their heads in disbelief.

"He was this happy-go-lucky guy," one said sadly. "Yeah, he was convicted of extortion but the guy never even carried a gun, for Chrissakes."

"I'll tell ya somethin' else," another cop asserted. "He was against the drugs coming into the neighborhood and made a huge effort to help keep the streets safe. And look what happened to him. It's a sin."

Local business owners came out in droves to pay respect to Sal's memory. Each one wanted their turn to express their own sadness. Their commentary can be summed up with just one declaration, "Sal kept watch over the neighborhood. He never hurt a living soul. We loved him and we'll miss him."

No shit.

Sal's sons began to fall apart. "My father was killed because he wouldn't let anyone sell drugs around the square," Billy told the newspaper in 1980. Yet Billy himself took up drugs, his comfort to self-medicate but he never lashed out at anyone. His brother was different. Ricky became more physical, acting out his frustration at the loss of his father by a cycle of violence and regret. Annemarie's efforts to help Ricky accept their situation were in vain.

"He'd punch a wall, throw something at a head and then break down...saying 'I'm so sorry, I'm so sorry.' It was hard to watch."

He would never again play the video of the family at Disneyworld that his brother-in-law took back in 1976. It was too painful. Both boys ended up doing time in the Massachusetts prison system and not without further complications.

Billy, for a short time, was incarcerated in Shirley Prison. He was eventually moved to another facility due to the fact that Moran, the killer of his father, was also at Shirley during the same time.

The Feds did the opposite for Ricky Sperlinga in 1991 when he was suddenly transferred into Shirley from New York's Ray Brook prison where he was doing time for selling angel dust - the same drug his father fought so hard to keep out of Somerville. The FBI considered Ricky a close associate of Howie Winter - still a subject hotly pursued by the government and Ricky's problems mounted as he was treated as a terrorist in jail.

The Bureau of Prisons had been moving Ricky from prison to prison, federal prosecutors visited him regularly to try and get him to talk about Howie. Why was Winter constantly at the Sperlinga home?

Howie Winter had been a fixture in the Sperlinga home for Ricky's entire life. After Sal's murder, his continued loyalty to the family of his best friend being viewed as some sort of criminal recruitment plan was abhorrent to the Sperlingas.

Bobby McCarthy believes that the Bureau put Ricky in the same facility as his father's murderer on purpose. "To get him to do something stupid and have something else to hang over his head, possibly get him to finally turn against Howie." Bobby remembers Ricky calling him from jail.

"He told me who was in the same prison as he was. He was so pissed."

"I told Ricky it could be a setup and to be careful. But the minute I hung up the phone my stomach went sick. I knew something was about to happen." Bobby knew Ricky's temper and the powerful punching prowess that he'd been fine-tuning since his father's death.

"Back in 1981, Ricky and I used to spar up the Somerville Boxing Club. I knew how he was."

One day in the Shirley mess hall, Ricky saw Moran seated at a nearby table. He could not control himself. Ricky carried his tray just past Moran, then dropped the tray and spun around. He hit Moran with such a monstrous blow that he broke both Moran's jaw and his own hand. He released years of pent up anger in one single blow.

The guards were on top of Ricky in three seconds. "That verified what I had thought all along," Bobby says. "It was a set up, and the best kind, the emotional kind."

Ricky was taken to the Hole, his broken hand unattended for several weeks. Annemarie finally discovered her brother's situation. "I called the Bureau immediately. I demanded to know why my brother's injuries hadn't been addressed and exactly why he had been put in the same prison as the murderer of our father." She didn't stop there. "I told them I was calling Diane Sawyer if I didn't get some answers."

The Bureau always plays dirty and this was one time that they got caught with their collective hands in the cookie jar.

The threat of national publicity jumpstarted the Bureau. That same night he was taken out of the hole and given medical attention. He was never charged in the attack of Moran nor given any additional time on his sentence.

Ricky Sperlinga eventually got out of prison but died unexpectedly in October of 2005, clouded by controversy and leaving a daughter behind.

Patricia Campbell Sperlinga did not live to lose her son. She suffered a series of strokes, finally passing away in January of 2005. "It killed me to see her that way," Annemarie says. "I would sit with her as she lay in bed and all I could think about was her hats, she had always been so fun and flamboyant. She was just a shell by the time she died. She never got over it, losing my dad."

Sal or "Salvy" as Willy refers to him, is buried in Oak Grove Cemetery. "I still miss him and I still go and see him now and then," Willy tells me. "I don't bring flowers, I never do to any grave. They just die anyway. But I do visit."

Willy pauses for a moment, leans back in his office chair, his hands folded across his belly. Then he closes our visit simply. "Salvy died penniless, he had nothing. All that money? He gave it all away."

In our city, drugs forever altered one family and an entire community. Not such an unusual story in Somerville, or any city for that matter, but still a tragic one. Sal Sperlinga was a bookmaker and sports fan that left behind a strong legacy of generosity and commitment to the streets and the people who inhabited them. He also left a poem his family swore he wrote during the time he was away, and even though the piece has been attributed to authors from Nelson Mandela and Martin Luther King Jr. to an unnamed Harvard student back in the 1940's and also hung on a wall in Mother Teresa's Calcutta orphanage, it pretty much sums up who Sal was. It doesn't matter who actually wrote it, Sal took it to heart and tried to make it part of his life. I think he succeeded.

ANYWAY

People are unreasonable, illogical and self-centered.
          Love them anyway!
If you do good, people will accuse you of selfish ulterior motives.
          Do good anyway!
If you are successful, you will find false friends and true enemies.
          Succeed anyway!
The good you do today will be forgotten tomorrow.
          Do good anyway!
Honesty and frankness make you vulnerable.
          Be honest and frank anyway!
The biggest men with the biggest ideas can be shot down by the smallest men with the smallest minds.
          Think big anyway!
People favor underdogs but follow only top dogs.
          Fight for some underdogs anyway!
What you spend years building may be destroyed overnight.
          Build anyway!
People really need help but may attack you if you help them.
          Help people anyway!
Give the world the best you have and you'll get kicked in the teeth.
          Give the world the best you've got anyway!

Howie Winter closes the sad chapter on the life and death of his dear friend simply. "There's always someone to replace someone, but to me, no one could ever replace Sally. He was just a beautiful person."

And me? I said before I come from a family of seven kids. My father was booking for Howie and Sal and the business is not always a job where you're making money hand over fist and stacking it in the attic, especially when you have nine mouths to feed. Some years were better than others.

*There were several bad ones in a row by the next time the December snow blew in. There was not enough money for food, clothes, heat **and** Christmas. My father was not a fan of charity and as long as no one went hungry, he wasn't the type to cry the blues about the sad fact that since ol' Santa Claus hadn't made much of a profit this year, there was one more chimney in Somerville that would not be accommodating any visits.*

Sal, however, did believe in Santa – or what passed for St. Nick on Winter Hill. In late December he went to see my father, spoke to him privately and when Christmas morning came, the seven kids in the Martini household woke up to all of the toys they had been fervently hoping to receive that year.

The winter I graduated out of the Santa years, my father made a special point to relate Sal's generosity to me. During one of Boston's traditionally crippling snowstorms, he and I were on our way to Sal's house on Ten Hills Road. For people down South, the whole idea of a white Christmas is a postcard experience - probably bundled up on a jolly horse-drawn sleigh ride across a beautiful woodsy landscape topped off with a romantic evening in front of a fireplace, sipping from steaming mugs while the flakes fall silently outside frosted windows.

*For us, it means one long season of adrenaline-fueled frustration: diligently digging down the sidewalk and shoveling to get to the car at a faster pace than the shit that is falling out of the sky. As a kid, it's especially painful because it doesn't just mean shoveling your driveway. It usually means shoveling **everyone's** driveway. In a community where there is already so little money, it generally doesn't mean anyone is going to pay you any vast amount of cash to do it either.*

My father chose this moment to confide Sal's donation to me.

"If it wasn't for this man, you kids wouldn't have had no Christmas the last two years. You don't ever say that I told you. You just be grateful. When we get there, you get out and you shovel his driveway. It's the least we can do."

*Apparently I was not interested in the least **we** could do since we wouldn't be shoveling – I would - and I argued vehemently. I felt it was below me to be forced to do this chore and have Sal's whole family as an audience to add insult to the perceived injury. Why should I have to be embarrassed? Sal had his own kids, let them shovel. I had my own shoveling I was already forced to do.*

In the end, my father gave up on me, probably because he couldn't give me a beating and drive at the same time. I didn't get out of the car.

At fifty-six, I've lived longer than Sal Sperlinga. I look back on that snow day now with much regret and more than a touch of sadness. I am ashamed I felt I was above the simple act of moving snow out of the driveway of the man who had quietly given so much to my family. I wish I had gotten out of the car and not only shoveled that day, but gone back many times.

The toughest thing about getting older is living with memories of things you didn't do when you were younger; and the fact that you're old enough to realize that you should have.

CHAPTER SEVEN

The Office at Marshall Motors

1968. I WAS sixteen and splitting my time between school during the day and getting into trouble in the afternoon. Occasionally hormones, combined with the lure of adventure upset that delicate teenage balance and I took a day off from formal education. I've never been a good liar, but I'm a damn good sneak and when I decided to pass on school one morning, I figured I covered my tracks pretty well. No one looked twice at me during supper that night.

The very next day, my father called me down Marshall Motors, the auto body shop where he worked. I didn't think much of it so I took my sweet time. When I walked through the garage door, Howie Winter and Stevie Flemmi were standing outside of my father's office, talking.

"Hey," I said. "Is my father around?"

Dead silence.

I knew these guys and they knew me. Yet no one said a word for a moment and then, as if on cue, both of them gestured toward the office. I should have turned and run like hell, but it happened that I wasn't nearly as smart as I thought. That was my first mistake.

"Thanks." I strolled through the office door. My father heaved himself up from his chair.

"How was school yesterday?"

I made my second mistake. I shrugged. "Good."

How many times have you heard the phrase "I got hit so hard I saw stars?" I don't think anyone can comprehend it until it happens to him. My father cracked me in the face so hard I was momentarily blinded by swirling white crackles – stars. I staggered backward and he grabbed me by the shirt. I hung in mid-air for a moment as I considered my next move. I probably should have thought a little harder.

"You lyin' to me?"

My father hated a liar. No matter what any of us kids did, all you had to do was own up to it – no matter how bad you fucked up – and he'd cut you a break. "You lie, you die," was his favorite adage. But I choked. Already in too deep, I forged ahead and made my third and fatal mistake.

"No, I ain't lyin' to you."

The old man yanked and my shirt tore completely away from my body. As I struggled to keep my balance, out of the corner of my eye I saw Boston's most dangerous men disappear like smoke. My father's rage was apparently deserving of privacy. That was the last thing I saw for what seemed like hours as my father gave me the worst beating I had ever received in my life. For a guy who has made his way much of the time with his fists, that's pretty profound.

The beating stopped when my father finally got winded.

"You skip school or lie again and you're gonna get the same thing. Now get home."

I was shirtless and had two rapidly swelling blackening eyes. Snot and blood slithered parallel snakes down my face. I made my way painfully toward the main door. The men turned away and I've always believed it was an effort to keep from embarrassing me any further, for which I was grateful.

I won't try to convince anyone that I never told another lie over the years but I can say, with no fear of contradiction, that I never skipped school again until the day I quit.

In 1967, Howie bought the garage on Marshall Street in Somerville and went into the auto body business, Marshall

Motors. He bought it in my father's name and the old man ran the operation for him. Whatever monetary arrangements were made were never divulged, it was a deal made between friends. I'm sure it was nothing more legal than a handshake – after all, it was Somerville and a man's word was his bond. My old man signed the business back to Howie in 1978.

Contrary to news stories over the years, the Marshall Street Garage was a legitimate auto body shop. One reason Howie bought it was to be able to stay located close to Winter Hill as a base of operations for his other endeavors, but he also wanted a working shop where he could put friends to work, service the neighborhood and make a legitimate profit.

It *was* a working shop, Howie *did* put friends to work, but the anticipated profit margin seldom panned out. The bulk of customers fell into one of two groups. Friends, mobsters, cops and politicians looking to trade favors – or Somerville residents who were sorely in need of auto bodywork but seldom in a financial position to get it. Everyone wanted to get his car fixed, but no one really wanted to pay.

Bringing Howie back to the garage is inviting an adult for a return visit to a childhood home now owned by another family. It could go either way.

When we drive up, I feel edgy. Maybe this wasn't such a good idea; perhaps it's too painful. His friends – Buddy, Sal, my own father – all dead. And some of the rest – worse than dead. The garage is empty now, the property for sale and in need of repair. I let Howie enter ahead of me and he immediately begins to check the status of his old hangout. The glass in the skylights above is broken. "Someone must've got up there. I had them covered in plastic," Howie notes tersely as he continues his inspection.

As I watch him, an elderly man in a Boston Celtics t-shirt and windbreaker, I wonder what a "civilian" might think if they saw us. Would they recognize the man John Kerry once called 'The Number Two Organized Crime Boss in New England'? He looks as if he could be a retired mechanic wandering through the place he once worked on repairing things – which I guess, is what he is.

I say, more out of nervousness than trying to jumpstart an interview, "We're inside Marshall Motors. All those stories and now we're here." Howie turns and a big smile appears on his face.

"Yup, here we are." I am relieved. I realize it's gonna go one way, and not the other.

"I bought the place in '67 or '68 and needed a guy to run it," Howie begins.

Bobby Martini Sr. was the man for the job. "He was meticulous and organized. And he hired some good body men." Howie also knew my father was a master at minding his own business, so much so, he ended up doing time for it.

Howie continues as he walks slowly through the garage. "He didn't do anything criminal, no. Nothing wrong." Big Bob, it seems, refused to answer the government's questions about alleged goings-on within the Winter Hill Gang. He was rewarded with eighteen months in prison.

"He went before a Grand Jury and refused to answer. He took the Fifth. They granted him immunity and brought him back to testify. He still took the Fifth. And they put him in, that's what happens." Howie turns back to me. "That's the penalty they make you pay, you know."

Somerville is a city of tests. Tests of strength, of family, of convictions, and mostly, of loyalty and the price to be paid. There is a harsh sentence that follows failure to meet the requirements of loyalty and no one is powerful enough to escape it. One test I passed by using my head, the other using my feet.

The phone rang insistently. I made every attempt to ignore it. I'd already been woken twice by my mother. She had a problem with her boiler I was to fix later that afternoon. Sick with a hangover from another night of partying, all I wanted was dead quiet. I yanked the

receiver to my ear. Before I even had a chance to croak "Who is it?" I
could hear my father's voice.

*"You lazy motherfucker, you think just because I'm in here I
don't know what the fuck you're up to? If I was out right this minute,
you'd be fuckin' dead!"*

My father was residing in the Lawrence House of
Corrections with sixteen months gone on that eighteen-month
sentence. He had reached his limit and was looking for a vessel
for his rising anger and frustration. Since I had answered the
phone, I was the lucky winner.

*"Your mother ain't got no heat! What the fuck are you doing
about it? Nothing!"*

*I was a grown man but that voice still turned my bowels to
water. My eyes focused on the clock. Three hours ago I spoke to my
mother and promised I'd make it by the afternoon, what was the
problem?*

"Dad, Dad! I spoke to her, I've got it covered."

"You ain't got shit covered!"

*He continued with a string of expletives even I don't feel
comfortable writing. Infused with the bravery of a lion tamer standing
far outside of the locked cage, I hung up.*

My father was going stir crazy. He was away from his
element, his wife, his girlfriend and most importantly, his small
kingdom in the heart of Somerville where his word was the law.
Used to being in charge, his reputation extended into the prison
system. When I visited, I felt that this must be what it's like to
enter the White House. I got the VIP treatment from prisoners,
guards and even the janitors – because of my father. He had an
immediate impact on anyone he met.

My father was harsh to his family, no doubt, yet there
was an element rending him incapable of neglecting the righting
of any wrongs he perceived within the community and it helped
to balance that harshness. His word was his bond. If he
promised something, it was written in stone. It felt good that
these men catered to me because I was Bobby Martini's son.

That's the point my upbringing brought me to - being proud of my reception at a house of corrections. However, it did serve me more personally later on, when I found myself in the same situation.

"I've got a great story," Howie laughs. "Your father called one day and wanted a swing set for the prison farm. He had been transferred over from Lawrence Jail because he wasn't on the most dangerous list and was already taking over."

The farm allowed the children of inmates to visit and my father started to obsess about the visitors yard. Little kids get bored easily and he thought if there was a swing set, it might make the visits go a bit smoother. Anyone who has ever been on the receiving end of a screaming toddler understands.

"I called you to rent a truck in Quincy. You told me that you didn't have a license to drive a truck, but I said there's only one way to learn," Howie reminds me. I did rent the truck, promptly backed into a door but finally rumbled down to the farm to deliver the swing set.

Howie became friendly with the prison bosses and often made loans to them at no interest. Most times he wouldn't be repaid but his borrowers were always happy to assist with a favor. So despite his incarceration, Bobby Sr. was occasionally treated to dinner on the town courtesy of Howie Winter.

"Howie would send the deputy in charge to Bishop's Restaurant [an upscale restaurant in Lawrence] for a nice meal – just as long as he took me with him."

As for my old man, Howie says, "Your father was in jail for not opening his mouth, even though he really didn't know much about the business that went on down the garage. He wouldn't even tell the investigators his name and a friend like that is hard to come by. Especially today."

Things turned quickly in the last month of my father's incarceration. One Thursday he called the Feds and told them he was ready to talk, but he needed a furlough for the weekend to gather some details.

"There's information on the outside I gotta get my hands on," he told the unsuspecting lawmen. "I'm thinkin' you guys want me to back up what I got to say."

The Feds were ecstatic. Someone fucked my father and the old man's fucking was their open-mouthed kiss. A truckload of secrets about the Winter Hill inner sanctum must be forthcoming. In their excitement to roll the Gang, they neglected to insist my father sign anything. I had no idea until I received a phone call from Howie.

"I want to see you, Bobby. Pal Joey's." Howie hung up.

I figured Howie had something special for me. I was right, but I was wrong.

There was a set of steep wooden stairs that led to the office over Pal Joey's. As I climbed, I saw Howie standing by the phone, as if waiting to dial. I tried to see who else was in the room, but it was dark behind him. I believe now it was a combination of heavy hitters. There were half dozen of them.

"Bobby, call your father and find out why he's leaving jail so early."

Jesus Christ, what was the old man up to? I didn't need any hints to convince me that what was happening at this moment was very, very wrong. Howie dialed and handed me the phone. After a few painful minutes ticked loudly by, my father came on the line.

"Dad, there's a few guys in front of me and they want to know why you're leaving jail early."

I knew what was coming and whatever I was to say to in front of this room full of men would seal the fate of both Bobby Martinis.

"I know which motherfuckers you mean! Lemme tell you something, I done almost a year and a half for keeping my mouth shut. I only got three weeks left. Why the fuck would I talk now?"

I prayed no one else could hear him ranting. I pressed the receiver hard up against my face to muffle his voice.

"And furthermore, tell 'em all to go fuck themselves. I got a furlough to see Stevie, but that's MY fucking business, so you can all fuck off! You tell 'em all I said that, too!"

Stevie was my father's girlfriend. He'd wrangled a pass to hop into bed with her, but he was so offended anyone would question his loyalty that now he was adamant no one knew his business! It would have been fine except that number one son was, literally, under the gun.

"So, Dad..." I tried to keep my tone light.

*He hung the phone up so violently I know it broke in half. I was freaking out. There was no way I was telling **anyone** to go fuck himself. I did the only thing I could to try and save my ass.*

I faked like I was talking to him. I could feel the roomful of eyes trained on me and if I'd ever considered a career in acting, this was my consummate audition. I laughed heartily – a "guys will be guys" sort of chuckle, told my father to enjoy himself and hung up. I looked over to Howie.

"My, uh, my father, how do I say this?"

"Go ahead," Howie said patiently.

"My father just got out to give his girl a jump. He couldn't wait no more." I grinned apologetically, as if embarrassed by the randy nature of my own parent.

The room exploded in laughter. I wasn't sure if they were laughing at my description or at my attempt at editing the conversation. Then Howie nodded at me," You can go now."

As I was walking down those wooden stairs I was sweating my balls off. By the time my sneaker hit the bottom, I was already running up and over Winter Hill. I had no idea what my father was really up to or what he had done to get that prized furlough.

But my father was a lot smarter than anyone gave him credit. I think he was testing his friends and they flunked. He did indeed get his furlough and trotted on home to Stevie for the weekend.

When Monday rolled around the Feds brought him in, anxious to hear his revelations. But he played the Feds just as he played with Stevie that wonderful weekend.

"Hmmm, I really don't got nothin' to say about anything."

They were aghast. The agents threatened him with more time unless he honored their deal, but he just laughed. "I don't know what you guys are talkin' about. I never signed no papers. I'm just a mechanic." He had them. He pulled one over on the Feds and there wasn't a damn thing they could do about it.

The victory was not as sweet as it should have been. The old man was disappointed his friends questioned his loyalty and angry his eldest son would...well, anything he could think of to be pissed off at me about.

He got out a month later, still pissed. On the day he was scheduled for release, I heard brutal pounding on the door of my apartment. I opened it to my own father pointing a shotgun at me. *"Hello, son,"* he said as he shoved the barrel up against the bottom of my chin.

"You never fixed that fucking boiler over at your mother's did ya, ya son-of-a-bitch!"

The boiler was repaired the day he complained about it but it seemed prudent not to argue the point. I stayed quiet while he railed at me for a full five minutes, until my own brain went from full-blown panic to simple acquiescence. I looked down the barrel and back at my father.

"If you're gonna pull the trigger, then do it now. Shoot and get it over with."

We stared each other down. It was a stand off. Finally, I eased out from under the gun and walked slowly into the kitchen. I busied myself at the stove, cleaning it with a rag over and over. I waited for the shotgun blast, but it never came. In the background, my father kept roaring, torturing me.

"You suck as a son. You're fucking stupid and don't deserve to live."

I cleaned that stove until the paint began to chip. When my fingers went numb I said, *"Do it then. Last chance. Kill me now or I'm leaving."*

He kept screaming, spit flying from his mouth. Wearing himself down, he dropped into a chair without missing a beat. I walked past him and out the door, leaving him and his shotgun sitting at the kitchen table. I walked the whole city of Medford before I finally came *home. My father and the gun were gone. I was so relieved that I sat down and my head dropped onto the kitchen table in instant sleep.*

I'd been terrified. I couldn't hit him because he was my father, yet he was going to shoot me – his eldest son (not that I am suggesting he should have shot any of the younger ones). I took the brunt of his frustration over the perceived lack of loyalty from his friends – a bunch of guys who were probably just as angry before they discovered why he'd left prison so abruptly.

The next time I saw the old man it was as if nothing had happened. The shotgun incident seemed forgotten, but it wasn't. A few weeks later, I was boozing it up and having a few laughs at a bar with my buddy Tommy Hersey. The door had a steady stream of patrons, but I was surprised to see my father enter, drunk, with a friend of his. He was seldom seen outside of the Pointer Post. Before I could greet him, he walked up and sucker punched me right in the face. The club went silent.

I felt tears forming in back of my eyes. I couldn't move. I've got a harsh quick temper. Or did. It's something I've learned to control over the years by compartmentalizing my anger but back then it was a ticking bomb just waiting for someone to hit that fuse. My father did, but I could not raise my fists despite the fact that I wanted to…bad. I sucked in my breath and carefully exhaled. "Is that all you've got?"

The old man exploded. His companion frantically held him back, eventually dragging him out the door. Tommy followed them. In an instant, he burst back through the door.

"Bobby! You gotta get out of here!"

Curious, I got up and stepped out into the parking lot. My father was wrestling with his friend over the shotgun in the trunk of his car.

"I'm gonna kill that little bastard!" He was howling.

I guess he was steaming he'd backed down the last time he was going to kill me. I looked at Tommy. "I think you're right, it's time to go."

I was barred from my own father's bar for about six months for either not fighting back or not being killed. I never have been able to figure it out.

Howie walks back to the empty room that was once "the office."

The office at Marshall Motors was where the Feds figured all the best-laid plans of the Winter Hill Gang were hatched. I ask Howie if there was ever a concern that law enforcement was listening in. Howie smiles. "We had equipment, [we'd] check the phones and stuff like that. Play the music loud."

Howie and his associates also practiced a unique form of cross surveillance that alerted them to the fact that the government was most likely eavesdropping. Winter Hill surveillance was somewhat less formal than that provided by the U.S. government.

"The lady across the street used to tell us if she saw anyone hanging around. In fact, one morning she came over to tell me that the night before guys in suits had actually broken in to the building."

"Was she a customer?"

"Well, no, not really." Howie hesitates for a moment, as if wondering if he should "out" his source. Then his voice drops and he grins, his moustache twitching. "She was the minister's wife."

He's quick to defend her. "Very nice lady. We used to take care of her. If she was walking down the street with heavy bundles, I'd send one of the kids over to help her, and to make sure her lawn was mowed, her driveway shoveled."

The break-in did little to alter the daily business in the shop. "After that we knew for sure that they planted something." Despite that knowledge, no one ever bothered to discover and destroy what were surely electronic listening devices hidden around the building. "They'd just do it again. We didn't care. We just watched everything that we said."

Winter Hill boys knew that the government couldn't resist listening in since as far back as the Civil War when Honest Abe Lincoln tapped into telegraph conversations. They couldn't prevent wiretapping, but they could make every effort to have some fun at the expense of the Feds.

"Here's what we did," Howie grins. "We had another office in Chelsea and wanted to make sure it was safe. So we rented an apartment across the street. The lease was in the name of a person who didn't exist."

He reminds me this was before computers, the pre-Google era of no credit checks. "Then we ordered a phone in the name of the tenant we created. After the line was installed, we did a little nighttime construction work."

The guys cut a hole in the apartment wall and ran the line back inside and down the side of the building. "At the bottom of the apartment house, we started to dig. We ran the line under the lawn and right out to the street."

After sundown, the men jackhammered a small channel across the street. "We ran the line right across into our own office. We did the exact same in reverse from our place back into the apartment. At the apartment, we brought the phone connected to the office inside, turned the ringer off, and sealed the phone into the wall. That way we knew it could never be used. Then we cemented the channel closed."

It wasn't long before the cops came knocking – at the wrong door.

"One day," Howie laughs, "We hear sirens and suddenly cars come down the street from all directions. They screeched to a stop in front of the building. Guns drawn, they busted down the door of the billing address of our working phone line."

The apartment was empty. Not only was it devoid of furnishings and tenants, there was also no telephone. Howie hoots and slaps his knees with his palms.

"We laughed our balls off watching the cops come out shaking their heads. As they'd been searching, we'd been busy taking phone bets. They never figured it out, even though they were standing on top of the pavement we had opened up. All they had to do was look down and they would have seen the terrible patch job we did!"

There have always been rumors about violence at the garage; that vicious punishments (other than the one administered to me) occurred inside the walls and away from prying eyes as retribution for transgressions.

Howie flatly denies the rumors. "No. No. No."

There are stories of Bulger and Flemmi using heavy auto wheel locks to administer at least one brutal beating to a hapless victim at the garage. The corners of Howie's mouth turn down. "That was when I was away, I believe," he says, referring to the time period when he was incarcerated and the two men moved into the garage, and in on Howie's operation.

"There were no beatings when I was here." That is the end of the beating discussion.

That is not to say that no disputes were hashed out at the shop, especially those involving one of the New York families. In the fifties and early sixties, the Genovese family was loosely connected to the McLaughlins. As the mid-sixties rolled around with only Georgie left, residing in Walpole, the Italians began to do business with Howie, his old friend Joe "Mac" MacDonald and Sal.

"We used to lay off some of our bigger debts to them, we gave them plenty." Most of that business Howie conducted right out in the open.

"They used to fly down and meet me at the airport restaurant. I'd give them or get a package and they'd fly right back."

The relationship was for the most part, polite and peaceful, but like any business partnership, occasionally there were problems. As powerful and expansive as Howie's bookmaking operation was, it was still a matter of grave concern when differences arose between the two New England entities.

Such differences could not be negotiated at an airport lunch counter.

"One time we had to arrange a meeting. Two guys from the New York mob come up and Sal and I brought them back to the office."

A private meeting was always cause for an additional level of caution and Howie exercised the home field advantage in preparation for his guests.

When the New Yorkers entered Marshall Motors for the meeting, they were more than surprised at the crowd that greeted them.

"Shocked, I think," says Howie, laughing. "We had called all of our friends, our own agents and some legit guys - I don't wanna mention names because they were just friends, regular citizens – in all, there were fifty Somerville men. Guys that were dressed nice, in suits and ties."

The New York gangsters entered the garage to the crowd milling around, doing business in groups across the floor. "They were all over the place!"

It's a pretty good visual. Tough guys from one of the biggest Mafia families arriving in Boston to neatly squash a beef with a couple of local yokels in an auto body shop. It should have been a piece of cake. Then they discovered they were completely outnumbered by what they believed was the Irish Mob – in reality, just some local bookmakers with a number of regular Joes thrown in.

"They walked in and you could see their mouths drop. The first guy turns to me and says, 'Who are all of these guys?'"

Howie winks at me. "I said 'Oh, they're just part of our boys, you know.'"

I ask Howie if the dispute was settled. He nods. "Oh yeah, they were out of here, and when they left, they were shaking. And no one even raised his voice."

There came a time at Marshall Motors when business problems were not so easily dispatched and there is one guy who witnessed it firsthand. Paulie Moran spent his teenage years working at the garage.

A self-proclaimed "punky kid from the projects" and hell-raiser, Paulie is now forty-eight and has been clean and sober for thirty years. "I got myself into some trouble and decided that I would never take a drink again, and I didn't." Paulie smiles. He's a survivor.

Open and friendly, he is unlike most New Englanders. He speaks slowly and deliberately, carefully choosing his words. Yet typically Yankee in another fashion, he repeatedly peppers his responses with the phrases "I kept my mouth shut, I minded my business."

Howie Winter was a major influence on Paulie's teenage years. In a twist of fate, a childhood crime birthed a relationship. In the winter of 1974 Paulie and a couple of his friends were indulging in a popular pastime; hurling hard-packed snow balls at passing cars. One driver did not appreciate the frozen missiles exploding against his vehicle so he hit the brakes and screeched to a stop.

"This old guy gets out," Paulie says, "and we think 'what the fuck is *he* gonna do?'" As the man threatened them with the cost of the damage, one of Paulie's ballsier friends sucker punched him. The driver was unfazed as the teenager's fist bounced off his mid-section. Paulie shakes his head.

"He just stood there. 'That's it? Is that all you got, kid?'" The boys ran, disappearing into the Somerville projects.

A week later, Paulie and a friend were shoveling snow when he noticed a black Cadillac carrying two men rounding the corner. As the vehicle slowly passed, he recognized the passenger; it was the same man his friend had assaulted. The kid decided to act first, so utilizing the wisdom that makes sense only to a teenager, Paulie raised his shovel and whacked the back of the car as hard as he could. The car braked to a stop. The door slowly opened and the driver emerged. It was Howie Winter.

Paulie blanched and immediately dropped his shovel. "We ran and we ran and we ran." The gentlemen made no effort to follow them.

The next day, a friend of Paulie's approached him with a message.

"Look, I don't know what this means, but Howie Winter wants to see you up Marshall Motors. Ya better go up and see what's what."

Paulie and his sucker-punching pal hustled right up to the garage. Howie Winter was and is still known as a man who seldom raises his voice above a normal decibel. "He did that day," Paulie says. "And I took it. At least I didn't cry."

Howie ended his tongue-lashing with, "You're going to pay for the damage by working here every day until you earn enough money to fix my car." Howie pointed his finger at Paulie. "And don't even think you can do it faster by cutting school. You come here *after* school."

"So I started working up Marshall Motors." Paulie was a hard worker, starting off by running errands, getting coffee and lunches for the men and learning a trade fixing cars. "I worked all through junior high and into high school."

Paulie soon found he liked the repair business. The men who conducted their own activities trusted the kid and he eventually became a fulltime employee.

"Joe Mac took me under his wing. There was Stevie Flemmi, the Martorano brothers – Johnny and Jimmy, and the only Jewish guy, George Kaufman."

He was friendly with Gertie, Howie's African-American secretary. One of few black faces on the Hill during that time, she was a perfect fit for a bunch of Irish and Italian guys, as well as Kaufman the lone Jew – and she took no shit from any of them.

"In about the tenth grade, I started to see things I probably wasn't supposed to. I seen lots of cops come in, getting their cars fixed, money passed. But I'd be given a hundred dollar bill to run for sandwiches and coffee and told to keep the change."

"There were other guys in and out. A guy from Southie named Whitey, a big fat guy named Fat Tony [when asked if "Fat Tony was mobster Tony Ciulla, Paulie shrugs. "I'd be lyin' if I said I knew his last name"]. There was a quiet guy, Jimmy Sims, always with Joe Mac until they both kind of disappeared." In this instance, disappeared means "went on the run."

I think people wonder when they read a story about a guy on the lam, as they used to say in the old movies. How does he live, get by financially? I found out during an aborted tropical getaway.

After a particularly nasty wide-awake week of partying from bar to bar in the early 1970's, Howie took his son Gary and myself aside. "How'd you boys like to go a little vacation?"

We hadn't been many places. Had it not been for the Marines and later working in the movies, I probably never would have left New England. But there were other factors to consider. We were on vacation right now. We had free run of the city, open bar tabs (as well as open tabs for other things), plenty of women, and were gainfully unemployed in a profession that could be easily identified by anyone. We were in paradise, where the hell would we want to go? However, it was Howie who was asking. Not Howie Winter from the newspapers, but Howie the father of my best friend.

Gary and I sort of shuffled around. Finally Gary spoke up. "Uh, where to?"

Howie allowed himself a very tiny smile. "Oh, just Fort Lauderdale."

"Florida?" Gary wasn't sure he had heard that right.

"Is there any other Fort Lauderdale?" Howie responded.

The Official Home of Spring Break? The land of bikini-clad women except for the women that we were sure went topless at every crash of a wave? Where the girls were? We packed so fast we could have left in an hour. There was a dress code, however, at least for the travel portion of the trip.

"Boys," Howie informed us sternly, "Each of you wears a sports coat. Don't show up at the airport in jeans and t-shirts."

We eagerly complied. Those coeds lining Los Olas Boulevard, the main party drag, would be looking out for the sharpest dressed men. In the car on the way to Logan, Howie pulled four envelopes from his jacket, handing two to each of us

"Put one in each of your inside coat pockets," he instructed. "We're going to make a delivery."

Through cryptic conversation, I learned it was someone on the run from law enforcement. Once we were walking through the terminal, I whispered to Gary, "What's in the envelopes?"

"Cash."

"Oh, OK." I stuffed the envelope in my jacket.

That was the Winter Hill way. You never questioned things that were none of your business.

It seemed like weeks, but the plane finally touched down and we were whisked to a hotel arranged for us. Howie collected all of the envelopes and said "OK, boys. Go on to the beach. I've got business."

He didn't have to tell us twice. We took off. After three hours of sun and boozing, we headed back to shower and change for the night. We hadn't exactly knocked the tops off of every woman we met but there were so many options, there was no way either of us would end up alone. Howie was waiting.

"Get cleaned up, we have to catch the next flight back to Boston."

It was the sound of our evening balloon bursting. We hadn't had ample opportunity to really turn up the Somerville charm on the girls littering the sand!

"Why?" Gary asked desperately.

"Something came up," his father shrugged. He didn't finish the last part of his thought that was probably, "And if you two think I'm leaving you here with no supervision after the shit you've been pulling at home, you're fucking crazy!"

We packed without a word. It turned out Howie was taking money down to Joe Mac who was in hiding for something he'd done *back in Boston. After I got over the fact I wasn't going to have my fun in the sun, I laughed it off. I was loyal to him and would have made the same trip again if he'd asked.*

I still feel the same way, although if he asked me to take a jaunt to Florida now, at my age, I'd probably spend the three-hour wait by taking a nap in a chair under the tropical sun. Maybe I might keep one eye open, just for fun. But I'd still go.

CHAPTER EIGHT

The Changing of the Guard:
Guns on the Run, Dead Indians,
and a Fast Turkey

BEING ON THE run is a lonely life and most guys screw it up because they cannot keep from contacting friends and family back home. There is also the matter of staying in business – whatever your business is – while skipping one step ahead of the law.

Joe Mac stayed in touch with Somerville by way of an elaborate pay phone system he and Howie worked out in the event that anyone was ever forced into an extended vacation.

The guys mapped out a series of pay phones in strategic areas. At pre-arranged times on fixed days, the Winter Hill guys would fan out across the public phone network between 11am and 2pm, each waiting for their specific phone to ring. No man monitored the same location more than once to avoid being clocked by ambitious lawmen. Weeks passed before a phone rang, but when it did there was a friendly voice to fill Joe's requests for cash or carry his orders back to his guys still in the real world.

Both Joe Mac and Jimmy Sims went on the lam after being indicted in a horse race fixing scheme, although Joe had a multitude of other sins under his belt.

Here's a Somerville Joe Mac bedtime story, courtesy of my father.

1993. I'm in the Post with the old man and a few stragglers. It's fairly quiet and I'm thinking of blowing this place for a bit more excitement elsewhere. After all, the night was still young and I figured at forty, so was I. At least I felt like it tonight.

"I got a little story for ya," the old man says as I look at my watch. "A Winter Hill story about cowboys and Indians."

Something in the back of my mind told me I had better stay and listen. Everything happens for a reason. Although I didn't know it that night, my father would be gone by the end of the year, as were the stories that were always both horrifying and hilarious. I pull my stool closer and belly up to the bar. Someone dropped enough coin into the jukebox to give us a nice 50's doo-wop soundtrack. The ghosts of the Five Satins begin to croon about the still of the night.

My father clears his throat. "Once upon a time..." And so it goes.

"Do you know what happened to Indian Joe?"

I shake my head. He nods. "That was before your time. 1973. 'Indian' Joe Notorangeli ran an independent gambling operation in the area back in the early seventies and his outfit was quite popular."

I was twenty in '73 but why bother to remind him?

Medford is just north of Boston. It's where James Pierpont wrote "Jingle Bells" in the nineteenth century and Lydia Maria Child took a trip to her grandmother's house and put it in a poem called "Over the River and Through the Woods." The home of Medford Rum ("best rum in the states," at least in 1860), New York's Mayor Bloomberg and Fannie Farmer, the chocolate queen (not to be confused with Frances Farmer, the notorious Hollywood outcast). The ill-fated Black Dahlia, Beth Short, left Medford as a young girl to become famous in Hollywood. And she tragically did.

Medford also boasts such dubious events as the only known Mafia induction ceremony secretly taped, one of the biggest bank and jewelry heists ever when a bunch of cops got together and robbed the Depositors Trust in 1980, and the story of Indian Joe Notorangeli and a little café called The Pewter Pot.

"*Indian Joe was raking it in and the guy from Southie started to hear about cash piling up. You know I never liked that guy, Whitey. Still don't.*"

I know. I've heard it for years.

"*That Southie bunch wanted a taste and Indian Joe wasn't sharing. He had his own thing going on and he wasn't going to bow down to anyone, especially an Irishman.*"

Indian Joe also had a brother – Indian Al. "You're kidding me, right? There weren't any Indians on Winter Hill in the seventies," I laugh and the old man cuts me a look.

"*They weren't actually Indians, those were their nicknames.*"

Maybe I'm missing something. "Did they have some kind of trademark, like swinging a hatchet over their heads when they threatened people?"

"*Don't be ignorant.*" *My father is getting agitated. I give it one last swipe.*

"*Did they look like Indians?*"

He considers this, finally, a fair question. "Naw, they looked like Cubans."

"*So why didn't they call themselves Cuban Joe and ...*"

My father interrupts me. "Do you want me to tell you this story or not? Shut the fuck up."

I shut the fuck up, but I'm thinking that no matter what the details, these guys have to come to a bad end. No offense, but if you're gonna be tough guys, you have to think up better monikers than to refer to yourselves as the Indians Joe and Al.

"*Anyway, Indian Al was running his own gang, separate from us. Extortion, some bookmaking with his brother. They couldn't even be considered real rivals, but Bulger, he didn't like no one doing nothin' he didn't get a piece of. But it was Indian Joe that was really getting under his skin because he laughed Whitey off."*

Whitey started dropping subtle hints around town that Indian Joe had two choices; fade away quietly or be faded. The hints came in the way of several assassination attempts but the not-really-an-Indian Joe proved to be fairly fleet-footed and stayed one step ahead. He did, however, take it seriously enough to lay low and moved up to Medford.

"But he kept running his book."

On April 18, 1973, Indian Joe Notorangeli ventured into the streets of Medford to get a bite at a local café, The Pewter Pot. Somebody saw him and that somebody made a call to Winter Hill.

"Joe Mac was the guy who took the call. The information was that Indian Joe was at the café. The Pewter Pot was always filled with customers. Joe Mac didn't seem to care."

Joe Mac and a companion set off for Medford Square. They tooled into town in a hot car and parked in a rare empty spot across the street from the café. Not twenty feet away, a Medford cop was directing the busy traffic patterns in his little police box.

"You remember those?" the old man asks. *"It was a box about two feet off the ground with one side open in a sort of rounded look, so the officer could turn completely around and see traffic from all directions. Anyway Joe Mac idles the car while the other guy strolls into the Pewter Pot, but not before locking eyes for a second with the cop. The cop felt like he knew the guy but couldn't quite place him."*

The man wore a yellow hard hat, sunglasses, fake beard and mustache and a long white meat cutter's coat.

By now, I've forgotten all about the next stop in my night. I want to hear what happens.

There were quite a few patrons in addition to Indian Joe when the man entered the cafe. He headed toward the counter where Joe was sipping his coffee.

"Hey Joe," the man called out. Indian Joe looked up, the guy pulled out a gun and seven patrons hit the floor, all averting their eyes. The killer blasted Indian Joe and then calmly went out the door.

Across the street, Joe pulled out of the spot as his companion ambled back to the car. Joe maneuvered into the flow of traffic. Waiting patiently for his turn, Joe caught the eye of the cop and the officer, blissfully unaware that a murder had just occurred, signaled for the hot box to come on through.

"In a couple of seconds patrons come out screaming. It sets off a chain reaction and other people in the Square start grabbing their kids and running like hell. The cop jumps off his box and runs into the café'. In just a second he realizes that he just let two murderers go free with the wave of his arm."

After that, most of Indian Joe's bookie braves fell right in line with their new chief from the Southie tribe. They'd rather work for an Irishman than join the Indian in his burial ground. Gang members who didn't were either killed, like James Leary, shot by Joe Mac in Ft. Lauderdale where he had run to hide and Al Plummer, blasted inside a moving car so many times by Whitey that his head nearly flew off his body.

"Wow," I say. "That's some story. But I have two..."

"Questions?" my father finishes my sentence. "Let me guess. One, who was the man in the yellow hat, right?"

"Yes," I answer.

"Johnny Martorano. And I'll take another guess. Who told me the story? Am I right?"

"You're amazing," I answer dryly. "Were you there?"

He shakes his head. "Naw. Joe Mac told me the first part, the part up until the murder."

He sips his beer and looks at his watch. "What are you still doing here? Don't you have something cookin' somewhere?" That's the Martini dismissal.

Not just yet. "Who told you the second part of the story? The guys getting away?"

Silence. He smiles.

Oh, wait a minute. I get it. "It was the cop, right? The cop told you?"

"I ain't saying that, you are. Me? I just think it proves my theory that cops can't even catch a cold when it slaps 'em in the face unless they got a rat to tell them it's coming. Now get out of here. I'm tired of yakking with ya."

Indian Al shortened his name to Al Angeli, but it wasn't an effective disguise. A year later, he was sent to join his brother in the Happy Hunting and Bookmaking Ground in the sky, thus shutting down both sides of the marginally successful Notorangeli crime empire. He is listed among the twenty-one victims of what the U.S. government calls the "Bulger Group" headed by James "Whitey" Bulger.

That was probably one of the last stories my old man ever told me.

Paulie ticks off more names. "Your brother-in-law Brian Halloran used to come up the garage; he was a tough, tough guy and not right – you could tell by looking at him. No one to screw with. When these guys showed up, they had me wash their cars at twenty bucks a pop, in addition to my pay. They treated me great."

He also got an education in how to treat people. Life in Somerville during Howie's reign was the ultimate classroom. "He helped everybody. I know of a lot of cab drivers around Christmas time who were up against it with their kids. I always saw him reach into his pocket. I don't ever remember seeing a single one of them paying him back."

It wasn't just the cabbies. There was another, rather select group that considered Howie their benefactor. A couple of guys who would go to almost any lengths to be considered employees of Howie Winter – the local winos.

Howie and I had been talking for months about my father, Joe Mac and all the rest, when one afternoon he mentioned a name I'd never heard associated with the Winter Hill Gang.

"Bobby, did I ever tell you about Fast Turkey Bob?"

I quickly scroll through our interviews in my mind. I recall "The Rifleman," "The Executioner," "The House Painter," "The Animal," Punchy, Gaga, Bobo, Chop-Chop, several Fat Tonys, a Fat Vinnie (with the "i.e."), a Fat Vinny (with a "y"), and even a Fat Harry but for the life of me, I cannot recall any mobster named Fast Turkey Bob.

"I don't think so, was he out of Boston?"

Howie laughs. "Fast Turkey wasn't a gangster, Bobby, he was sort of a valet, I guess is the best way to put it. But secretly, I think he wanted to be an enforcer."

Back in the sixties, Howie used to do his bookmaking in the back room of the 318 Lounge on Marshall Street. This place would change names, becoming Pal Joey's in the seventies and then El Sid's in the 80's.

"Every day I'd drive up and there would be this wino called Fast Turkey Bob holding a parking place for me. Just standing there, flapping his arms so no one would pull in."

Howie always gave Fast Turkey a few bucks.

"It's not that I condoned his lifestyle, but there something that made me say to myself, 'there but for the grace of God, it could be me there instead of him.'"

I ask Howie how Fast Turkey Bob got his nickname, but he doesn't remember.

Fast Turkey's loyalty knew no boundaries; he almost tore a lady's head off because she parked in what he had deemed Howie's spot. The woman drove off scared shitless. Howie was Fast Turkey's sole concern and nobody parked in his boss' spot. Howie got a kick out of their daily routine.

The wino would eventually retire for the evening with a contingent of other drunks. They snuck into Marshall Hall to sleep in the coal bins. As a kid in the fifties, I remember having to shovel the coal in the furnace to keep the family warm, and the bins were still in use.

Howie continues. "From time to time another wino by the name of Rebel hit me up for money as well. One day I gave him a couple of bucks. I didn't think anything about it but apparently ol' Fast Turkey Bob was watching from down the alley and he didn't like anyone bothering me."

As the week passed, Howie realized it had been a while since he'd seen Rebel. When he pulled up to his spot being held by his alcoholic valet, "I asked him if he'd seen the Rebel lately."

The wino pulled himself up into an authoritative position and replied, "That Rebel won't be bothering you anymore, Mr. Winter."

"Fast Turkey," Howie said, "What in the hell are you talking about?"

"I saw him pestering you so I waited for him to hit the coal bins. After he went to sleep," Fast Turkey continued conspiratorially, "I boarded him in. I nailed it so good it would take a sledge hammer to get him out!"

Howie was aghast. "How long has he been down there?"

Fast Turkey Bob thought for a long moment. "Two or three days, I don't remember."

The wino's loyalty did not have the desired effect on Howie. "I told him to get his ass over to the coal bin and let Rebel out immediately!"

The personal valet did as he was told.

"I was sick to my stomach that the old wino was dead."

It was a relief when Howie saw the two of them coming staggering back down the block.

Howie appreciated the old guy's loyalty, but he'd always preached about not hurting anyone over money, it could have happened without him even realizing it. Back stabbing and double-dealing it appeared, was not confined solely to the established New England crime circuit nor to the Federal Bureau of Investigation. It also happened in the most unusual of places.

"After that, I knew I had to keep a sharper eye on what was going on in the street. It was a good lesson, but it still gives me a laugh all these years later." From that day on, Howie made sure both of the winos received daily pouches of money so as not to offend either of the street warriors.

The cops asked for other favors. "It wasn't just patrolmen, it was detectives too. They all came in asking, all the time." Paulie is obviously uncomfortable with the subject of law enforcement.

How many cops came in looking for help?

"Just...more than you would want to know."

Didn't Paulie realize he was working for an extensive bookmaking operation?

He laughs, a bit embarrassed. "No. I figured they [Howie] were people who loaned money, like loan sharks."

It wasn't until indictments began to roll in and the press made the Winter Hill Gang a household name once again that Paulie began to get a handle on the actual professions of the men he worked for over the years.

"I didn't really know what Stevie and Whitey's game was. I thought they were like the musclemen. If you didn't pay, those were the guys who went and got the money. I always thought he was the boss. But I minded my own business."

Life continued at Marshall Motors for Paulie Moran, the former snowball hurler. The more of his own business that Paulie minded, the more business unfolded in front of him. "One thing I began to notice is that cars would come in one way, and they'd never leave. It was a..."

Chop shop?

Paulie finally gives in. "Ya, it was." He laughs. "Parts were sold off. Then they had this Cadillac salesman. Those Caddies come in one way, leave another and then come back a second time! All smashed up, then they called in the adjuster."

The adjuster got a couple of hundred dollar bills to "adjust" the vehicle. Then the car would disappear for good. So the owner got paid for the repair and then for the theft.

"Or maybe a beautiful car rolled in and we'd take it completely apart. Then I'd deliver parts all over town and over to George's place on Lancaster Street. I went everywhere except for Southie. Whitey and Stevie kinda kept that to themselves, where they conducted their other business."

Bookmaking, loan sharking, chopping, it was one stop shopping at Marshall Motors. "Well, they had cops, state police, Feds all on the payroll so they did it all under one roof."

In the late seventies, Paulie was still at Marshall Motors but the landscape had begun to shift. Howie and Sal had been convicted of extortion in the much-debated "Pinball Case" and were awaiting appeal in jail.

The old guard was replaced. "Whitey and Stevie were there with both the Martoranos." As the new command began to take hold at the garage, changes were implemented. Some of the visitors had to wait on line outside of the office and there was an elaborate system as to who gained entry first. "There was guys they didn't want in the office at the same time for whatever reason."

Bulger's propensity for micro-management and control were evident from the start. These new guys "ran things differently. It was no nonsense."

Under Bulger, Paulie says, "You knew when those guys went into that back room for meetings, it wasn't gonna be nice. I saw guys come out of there," Paulie pauses and shifts uncomfortably in his chair, "looking as if they had been...like they had been...you know," He runs his right index and middle fingers down his cheek, "Crying." That's not easy to admit in Somerville, even though we were a predominantly Irish burg. "And more," Paulie says. "Noses twisted, bleeding. You knew Whitey meant business."

But didn't Howie mean business?

"Not that kind of business," Paulie replies tightly.

Paulie saw one such brutal beating firsthand. That incident when Whitey and Stevie beat a guy with a heavy lock. "Howie was away then. I had never seen nothing like that before."

The appearance of the back office itself changed as well. "I started seeing stacks and stacks of money piled up. And stuff normal people wouldn't have; meters, so they could tell if someone else was listening, a TV in the corner they used to turn on [to muffle the sounds]."

There was also the legendary trap door. A covered hole in the floor of the office for access to the furnace, over the decades it has gained the unsubstantiated reputation as a dumping ground for uncooperative business associates.

Paulie spent the next few years learning the likes and dislikes of his new bosses. "Johnny Martorano liked to drink and if he was drinking one night, the next morning he'd want two coffee frappes from Brigham's and a sandwich from Primo's where they'd pull the inside bread out of a sub roll and fill it with egg salad."

This particular detail makes me laugh, but it's clear Paulie doesn't find any humor in special orders. "You know, you're laughing, but that's how he wanted it."

I get the feeling that it really wasn't a laughing matter and perhaps Paulie had learned the preferences of the men the hard way.

Bulger and Flemmi's particularities don't fit with their much-publicized reputations as mad dog killers. "They were kinda health conscious," Paulie says. "They'd drink tea." All of the men had to have their specific requirements met. But despite catering to the men's needs, Paulie had little personal interaction with them.

Paulie's status with his new bosses was elevated. "I'll never forget this. Johnny and Jimmy were there, Whitey and Stevie. The garage door was down. A big Ryder truck pulled up outside with the horn blowing."

Paulie looked outside and suddenly the back door of the truck opened up. Twenty to thirty guys jumped out and broke down the door of the garage.

"I was scared stiff. I know now it was a raid, but then I had no idea what was happening. I was seventeen and these guys came barreling in, guns drawn."

The kid immediately raised his arms in a surrendering gesture, broom still in hand, and stood shock still, while the law swarmed all over the property. The men were rounded up and hustled out of the back. One officer grabbed Paulie by the front of his shirt and lifted him up, demanding the kid identify himself. "I wouldn't say anything. Jimmy saw the guy and started yelling 'Put the kid down, he don't know nothing! He just cleans up, leave him alone!'"

The officer released his hold on Paulie, all the while taunting him, "You must be one of their punk kids," while the search continued. As the men were taken into custody, Paulie asked Jimmy what should he do. "Should I lock up?" Jimmy instructed him to secure the garage and set the alarm after the law had left.

"So that's what I did. Not long after, I had to run some things over to George Kaufman's garage."

Kaufman was delighted to see the him, "'Hey kid, I heard you kept your mouth shut. They say you had tears running down your face, but you kept your mouth shut.'

Paulie smiles. "And I did. And after that, the men looked at me differently. I started to feel like I belonged to the new management, that I was accepted."

His teenage years waning, Paulie began looking for a way to raise money to buy his own tow truck. "Joe Mac had taken me under his wing but he had disappeared. Howie was away as well. There was only one guy left. Joe Mac's brother, Leo. He was sort of an odd duck; never really said two words to anyone. He never even said hi to me in all the years I was there."

I remind Paulie that Leo had done something like twenty-eight years in prison, which may have had something to do with his lack of demeanor. Paulie shrugs as if to say that was no excuse for rudeness.

"Ya, but he never spoke to me so I never would have thought of going to him. In the end Young Howie lent me the money and I got my own truck, working right out of the yard at the garage."

"Some time went by, Joe Mac was arrested in New York when he was on the lam. I heard he was dressed as a nun and carrying a machine gun."

Despite the arrest, Joe Mac made his way back to Somerville, like the homing pigeons we all seem to be and appeared at Paulie's on Thanksgiving with an envelope of money – two thousand dollars.

Paulie remembers opening the front door and thinking, "Here he was again. I invited him in for dinner, he told me he couldn't stay but he handed me the envelope."

Joe Mac had tears in his eyes as he refused the offer of a turkey dinner.

Paulie shakes his head. "Joe said, 'I wish I was around when you needed help.' I told him I was all set, I was OK. He asked why I hadn't gone to his brother Leo. It seemed that Leo really liked me; he just never talked to anyone, but had kept Joe up to date with my life. He made me keep the money even though I didn't need it. I tried to return it several times over the next few months, I'd see him walking his little dog down the street, one of those skinny hot dog kind of dogs, but he finally told me to stop being a thorn in his side and just keep the money. He'd keep on walking, just Joe and his hot dog."

The image of stocky Joe walking his dachshund down the street sticks in my mind, right next to a mental picture of big, burly Sister Joe Mac, the gun totin' nun.

"I always shoveled his walk in the winter after that. I shoveled Leo's too."

Unlike me with Sal, Paulie took advantage of the chance to show his gratitude. I felt a twinge of envy when he talked about shoveling the snow. It was just so easy to have done.

"Years later I found out that Joe Mac, the guy who cried because he wasn't around to help me buy my first tow truck, this guy who was a gentleman to the neighborhood was..." Paulie stops for a second as if deciding whether or not to go on and finally says, "Well, he was a stone cold killer."

Yeah, he was. A friend I interviewed for this book asked me not to name him, so I won't. But he did give me this insight into Joe's involvement with the Winter Hill Gang.

"Joe hated Whitey even though he did business with him. The relationship was what he called 'an evil necessity.' He called him 'that bum from Southie' and a coward," my friend says.

Joe Mac snorted disgustedly when anyone referred to Whitey as a tough guy. "Tough guy? Bullshit! Pussy is what he is. He liked to drag that big machine gun around to make his dick seem bigger."

Apparently that was not a problem Joe Mac suffered from.

"Me? I use a pistol. If I gotta kill a guy, I walk right up to him, press that gun against his head and that's the last thing he sees – my face. Then I pull the trigger and then – nothin'."

According to my friend, Joe wanted to ice Whitey, but Howie demurred. "Leave it be, Joe," he said. This was back before Whitey's own murders surfaced. I haven't asked him, but I wonder if Howie knew then what he does now, would he have answered differently.

But yes, Joe Macdonald was a stone cold killer. Back before he took that turn, however, Joe Mac was a war hero. During WWII he had two ships shot right out from underneath him. His baby brother was on the second ship with him and was not as lucky as Joe. He didn't survive and haunted Joe until he died.

Paulie shrugs. "It's all very sad."

He closes with some simple thoughts, mystified about how it all turned out. "That's where I got my education. I learned a lot. Howie, I'm still friends with, he's a gentleman. No question there. But Whitey – he's a rat. And Johnny Martorano," Paulie pauses, his conflict evident.

"I can't believe the stuff Johnny did, I used to wash his car, and he was very, very good to me. He never struck me as a killer. He was like a gentle giant. I knew his son Vincent, a great guy. I knew all of their kids. I was a kid at the same time. Hell, I used to take all of them for ice cream."

I also know Johnny, and although I haven't seen him in years, when I was younger I spent time drinking and laughing with him, John Callahan and the boys. I never had any hint of what was to come and all I can say about Johnny Martorano is that he was always decent to me.

Paulie looks sad for a moment, remembering the man who stood up to the law in an effort to protect the kid from being tied into their activities. "Jimmy Martorano was a class act, I met his father, knew his kids. I remember when Jimmy's son died of carbon monoxide poisoning, him and his girlfriend in their car. A great kid, a football player. It was very sad. It broke Jimmy's heart."

It was a horrible mishap. In 1983 Frank Martorano and his girlfriend, both just nineteen years old, were overcome by carbon monoxide as they sat together chatting in a car one night in the small seaside town of Scituate, Mass. Found with their arms around each other, the girl survived, but Frank did not. The high school sweethearts were, according to all accounts, deeply in love, and the tragedy was an accident. Loved by his Rebecca Road neighbors and described as a handsome and kind-hearted football player planning to go into the service, Frank's quote under his photo in his girlfriend's high school yearbook was the lesson, "You never have a second chance to make a good first impression."

Neither Paulie nor I say anything for a few moments, the hopeful poignancy of the young man's message washes over us.

The sadness Paulie exhibited for the aforementioned dissipates when he is reminded of Stevie Flemmi. "Stevie's a rat. I have no respect for him. I knew both girls he murdered. Debbie [Debra Davis] used to come to the garage, a beautiful girl. [Debra was strangled by Whitey at the behest of Stevie when she began dating a Mexican]. And I knew Deborah Hussey, who we thought was Stevie's daughter." [Deborah Hussey was actually Flemmi's stepdaughter, murdered by Whitey and Stevie in 1985].

Davis was strangled; fingers and toes hacked off, all of her teeth removed. I've been told by more than one of the neighborhood guys that in the pre-DNA days that relied solely on dental records, Whitey yanked so many pearly whites Stevie presented him with the horrifically useful gift of a sterling silver tooth puller.

There has been much speculation about the relationship between Bulger, Flemmi and Howie Winter over the years. As decades rolled past the glory days of Marshall Motors, revelations about Whitey working as an FBI informant have led many to believe that it was indeed he who enticed the government to turn its attention on the pinball incident that initially sent Howie to prison.

"To say that Whitey and Stevie were rats to get rid of Howie, back then I figured...no."

Paulie Moran, the kid who used to sweep up and run for coffee frappes has had a long time to reflect as he has learned more about the men.

"But now, seein' what happened, after it all come out, yes...I see why they wanted Howie out of the picture. They'd have complete control. They were people who were feared, they just did away with..." Paulie stops short. He doesn't elaborate. He indicates I should know what he means, that Bulger and Flemmi did away with anything or anyone in their way.

"Good men got hurt by them. Those two? No respect. Howie was feared, but Howie was a gentleman who was always respected. That was the difference."

Howie Winter is indeed a gentleman. As we walk around the garage, each immersed in our own memories, he reminds me of the incident that precipitated my own father leaving his employ back in the late seventies. Everything in the garage reminds me of my father and our relationship. He wasn't the gentleman Howie is, but I loved him as I love this old man.

"Your father worked the movies," Howie begins.

I work in the movies; I'm a Teamster for films and television.

"I didn't know that." I am mystified by the things I do know about my past and confused by the things I don't.

"Oh yes," Howie tells me. "He was quite a capable guy. The movie electricians used to bring in all kinds of stuff for him to fix, and the guys with those movie sets used to put them over there." He points to a corner. "Yeah, your dad, he worked the movies."

That's right, I do remember. My father's career in entertainment was cut short, though. He was working on a movie and got into a beef with Gus Manning, the business agent for Local 25. Apparently my father felt that Gus was screwing him somehow. Instead of filing a grievance, my old man dealt with his problem in a more direct way – he cracked Gus across the face and that was a wrap for him.

Marshall Motors. Loan sharks, bookmakers, chop shoppers, teamsters AND film technicians, set decorators - then eventually turncoats, murderers and FBI informants. Wouldn't conservative critics of liberal Hollywood have a field day with this?

Howie looks at an empty space where tools once resided. "He liked everything just so, your father. Did you know that?" Yeah, I knew that. As a kid, he'd rip me apart if I lost a single nut or bolt out of his inventory.

"When did my old man leave here?" I ask Howie. "Do you remember?"

Howie doesn't say anything for a moment.

"Whitey didn't like your father, Bobby," he says suddenly. "He wanted him out of here."

"Really? I didn't know that." My old man rarely mentioned Bulger but I knew he had no use for him. I find it hard to believe that little Whitey had scared off Big Bob. I have heard Whitey described as "pure evil," but I had seen my old man in action. That would have been a match made in hell.

"Do you remember Buddy White?"

Buddy White was the chief of detectives in Somerville during the seventies and another childhood pal of Buddy McLean and Howie's. White was no one to be fucked with and although he was a friend of the Winter Hill boys, he wasn't afraid of them. He wasn't afraid of anyone.

"I don't know what it was but I remember there was an incident," Howie says. "I was away on vacation at the time. But I remember someone told me, Whitey tried to bully Martini around and Buddy White heard about it and came up and laid it into Whitey."

"I never knew any of that stuff," I reply.

But I think, "Wow, if the old man knew then what Whitey was to become, would he still have been stubborn about being pushed around?" Yeah, probably.

Howie nods. "Oh, yeah. Buddy took Whitey outside and told him 'If something happens to Martini, then the same thing is gonna happen to you.' Whitey acted as if he didn't know what Buddy was talking about, but he did. And that was the end of that. They didn't bother him again, but I think Bobby had enough of their shit. He just wanted to leave on his own timetable and we remained friends. [Whitey and Stevie], they didn't want any guy that had any balls around them."

I shake my head. "But my father was no shooter so they had nothing to fear."

Howie smiles at my naivety – my assumption that one must be outwardly aggressive to be feared, something I am still working to reconcile in my own life. "No, but he was a man of his convictions. You weren't gonna bully him around. He didn't take any shit from anybody even though he never did anything violent. He didn't need to."

Howie is talking about my father, but he's talking about himself as well, he just doesn't acknowledge it. He takes one last look around and gives a small wave to the empty building and all of the ghosts still residing there: Sal, Joe Mac, George, the New York gangsters, my father, and the rest of the guys. Howie has also had enough. He's a man who likes to keep moving forward. Me, I just keep moving.

"Now Bobby, you know what I think. So let's go to lunch."

"OK, Howie," I reply.

So Howie Winter and I open the door and step back into the present, closing the chapter on Marshall Motors.

CHAPTER NINE

A Horse Is a Horse, of Course
The Race Fixing Trial, Spread The Word

IT WAS 1974, more than four years after the massacre at Kent State. I was driving through Harvard Square with Howie and my father. Our troops had supposedly been withdrawn from Cambodia but anti-war activists still claimed the streets and made up most of the foot traffic.

As we drove through the Square, I could picture the riots of the sixties, the clash of the cops with the peace advocates against the soundtrack of "There's somethin' happenin' here." The cops took no prisoners and if a hippie with long hair and beads crossed the line, he was assured a spot under a nightstick. Later on, when I became a cop, I wondered why we called police batons nightsticks; many of the guys also utilized them generously in the daytime.

I'd seen it unfold in snatches on TV. Not in person, I was already a teenage Marine on the run from Somerville. But even if I'd been home, I wouldn't have been an eyewitness. Back at home we were waging our own wars daily and had no spare time for the police and peaceniks battling it out in Boston.

"When I was in the Marines, you'd never have seen anti-war bullshit," I heard Howie grumble, but who could relate to it? If Kent State was already history, WWII was another century. Perhaps it was *some vague reference to the fact that I had not been to Vietnam myself, my real age of sixteen having been revealed; instead I served stateside.*

The three of us gawked as a guy wrapped in green cellophane (and not much else, to the chagrin of my father) marched up and down the sidewalk. The sign around his neck read "I Am Mother Earth, Love Me." We burst into laughter.

We stopped at a light and a group of kids passed by. Girls with long straight hair and voluminous thrift store coats flapping despite the fall wind. They hung on the arms of longhaired guys in jackets covered with symbols: peace signs, smiley faces and the upraised middle finger.

My father snorted. "Jesus, the guys look just like the girls. Who the fuck can tell the difference?"

I certainly could. The braless state of the girls was evident as they bounced by.

"The world is changing," Howie mused. "Things are gonna be different."

Across the rest of the country, they already were. The gunfire in the Ambassador Hotel kitchen assassinated the last hopes of the New Frontier and the Summer of Love. The war crawled to a bloody end, as did the presidency of Nixon. The Watergate Hotel was broken into and The Brady Bunch was canceled. Ted Bundy was on the loose. The Black Panthers had a woman in charge. Kidnapped heiress Patty Hearst burst into a bank proclaiming, "I'm Tania! Up against the wall, motherfuckers!" Bobby walked over that hill with Abraham, Martin and John, and now Boston mournfully boasted two dead Kennedys instead of just one.

My father folded his arms and grunted as the light changed. "Not in Somerville."

I had to agree. Somerville would never be like the rest of the country. Despite the world struggling through social evolution, things in Somerville remained the same. It seemed outside forces would never touch those four square miles. But I was wrong.

Howie glanced over at my father. "Bobby, I've got a good pick tonight on a horse. I need you to put out some action in the streets, but nothing with our offices, if you know what I mean."

I sure as hell did. So, as usual, I figured I'd jump right in. I leaned forward. "I got a few bucks."

Howie's eyes slowly rose to the rearview mirror as my father turned almost completely around in his seat – no small feat for such an enormous body. The message was eerily the same. Shut The Fuck Up. Not only did I shut the fuck up, I sat as far back into the seat as I could, hoping that some cloak of invisibility would cover my grievous error. I didn't say another word as we drove.

I was twenty-one years and had done the same number of months in the Marine Corps. But sitting in that backseat, I had no idea what life had in store for me. If it were up to those two guys in the front, I would definitely not be hanging around with them for any long period of time.

Howie and I have ventured out for our interview regarding what came to be known as the "Horse Fixing Trial." A twenty-something waitress weaves us through the busy Millbury steakhouse to a comfortable booth in the back. We're seated against a window and outside the sun has made a brief cameo to light up the snowy parking lot this winter day. Howie studies the menu.

Dubbed in 1978 by Sports Illustrated as "Racing's Big Scandal," Howie and twenty others were indicted on charges of bribery and extortion. It was the final nail in the coffin of his empire, no matter what you believe that empire to have been, and resulted in convictions tinged with conflicting versions. Yet the evidence produced was the testimony of one single individual.

I'm starting to wonder why I decided to write this book. It's been one long year of asking friends uncomfortable questions. I sigh audibly.

Howie puts down the menu. "Bobby, what are you having?"

The waitress bounces up at the exact moment I blurt out, "When did you meet Fat Tony?"

She smiles brightly albeit uncomprehendingly. In the spirit of Christmas (and a good tip) she snaps to attention and turns to Howie. "Pleased to meet you, I'm Kelly!"

It didn't matter that Howie isn't an enormous fat man. This is Massachusetts where everyone has a nickname and half the time they don't relate to anything you can easily recognize. Take for instance a guy called Skinny. He might have been coined Skinny because as a kid he skinned his knees all the time, or his dick is too small, or for no reason at all.

Howie rolls his eyes at both of us. "I'm not Fat Tony, but I am hungry, so let's see..." He orders us a couple of steaks. Then he turns his attention back to me. I clear my throat and start over.

"When did you meet Tony Ciulla?"

And so the horse race fixing is on the table. "Through my ex-wife Sissy," Howie says.

He hadn't lived with Sissy since the guys went underground during the Gang Wars. "We got married way too young," he says. They'd had a rocky union, but as is typical for where I come from, they had never divorced. Instead they lived apart until Sissy's death in the early nineties.

"Sissy," Howie continued, "Asked me to do a favor for Ciulla, who was married to one of her girlfriends. He was in trouble, owed some bookmakers money. I needed that like I needed a hole in the head but for Sissy I'd do anything. So I called Ciulla. We arranged to meet down Chandler's Restaurant. He was one big man."

Fat Tony was six foot three and weighed, so he claimed, only a scant three hundred and fifty pounds, and yet was constantly dieting. Or insisting he was. He put away so much food the sheer volume of it rivaled his gambling debts. He was a Boston native, son of a horse playing fish peddler, so he had the ponies in his veins and at present, no cash in his wallet.

Tony claimed he was funded by Philly Mob boss Angelo Bruno. Born in Sicily, Bruno was known for settling matters by reconciling differences as opposed to the more popular method of removing limbs. Bruno rose to become the only mobster to gain a seat on the famed Cosa Nostra's Commission who was not a member of a New York Family. Like Howie, Bruno was accepted by his peers despite not being a carbon copy of them.

"Ciulla was a degenerate gambler," Howie grimaces. "He bet everything, owed everybody. Horses, dogs, football, baseball, you name it. This time he was down to the wire."

Fat Tony was also an associate of another Fat Tony, Genovese Family bookie Anthony "Fat Tony" Salerno. But even this connection wasn't keeping Ciulla off the ropes. He was deep in debt.

"What was I gonna do?" Howie shrugs. "He was from Boston. Our wives were friends. I made a call on his behalf and bought him some time." Ciulla got his reprieve but it wasn't long before he came sniffing back. It would be very helpful if Howie's office would make several bets for him. His credit wasn't very good.

"Sal and I were doing well in the mid-seventies, we didn't need extra heat. And Sal didn't like Ciulla. But I did find out he'd been in the horses for some time. I was interested in that business."

Ciulla and William "Billy" Barnoski from Somerville were convicted of conspiring to fix a horse and got one year in the Cambridge House of Corrections back in 1972. In '73 Fat Tony and Billy were again convicted, this time for doping horses in Rhode Island.

"Ciulla was barred from over fifty tracks and was unable to place a bet. To say he didn't have the most sterling reputation is probably an understatement. But he did know his horses. I told him I'd think about it. In the meantime, I began considering how much money I might make almost legitimately if I bought and ran my own horse." Howie was a realist and knew the bookmaking business might not last.

He'd worked down by the South Boston piers in the late fifties with a guy by the name of Peter Demetri and they'd stayed friends over the decades.

"Peter and his brothers, Charlie and Jimmy, already had a few licensed horses and were big into racing. With Ciulla's knowledge of horseflesh, he could help us buy a quality winner."

"My idea was to train the horse privately until we were sure we had the best chance to take the win." He approached Peter with the venture – and his theory. Run it as a true "dark horse" and let it outclass the others for the big win. It wasn't anything new; owners, trainers and jockeys had been doing it since the ancient Romans raced chariots.

Peter readily agreed. His secluded homestead in North Reading was the perfect spot. Howie set up a meeting with Peter and Ciulla. The fat man was immediately enthusiastic.

"I know the horse, cost ya thirty grand and worth every penny," he wheezed to Howie. "Just leave it to me." They did. Peter's two brothers were just as enthusiastic.

I couldn't wait to hear about the horse in question. "What did you get for thirty thousand?"

Howie picks his steak knife up off the table and jabs it into the air. "What did we get for thirty thousand? We got a TWENTY thousand dollar horse!"

"That doesn't sound like a very good deal to me!" Kelly muses as she puts the sizzling meat down in front of us. "That's a one third mark up!"

We both stare at her.

"Can we have a couple of beers?" I ask.

She nods and whisks away. Howie bursts into laughter. "The waitress figured it out right away, but Peter and I?" He makes a slashing motion with the steak knife. "No idea."

"I found out much later Ciulla pocketed our ten. He was screwing us from the jump. But at the time, we were thrilled. We even built a regulation size track up at Peter's house to work our horse away from the eyes of the local trainers."

As their new acquisition, Spread The Word, began to train, Ciulla became a mainstay at the North Reading farm. Peter's son Young Jimmy (yes, he's called Young Jimmy so he wasn't confused with his Uncle Jimmy) was very familiar with the fat man.

"My father was always outside grilling for his friends. Howie and Tony were frequent guests. My father loved Howie and he took a liking to Ciulla. They never talked business in front of us kids, they just hung out. But there was an incident that really soured my father."

Peter had flown to Philly to attend a horse race with Ciulla and his constant companion Barnoski. When he opened the door to the hotel suite where they were staying, he walked in on Barnoski viciously beating up a jockey. The hapless victim was being pummeled, blood streaming across his face.

Shocked by the brutality, Peter immediately flew home. He and Howie bought a horse with the help of Ciulla and, by proxy, Barnoski, but Peter had no idea that it would come down to physical intimidation in order to win. Sickened, he wanted out of the partnership.

"Everyone knew there were going to be some improprieties to win. They weren't babes in the woods, but my father and his brothers were licensed horse owners."

It was not an isolated incident. Victims later testified Ciulla sent Barnoski out to deliver "a few slaps" to jockeys and trainers who balked at the race fixing requirements. One trainer, Vernon Ewalt, said that he needed twenty-six stitches to close his face after one such "visit."

Barnoski did have his fan base, though. Recently I was having a couple of beers with my good friend Spike Leva when

Billy's name came up. Spike's uncle used to run with Barnoski. A bad motherfucker, we both agreed.

"But," Spike says, "You could never convince my grandmother of that. I was at her house one night when Billy and my uncle came in. They were all bloody. Head to toe, blood all over their clothes. My grandmother didn't say one word as they began to clean up. Suddenly the cops were at the door."

The officers arrested Spike's uncle and Barnoski for attempting to beat a man to death with baseball bats. Spike shakes his head. "After they left, Grandma looks over at me and says disgustedly, "Can you believe what those men said about Billy? He's a nice boy, he'd never do anything like that!"

We both roar at his grandmother's judge of character. I got a kick out of that story, thinking brutal Bill Barnoski was actually a favorite of little old ladies.

Peter began looking for a way to ease out of the deal. He didn't want to disappoint Howie or leave him holding the bag, and he was sure that Howie wouldn't condone what he'd seen, but all the same, he wanted out and the best way would be to go to Howie and speak to him directly.

"I know he agonized over it. Before he had a chance to resolve it, he died. He didn't live long enough to see his horse win the following February of 1975 at Garden State," his son says sadly.

"It was a damn shame," Howie drinks his coffee as Kelly clears the table, wisely keeping her thoughts to herself. "The horse was set up for Garden State by holding him back at Rockingham. We held him back for three races, finishing last or close to last in all three."

Spread The Word won in New Jersey by a length and a half, as expected. What Howie did not expect, however, was that not only had a portion of the other jockeys been bribed by Ciulla to hold their own mounts back but that the fat man had brought in runners from all over the country to place bets on the horse. It was one of Ciulla's biggest scores.

Talk about Spread The Word heated up. Less than a month later, the horse was scratched from another race due to rumors that ownership of the animal was really Ciulla's and not those listed on paper.

"A lie," Howie fumes. "We paid for the horse. We *overpaid* for the horse."

Ciulla was still viewed by the Feds as the ringleader of a group that consistently fixed races and drugged horses. He had the resume to prove it. But they were having a hard time coming up with anything more recent than innuendo and got their big break when an unrelated jockey's agent passed a bad check.

The jockey's name was Peter Fantini. On the Fourth of July in Atlantic City, Fantini jerked the reigns of a horse as he came out of the gate so hard that track officials questioned him. At the same time, his agent was picked up for passing bad checks. No one wanted to go down for their own crimes, so they offered the racetrack officials and the law one better. They would bring them a guy named "Tony" who was fixing races all over in exchange for skating out from under.

The Feds were in horse heaven. Fantini agreed to be wired and arranged a meeting with Ciulla. He encouraged a conversation with the race fixer and blew Ciulla's whole operation wide open. Horses, jockeys, trainers, names, names and more names. Ciulla had a stable of jockeys around the country that held horses back for prearranged fees. By the beginning of August, a warrant was issued for Ciulla and Barnoski on numerous incidents of sports bribery and conspiracy.

Ciulla discovered the Feds were after him and he – yes – went on the run. But he wasn't a true Somerville guy. He knew nothing about laying low, didn't have any talent at disguising himself - there are only so many places a 6'3" three hundred and fifty pound guy can hide – and he couldn't resist keeping a hand in the racing game. He was arrested at the airport in San Francisco as he was awaiting a plane to Philly to fix a few races.

Thanksgiving week of 1975 found Fat Tony none too pleased to be eating his turkey dinner in jail.

Ciulla got four to six years. After twenty-two months, Fat Tony had enough of poor cuisine. Ciulla's jockeys may not have known how to hold 'em, but Fat Tony sure recognized when it was time to fold 'em. He began to write the song that he eventually sang for the Feds.

Ciulla told the press he was afraid he would be executed in prison before he could serve his time. By who was never disclosed, but in reality, Ciulla just wanted out of the joint. All he needed was someone to pin everything he knew on. That someone had to be – as much as it pained Ciulla to admit to himself – a bigger fish than even he in the eyes of law enforcement, and a person who wouldn't come knocking on his door. He had just the guys! Two of them were already safely tucked away in prison.

Howie Winter, Jimmy Martorano. Both locked up. And the list could fan out to encompass such a cast of nefarious characters with impressive criminal resumes that Ciulla could keep himself and his wife on the federal dole for years to come.

There was Joe Mac who was not only already on the run for theft of rare stamps but also featured on the FBI's Most Wanted List, and his old running buddy Barnoski who would be sure to hit the road. This was also a chance to get back at some guys who had embarrassed him in Vegas. And a plethora of minor Winter Hill players – those guys who were now rising in the ranks since Howie's pinball conviction – guys like Whitey, Stevie and Johnny Martorano. Might as well throw them in, as there was no telling how powerful they would become while Howie was in absentia.

While Ciulla's brain churned Tom Daly, a Boston FBI agent, was nosing around Massachusetts amidst rumors of race fixing within six northeastern states. The same agent from the pinball investigation. The fat man put the word out. A deal was struck with Ciulla – testify and get immunity, a reduced sentence and the mother of all trophies – relocation in the Witness Protection Program.

In 1977 Tony agreed to sing that song of such great magnitude and deceit, that he claimed he would eventually be able to write a book about his life in the Winter Hill Gang.

He started with Spread The Word, withdrawn from racing after one big win. The indictments were handed out quicker than lottery tickets. Despite the speed of the printing, Johnny Martorano stayed one step ahead for the next sixteen years, escaping down into the steamy Miami tropics until he was eventually caught.

Howie was in the Worcester County jail awaiting transfer to Concord Prison when a guard appeared, a grave look on his face. "Howie, your lawyer is here to see ya and he don't look happy."

Howie knew right away the man wasn't fucking with him. As soon as he entered the visitors' area, the attorney looked up. He was nervously smoothing a newspaper on the table in front of him. Howie sat and waited. Bad news need not be rushed; he just hoped it had nothing to do with his family.

After a moment, the lawyer slid the paper across the table to his client:

21 INDICTED IN $1.3 MILLION
RACING SCHEME

FBI agents after more than a dozen suspects in a $1.3 million racing scheme involving horse tracks in five eastern states. Fifty-one counts of bribery and racketeering.

What the fuck? Where?

Garden State Park in New Jersey. The leader of the alleged scheme was identified as Howard

T. Winter, a reputed leader of organized crime in the Boston area.

Both Martoranos, and Barnoski were indicted. Vegas casino executives Mel Golden and Elliot Price. And jockeys, horse owners and the Demetri brothers of North Reading, Mass.

Howie's mind went blank in one of those infrequent yet crippling moments when one suddenly wonders if he's gone mad. He blinked. The newspaper was still in front of him:

Anthony Ciulla, who was not further identified, was named as an unindicted co-conspirator.

Howie knew then what had happened. The words "unindicted co-conspirator" were the media's polite way of saying "he who is also in the shit and looking to shift blame fast." What he didn't understand was how holding back one horse in one race had ballooned into over fifty counts of bribery and conspiracy and how the hell everyone else was involved. What had Ciulla gotten them into?

Anthony "Fat Tony" Ciulla took center stage in his own opera for seventeen long days of testimony. He talked so fast and for so long that inaccuracies began to reveal themselves.

Ciulla swore under oath that he met Howie, Jimmy Martorano, Barnoski and the Demetris at Marshall Motors to divvy up profits in the amount of $250,000 in February of 1975.

The defense submitted evidence to the contrary. Not only actual hotel bills, but also a home video of Howie and Jimmy in Florida during the same period. The Demetris were shown in an irrefutable photograph on a Boca Raton cruise tour during the time Ciulla swore he met with them in Boston.

Ciulla insisted he'd spoken to Vegas casino executive Elliot Price from his Rhode Island home on a date he was actually in Vegas himself. Price's attorney presented hotel bills and signed restaurant receipts to back up Ciulla's location.

As the attorneys argued back and forth, a surprise move shocked even Ciulla: Whitey Bulger and Stevie Flemmi remained unindicted. He'd told all kinds of stories about those two – not just in court, but also to the FBI directly. Yet they remained at large. He was mystified.

The trial itself had a few light moments, even if they were concealed from the judge and jury. Recently, I pulled into the parking lot of the Big Dog Bar in North Reading after working a thirteen-hour truck driving shift and saw Charlie Demetri standing in the doorway smoking a cigarette.

No smoking in the bars any more, which is a shame. I don't smoke, except for the occasional cigar, but there's something about the smell of cigarettes and overflowing beers wafting across a warm crowded barroom while the jukebox pounds in the background against the laughter and war stories of patrons. Now bars empty out on and off as the patrons file out en masse to smoke together. Strangers that wouldn't look twice at each other inside will share small talk as the smoke off the Marlboros rises skyward. Nobody wants to be alone, I guess, even smokers.

"Charlie! It's me, Bobby Martini!" He laughed and I parked my truck. I got out, gave him a big hug and the regulation half-a-cheek kiss.

I walked in and sat down with Charlie and his wife. On that night I was still considering writing a book about Somerville so I started to push him a little about the old days.

After a few minutes, Charlie finally looked up over a sip of Scotch and said, "OK, OK, Bobby. I've got a good story for you." Peter Demetri's surviving brothers Charlie and Big Jimmy were on trial as co-defendants with Howie.

"We were in court one day," Charlie began, "and Howie noticed Big Jimmy was getting very anxious at the table beside him."

Big Jimmy is Charlie's brother. Young Jimmy is their brother Pete's son. All of them are partners in the same business, so it helps to differentiate between the two. And, up north, we all name our kids after us and our brothers and uncles, so it tends to get confusing.

The Demetris, by the way, are not members of the familiar Somerville fraternity of garden-variety criminals you have been following throughout my pages. The Albanian Italian-Americans are successful, well-respected businessmen, a reputation that survives today. They loved the ponies, though, and would travel all over the country to see their horses race. Such was their devotion that not even a horse fixing trial could dampen their enthusiasm. Howie finally became distracted by Big Jimmy's fidgeting.

He leaned over and whispered, "Why are you so nervous?" He meant "Why are you so nervous other than being on trial for race fixing?"

Big Jimmy leaned back. "We got a horse running at Suffolk today and I gotta place a bet!"

Howie nodded. "Jimmy, get the fuck out of here and put in a bet for me too!"

That was all Big Jimmy needed. He motioned his lawyers over. "I don't care how you do it but get us the fuck out of here. We got a horse running and he's a shoe-in to win."

Lawyers, as I am sure that anyone ever represented by one knows, uncoil like vipers when the clink of possible cash is heard. They only had one question, "What's the name of the horse?" The attorneys immediately played the favorite card of first graders the world over – recess.

"Recess, Your Honor. We need one. We have to have one. When? Uh, pretty much right now!"

Somehow, between a flurry of motions, double talk, and something that could only be labeled "confusement", the judge adjourned until the following day. As the Demetri brothers stood, their lawyers were already speeding off through the double doors.

By the time the boys got to the track, their dream team was already ensconced in their seats waiting for the race. The brothers shrugged, placed their bets and joined their legal representation.

The horse won and the lawyers walked away with a cool five thousand, thanks to the tip given them by their clients. The brothers made quite a bit more, as did Howie.

"Quite a bit is all I'll say," Charlie demurs when I ask.

When the jury came back and the dust settled, and after even Ciulla admitted to errors in his story, Howie was found guilty along with Jimmy Martorano, the Demetris, Elliot Price, Mel Golden and plenty more guys. The defendants were shocked by the verdict. Barnoski was left off that list as he decided to utilize his own personal version of the Fifth by skipping town. Billy stayed gone for five years.

Back in the steakhouse, Howie puts down his fork. "So what really happened?" I ask.

"That piece of shit Ciulla lied about a lot of the guys that he told the Feds he did business with."

Yeah, and I know one of them. "Jimmy Martorano?" I say.

Howie nods. "Jimmy and I were partners in Chandler's Restaurant. We remodeled the old hotel and built apartments on top, and that's the only dealing I ever had with Jimmy."

The law was always tying Jimmy in with his brother Johnny. Jimmy and Johnny were "Irish twins", born just eleven months apart, Johnny sliding into life first. They were so close in age and their birthdays fell in such a way that they were in the same high school class. Jimmy, although he had amassed his share of jail time, was nowhere near the big fish that the Feds thought his older brother was.

"Johnny was there on Marshall Street," Howie says as he waves the waitress and dessert menu away. "And from there he would work the office and put the bets in with the different bookmakers that we knew. That was all Johnny had to do with this. Then the fat bastard brings into the mix Mel and Elliot from Vegas. Nice men. Businessmen."

Kelly is not to be deterred by our inattention to her. "Have you been to Las Vegas? I want to go someday! Is it cool?"

Yes, Howie assures her, it is very cool. Or it was back in the day, but why disappoint the kid? As Vegas struggles to revive its "What Happens In Vegas" image, it's really like Branson, Missouri now, but with more neon. He orders coffee so we can escape a full description of the wonders of Sin City.

"Back in those days," Howie says and laughs, "You know the days I mean, Bobby? When it really did happen in Vegas and really did stay there?"

I laugh. I do remember.

"I used to send fifteen or so guys every month out on junkets. I would approve a credit line for them with Elliot or Mel."

Golden was short for Goldenberg. Originally from the Brookline area of Boston, Mel was a successful casino executive and a big time gambler who rarely lost a wager. I was lucky enough to be one of those guys on a junket back in the seventies, just on a smaller scale. Howie sent his son and I out and Elliot and Mel took great care of us, making sure we were on the VIP list for every show. It was a big deal for two young guys from one of the largest white ghettos in the country to be ushered to the head of a long line of waiting patrons and seated at a reserved table directly in front of the stage.

A few years later I went back to Vegas and phoned Mel. He was getting on years but he took my call and after reminding him who I was, I asked if he could snag me tickets to a couple of shows.

The ultimate gentleman, Mel complied but it was clear his patience with the young Turks of Boston had come to an end.

"Now," he said heavily. "I am done with you, no?"

"Yes, thank you sir." Far be it for a Martini to wear out his welcome, unless of course he is in his own hometown. I never saw Mel again.

While researching the book, I unearthed an article from a 1938 Massachusetts newspaper. A Mrs. Charlotte Goldenberg from Boston, age 19, petitioned the court for an annulment to her very recent marriage. She claimed that her husband, a Melvin Goldenberg, admitted he'd only proposed marriage so he could "boast he could be married within two hours." The annulment was immediately granted. If marrying a girl you met the same day doesn't sound like the ultimate wager, I don't know what does. I've tried to track down anyone who can verify that the groom grew up to be Mel Golden, but I cannot. If they are one in the same, it was a helluva way to start off a gambling career.

Fat Tony was always up for anything that was free, marginally free or gave the appearance of free. During the early seventies he called Howie from Vegas to see if he could dip into that VIP champagne glass. "He'd already blown his first comp and then ran through a line of credit." Howie shakes his head. "And that's how the Feds got casino executive Elliot Price involved."

CHAPTER TEN

Tumbling Dice,
The Fat Man's Opera, and The Price of Vegas

ELLIOT PRICE WAS another Boston guy, one who made good.
Successful and well respected until Ciulla came along. Elliot is
gone to that place in the sky where everything truly stays once
you get there, but his nephew, Eddie Accomando remembers
what happened.

A first generation Italian-American born in 1949, Eddie
has what I've come to think of as a typical upbringing...for
Somerville, I mean. "My family wasn't the kind you see on TV,"
Eddie says.

Whose is, I wonder.

Eddie works for a well-respected investment real estate
company. Relaxed in a button down and slacks, he's seated
comfortably in his den. He's got a full head of dark hair and a
pleasant friendly face. He's entertaining and speaks like a
historian with a sense of humor and, as most of my subjects,
very matter-of-fact about his relatives' lives. Yet Eddie speaks
with a twinkle in his eye, yanking the family skeletons out of the

closet for one last dance. You can't help but get caught up in his enthusiasm.

"At the end of the fifties, the Mob, whatever you call it, was – what I saw in my own circle – not the violent entity we've come to know. Their business was predominantly gambling after Prohibition. You didn't hear of men disappearing or dying. The neighborhoods were safe, no drug dealers."

The men worked to keep the streets where their children played crime free. "Sal coached my Little League team. You never would have guessed he was a gangster. If he had been in Vegas, Sal would have been a successful casino executive!"

Eddie takes pause at the use of the word gangster. "There is quite a bit of difference between gangsters and bookmakers. Sal was a bookmaker. They [Howie and Sal] did what is legal now in ninety per cent of the country. They took action, gambling. There wasn't all this violence you have now."

A kinder, gentler Mob, as I've heard it described a time or two.

Eddie's not defending the way of life; merely illustrating a time when the crime organizations were directed by the first generation of men who went about their business quietly, one step ahead of the law but not necessarily having to worry about also being one step ahead of the undertaker. That all blossomed later, as the decade came to end.

"We never saw any violence until the Irish Gang Wars, as you know," Eddie reminds me.

Yeah, I know. We...the fuckin' Irish.

I ask him about his uncle, Elliot Price, the former local boy and Las Vegas casino executive who became one of Howie's codefendants in the race fixing trial.

"Elliot Price was, at one time, Meyer Lansky's accountant," Eddie begins. "He met my aunt Nana through friends and fell instantly in love. Their first date was to..." Eddie smiles, pauses. "It was what you would call an organization party."

A huge Mob buffet, dining and dancing. I'm familiar.

Elliot's beloved was the niece of New England crime boss Filippo "Phil" Buccola. "They had to get permission from both of their families to marry. The Italians and the Jewish."

Normally such a marriage was frowned upon, but in this case both sides of the crucifix decided that with the "organization" preparing to expand holdings across the country and into Vegas, keeping the marriage in the Family ended up overriding any pesky differences over whether or not Christ came out of the cave after three days.

Elliot was a genius with numbers. And although his name eventually became showcased on any number of so-called Mafia watchdog websites, there was quite a bit more to Elliot. He also was a World War II hero.

"He was awarded the Purple Heart several times. But my uncle was also a great mathematician. So he was brought into the business and subsequently he made a place for another great numbers guy, his friend Mel Goldenberg."

The business was, of course, bookmaking. Abraham "Abe" Sarkis, along with his partner Ilario "Larry Baione" Zannino were Boston's biggest bookmakers in the forties and fifties. They were powerful and their close ties to the Gambino Family also made them a partnership to be feared.

"Abe brought my uncle into his organization as an accountant. Elliot got such a reputation that a certain fellow from Florida made a special trip just to see him in action."

Elliot asks me if it's acceptable for him to say the name of the man and I tell him yes. This is a collective memoir, not an indictment and anyway, most of the players are beyond caring.

Meyer Lansky, the most notorious Jewish mob guy of all time took a liking to Elliot. The old gangster brought him down to Florida in the early fifties to run his "carpet joint" casinos. Carpet joints were luxurious locations (hence the carpeting), but not exactly legal. Lansky was lying low as he had his eye on Cuba as a new gambling mecca. He needed a place to set up shop in the meantime and the endless South Florida summers seemed perfect. Lansky began work on The Riviera in Cuba with his friend President Batista. With Elliot's help, The Havana Riviera opened as one of the largest, most opulent casinos in the world.

Lansky also had ties to the Detroit and Cleveland mobs. The Feds tried in vain to nail him along with Vincent "Fat Vinnie" Teresa for gambling in the early sixties. Fat Vinnie, not to be confused with Fat Vinny, Fat Tony or the other Fat Tony. We Italians just cannot move past the nickname thing. The scene in Goodfellas when Henry Hill describes the various nicknames of his pals is hilarious but also painfully true. I guess no one has a given name that we feel shouldn't be enhanced.

With the fall of Batista, and Lansky once again in the headlines, Elliot became a target. The guy who keeps the mob's books is ultimately more important to a prosecutor than the boss. "The Feds were unhappy they couldn't peg my uncle," Eddie says, "and they made sure he knew it." Elliot finally headed west to Vegas with Lansky's blessing.

"He became Vice President of Gaming Operations for Caesar's Palace. It was a well paying job with a bonus, I believe, of 2 per cent of the proceeds the Casino brought in. The only connection that Ciulla had with Elliot was that Howie told him Ciulla was all right to comp. By comping, I mean that he'd get a credit line in Vegas. Howie wasn't asking for Ciulla to get a free ride. If he lost he would have to come up with the money the following week."

Comping is a common avenue for the casinos to lure any potential high rollers into Sin City. One of the few guys to ever to fuck it up was Fat Tony.

Mr. & Mrs. Fat Tony hit Vegas on Howie's say so and when the portly man started betting, he immediately started losing which gave way to a loud belligerence. While back in Somerville, Howie had no idea what was going on, it had to be more than embarrassing for Elliot on the front lines.

Ciulla insisted he was mob connected and nobody was going to fuck with him. He was right to a certain extent, although it had nothing to do with any connections. Casinos do allow high rollers a certain amount of misbehaving – up to a point.

"He got out of line once and then twice. My uncle ignored him but when Ciulla started the third time, my uncle threw him out of the casino and told him never to come back."

Ciulla mother-fucked Elliot up and down as he stood on the sidewalk of the Strip. It was the usual diatribe from the ejected – Tony would get him back, he'd make all those motherfuckers pay for disrespecting him.

Elliot Price was no stranger to federal investigations. In 1966 the LA Times published a story revealing a series of meetings in Palm Beach, California during which high ranking Mafia men like Vito Genovese and Fat Tony Salerno met with several casino execs – including Elliot Price. Although the Feds probed, they could find no evidence of wrongdoing. Even their star witness Victoria Lockwood, a Vegas showgirl also in attendance, testified there was no talk of gambling. Formerly in a self-proclaimed "suicidal mental condition," Miss Lockwood agreed to testify with immunity but revealed only that she once saw a gentleman using the phone. The government had triumphantly seized a half a million dollars from Elliot's safety deposit box as "evidence" and were publicly embarrassed when the court ordered the money be returned as legitimate private funds.

Since Palm Beach, Elliot took even further care to distance himself from any breath of illegal activity. But Howie was an old friend from the neighborhood and what could the harm be to extend some credit? The harm was that Ciulla suddenly claimed he'd met with Elliot to discuss fixing horse races.

"Shit, Bobby! My uncle was making $250,000 a year. He didn't need to bet horses. As a matter of fact, he hated to gamble, period."

Obviously Elliot wasn't afflicted with one of the other popular Somerville diseases; the irrational belief that the big win and a whole new life were just around the corner.

It was the phone that turned out to be the weapon. Ciulla used Elliot's private phone at the casino to call Howie asking him to speak to Elliot on his behalf and comp him. When Elliot's phone records were pulled, there was the connection.

Eddie shrugs. "Elliot was astonished the Feds were even interested in his phone records. He was mystified at where their information came from. But we found out later they'd been tipped off by their favorite informants who offered them a pencil to connect any dots. After all, keeping Howie in prison was a feather in the cap of the FBI and a monkey off the back of the informants – Bulger and Flemmi."

Bulger was taking over Boston. Howie Winter was behind bars but he'd eventually be out and perhaps not only looking to regain his throne at Marshall Motors but also to do a clean sweep of the streets. To borrow a phrase from Jimmy Buffett, "The Order of The Sleepless Knights" had a great deal to worry about, unless Howie remained firmly ensconced as a semi-permanent guest of the government.

As they did with Howie, the Feds wanted to find out exactly what Elliot knew about all things not connected to the alleged crime at hand. Race fixing took a back seat to their questions about Elliot's association with bigger fish, like Meyer Lansky.

"They were flat out pissed my uncle wouldn't talk. They wanted Lansky more than anyone and here they were, with Meyer's own accountant in front of them refusing to turn the key."

Elliot was convicted of the charges levied upon him.

Three days after his trial, Ciulla did an interview with a local newspaper telling all in a completely different fashion from his sworn testimony. Elliot's horrified defense attorneys immediately presented the judge with the article and noting the inconsistencies – asked for a new trial. The court denied the motion. The general opinion is that due to all the public pressure and the magnitude of the supposed criminal activity throughout this event, it was better to let sleeping dogs lie in jail.

Elliot Price did not do any jail time. The conviction cost him his executive license required to run a casino in Vegas. Few men were granted them and Elliot was one due to his integrity, connections and his wizardry of the casino gambling facilities. He later became marketing director of the Aladdin Casino in Vegas in the 1990's.

"I miss him very much. In this lifetime there can only be one Elliot Price," Eddie concludes simply, a smile on his face. "That's it, Bobby."

The snow starts to let up and so do I. As I trudge out to my truck, I feel as though I've been living in a bubble throughout my life in Somerville, but maybe I just didn't pay enough attention to anything outside of my circle of friends to learn anything.

The Demetri brothers were found guilty at the trial but their convictions were reversed in October of 1981. Charlie is a still a successful guy. His brother Big Jimmy, as we began this book, was struck by Lou Gehrig's disease. Big Jimmy was as strong in spirit as he was back when his body still obeyed him. He communicated with his family by blinking his eyes. He looked forward to Charlie coming over every week and betting the football games with and for him. Gamblers take their bets very seriously.

In August of 2008, with his family beside him, the doctors shot Big Jimmy with morphine and shut off the life support. He opened his eyes one last time and then passed quietly on.

Billy Barnoski couldn't help but to break the law. Five years after he blew town, he made an illegal u-turn on a road in New Hampshire and got pulled over. That cop must have shit his pants when he ran Billy's license. Billy was tried, convicted and headed off to the slammer for three years.

After his release in 1987 Billy migrated back to Somerville, hoping to get back into the rackets. I was a still a Metropolitan Police officer when I got a call from him.

"Bobby, can ya fix a ticket for me?"

Here we go again, I thought. You know what the biggest problem is for a guy from the streets who is a cop? Ticket fixing. You run the streets with packs of guys your whole life, then one day you're a cop. You're the goose who can lay the vehicular golden egg and everybody wants to get into the nest. My father's friends were the worst. I think the old man was thrilled I became a cop for the sole reason that he figured none of his buddies would ever get another ticket.

I sighed internally. "Lemme see what I can do." *Because he was a friend of my father's, I didn't want to just end the conversation curtly so like a dumb fuck and as usual, I start talking.*

"Hey, you been over to the new sub shop in Arlington Center? They got the best veal parmesan sub I ever had."

"No shit, huh?" Billy answers.

Anyone who knows me wouldn't find that out of character. Twenty years later I'm still on the hunt for good, cheap food.

"Listen to this, they even got half subs there, too."

That's also big news in New England. One can be hungry and frugal at the same time. It's our birthright. Billy promises to check it out and we say goodbye. A couple of weeks later, there was a knock at my front door. I opened it to two state troopers.

"Officer Robert Martini?" Uh oh.

"Do you know a William E. Barnoksi?"

Fuck, did he rob the sub shop? They had to be raking it in on that half sub deal.

The conversation deteriorated. They threatened me with losing my job if I didn't cooperate and immediately disclose my relationship with Barnoksi. I was so pissed I threw them off the porch.

In a few days I received a letter to appear before the Grand Jury in Middlesex County. In the past I would have ignored it completely. But as a cop I had to show up. When I arrived, I was ushered down a hall with the prosecutor. He bore a remarkable resemblance to Paul Rueben's character Pee Wee Herman but had none of the charm. He carried that small guy's complex on his shoulders and once he took one look at me, I knew this wasn't going to go well. I pitied the poor bastard who was on trial and I wondered if it was someone I had arrested for drunk driving or some other embarrassing infraction.

"Listen, I've never done this before," I said as he strode ahead. I'd never had to testify in the trial of anyone I had arrested. We entered a large room and at least a dozen spectators already seated.

"Sit down, Officer Martini," the prosecutor said officiously. I started to take a seat near the spectators. "No," he said tartly. "Over here."

I was sworn in and sat in the chair. Even when I was seated, I towered over him. He frowned at me and at the disparity between our sizes. I tried to slide down a little in the chair.

"I'm a little nervous," I explained. "I've never done this before."

"What, tell the truth?"

"Well, sure. I'm a police officer. I tell the truth all the time."

The spectators were all craning their necks to take a look at me. Not good. I flashed my best Somerville smile at them. One lady almost fell off her chair. "Name?" the little prosecutor snapped.

"Uh, you know who I am, you just called me Officer Martini."

"Are you acquainted with a William E. Barnoski?"

"Billy? You mean Billy Barnoski?"

A wormy smile crawled across his face. "He's a friend, Officer? How well do you know him?"

Suddenly I realized this wasn't about anything that I knew about, had been involved in, or had even heard about. He was looking for someone to go down. It wasn't going to be fucking me. I leaned forward in my chair; hands folded, and put on my most earnest little boy face.

"Gosh, I don't know him that well at all. He's a friend of my Dad's."

The little man shoved himself closer. "When's the last time you were out with Mr. Barnoski?"

I kept my face benign. "I've never been out with him. I saw him a few weeks ago at the Pointer Post," I turned so the spectators could hear. "A place veterans get together and talk about old times."

The prosecutor rolled his eyes. "Officer!" he kept saying "Officer" in that way you see on TV when some overbearing IA guy is trying to make Frank Furillo look like Attila The Hun. This was turning into a bad TV movie of the week. "Officer, while you were visiting with all of these guys..."

"Veterans," I retorted. Two can play at that game.

"And where were you sitting during this visit you made to the veterans?" he spat back.

"On a barstool," I said innocently. The room burst into laughter.

"Officer, I'm sure the streets of Somerville are entertained by your wit, but here it's not doing you any good! Where in the bar were you seated on a barstool in reference to Mr. Barnoski?"

He had found my button and was leaning hard on it. He was making me feel stupid. It's the one thing that drives me into a rage, but I was mindful of the audience.

"Down the Pointer, you just sit in one seat for a short time. I'm sure that sometime during the night I would have been seated next to Billy, but I really don't remember."

"So, you don't remember having a conversation with Mr. Barnoksi about a submarine sandwich? Which everyone knows," he paused dramatically, "is street code for a kilo of cocaine!"

Before I could form an answer, he shoved ahead, right in my face. "And didn't you tell him about a half of a sub and doesn't that mean a half key of cocaine?"

Cops and cocaine; that deadly combination. Audiences eat it up; those who live it eventually die by it. I could feel the spectators turning on me. And I was feeling stupid. I stared him full in the face.

"I am just a traffic cop who pulls over people for speeding and usually gives a warning. I don't make enough money to live on, so being able to buy a half a sub instead of having to spring for a whole one is a big deal. I told Billy, in fact, I've told everyone I know." That was the absolute truth.

The people listening were folks who also appreciated a half a sub and a few extra bucks as well. It was painfully obvious the prosecutor's fishing expedition was humiliating to him. As I was finally excused, the prosecutor scowled at me. He'd gotten nothing and was fuming. So was I. In the end, he got the last laugh. It wouldn't be long before I was prosecuted for my own crime – the one I did commit. When I walked into the courtroom, it was the same little prick who smiled tightly at me from the other side of the room. That day I left with a sentence of two years in prison, to be served on the weekends, despite the fact that he wanted me to go away for ten. He wasn't happy and neither was I.

To this day he probably goes to sleep at night thinking of how he managed to get me on something, even if it wasn't for sub sandwiches and cocaine. I go to sleep at night wondering how the fuck I managed to end up in prison. And where I can get a nice half sub for a couple of bucks.

While he was in prison, Barnoski had numerous conversations with his friend Chucky Flynn, who was also still on the inside, about his plan to become the new king of The Hill. The former partner and business heir of Indian Joe Notarangeli, Jackie McDermott wasn't about to give up the niche he'd carved out. But there was talk the Feds had spoken to Jackie about the conversations they'd taped between Barnoski and Flynn.

Jackie was a good friend of my father's and I find it hard to believe he was speaking to the government about anything. But paranoia was always the word of the day when it was linked with "Feds" and it was enough to make the most standup guy fear retribution from persons unknown. One late night in 1987 at the Pointer, Jackie was deep in conversation with the old man.

They were hunched over the bar. "It's bizarre," Jackie was saying. "They musta called me at least four, five times in the last few weeks. Every time I pick up the phone, this guy says 'We're gonna hit you and your son Peter.' Then they hang up."

My father grunted. "What the hell for?"

Jackie shrugged. "For the life of me, I can't figure it out. What kind of dumb fuck keeps callin' ya, sayin' he's gonna hit you and then just hangs up and calls you back later?"

Inaction is frowned upon in the Somerville I grew up in. "You got a good point there," Bob Sr. agreed, putting his serious face on. "You call the cops?"

Both men started laughing. "Yeah, right. I'm calling the cops!" Jackie yelled uproariously.

Later on, my father asked me to lead Jackie back to the highway. I never saw him again.

Barnoski, his wife Donna and two other thugs went to Jackie's house and what occurred prior to his son arriving home is sketchy but when Peter McDermott opened the door late that evening, he walked into a tense situation. Jackie was insisting the roads were bad due to weather and Barnoski was drunk, he should stay the night. Instead of accepting the offer, Barnoski pulled a gun on Peter and said, "Die motherfucker!" As Peter fell to the floor, he could hear his father begging, "No, Billy, please don't."

Barnoksi replied, "Relax, Jack, they're only blanks." Then he killed Jackie.

Peter survived and testified. Barnoski was convicted of killing Jackie and put away for life.

Howie and the others appealed their convictions. New evidence had come to light. A freelance writer named Margaret McCarron had contacted FBI agent Tom Daly requesting he put her in touch with Tony Ciulla to discuss a book project. Ciulla called back immediately and told McCarron if she would give him $25,000, they'd be in business as creative partners.

McCarron delivered a $2000 deposit (and wisely acquired a receipt) and their partnership began. She testified that during negotiations for the yet-to-be-written book and film rights, Ciulla confided to her that he was going to make millions off the story. Through McCarron's literary contacts, they had already submitted a treatment to Bantam Books and Columbia Pictures.

Ciulla told the writer that Tom Daly, the enterprising FBI agent, was a close friend and Ciulla said whatever the government wanted him to in court. That wasn't all he told her.

"He told me that he had lied during the trial [involving] Elliot Price and other defendants and that he had brought the Vegas people into this case because he had been down to Vegas and had become drunk and disorderly and that he had lost a lot of money gambling and when he went to get additional credit, he was turned down and that this was the reason why he felt that he would rather bring those people into the case than others to whom he felt a personal loyalty."

Ciulla huffed, "My credibility is the most important thing to me because when I get out of this fucking [witness protection] program I am going to get my money for my story. It is my story and I'll lie whenever I feel like it."

He needed convictions to bolster the book sales and the bigger the names, the better the book would sell. Then Ciulla dropped the bomb on McCarron. He presented her with an agreement in which he had struck her rights to future TV and film earnings from their contract. McCarron was horrified and called Daly. The agent told the writer he'd washed his hands of the race fixer and nothing could be done.

As soon as McCarron went up the food chain and swore to her story in an affidavit, Daly did likewise. He insisted he had no idea she was writing a book when he received her inquiry call and had no idea what she was talking about. Ciulla denied the partnership as well, despite the $2000 deposit.

The affidavit from Daly, the heroic government agent, minimized that of an "opportunistic" hoping-to-go-Hollywood writer and the motion for a new trial based on this evidence was denied. Ten years later, the truth of who Tom Daly really was seemed evident.

That's probably one of the biggest sins of this whole fucking debacle because, like everything we've come to know about the second generation of Winter Hill, Daly was just another John Connolly. In 1988, Boston Globe reporter Kevin Cullen, detailing a "Spotlight" series on Whitey Bulger, received a call from Daly. Another Globe reporter was trying to get in touch with Ciulla about the unindicted race fixing co-conspirators Bulger and Flemmi. The paper was beginning to unearth a strange relationship between the mobsters and the law and eventually broke the whole sick mess wide open in 1997. Daly told Cullen, according to the reporter's testimony, that he had a message from Ciulla.

"I took it as a threat," Cullen said. "If we embarrassed [Bulger] or wrote something that wasn't true . . . He would think nothing of clipping me," Cullen said Daly told him.

Daly took great pains to explain to the seasoned reporter that just because Bulger hadn't been indicted didn't mean he had any relationship with the FBI. Bullshit. Then why not tell it to the judge? The state declined to call Daly in to refute Cullen's accusations. One other thing, Daly was one of the first to defend accusations against John Connolly when his relationship with the Mob came to light. Connolly and his pals were responsible for insuring that Bulger and Flemmi – named by Ciulla in his laundry list of pony phonies – were never indicted on a single race fixing charge.

Who are the fucking bad guys anyway?

Ciulla's book and movie deal options collapsed. Despite the fact Sports Illustrated had coined him "The Greatest Race

Fixer of Them All," Ciulla rated only a quick piece on Geraldo and a few articles in the newspapers. There's more to say about him, but I'm not giving him any more words. I'm pissed off I had to write this much.

Tom Daly retired from the Bureau. Joe Mac passed in 1996. Mel Golden is gone, too.

Elliot was still furious a decade after the trials. Even though his two-year sentence was eventually revoked and reduced to probation in 1982, he was appalled. He was adamant that he hadn't fixed a race - ever. He wanted to be exonerated. He went to see Anthony Cardinale, a successful respected Boston defense attorney who has had his share of underworld clientele. He is also a friend of the neighborhood.

Eddie and I had another conversation about his uncle. "He died," Eddie says sadly, "before the case could be re-opened. It's a shame, all of it. People lost everything, guys spent years in jail that shouldn't have - all in the name of the protection of Whitey and Stevie by the federal government."

He has the last word on the subject of local gangsters.

"I don't know who is or isn't, who was or wasn't what you call a real gangster. All I can say is that when Howie and Sal were walking the streets, those streets were safe. Drug dealers stayed away; there wasn't any street violence. The minute Sal was gone and Howie was inside, it all changed and it's never been the same since. So who do you think were the real bad guys, Bobby?"

Back in the steakhouse, I look across the table at the elderly man who finally gave in and is spinning a tale of Vegas glitz and glamour for the young waitress because he knew it was what she had been hoping for all along. I reach for the check, but they wave me away. He's already paid.

He finishes his story with a flourish and gets up, pulling on his jacket. We bid Kelly goodbye after Howie admonishes her to complete her degree in accounting. Good jobs, he says, are hard to find without a proper education. He walks slowly ahead of me, out into the darkening afternoon. Who do I think the bad guys were? Eddie's question echoes in my head.

Howie walks carefully over an icy patch of parking lot, pausing to point it out to me. "Careful, Bobby, you don't want to fall." He reaches a hand out to make sure I don't slip.

Who were the bad guys, I think as I walk. *Who are they?* If the standard is based on crimes, it's all of us, but also all of them. A friend of mine told me a story. Her college roommate is divorced and lives with her children and longtime boyfriend. The roommate recently found out one of her sons is gay. The roommate went to her mother, crying.

"It goes against everything I believe. My pastor agreed. He said it's a sin, my son will go to hell."

The elderly mother listened patiently to her daughter's story. Then she looked the daughter in the eye and asked, "Do you think you're going to heaven?"

Her daughter was shocked. She attends church regularly with her whole family, tithes, does charity work and studies The Bible. "Of course," the daughter stammered.

The mother shook her head. "Not by your own standards, my dear. Your pastor preaches that living with a man you're not married to is a sin."

"But," the daughter tried to explain. "That's different."

The old broad wasn't buying it. "A sin is a sin is a sin. There isn't any gray area. It's like being pregnant, either you are or you aren't. We're all sinners. The only thing that makes it worse is when you sit in judgment of others. That's when you fall from grace with God."

Even though I don't think not being married is a sin and I don't have a thing against gays; I got the mother's point right away. We're all sinners. But there's a difference between fucking yourself – which is between you and God, and fucking other people for your own gain.

Fuck, I may not know who all of the bad guys are but I know the good ones when I see them.

And no, I don't want to fall.

CHAPTER ELEVEN

Witness Unprotected,
Brian Halloran

THIS IS NOT so much a story about Howie Winter, but in chronicling his history in Somerville, there is a thread woven throughout that era. A thread that began to unravel the reign of Whitey Bulger, just as, many believe – myself included - that Whitey unraveled Howie's.

Edward "Brian" Halloran.

I only knew Brian Halloran a few short years, but I had more violent experiences alongside him than I did with any other person in my life.

1977. Brian gave me a diamond ring for Christmas. For such a macho bunch of burgeoning thugs, it's now funny to look back and realize we thought nothing of exchanging gifts of jewelry. It was an expensive gift, but Brian brushed it off. He hadn't paid for the ring.

"Bobby, the Jews fly into Logan with belts around their waists crammed with diamonds!" he confided to me. He was talking about the scores of Orthodox jewelers who did business in the city. "They're so cheap, they take public transportation."

*The Jews were a constant source of amazement for Brian. "They wear them goofy hats and don't even carry no guns!" he exclaimed, astonished. "They think God don't want them to." God must have special rules for each sect; because for us, it was a cardinal sin **not** to carry at least one gun at all times.*

"I got a connection in the jewelers building in Boston. You interested in making a score?"

I was twenty-four. I was making money in various ways that didn't involve actually having to appear at a job site and doing pretty well at it. And anyway, it didn't matter. My response was the one required in an environment that judged you solely on whether or not you had any balls.

"Sure."

Brian nodded. "Me and two guys tagged two Jews at Logan. I punched 'em in the face, the others grabbed diamond bags and we all jumped on the train." It was just that easy, he kept assuring me.

That was only partially true. There was a complicated fencing process for this particular brand of "ethnic" goods as any robbery was quickly circulated throughout their close-knit circle. There would be instant revenge from their own mob connections in New York. Brian took a huge risk by robbing them.

We had a dry run after discovering the cautious jewelers had begun cabbing it to and from the airport in an effort to protect their wares. I borrowed a motorcycle from my friend, warning him it might not come back.

Brian's fellow Mullen Gang member Jimmy Mantville would follow the jewelers' cab and stage an accident, effectively cutting off traffic in the Callahan Tunnel. I'd drive the bike with Brian on the back and as we approached, Brian would jump off, reach into the cab and grab the belts.

One afternoon we went on our final practice run. Brian stuffed two guns into my belt. Why two guns? Back then I am sure we were convinced it was the God-given right of the Irish.

"Aww, don't whine, Bobby," Brian admonished me. "They're not even loaded, this is just practice!" I mounted the bike, following closely behind Brian's Caddy when it began to rain.

As we made a sharp turn, I hit a wet sewer cover. The bike spun and lay down like a pile of bricks toppling off a truck. The handlebars jammed into my ribs and I couldn't catch my breath as my body skidded across the pavement into the opposite lane. Brian didn't even brake; he drove off, weaving through traffic. Cars whizzed past, drivers laying on horns and barely missing each other trying to avoid hitting the guy on the ground with two guns sticking out of his pants like some Clint Eastwood wannabe.

After a few excruciating minutes, I got myself and the motorcycle upright and went after Brian. By the time I found him I was scraped up and bloody, wet and pissed off.

"What the fuck, Brian? Why didn't you stop? I was almost killed! Didn't you see that I…"

He laughed, interrupting me. "I didn't see you lay it down. I thought you were right behind me!"

That ended it for me. I returned the battered bike and walked away.

Brian didn't. One night in 1980, I was partying and raising hell with him and another friend, Billy. The next day I was forced out of a dead sleep by the phone. I remember groggily picking it up.

"Yeah?" I managed to mumble.

"Bobby, it's Billy."

Billy. Billy. It took me a second until my friend's face sort of swam into clarity. His name isn't Billy, but that is what I'll call him here.

"What happened?" Something had to have happened. No self-respecting partier would be so harsh as to kick off the hangover process of another without a damn good reason.

"I'm in Charles Street."

I was instantly and fully awake. Jail. Uh oh. What did we do?

This must be bad. Assault, public drunkenness, busting up a bar; these were all offenses that could be easily admitted and even bragged about via telephone. This was something else.

At the Charles Street jail, my friend told me what happened. "Brian had this plan. I wanted to call ya, but Brian said no, so I got my buddy Vinny and Jimmy Mantville. We went down to rob the Jews."

Oh shit.

"Jimmy cut the cab off in the tunnel, but he kinda overshot. Brian was in another car for us to jump into. So me and Vinny hit the cab. Vinny sprayed the jewelers with Mace and I grabbed two cases, when all of a sudden we was surrounded by the Feds."

Two ATF agents just happened to be in the cab behind the jewelers.

"I had a gun in my sweats and couldn't run too good. Vinny jumped in the car with Jimmy. But Brian was nowhere to be found."

Billy was standing in the middle of the street, a gun in his pants and two cases filled with $200,000 in jewelry when he was grabbed by the Feds. Everyone else got away clean.

"What did Brian say?" I asked.

"He said he couldn't get there in time."

Billy ended with five to seven in Concord Prison. He never gave the others up.

Did Brian have a hint the Feds were onto his plan? Or was it simply coincidence that agents just happened to be directly behind the cab carrying the jewelers? No one ever asked.

It was years later, after Brian, who eventually became my brother-in-law, was already in the ground thanks to Whitey Bulger, that I thought about my own bungled rehearsal. I should have asked, "Hey Brian, if you didn't see it happen, how did you know I laid the bike down?" But I never did.

1970. I was a seventeen-year-old Marine stationed at Camp Pendleton in San Diego, when I got a call from my father. "There's a friend of mine up Terminal Island. I want you to go there and see if he needs anything." Terminal Island is a prison not far from where I was stationed.

"His name is Brian Halloran and he's doin' seven years for bank robbery. He needs company."

Brian and a couple of Boston guys had actually robbed seven banks in California, but no one was really keeping score. I had no interest in hiking it up to the prison but the long arm of my father reached across the country, so when he said do it, I still did it – whatever "it" happened to be.

"Will he know I'm coming?"

"No," my father said.

"Does he know what I look like?"

"Naw."

I sighed the deep sigh of teenage intellectual superiority. "Well, how will I know him then?"

My father laughed. "Oh you'll know him." He hung up.

The next Saturday I rode up to Terminal Island. I sat in a crowded waiting room forever, getting pissed off at blowing my Saturday waiting for someone I'd never met. I played a game, watching each prisoner come through the iron bar door.

Three big bald guys. Nope. Another covered in tattoos. A black guy the size of a train – definitely not. Man after man entered. Then this massive guy with shaggy hair came through the bars and looked around. He had eyes like a shark – flat, black, emotionless. The muscles in his arms twitched like he was ready for a fight. God Almighty, please don't let this be my father's friend.

I got up and approached him, careful to stand a few feet away. "Brian Halloran?"

He looked at me curiously. Brian's eyes cut right into your head and stabbed the breath out of you. I couldn't think of anything to say. I was a high school dropout who ran off and joined the Marines. I had no idea of the world that Brian was actually in, but just looking at him made me freeze.

"Yeah. So?" he said.

"I'm Bobby Martini's son. My father sent me to see if you need anything."

Brian stared at me. My mouth got dry like it still does when I get nervous. I managed to croak out, "So...uh...Brian...do you need...uh...anything?"

His eyes relaxed a little. This wasn't anyone challenging him. This was the son of one of his closest friends. He shook my hand.

"C'mere, siddown." We walked to the nearest bench and he thanked me for coming.

"I come out here for a coupla weeks, but the state of California like me so much, they're keepin' me seven years." Brian grinned and it softened his face, but the prehistoric shark eyes stayed dark.

We shot the shit for an hour and I enjoyed talking to him. He had a matter-of-fact attitude about his incarceration as he'd gotten away with so many crimes prior to this conviction. He told me the details of one spectacular crime that was already Somerville legend, starring Brian himself and a local cop.

Brian was the wheelman for a bank heist on Winter Hill for a group of Canadians who had migrated down to Boston on the robbery circuit. Something went wrong inside and before the would-be robbers could escape, the bank was surrounded. Outside in the getaway car, Brian watched the cops screech in and realized his cohorts didn't have a chance. He calmly reached over, picked up the M16 rifle on the seat and began shooting. Brian held the law off until he ran out of ammunition. In what would become the typical routine for him, once he saw that he could be of no further assistance to his former partners, he got away. The Canadians were not so lucky and were rounded up by the police.

Younger MacDonald was walking his beat at the bottom of Winter Hill when a frantic spectator ran breathlessly up to him, "Officer, there's a robbery goin' on at the top of the Hill!"

Younger calmly glanced up the Hill and told the Good Samaritan, "I'm on my coffee break."

Bank robbing has always been a major leisure time activity for Boston's amateur, as well as career-minded criminals so one could almost say that Brian came by it honestly. I know guys from Charlestown who actually brag that their burg has been hailed by author Chuck Hogan, among others, as "the bank robbing capital of the United States." At that time, even a bank robbery was not such an unusual occurrence that Younger felt the need to go charging up the Hill.

Younger, when he was not ignoring a robbery in progress, also used to make the sauce for the VFW. One time I saw him flick his cigar ash into the pot.

"What the hell are ya doin'?" I asked.

He winked. "Gives the sauce a nice taste." He kept stirring.

Not much I could complain about. He was right; the sauce did taste great.

"The sauce here," Brian snorted disgustedly, "is nothing to write home about."

When our time was up, Brian was appreciative he had not spent the afternoon alone.

"Thanks for the company." He gave me a big hug and said, "I'll see you soon, pal."

"I'm in the Marines!" I called as the guard led him away. I was a grown man and never going back home. I was going to be traveling around the world. "I won't be here long!"

He turned his head and threw back a laugh. "Ya, neither will I, kid. See ya in Somerville."

Two years later my tour was up and soon after both Brian and I were back home.

Brian, originally a member of South Boston's infamous Mullen Gang gradually drifted toward Marshall Motors. I was in my early twenties when I began to see him regularly at my parents' on Hudson Street. In the early seventies my father staged huge clambakes in our little yard for such attendees as

Howie, Sal, Joe Mac, and the rest of the boys he hung with – Brian one of them.

My father liked to entertain in his own way, getting loudly drunk, singing Irish songs and busting everyone's balls. I set my sights a bit higher and activities that didn't involve getting laid were a waste of time. I had completed my stint with the Marines that began when I was sixteen (just to escape the brutal excessive beatings I received at home), got my high school diploma in service, graduated from Chamberlayne Junior College and was back home trying to figure out what to do next.

Years later I'd be ensconced in the life unfolding in my backyard but for now I was just a visitor.

In 1975 that began to change. Brian and I found ourselves on the same softball team that the boys down at Howie's Chandlers Bar and Restaurant had put together. Chandlers was on the ground floor of a former hotel on Columbus Ave. in Boston. Howie and Jimmy Martorano were partners in both the bar and the building and they eventually turned the hotel into rental apartments. Gary Winter regularly brought all the kids who were hanging out in Somerville's Belmont Park into the city to help in completely gutting the building. Gary was his father's construction foreman and did a great job. He was dependable and everyone liked him. Of course, most importantly, he also played softball.

Gary, myself, Gary O'Brien, and Willy Medeiros represented Somerville for Chandlers, along with Jimmy Martorano, Brian Halloran, Tom and Brian McNeeley and a few more from the Boston contingent. The McNeeleys were big huge bastards, tough-as-nails local boxers. One game we were scheduled to play was on the same field that Harvard utilized. As we were practicing, the Harvard soccer team trotted out onto the field and informed Brian Halloran that the field was theirs and had to be vacated for Harvard to play.

Brian Halloran and Brian McNeeley looked at each other, then at the considerably younger kids and gave them a simple answer.

"Go screw."

The McNeeleys and Brian then went one step further to make sure that their point had been made. They sauntered over to the goal posts, ripped them out of the ground and threw them over the fence. The kids from Harvard proved to be just as smart as one would assume Harvard attendees are – they did not say a word. We proceeded to play as planned without any further interruption.

After the game, we took a shortcut through one club in Kenmore Square to get to another, not unusual for making the rounds through Boston's bars. As soon as we entered the first club, a dozen or so big guys in full softball gear, we realized we had walked into a venue that was hosting a special event.

A fashion show.

An all black fashion show.

The main room was impressively decorated for the event with a professional runway cutting through the center. It was filled with nothing but well-dressed African-Americans. Boston, at that time, was not only not a town where whites from Somerville and Charlestown regularly co-mingled with blacks from the city, but to appear to be crashing an obviously carefully planned private affair was unheard of and uncomfortable for both groups.

No one said a word to us as we strolled through the front door and out the back.

The reputations of Halloran and Martorano preceded them wherever they went. Today an incident like that would completely embarrass me, but at twenty-two all I felt was some incredible power just to be able to do this – walk casually right off a muddy ball field and through a place I had no business being without giving a shit, almost daring someone to call me out. I was too young and cocky to realize I was gravitating toward a very dangerous circle. I was a boy in a man's world and it would take most of my life to realize how deadly it could have been for me.

As years passed, Brian starting hanging down the Pointer Post regularly. A man's crimes were never a factor in my old man's friendships. Crossing him, however, was a different matter and that came into play when Brian took up with my sister Patty in 1977.

"I was the secretary at Boston Thermal King when I was nineteen," Patty Martini Halloran Macarelli says. "I worked for Charlie and Jimmy Demetri. He was their friend and used to drop by. That's how we really met. He was thirty-four. We got married a few months after we started dating."

At forty-nine, my sister Patty has lived the kind of life that built the Lifetime Movie Network empire. She suffers from numerous physical maladies, as well as the fallout from years spent as Mrs. Brian Halloran and subsequently as his widow. She's a no bullshit chick with riveting eyes and has absolutely no reservations about chronicling the history of Halloran. Nor does she make any attempt to gloss over her own family, or her husband's activities.

What motivated Patty to marry the convicted bank robber fourteen years her senior?

"It was," she says, "a combination of things. I thought I was crazy in love with him. And it was infatuation with the circle of people. Going out, having money. Dad was very strict. I wasn't allowed to date, wear halter tops, have my ears pierced. When I started going with Brian, it was new and exciting."

She pauses for a second. "But it wasn't too exciting after it was all over." And before it ended in a hail of bullets four years later, there would be plenty of pain and suffering.

Both Brian and Patty knew that the news of their marriage wouldn't go over well with our parents. "So we eloped and went down to Florida. We stayed seven months." It was a good thing, because, as expected, the news was not well received.

"Dad was bullshit. He couldn't believe Brian married his daughter without his consent."

Patty is reticent to talk about our mother, saying only that "she got married young, and she was known as the best looking wife up Winter Hill. And Mom never liked Brian."

There were other issues as well. At first there were expensive restaurants, trips to Los Angeles, and plenty of spending cash.

"I was the oldest girl in a family of seven. My mother was sick a lot so I had to do housework, cook meals, and watch the kids. Then all of a sudden, there I was in my Mickey Mouse t-shirt, jeans and suspenders shopping on Rodeo Drive in a Rolls Royce, staying at the Beverly Hills Hotel." Patty grins.

"I'm amazed at the places I went. But," she adds sagely. "I always looked for the bargains."

I laugh to myself. Another New England idiosyncrasy – the compulsion to talk about how much things cost. But unlike our counterparts in - say, L.A. - we enjoy bragging about how *little* we've spent on something. It's the way we are. The actual thrill for my sister was not shopping in one of the wealthiest shopping districts in the country, but that she found things on sale.

"With Brian the cash came and went quickly, but when we did have it – he spent it." The first months of their marriage, Patty was lonely in Florida so Brian flew her girlfriends in to visit. But he was also very jealous. Almost immediately, Brian's darker side became evident.

More than once I pulled him off an innocent Pointer Post patron who'd made the mistake of striking up a conversation with my sister. Paul Rastellini was a close family friend of ours and he and Patty grew up together. They shared as adults the silly kind of jokes that come from childhood. Brian beat him badly one night simply because he overheard their casual banter.

Brian need not have worried about my sister and her honor. In fact, my money was on Patty in a street fight. One night during a scuffle at a house party, the cops were called to settle down the partygoers. Patty was incensed at the law interfering and got into a scuffle. She threw three cops off the porch. If she hit you, you felt it, and if she was in a mood - she'd drop you. It probably came from five brawling brothers who didn't sexually discriminate in their choice of opponents – any sibling would do in a pinch.

The couple had plenty of what the police call "domestic altercations" but as hard as she went at it, he was too strong for her. She got her share of black eyes during their brief marriage and Patty was careful to avoid the Post until she healed. The old man would have gone after Brian and the consequences were sure to be deadly on one side or the other.

"Brian had his own pain," Patty says earnestly. "He lost his mom when he was twelve. They were very close. It snapped something inside him. It's not an excuse, but he never did get over it. And he was angry for the rest of his life."

Brian was definitely angry. I experienced it firsthand. We had words in a bar, one of those incidents usually forgotten the next day. Brian did not forget about it the next day, or even the next week. He put the word out he was after me and I became very cautious. This was during a period when I ran and boxed every day. Each time I left the house, I had a .22 caliber in my right hand covered by a long-sleeved shirt. I actually ran with that gun in my hand until Brian forgot he was mad.

Brian didn't need an excuse for violence but he'd use one if it were convenient, especially if he felt he was vindicating one of the boys. For example, Gary Winter was down the Post drinking with Jackie Hughes, a Harvard hockey player who eventually went pro. The drinking soon gave way to an argument. It took less than five minutes for the difference of opinion to escalate to a fistfight. The fight went on for a while, as other patrons moved away to continue imbibing in relative safety. Jackie was just too big for Gary to take down and he finally gave in. Everyone assumed the skirmish was over.

The next night I was working the door at the Post and things were nice and smooth. I was about to relax when Brian and another buddy showed up. Shit. Now the night could go either way.

"Bobby, I need to talk to ya in private."

I sighed. He'd chosen the only secluded space in the joint – the girl's bathroom. It was small, and my father had installed a rug from floor to ceiling. The old man loved rugs, it was his personal form of interior decorating (probably because he could combine his idea of fashion with soundproofing) and he paid great attention to the detail. His best friend Clem Salvi was a rug specialist and Big Bob took full advantage of Clem's talents. In the Harley room, devoted to all things Harley Davidson, Clem had also rugged the walls, but with a motorcycle artfully carved into the weave. It was quite a spectacle.

In the bathroom, Brian pointed at me. "Where's Jackie Hughes?"

I shrugged. "Why, what's up?"

Brian reached into his coat and slid out a long, shiny ice pick. "See this?" He slashed the air between us with the pick. "I'm gonna stick him right in his eyes as soon as that prick comes in! He had a fight with Gary and I can't let that go."

This was dangerously ridiculous, even for Somerville. I got right in his face.

"Yeah, so what? Does Gary have any idea what you're up to?"

Brian grinned proudly, his face a creepy smashed up Jack-O-Lantern. "No, he don't."

Those crazy eyes bored into me, but I wouldn't back down.

"No Brian! You ain't gonna stab Jackie in here or anywhere else. It was just a friendly beef."

During our back and forth, Brian's companion pulled an ice pick from *his* coat. Twin shiny points perfect for removing a set of eyes. I tried to watch him while I was nose to nose with Brian.

"I don't give two fucks what you say, Bobby, it wasn't right what Jackie did, and it ain't right for you to tell me I can't stab him."

The moment was thick between the five of us: me, Brian, his friend and the two gleaming picks. Seconds felt like hours. Eventually Brian sighed, "Well, if we can't stab Jackie, can we stab Rico?"

Poor Rico was just a local kid that crossed Brian years before. I wondered if we were all going insane inside the girls' restroom of a tiny bar in a small New England town; a Stephen King novel in the making. I gambled on my brother-in-law status and the fact my sister wouldn't be too thrilled if her husband stuck the family ice pick into her older brother.

"No! You can't stab Rico either! What the fuck is wrong with you, Brian?"

"All right," he whined dejectedly. Brian signaled to his friend and the picks disappeared.

Later that evening, our mutual buddy Ibby Alewood sat down next to me at the bar. "Christ, Bobby. You're crazy to talk to your brother-in-law like that! He's just a psychopath."

For a short time we worked together making collections for shylocks. When a customer didn't have his payment, I never strong-armed him. I'd just say, "Wait 'til you see the next guy that comes to visit you." That would be Brian.

I didn't last long. When I returned and the loan shark asked for the cash, I had to tell him the client was broke. I couldn't bring myself to become physical over money.

"Well, what did you do about it?" he'd demand.

"I told him wait until he sees the next guy that comes to collect. So you better send Brian."

The shark smiled a moment before he fired me. "You're in the wrong business. You don't have the stomach for it. Brian, he's the kind of guy who knows how to get people to pay up."

I'll admit at the time, my ego was a bit bruised. But after the ice pick incident, I had a vision of some poor bastard dead on the ground; two bloody holes the only evidence of where his eyes used to be, all over a couple hundred bucks. I realized the loan shark was right; about the stomach part anyway.

Brian was decidedly unbalanced. He was driving a car with a friend riding shotgun — I'll call him Rod — and two guys in the back. Supposedly going for drinks, the real plan was for Brian to take out one of the passengers on orders from his bosses. When the car stopped at a light, Brian casually turned and shot one of the guys in the head. Blood splattered across the seats and the shaken seatmate of the now dead man. It was Rod who confirmed what happened next, and I believe him.

"I whispered to Brian he'd shot the wrong man. I couldn't believe it. The victim was just a guy looking for a ride to a party. Now we were really in the shit. Brian looked at me, shrugged and shot the other guy. 'Now we're outta the shit' he says. Then the light changed and he kept on driving."

But that was in the past. Married life put new pressures on Brian. He was a man used to taking what he needed and getting more when he felt like it. Now with a wife he had regular expenses.

"Did you know what Brian did for a living when you married him?"

My sister gives me a look. "I knew he had robbed a few banks in the past, but I figured he did his time, he was over all that. It was Somerville, after all."

Yeah. It *was* Somerville. "When did you discover he wasn't making money the usual way?"

"Bobby, I didn't ask, didn't think about it. I was nineteen years and look who my family was? You didn't ask until suddenly you got yanked into it. Then ..." she taps her forehead, "you start thinking."

"What made you...?" I tap my own forehead, mimicking my sister. She gives me the "Quit it!" look and keeps talking.

"Let's see, it took me a while to figure this one out but when I did, I was pissed. He'd steal a set of keys from a parking lot, take somebody else's car, go rob. And then..."

"Wait a second," I interrupt, "Rob who?"

She shrugs. "Whoever."

"Just rob anybody in the street?"

Patty rolls her eyes at me like I am an idiot. "Not in the street. It had to be something more than that, Bobby. I mean, what are you gonna get on the street?"

I tell her that's what I am trying to find out, but she dismisses me, lighting a cigarette.

"I am *trying* to tell you something, *Bobby!*" she says angrily, blowing smoke. "Anyway, I drive him to a parking lot and the guy who usually gets the keys wasn't there; he was on break or whatever."

She must be talking about a parking lot attendant but God forbid I should interrupt her again.

"Uh huh, so then what happened?"

"Bobby, you know me at that age, I was so naive as far as stuff like that went, crimes, I mean."

I wonder about that, but again, I let her talk.

"Brian says, 'Look here Patty, this is what you're gonna do. A friend of mine is gonna leave me his car so I can run an errand. When I pull out, you follow me. And when we get to the place where the errand is, I'm gonna leave that car and get into ours. Then you drive away as fast as you can.'"

Patty lights another Marlboro. "Thank God he couldn't get keys. Because I realized what we'd been up to! No one would have believed that I didn't know what was going on. What a guy."

Patty reminds me of more stories: the time Brian robbed a suitcase full of coke and cash from one party only to have it stolen from him by another.

"He wasn't what you would call a real successful criminal," my sister shrugs.

Patty tells story after story and we laugh in spite of ourselves. It was a crazy, crazy time. Brian is, like most of the guys in this book, local legend. We were all touched by him and we all participated in his crimes, unwittingly or not. And we all, I believe, are responsible in some way for his death. Finally it's time to move on from the late seventies and into the first couple of years in the '80s.

1981. In April, Brian put the word out that he needed help with a job. I wasn't too keen on even listening. His "jobs" had a way of falling apart, usually at the expense of his "employees." Three years earlier, Brian convinced a guy you may be familiar with — let's just call him "Luke" - to rob Boston's popular Anthony's Pier Four restaurant with him. I will leave his real identity to your imagination.

Located on the Boston Harbor Pier, Anthony's was and remains to this day, a favorite hotspot for politicians and celebrities. Opened in 1963, its popularity eventually catapulted the eatery into one of the highest grossing restaurants in the United States.

"Ninety grand in the safe," he said. "An easy score." This popular establishment was a high profile spot and to attempt to rob it was a lousy idea. But Luke had a marriage on the rocks and needed the money. Without naming anyone else in this idiocy, suffice to say that another friend and Luke dressed up in some half-assed security guard shirts Brian had provided without stopping to wonder if anyone would notice their torn jeans, strapped on a couple of gun belts and (this is hard to write, trust me, as there is no statute of limitations on stupidity) fake mustaches.

Brian drove the hot box and had a .45 caliber along for the ride. It was ten o'clock in the morning and the plan was to slide in and out with the cash, one step ahead of the ten-thirty scheduled armored car pick up.

They finally arrived at their destination.

"Just go in and tell 'em you're there to collect the weekly receipts."

"OK," the hapless guys agreed. So they did. Right through the front door. Brian had instructed them to go directly up the set of stairs on the left to the payroll office.

They couldn't find it.

There was no payroll office. After a beat of confusion, they traipsed back down the stairs, wondered around and suddenly found themselves in the kitchen where they surprised the manager and eight cooks.

The manager was a young guy, six foot five. He stared at the men expectantly at first and then his face fell as his eyes first took in the "uniforms" and then the guns.

Luke cleared his throat. "We're here for the payroll."

Wordlessly, the young manager pointed toward a doorway and a steep staircase past the kitchen. Luke stared for a moment at the staircase and shook his head. Something was wrong. Luke's partner, a recently graduate of Walpole Prison, was nervous and sweaty.

"Move to the doorway," Luke barked at the manager. He could tell by the kid's face he was either scared stiff or doing a good job of acting. Luke started to feel a set up. He put his hand on the gun, looked at his shaking partner, then back at the kid and said, "We've got to go."

The three walked calmly out the back door together toward the waiting car. The kid was afraid that the robbers were real thugs and that he was going to go for a ride. Luke felt bad, the kid reminded him of his younger brothers. Luke turned and said, "Thank you very much."

The kid nodded his head like a bobble doll and the guys jumped into the car. Brian pulled out, turned a corner and screeched to a stop. They all bailed out, the boys tearing off their "disguises." They walked across the street to a coffee shop and no sooner did they slip in, when the cops converged on the eatery and the getaway car.

Luke stared at Brian.

"What the fuck? Brian, who set this score up? We were set up, no way the cops could get there that fast."

Brian just laughed. Creepy. Luke eventually did make the money he so sorely needed and paid dearly for the profit. That's another story.

Brian was always tossing down the gauntlet, testing your balls. You never knew when to take him seriously. He and I were boozing hard in a local bar one night and he asked me if I wanted to go to Tulsa and make ten thousand dollars.

"What do I have to do?" I asked suspiciously. Brian raised his glass casually.

"Whitey wants me to go and kill a guy from Tulsa." Brian's involvement with Bulger and Flemmi is well documented; he worked as an enforcer for them.

I stared at him. "You gotta be shittin' me. You want me to fight someone, that's one thing, but..."

Brian cut me off, laughing, shaking his head. "Martini, you'd believe anything."

I took some offense at that, but had to admit he had me going. We continued drinking and I forgot all about it.

CHAPTER TWELVE

Dancin' with Mr. D
The Luck of the Irish Runs Out

ON MAY 27, 1981 Roger Wheeler, the new president of World Jai Lai, was gunned down outside a Tulsa country club. Joe Mac later told my father that it was the easiest hit they ever did. He and Johnny Martorano flew to Tulsa and were waiting for Wheeler at the club. Johnny walked up to the side of the car and in a flash Roger Wheeler was dead. Joe was back in Boston before anyone knew they were gone.

Why Mr. Wheeler was killed is a long story and found in its entirety in scores of other books. Suffice to say after the hit was completed, the shit hit the fan for Brian. Whitey Bulger originally tapped Brian for the assignment. Now the only way to insure nothing was ever said about Bulger's involvement would be to fire Brian permanently. Whitey put out the word that Brian was a rat, an unreliable talkative cokehead that had to go — although up to this point Brian hadn't spoken to anyone.

Bulger sent one of his cohorts over to inform my father of the situation and even though the old man had tremendous animosity towards Bulger, he still didn't know what the truth was. Brian was his son-in-law. But if he'd broken the code of silence, then there was nothing that could be done except to protect my sister and her children.

My father never discussed the visit; yet over and over it's been repeated in local barrooms and pool halls. It was just recently I spoke to the one source still living and not on the run or incarcerated, who confirmed it. Bob Sr.'s best friend Clem Salvi.

Clem is a man of few words and his taciturn presence is sometimes hard to get past, especially when asked about anything regarding Winter Hill. He is also a loyal friend who agreed to answer a few questions because he knew how important it was to me.

"Clem," I ask "what about Brian Halloran? What can you tell me about Brian?"

"I didn't know Brian." He waits.

I try another angle. "Clem, what did my father say about Brian being killed?" When he doesn't answer, I push one more time. "Didn't someone speak to him about it before Brian was murdered?"

Clem points at the video camera I use for interviews. I'm a terrible note taker and DV has become my editorial assistant, the keeper of the information log so I tell the stories as they were told to me.

"I can't say on TV," Clem eyes the camera suspiciously.

"It's just video, Clem, so I can remember what to write," I say patiently. "You know how I am." He considers this and finally gives me a little information.

"Some people come down and told your father they were going to do something about Brian."

I interrupt Clem. "What people? Whitey?"

"*Some* people who would know," Clem says sternly. "Your father said to them 'As long as my kids aren't in the car.'"

So perhaps Big Bob knew what was in store for his son-in-law and rationalized it by telling himself "some people" were going to do what he himself had not. Deep in his heart, I think he knew Brian had spiraled so far out of control he couldn't come back.

The word was on the street and Brian began to unravel at an alarming rate with good reason.

"Patty, when was the first time Brian was shot at?"

My sister thinks. "Quincy, in 1981, I was pregnant with Justin and sitting in the car. We were going out. Shaun was a baby. I had him in my arms and Brian had gone to the back to take out the trash."

Patty waits for a beat, lights another cigarette. I wait with her.

"All of a sudden I heard these sounds...like pop, pop, pop. Brian came running and got into the car. He was all shook up. 'Someone's shooting at me!' he kept saying. So we took off to his father's house. And then we went..."

I stop her. "Wait a sec, you went to his father's house, what happened there?"

"We left and went to the mall."

That's my sister. A baby in her arms and another on the way, someone tries to execute her husband as he is trashing a bag of dirty diapers and they go straight to the mall.

"Don't give me that look," she warns. "I was trying to block it out. Anyway, when we finally came home the whole complex was surrounded by police. I don't know if the FBI was there. They were looking at bullet trajectories. One cop pointed to some splintered wood and said 'If just one bullet ricocheted, it could have hit your wife and child.'"

"Did Brian say who he thought was shooting at him?"

"No. He didn't want to talk about it."

My sister was married to a drug-crazed maniac, running from the law, the Feds and the Mob. She had two babies. Twenty years ago, I wouldn't have thought twice about it. Now I'm a grown man, a father. Why the hell didn't she get out?

"Brian made it very clear that if I were to leave, it would only be in a box." My sister is almost defiant, daring me to comment. I do not, whether from shame or regret. I just nod.

Patty confides in my partner something she does not bring up during our interview. "My father wanted my brothers Bobby and Leo to kidnap me and the kids. But Bobby said no, they wouldn't do it." When asked if she felt hurt about her brothers' refusal, my sister's response, I am told, is immediate and vehement. "Absolutely not! Brian would have killed my brothers. He would have found me and then he would have killed my brothers."

I don't remember the incident, probably because I don't want to.

She tells me of one other attempt on her husband's life. Patty and the kids were visiting Brian's state trooper brother Barry and his wife Karen when Brian pulled up in the driveway. "The car, our maroon Cadillac, was shredded, that's the best way I can describe it."

Brian had been at a nightclub and as he exited and walked toward his car, another vehicle pulled alongside, spraying bullets. He dove under the car and rolled up against the curb as the assailants tore off.

"Bobby, the inside of the roof, the car seats; there must have been hundreds of bullets. I don't know how he survived."

"Did Barry say anything?" I ask.

"Oh yes. Barry was upset. It was terrible. You had to see this car. 'Brian,' Barry said. 'You have to get out of this life.' But that's what he tried to do. And look what happened."

I have to think this is debilitating for my sister. Patty is five years younger than I and although my remaining family is not particularly close, she is sharing the most intimate painful details of her life on camera with me.

"Do you want to take a break?" I ask.

"Nope. Go. Ask." Patty is tougher than me sometimes.

"Tell me what you know about George Pappas."

George Pappas was a twice-convicted drug dealer gunned down at Boston's Four Seas Chinese Restaurant on October 13, 1981. John Salemme and Brian were charged with the murder.

"Pappas was bad news. He used to come around and ask Brian to take a ride," Patty sneers. "I never liked him, that dirt bag. John Callahan told me, 'Keep Pappas away.' But what could I do?"

John Callahan was the former president of World Jai Lai and a good friend of Howie, my father and just about everyone else on Winter Hill. Howie still has a photo of John in his kitchen. He was ousted from Jai Lai due to his alleged Irish Mob connections and under a cloud of suspicion regarding profit skimming in Florida and Connecticut — Whitey and Stevie's operation. Callahan was also the precursor to Roger Wheeler...from Tulsa. Patty and John got on very well.

"Callahan really liked me. He used to say, 'Patty, you are the only wife allowed around. I'm trying to put him [Brian] on the straight and narrow.' Which he was. He was trying to keep him in line, doing the right thing because Brian had a family."

Here's where that line between the reporting of the federal government and Somerville history part ways. The FBI claims that Brian Halloran came to them and told them Bulger, Flemmi *and* Callahan came to him about terminating the presidency of Wheeler. Supposedly Bulger changed his mind about the reliability of Brian and sent Callahan back with twenty thousand dollars in cash as a conciliation move for cancelling his involvement in the contract. "I never saw twenty grand," my sister argues.

Brian invited me to go to Tulsa for $10,000, although he never mentioned the name of the intended victim, to replace him on a job that Whitey was farming out. The cash had to have a source.

"Well, what had happened was, the night that Brian shot him..."

"Hold up, Patty. Brian told you he shot George Pappas?"

"No," Patty says flatly.

"Then how do you know?"

"I'm not a nitwit, Bobby! Anyway, he didn't come home all night. The phone rang about six in the morning. It was his father. He said, 'Yo, is the Big Guy home?' I'm trying to lie because I didn't want him to know Brian was out partying all night — is what I thought. I say, 'No, he's not home.' He said, 'Oh Jesus! I just watched the news and someone got blown away in Chinatown.'"

The investigation was quick and easy. "The cops had found the car because Stupid [Brian] had left the keys on the table in the restaurant! It was the car that the Demetris rented for us since the Cadillac had been shot up. The phone rang again. My husband. He said 'Go in the closet, there's a box. And it's got black wires and a ski mask in it. I need you to get that box and come over to Michael Donahue's.'"

Michael was a friend of ours, the son of a Boston cop and a good guy who, because of his friendship with Brian, later ended up at the wrong place at the fatally wrong time.

Patty continues. "So here I am, the box, a newborn, a toddler, no license. I drove over. And when I get there Brian says. 'They think I shot Pappas,' but he denied it. And while he was denying it, the cops were raiding my house. It's a good thing I got it out because they tore it apart, down to the baby's room."

"It was ugly. I'll tell you one thing though. My jewelry was laying around and they didn't touch it. I'll give them that. They didn't touch my diamonds."

After not touching Patty's diamonds, the cops moved on to the Demetris. Poor Charlie and his brother Jimmy were two of the best guys in the world. When the cops asked who had their rental car, they couldn't lie. Charlie said later "That's the last time I ever rent a car for Halloran."

No shit.

An old friend I'll call Lucky Lou is puffing on the last half of a decent priced cigar at a backyard cookout. Tanned and still teetering on the good side of overweight, he is one of the luckiest guys I know. Twice he escaped death while hanging with Brian and twice lived to tell about it — yet he rarely does.

"Hey, how you doin', Bob?" Lou's got one eye on me and the camera and another on the kids fanned out across the lawn in various stages of horseplay. We're the same as any parents — what we lived through is what we fervently pray our own kids will avoid so we're trying to keep them out of earshot.

In the background, the only kind of music we ever listen to — oldies — is blaring over the sounds of the wives laughing at some story that is probably about one of us. I think how bizarre it is that suddenly and without advance warning, bands like The Stones and Aerosmith are old people's music and the music we used to think of as oldies — Frankie Valli, The Coasters, and Bill Haley — is now ancient history. As for the current top forty, rap all sounds the same to me and the kids cannot discern the difference between Bob Seger and Bobby Darin. One generation's icons are just plain white noise to another, I guess, but we old Somerville boys refuse to keep up with the musical times. Secretly I do listen to Counting Crows and Kid Rock, I actually own Billy Idol's album he released at age fifty, but I don't admit it in public and keep my loyalty with the sounds of the past.

This get together reminds Lou of another, despite the lack of drugs and the multitude of children.

"Want me to tell you about the night Brian went crazy, Bobby?" he asks me.

"Which night?" I reply. There are several I can easily recall and many more that I don't.

"There was a party one night at Howie's house. The old man [Howie Sr.] was out for the evening and it was like eight or ten of us guys. We were all getting smashed, getting...you know, we were doing our demons."

Now that we've all grown up and wised up, here in the middle of a yard full of little kids it is uncomfortable to discuss our younger, wilder days.

"It was two or three in the morning. Brian was sweating, nervous. In the middle of the conversation, out of the blue, he says, 'I love to rob banks.' It was very strange; you could see the coldness in his eyes. I remember that everyone just sort of paused."

Brian was that way. He could grind all activity in a room to a halt. Lou tells me that later on, the supply of entertainment was depleted and he and Brian decided to pay a visit to the local dealer.

There was a guy in a wheelchair in the projects who supplemented his disability by dealing out of his small apartment. The identity of his supplier was a mystery as the kid rarely left his home, but he made a decent living, as he was always available and always stocked up. He was also a frequent visitor to the local jail.

Paul Martins is also at the backyard party. A successful plumber, he remembers the wheelchair-bound dealer's impact on the local police department. "I can't remember his name for the life of me but I do remember that this kid was arrested so many times that the judge got sick of the cops having to struggle with finding a place to put him and his wheelchair."

The police department was ordered to remodel a jail cell to make it handicapped accessible. Paul describes the set up. "They even ordered a handicapped toilet, one stainless unit that came all the way from California. It was low enough and easy to get from a wheelchair right onto the john."

The coke dealer had a comfortable home-away-from-home during his many incarcerations.

"Yeah," Lou agrees, "everybody knew this kid. But Brian wasn't quite sure where his apartment was, so I drove with him."

Brian and Lou drove through the pre-dawn streets, Brian sweating and becoming more irritated with each turn, convinced that the reason the party had run low on "demons" had to do with him being shorted by the crippled coke man.

"We pulled up outside of the kid's apartment. Brian got out, and reached under the seat, pulled out a sawed off shotgun and loaded it. 'I ain't paying for nothin',' Brian said. 'I'm gonna kill this kid.' I was scared shitless, I didn't know what to do and I didn't want to walk into that apartment with him."

As they stood at the trunk in the silence of sunrise, a lone car came down the street toward them and stopped. Howie Winter got out.

"Brian," Howie said quietly. "Put the gun away."

Nobody moved.

"Brian," Howie said again. "Put the gun away, get in the car and you boys get home now."

Brian nodded and slowly put the gun back into the trunk. Howie nodded in approval. "That's it, that's good. Now get on home."

The boys got into the car and drove straight home. "Brian never said a word," Lou says. "He was completely calmed down."

Days later, Howie told Lou that he'd come home the night of the party and gone directly upstairs to bed, leaving the younger guys to their own devices. A few hours later he got up for a drink of water and came downstairs. The party was much more subdued. Buckling under Howie's questioning, one of the guys admitted that Brian had left and seemed more out of sorts than usual as he headed down into the projects. Howie immediately got dressed and got into his car.

The end of Lou's story is chilling. "I will always believe I was very lucky that night, that Brian probably would have come out with the shotgun, with the bag of coke, but without me."

"He would have killed you?" I ask Lou.

Lou shrugs. "He was crazy at the end. Brian Halloran could walk up to you and say 'Hi,' one minute and shoot you the next." He gnaws on his cigar, blowing a cloud of smoke upwards. "That's actually a fact, by the way. Remember what happened at the Chinese Restaurant?"

George Pappas. I remember.

"Well," Lou says, "That night a few of us guys were drinking in a bar when Brian leaned over to me and said 'I want to go get Chinese. You wanna go?' I didn't so I said 'I'm just gonna stay and have a few more drinks.' The next night I read in the paper that Pappas had been murdered and you know the rest. No witnesses."

Lou shakes his head and doesn't say anything else.

In the sun-dappled backyard, The Tokens sing about a lion sleeping tonight and our kids dance and weave through the sprinklers. I feel cold.

Fueled by panic and coke, Brian believed him when Bulger whispered the drug dealer was seen coming out of the federal courthouse and must be a rat. Whatever Pappas was ratting about was inconsequential in Brian's deluded mind. Bulger didn't know for sure, I'm told, but it was an easy way to set up his former would-be assassin. Besides, Bulger had his own informant, Boston FBI agent John Connolly. Connolly was the handler who assumed that Whitey worked for him, feeding him information about New England Mob figures when in reality, Connolly worked for Whitey, repeating his gossip and assisting Whitey in slowly dismantling all operations except for his own. It was a double blind experiment in the lab of Winter Hill. Everyone involved was ratting to someone who was ratting to someone else and not one person knew what was really going on except for Whitey Bulger.

Brian surrendered to the Boston police on October 29, 1981.

"Patty," I say very carefully. "What was the deal between Brian and the FBI?"

Rat is the word. Men have died rather than be tagged with that name; Howie took the chance of rotting in prison rather than turn over. Maybe from where others sit, it's hard to understand. But that's the way it was...and still is here in Somerville and inside all of us.

Now my sister and I start up the final slippery slope together.

State trooper Jack Towsey was a friend of Barry Halloran's and knew people at the Bureau. Brian wanted to buy some time to stay alive until he could figure a way out of his situation. "He had nowhere else to run because no one else could protect him. And he thought the FBI could."

"And he was scared?" I ask, more as a statement.

"I just said that he was shot at twice, Bobby! Pay attention! He was a walking target."

Almost immediately the Hallorans were whisked off to a safe house. "[Agent] Leo Brunick was one of the guys interviewing Brian. He said, 'Brian with all this stuff going on, let me have you talk to this guy [another agent].' And one thing led to another and soon we were staying down at the Cape with Jack and his girlfriend. We had to stay downstairs while the FBI and them met upstairs."

"What did they want?"

Patty smiles. "For Brian to name names."

"Did he?"

"No."

"What did he tell them?"

She laughs. "As little as possible."

"Did he talk about Whitey and Stevie?"

"No way," she is adamant although various witnesses state otherwise.

"Howie?"

That doesn't go over too well. "Are you kidding me? Howie was his friend, Bobby." Howie's name does not appear in any court transcripts or witness statements.

"Well, what happened?" I ask.

Patty patiently explains the game. "They weren't offering Witness Protection. Just a safe place until they got real information. So we moved from house to house while Brian was stringing them along."

What was the payment for such a service, I wonder.

"Like a hundred dollars a week and I was told I should be happy I was getting anything at all." The Feds grew impatient with the vague informant, so according to my sister, they pushed Brian.

"They had him wear a wire. But he kept giving them the run-around and that's why they wouldn't put him in full protection. After [Brian died] the Hallorans claimed we didn't go out of state because I refused. But that wasn't true. It was because he kept pulling their chain and they knew it."

My crazy brother-in-law was stalling simply to stay alive. The Feds switched tactics.

"They fed him a lie." According to his wife, the Feds presented a purportedly authentic wiretap recording in which Brian's unnamed potential executioners had spotted him away from the safe house.

"They played him a tape and he heard, 'Yeah, Halloran's here at the pier, but he's with his wife' and supposedly, the answer back was 'we don't care, we'll get her too.' He couldn't think it through and realize it was all bullshit, fabricated. So he panicked."

During this time, none of us were allowed contact with Patty, not even my parents knew where they were. Used to talking to my mother daily, suddenly she wasn't allowed to call at all.

"I couldn't contact nobody. Ma and Dad were devastated. Ma use to talk about it until the day she died." Patty was cut off from everyone. Even if she'd left Massachusetts with Brian, it wouldn't have mattered. She'd still have been in the same state of isolation — isolation that was getting to Brian as well.

We are close to the top of the slope now. I'm not sure I want to keep going but I have no choice.

"What happened on that last day, Patty?"

Brian made a series of phone calls from the safe house and set in motion the last few hours of his life. "It was around three in the afternoon on May 11th [1982]. We were alone with the kids. Brian kept saying 'I'm going up to Boston to see Charlie and Jimmy, I'll get a car.' We had use of a car for errands but he didn't want to owe the Feds anything. He called the Demetris but there was no way they were giving him a car after Chinatown. He called the FBI and told them he'd had it. And finally, he called Michael for a ride and that," she looks at me, "was that."

"He left after three and I was alone until eleven when the news was coming on. He never left me alone without at least calling, even if he was out partying."

The temporary home Patty was living in was deep in the woods with huge glass windows; a strange set up for a safe house. "It may have been owned by a doctor," she muses. "Anyway, I kept looking outside for someone to drive up. I had just put the baby down and Shaun was asleep. I heard a knock. I froze; I couldn't turn around. I thought maybe I was going to die right then."

Patty slowly opened the door. It was Barry's wife Karen and trooper Towsey.

"For a minute none of us said anything. We all looked at one another. Then Karen took my arm and said, 'Patty, Brian's been shot.' And I just looked at her, waiting. 'He's dead,' she said. I ran to the bathroom and got sick. I stayed in there for a while, throwing up. But then I had to get up off the floor, I heard the baby crying and so..." her voice trails off.

There is silence in the room. We Martinis are not known for long stretches of quiet. We have a need to fill up the space between us with something. I fidget for a few seconds. Finally I can't take it.

"And?" I say, which comes off colder than I wanted it to — another Martini trait.

My sister looks at me hard, snaps it right back. "And? We packed up everything; all of our clothes, the kids' toys and Karen took me to her house. The Hallorans took care of everything else."

"So you moved out of the safe house right away?"

"Oh yeah, Bobby, I had to," my sister says simply. "The FBI made us."

"Didn't they give you any money?"

Patty laughs bitterly. "Their employee was blown away, they didn't give severance pay. They certainly weren't gonna support me. It was, 'Take off, starve, freeze to death, do whatever you're gonna do.' So I went to Karen's, cried for three days and then started the process of trying to block it all out."

The hapless Halloran starting spinning out of control from the moment he was charged with the Pappas murder, the man Bulger insisted was an informant. Brian knew he'd be convicted. In desperation, he went to the Feds hoping to string them along while he tried to figure out how to bankroll his escape. Later on, former Bulger associate Kevin Weeks testified that during this final period in Brian's life, Halloran was "threatening [certain people] with naming them as the killer of Pappas if they did not give him some money" and he was "robbing people of coke at gunpoint." Brian had lost all patience and had decided it was time to make his move. He called the Feds and told them it was over.

On the last day of his life, Brian met up with Michael and together they were gunned down just steps from the Pier Grille. They were in Michael's blue Datsun in the parking lot when a Chevy pulled up from behind — a curly haired mustached man yelled out "Brian!" and three men sprayed bullets into the Datsun and its occupants. The Chevy was a "hit car", souped up engine and a device straight out of a James Bond novel that could, with the flick of a switch, spray oil from behind, creating a slick for anyone chasing it to have to maneuver. Michael J. Donahue was instantly beyond help as a high velocity bullet blew through the back of his head. Brian staggered out of the car and, like a low rent Sonny Corleone, spun and danced in the air as gunshots tore through his body. He fell facedown onto the ground, blood gushing from what seemed like everywhere.

A frantic motorist flagged the cops down. Officers arrived on the scene less than a minute after the last shot. They tried to staunch Brian's wounds as they called for an ambulance. In moments the pier was crawling with more uniforms, news crews and detectives. Detective Sergeant Bo Millane was one of them. Well acquainted with both Brian and Michael, when he saw nothing could be done for Michael, Bo claimed he jumped into the ambulance with his rapidly expiring friend — something the ambulance driver insists never happened.

"I said 'Brian, who did this?" Millane testified later. Then the forty-one year old bank robber, alleged murderer, son, father and husband supposedly whispered his last four words. "Jimmy Flynn from Weymouth." Brian never regained consciousness and was pronounced dead in less than an hour. The Halloran family minus one was out of what they thought was a safe house before dawn.

There were two hundred people at St. Ann's Church on May 15, 1982. I was one of them. Reverend Richard McLaughlin prayed, "Forgive him whatever sins he may have committed in weakness." Brian's Teamster brother Kenny gave a eulogy denouncing rumors Brian was an informant and also made reference to Brian's tumultuous and violent life when he said, "You hear things, but the only one who can judge him is the person up there," pointing toward heaven. He was clearly upset about accusations because his family had been brought up within the code of silence. If Kenny, or any of us, had known how many times Brian's enemies had tried to kill him before he finally gave in, possibly only to save his family, we may have felt much differently about Brian breaking that code.

My own father didn't attend the wake or funeral of his grandchildren's father. I want to believe he would have gone if he knew then what we all came to learn about Whitey, Stevie and the FBI.

Patty disagrees. "My father was done with Brian long before the whole thing with the Feds. Dad didn't like the way Brian treated me and he disowned him."

Patty and her boys bounced around. "I stayed with my brother Leo and his wife for a time, but they had just gotten married. They had a small apartment — I had a crying baby. It didn't go so well."

I can tell there is more she would like to say on the subject, but she doesn't.

I feel the story begs for more detail. A reader, I think, would want to know what happened when Patty called our mother, told her that she'd gone from wife to widow in just one short afternoon. How did our father respond? What did we say to each other?

Honestly? Not much.

My family is from Somerville. From as early as I can recall, each person's safety and sanity has been tied to personal survival. My parents were young teenagers when they began a household that eventually expanded to nine. My father was rarely home and my mother's life can best be described in two parts. During the first, she gave birth and attempted to raise seven children with a husband who was rarely home or an active participant after conception. There weren't enough daylight hours for her to dote on any of us. Mom also suffered from a variety of illnesses and as the oldest I spent much of my preteen years rounding up the littler kids.

The second part of her life was eaten away by the knowledge that the same man was now living with another woman. Her illnesses continued yet she often took a few drinks to ease the pain of a different kind. I have come to believe the only time she was genuinely happy as an adult was the eighteen months my father was incarcerated. He wasn't with her, but he wasn't shacked up with his girlfriend either.

As I passed into adulthood and my father changed residences, I became more of a surrogate husband than a cherished son. I spent countless hours with the phone pressed to my ear, listening to her rail against the old man and much of my spare time completing "man of the house" chores at her house. My marriages, subsequent divorces and my own jail time passed with little commentary from my own mother. Her whole world shrank to her personal day-to-day survival. I loved my mother as I did my old man and I know that although they didn't say it — they loved me. That has to be enough.

My siblings and I were not particularly close when we were younger. We ran with our own groups of friends. As we aged, I believe the impact of the combined deaths of two of our brothers have kept the distance between us intact today. The closer one is in proximity to loss, the greater skills required to survive.

Brian's life did not pass without pain and regret within all of us who knew him. It was, however, Somerville and so we did not talk about it.

Eventually Patty rented a tiny place with money she got from Social Security. "The only people who would rent to me were a couple with five kids. If it weren't for them, I'd probably be dead. My father helped. Bobby, you did too, but there still wasn't much. I did the best I could, we got by."

She avoided the press and settled into survival. About three months later, John Callahan was shot to death in the parking lot of Miami International Airport by his old friend Johnny Martorano and folded into the trunk of a car to swell in the tropical heat. [Johnny admitted to killing both Callahan and Wheeler eighteen years later.] Soon after Callahan's rotting body was discovered, Patty got a visit from the FBI.

"I just put the boys down for a nap and this FBI agent came to my door. Of course, I don't remember 'em, you know what I mean? They all look the same to me." Patty grins. She had and has the same regard for the Feds as they had for her husband. A thug dressed in a suit and tie is still just a thug.

"I opened the door to this guy in a suit and he says 'Mrs. Halloran?' and I said 'Yeah?' not even thinking. He flips his badge..."

"What did you do?" I ask. I'm hoping this is one of the great Patty stories like when she threw the cops off of the front porch. My sister knows what I'm thinking.

She wags a finger at me. "The boys were sleeping." She says sternly. "I said 'You might as well come on in.' Right away he's asking questions about Callahan. I don't know what they expected — I was Mrs. Brian Halloran, but not *Brian Halloran*. I had been down this road before. I sent him on his way."

A few days later, Patty received a call from the FBI requesting a meeting. Patty began to get nervous. "I didn't want them back in my house. So we met at the Assembly Square Mall." Patty packed up Shaun and Justin and dutifully headed off to meet the government agents. Another trip to the mall.

"What could I do?" she demands. "I didn't have a babysitter."

Why, I wonder, did Patty go to meet with the very group of men she was convinced had aided and abetted the execution of her husband?

"One — I was curious as to what they might want. These guys knew me pretty well so I was surprised they called. Second, I knew if I didn't settle whatever that was once and for all, they'd keep at me and I didn't want that."

Patty drove to the parking lot, and with her children got into a car with two agents who had been handling Brian during his brief tenure as an informant. They didn't waste time with condolences. The subject was Callahan's murder. But Patty had no information about Callahan or any of the men she was once so close to in the past, at least none she chose to share. Then the agents did something strange.

"They handed me a thousand bucks, Brian's departure gift. 'This is what we owed your husband for his services,' one of them said to me."

"Was that it, Patty?" I find it hard to believe the government got the last word in and I am right.

"Oh no, I thanked them for the money, the bastards," Patty snorts. "And then I told them that not only did I not know anything — if I did 'I wouldn't tell you nothing. The day my husband called your office, *you guys killed him.*' Then I grabbed my kids and went home."

Any hopes the FBI had that Patty Martini Halloran, like her dead husband, might just have been desperate enough to hop on the Feds' payroll or provide information about the activities of dozens of men drifted away forever with the exhaust from her departing car.

Howie was away during the time Brian and Callahan were killed.

"Patty, do you think if Howie had been on the street that Brian would be alive today?"

Patty shakes her head slowly. "No."

I'm surprised. "You don't think he could have stopped it?"

"Callahan, maybe. In fact, I'm pretty sure that had Howie been out, Callahan would still be alive. But Brian? No. I think that Brian had just pissed off too many people. Anyway, I kept moving."

My sister Patty was once a star athlete who sparkled on the high school track team. Suddenly she was a grief stricken twenty-four year old widow with two children. Patty worked at burying her past. She had little direct contact with the Hallorans.

"They blamed me. They say that if I went away with him that he'd be alive today. And what they don't understand is they weren't gonna grant him the Witness Protection. We just couldn't get it."

Not everyone turned his back on Patty. Brian's brother Dennis reached out to her in the months after Brian's death.

"Dennis is great, he always was. He came over and said 'Look Patty, you've been through a lot and we'd like to take the boys. You keep the Social Security. I'll take one and Barry will take the other.' He meant well, he really did. But Dad flatly refused. 'No way! The Hallorans are not getting those kids!'"

Halloran family friend Jean worked to keep a relationship going with Brian's sons. "She picked the kids up every weekend. Took them up to the Hallorans."

Patty's own fragile relationship with the Hallorans finally deteriorated completely.

"The boys visited for years till they got older. They were still in contact with Brian's family when one day Barry said something, something like, 'if it wasn't for your effing mother, your effing mother was the one that got my brother killed.'" Patty stops short of going for the gold with the "F" word, surprising me, because of the naked pain and something like regret slipping across her face.

"They hate us, Bobby. They hated Dad. They always hated Dad. They blamed him too." My younger sister looks right at me and spreads her hands out in supplication, as if asking for my help.

"But Bobby, it's *all* of our fault — *theirs and ours* — because he lived the life he lived and none of us ever tried to stop him."

We sit in silence. She's right, we didn't. Not the Hallorans, not Patty, not my father, not me.

Two years after Brian died, she met and married Somerville cop Joe Macarelli and had another boy. Their marriage sustained her pain, her three sons are grown, but the years have not been kind to Patty Martini Halloran Macarelli despite her second chance. We lost two of our brothers — Eddie and Joey — to AIDS, a nephew, both of our parents and recently my oldest son. Our family has had more than its fair share of pain, but Patty's is twofold.

"I see Brian in my boys and I still dream about him after all this time."

Patty, like most of us, is still suffering with the long-term hangover of Somerville's bloody history and the questions that are buried along with Brian Halloran.

How was it that from an undisclosed location deep in the woods off the Cape that no one knew about, save the FBI, Brian left in the late afternoon and was dead before the nightly news? There are several documented facts that, despite published books with differing opinions, thugs turning on each other and pointing fingers all around, news reports and court transcripts, are not in dispute.

One, Whitey Bulger was in bed with his childhood friend FBI Special Agent Connolly. Connolly was indicted in 1999 on charges of alerting Bulger and Flemmi to developing investigations into their crimes, falsifying FBI reports, and accepting bribes. In 2000, he was charged with racketeering and a bevy of other offenses. In 2008, the G-man was convicted of second-degree murder for his participation in the eradication of Callahan. Two, Connolly, although not Brian's handler, had access to all communications between Brian and the Bureau.

And three; in 1998, John M. Morris, former supervisor of Boston's FBI's organized crime task force, testified that in '82 he told Connolly that Halloran was talking about Roger Wheeler. Morris testified, "Everyone was questioning Halloran's reliability and truthfulness. I questioned Connolly for his take on it." Connolly insisted his informants had nothing to do with the Tulsa job or Brian. But he was suddenly in possession of just the information Bulger was looking for — the location of Halloran.

And *somebody* asked Brian to travel to Tulsa for at least $10,000, not a typical vacation getaway for Somerville thugs —

paid or otherwise — because I *know* he asked me to go and there was no earthly chance it was coming out of his own pocket.

Patty believes this is an FBI no-brainer. "Bobby, he called them when he was at the Pier. A [WCVB] Channel 5 reporter told me afterward, 'Picture it Patty, Brian's calling the FBI, and whoever answers the phone turns around and yells out, 'Brian Halloran on line three, he's down the Pier.' So it's being announced through the whole place."

I have an idea what an outsider may be thinking — Halloran got what he deserved. After all, he was awaiting trial for murder and had a history of other crimes for which he was yet to be judged. But for federal law enforcement to allow, if not help arrange for the hit of one criminal to pacify another bigger criminal fish is a travesty. The FBI is culpable, I am convinced, of participating in the execution of Brian and Michael, thus wiping out yet another avenue of gaining information about the crimes of Whitey Bulger. In the end, Brian was someone's son, someone's father and husband, and still entitled to stand trial for his transgressions.

Even to this day, the FBI in Boston can't live down the corruption that plagued the agency for over thirty years. In 2000 The Boston Herald obtained copies of FBI reports regarding the murders that had been locked away for eighteen years. Two witnesses who happened upon the scene as the shooting began reported seeing a late-model black sedan, the kind usually driven by the Feds, helmed by an individual "in businessman's attire." The same vehicle blocked the witnesses' car from approaching the scene and glided away just behind the "hit car" after the shooting was complete. Stevie Flemmi reportedly told several of his friends that it was common knowledge that FBI turncoat Connolly was "in the area" when Brian was taken down. This information was never made available in the days, weeks, months and even years after the murders. Nor did it come to light during the trial of Jimmy Flynn.

James P. "Jimmy" Flynn knew that he hadn't been anywhere near the Pier on May 11th. He also knew he certainly hadn't killed Halloran or Donahue. So when he heard his name broadcast as the suspect in the dying declaration of a victim bleeding to death from between ten to twenty-one bullet wounds (depending on your choice of news networks), he did the only sensible Somerville thing — he blew town.

Sure, he was innocent, but he also had a police record for activities like counterfeiting, bank robbery and gun charges, as well as a reputation as a member of the Winter Hill Gang from as far back as the Howie years. Coupled with the rumors that Whitey and Stevie were double dealing with the FBI, Jimmy knew lawmen would be racing to close the case before the investigation went any deeper. Any Winter Hill-er would do in a pinch. It took the Feds two and a half years to catch up with him and when they did, he was held at the Charles Street jail for eighteen months. The guy in the next cell was Patriarca underboss Gerry Angiulo. The two spent hours swapping stories about the old days when stand up guys either admitted what they had done or clammed up —and most certainly did not wear disguises.

The Feds knew Jimmy was innocent, even the ambulance driver proclaimed there had been no one in the vehicle to hear the alleged "dying declaration." Jimmy's wife Carol took the stand and swore her husband had been home with her. Jimmy's daughter repeated what her mother had told her and indignantly punctuated it with, "Of course it's true, my mother does not lie!" Jimmy even had two state troopers vouch for him.

The FBI allowed Jimmy to be indicted and put through the painful spectacle of a murder trial. He could have easily ended up like Joe Salvati and Peter Limone, two guys who did over thirty years for a killing they didn't do until it came to light the Boston end of the FBI was once again involved in a frame up of the men and they were convicted, partially, on the testimony of federal informant Joe Barboza.

But Jimmy was eventually acquitted of Brian's murder thanks to an attorney named Richard Egbert and a mobster called Kevin Weeks. Weeks is a former Bulger associate, mobster and author of the book *Brutal: My Life in Whitey Bulger's Irish Mob*. Weeks cooperated with the authorities and gave information leading to the discovery of multiple murder victims of Bulger and Flemmi. In exchange, he received a lighter sentence for his involvement in the crimes — one was the murder of Brian (referred to as "Balloon Head" by Bulger) during which he was the lookout. Weeks testified he signaled Bulger by walkie-talkie that "the balloon was in the air" — Halloran was out in the open. Weeks also testified Whitey wore a disguise — a wig and moustache and that Whitey laughed later the same night, yeah, he did look "a lot like Jimmy."

I'm hard pressed to find more than a handful of good comments about Brian but one came from Howie himself. It's difficult to read his expression when I bring up my former brother-in-law. His face is a cross between sadness and protective loyalty.

"Brian," I begin tentatively, "was a pretty dangerous kid." I repeat a few stories that culminate in Brian's explosive behavior.

Howie doesn't bite. "Bobby, I never saw Brian like that, hurting people just to cause pain. I think at the end, when he was really into that shit [drugs] his whole personality changed. For many years Brian was well liked and not just by the neighborhood. The whole Boston Bruins gang — they loved Brian.

"Brian," Howie reminds me, "was a colorful guy when he was younger, at every party, sang great Irish songs. Brian was a different guy back in those years."

I remind Howie of Brian's violent history but he just shakes his head.

"I never saw him like that, that's all I can say. I'm not disputing anything that happened, but he was never the way they wrote about him when he was with me. He wouldn't hurt people for money. If he had to defend a friend he would have."

"What about Whitey? Do you think Brian was Whitey's pawn in Wheeler's murder attempt?"

Howie's reply is simple and strangely apologetic. "I don't know, Bobby. I was away by then."

I press a bit further. "What about the story when Brian shot the wrong guy in that car?"

Howie turns away as if he's done but then turns back to me. "No," he shakes his head. "No. I don't believe that, Bobby. Who told you that story?" he asks sternly.

It's my turn to shrug. "Brian did."

"Hmm," is all Howie will say.

I don't want to push any further and while I'm waiting for a better question to come to mind Howie says suddenly, "It was the shit, Bobby. Drugs. It makes a man completely different. All of a sudden you look over at a fellow you've known for years and you can't recognize him. You want to, but you can't. He's a stranger. You keep hoping the first man will reappear, but generally — he doesn't. Brian went away from us and then he never came back."

I can't argue with that.

Jimmy Flynn is a friend of mine, and a guy that knew Brian well. We work together now, but we never talk about Brian Halloran.

Sometimes, late at night after a few beers, I think about Brian and those last few moments of his life. I remember seeing the news; the TV camera caught Brian being loaded into the ambulance down by the waterfront. I saw his belly going up and down as he struggled to breath, it was unbelievable that he could still be alive. Did he go to his grave believing that it was Jimmy Flynn who gunned him down? Or did he recognize Whitey in those last few minutes? If he did, was it just dumb hope that he just might survive and the thought of Whitey coming after him was somehow far more terrifying than throwing Jimmy in? I don't know. And I don't ask my sister, because she doesn't want to talk about it anymore.

I also think about a boozy conversation in a crowded, noisy bar many years ago, and my brother-in-law's offer of a job in a far away place called Tulsa that was played off as a joke. But I try very hard not to.

CHAPTER (LUCKY) THIRTEEN

Stabbings, Sticks and Stones:
Everybody Gets Stuck Eventually

"BOBBY, YOU WERE stabbed once, weren't you? You and my son Howie?"

"That was my brother Leo," I reply. "Young Howie the next time. Timmy Russell was shot. But everybody gets stuck eventually."

Howie nods thoughtfully. "I guess you're right."

Timmy Russell was shot in Charlestown.

One evening a group of us crossed the line of community demarcation and attended a house party at a third floor apartment in Charlestown. The bitter rivalry that began in 1843 when Somerville separated from Charlestown to become its own entity and was fueled by the Irish Gang Wars of the sixties was still firmly in place in the seventies.

Events that crossed our imaginary boundary lines were as organized as a Secret Service blueprint and the guest list was fine-tuned to invitees known to be able to co-exist (and party) safely together.

The party was in full swing when a pounding on the front door cut through the loud music. I grabbed the knob and swung the door open to face six Charlestown guys. They insisted they were coming in and we countered with the usual, "Go screw" — the Somerville equivalent of "Fuck off." The two camps tossed back some macho insults and I slammed the door. The ejected group tromped down the stairs and the party picked up from the point of interruption.

It wasn't long before a series of street debris missiles began sailing through the windows of the apartment. The locals were not taking their lack of invitation very well and were making their presence in the street below known in the form of bottles, cans and other street trash. Not to be outdone, the partygoers started winging household items down at the troublemakers. A friend of mine named Timmy Russell and I decided to try and stop the battle before someone got squashed with a television. We ran down the three flights and out onto the stoop. I began talking to what seemed like the most reasonable of the guys when another jumped forward and hit me across the head with a heavy rusty venetian blind.

That shut me up and I hurled myself into the crowd, fists flying. I was pounding anyone I could grab while a crowd formed at the window above, yelling and cheering. Then a scream, "GUN!" I spun around and stared.

A Charlestown thug careened around the corner toward us. In his hand was a gun with the hammer cocked.

"Fuck!" I think I yelled. I grabbed Timmy and yanked him out of the fray. We slammed back through the front door of the apartment and banged the door closed just as the shooter pulled the trigger. Shots exploded into the front door and Timmy's hand ran red. A bullet went right through his wrist and blood sprayed both of us.

We fell backward, found the cellar door and threw ourselves down the dark stairway. In the blackness I fumbled around to get my shirt off and wrap it around Timmy's oozing wrist. We struggled to keep quiet. The iron odor of blood was overwhelming.

It wasn't long before there were dull footsteps above our heads.

I've had my share of fear over the decades. Usually I have a decent reserve of bravado I can call upon to quell that fright. But this night I was more afraid than I can ever remember. Timmy and I were just a couple of guys who started the evening with no other desire other than to whoop it up and have a few laughs. Now it would end in a basement execution because we wandered behind enemy lines. I closed my eyes, smelled the blood and waited for the gun.

"This is the Police. Is anyone down there?"

I wanted to cry with relief. Outside another cop and an ambulance were waiting. The medics grabbed Timmy as soon as we hit the street.

"Who shot at you?" One of the cops demanded. We shook our heads and stuck to the code.

"We didn't see a gun."

Then I was astonished. The Charlestown guys returned — marching toward us as if angel dust blind to the presence of the cop. The shooter was leading the pack. With a healthy prehistoric howl, I threw myself at him and punched until I trapped him up against a car. While the cops stared down the others, I beat the shooter for a good ten minutes until the officers decided it was enough. They even allowed Timmy to get a few good pounds in on a couple of other guys. They were Charlestown cops, we were Somerville boys, and the invisible treaty dictated we should have been beaten out of town. But the unfair advantage of a gun introduced into the fight changed the rules.

It was over as quickly as it started. The gang scattered, Timmy went to the hospital and I headed back to the relative safety of Somerville.

My brother got stuck because of my ego.

On a weeknight in 1977 the Club 3 on Somerville Ave was packed solid. My brother Leo, Tommy Hersey, Jackie O'Keefe, all the regulars were pounding back beers. There may be work tomorrow, but tonight we were celebrating another softball win. Or loss. It really didn't matter. During the late 70's I was down there five times a week.

I was sitting at the bar listening to a buddy brag about the amazing (and imaginary) clutch hit he insisted he'd made in the sixth inning when my younger brother Eddie blasted through the door.

"Bobby! Listen, I gotta tell you something."

It was a tough choice. I could tear myself away from a bullshit story and certain boredom, but the alternative could have it's own ramifications.

The words "I gotta tell ya something!" from Eddie could range from "The reason your car is missing is a group of gypsies came by and stole it! I swear to God, I tried to stop them! I can get it back for a few hundred bucks!" to "I gotta tell ya something! Mom and Dad have just been abducted by aliens and I need $1000 right now or we'll never see them again!"

As Eddie yanked on my jersey, I decided a little excitement was preferable from my eyes glazing over. Eddie was flushed, his face a serious knot. He looked a little scared.

He gulped air, trying to catch his breath. "I just run all the way up from the projects!"

"You ain't taking my car, Eddie! I got fuckin' work tomorrow and I ain't taking the bus again."

Truth was, I probably wouldn't make it to work the next day, but if I told Eddie he'd just hammer at me until I gave in. Strangely enough, I didn't show up at my job after all, but it wasn't due to my brother. Not this brother anyway.

"No, no, not the car, I don't need the car, that's not what I'm tryin' to tell…" Eddie paused and then charged ahead. "Well, actually I might need to borrow…."

I held a hand up, cutting him off. "Eddie, what did you come here to tell me?"

"I was down the projects and Butchie is motherfuckin' you all over the place. Says you're a loud mouth, an asshole, and…" he paused again for effect.

Butchie was a loud mouth and an asshole himself, I shrugged. No new news there. We prided ourselves on noisy bravado and were all on this side of being an asshole at one time or another. Those weren't fighting words.

Butchie isn't the man's name, by the way. It's the nickname I chose to use. He's still around and like most of us, is far different as an adult than he was as a young guy.

"And," Eddie continued, lowering his voice just as Leo leaned into the conversation. "Butchie says you can't fight worth a shit!"

*Now those **were** fighting words.*

In Somerville insinuating a guy can't fight was the equivalent of saying he dressed up in his old lady's clothing and paraded up and down the street. Sorry to admit it, but that's the way it was.

I slammed my beer down and the place went silent. OK, maybe not the whole bar, but down my end of it every mouth dropped wide open. My brothers, Tommy and Jackie all stared at me.

"Fuck him. Let's go!"

Still in our softball uniforms, we slammed out the door and jumped into my car. Eddie stayed behind, no doubt to convince someone he needed to commandeer their vehicle to follow us.

Butchie was six feet and two hundred and forty pounds, bigger than me but it made no difference to my bruised honor. He was holding court in the project parking lot when we screeched up. I jumped out of the car and went after him. I didn't need to say a word. He knew my baby brother had tattled on him. In seconds we were pounding each other, both sides of friends taunting the other.

As we went at it, Butchie's girlfriend leapt from behind and straddled my back. She sunk her fingers deep into my neck and tore off my regulation 1970's gold chain as I staggered to keep my balance. Butchie took the opportunity to land two good punches before I managed to toss her off.

Two of his Charlestown buddies joined in and I managed to knock them both out (Goddamn it, I was grunting to myself, don't tell me I can't fight!) but Butchie was another story. He wouldn't go down.

One of the guys on the ground didn't stay there. He came up with a knife in his hand and lashed out at the body closest to him, ramming the blade. It tore easily into Leo's back, just above his kidney.

As the knife slid out blood spurted in a huge arc; that familiar smell immediately sickeningly sweet. Leo fell to the pavement, his hand grabbing at his back. I forgot all about Butchie and reached for the knife. It sliced my hand open but its owner and I danced a moment as I gripped at the handle. I yanked as it gave way, tearing bits of my skin as I pulled.

"Lemme give it back to you, motherfucker!" I was screaming as I raised the blade.

The very wise Jackie grabbed and twisted my hand, releasing the knife. He snatched it off the ground and tossed it high into the air, toward the roof of the projects. It spun end over and I remember staring as it rotated in the sky. It landed on the roof with a clatter.

Tommy pulled a bat out of the car and tossed it to me. He held the offender down while I hit him. But my rage was distracted. I had the feeling I'd forgotten something important that was nagging at the edges of my brain, like an irritating itch.

Then I remembered Leo.

On the ground, my younger brother (they were all my younger brothers) had an arm twisted behind him, eyes squeezed tight. Blood was pooling underneath him.

"Bobby," his voice was a quiet, desperate panic. "I'm bleeding bad."

This was bad. Real bad. The opposing team scattered. We loaded Leo into the car and Tommy, who was always the best driver, tore off for the hospital. He ran the lights and weaved in and out of traffic as I pressed my hands hard against Leo's wound.

"Am I gonna die?" Leo asked as Tommy jumped a curb turning a corner.

Blood was all over both of us, mixed with that post-fight sweat and now fear.

"Not unless someone tries to cut Tommy off," was all I could think of to say.

At Mass General, I slid out from under Leo and banged through the emergency room doors. My white uniform was stained with grass and blood, my hand dripping a trail behind me. I didn't stop until I hit the desk.

"Please!" I howled at the nurse. "My brother...stabbed...needs a doctor."

She grabbed two orderlies and they rushed to the car with a stretcher. As they wheeled Leo by, I heard him say weakly, to no one in particular, "You should see the other five guys..."

One orderly shook his head. "You fuckin' Somerville guys."

I stood watching my little brother get smaller and smaller as he was rolled down the hall. I was dripping red steadily and when I raised my hand to wipe the sweat off my forehead, I smelled that smell, saw the blood. I better sit down, I thought.

The next thing I knew, I was being stitched up.

Afterward, I sat in a small uncomfortable plastic chair in the waiting room as the surgeon tended to my brother and had a weird feeling of déjà vu. It was barely a year since I'd been in this same room, waiting for another surgeon to work on a different guy. Young Howie, Howie's son.

It was Bunker Hill Day, actually a legal holiday in Boston. Banks close, union shops shut down. We take the commemoration of the battle that kicked off America's fight for independence seriously. I once worked on a movie with producers who were shocked to realize they had to pay double time in order to get the crew to come to work on Bunker Hill Day. It was in the Teamster contract.

We're also big parade fans; we'll parade for anything, but the Bunker Hill Day Parade pales only in comparison to St. Paddy's. Young Howie and I bit the bullet and with a couple of buddies crossed out of Somerville and into Charlestown — the location of the parade that year.

We were hanging on the corner, joking and looking at the girls in short skirts march by when some idiot out of the Charlestown crowd pointed a finger at me. "Hey, you!"

I pointed at myself, "What, me?"

He pushed forward through the revelers.

"*Yeah, you. What the fuck ya doin' here? You're one of them Somerville assholes!*"

I spread my hands. "*We don't want trouble, we're just watchin' the parade.*"

He came toward me, picking up speed. "*You ain't watchin' no parade in Charlestown!*"

A fist came up and he threw a punch at me; but I knocked him out and we disappeared into the crowd, laughing at the audacity of the kid. We walked a half block and Young Howie was still grinning when suddenly he arched his back and pitched forward awkwardly. Apparently my punch had no long-lasting effects, as the Charlestown kid recovered to follow us and jab-stab who he thought was me. As the sidewalk turned red, the sticker slipped back into the crowd.

It resulted in another high-speed blast to the stitch factory wheeling around the blocked-off streets of the parade route. Young Howie survived that fight and as I sat waiting for Leo, I hoped God gave me one more pass.

Leo almost died during the night. They stitched him but missed his insides continuing to bleed. By early morning he was back in surgery and the second time was a charm. And I didn't make it in to work that day, although I did get a call from some poor sucker looking for his car. Eddie had borrowed it.

The guy I hit with the baseball bat went to the hospital too, but he walked out the same night. So high on angel dust, he didn't feel a thing and had no idea what had happened.

After Leo was released, the incident was forgotten. Maybe not forgotten, but we didn't talk about revenge or what ifs. Except for our scars, it was as if it never happened.

I was too ashamed for thoughts of revenge. Because of my pride, because I couldn't bear anyone thinking I wasn't the toughest bastard in Somerville; I almost caused the death of my brother. It was a stupid mistake and I've never forgotten it; never again allowed myself to be suckered into a physical altercation because of pride. Over the years tougher guys than Butchie have tried but I don't bite. Sticks and stones just like they told you in school.

There is another reason besides shame that people make the decision to forgo revenge, although seldom does someone choose this route. Blind anger is such an immediate and visceral reaction that it is almost impossible to forecast the domino effect of revenge wreaked. Almost, but not always. Howie Winter falls into that category.

Howie lets out a breath out and nods as I finish telling my stories. "I remember both of those incidents. I was stabbed too, very badly and I almost died."

1968. Howie, Brian Halloran, and Buddy McLean's son Jimmy were at an after hours bar in the North End. Jimmy McLean was walking a tightrope of borderline bad temper since the death of his father, but Howie overlooked what, in Somerville, was considered an idiosyncrasy. He'd loved Buddy like a brother and subsequently his son as a nephew. After a few drinks, Jimmy began arguing with another patron. The word exchange quickly turned to blows.

"So," Howie recalls, "I tried to break it up. Then I felt something in my back, like a stick. I felt it through my clothes," Howie grimaces, a hand to his back, remembering. "It was almost numb, a numbing wetness."

As was and still is the custom in many neighborhood joints, no one called the police; instead the combatants scattered at the sight of first blood. Brian and Jimmy loaded Howie into the car and retired to his house.

There, "due to the lateness of the hour and varying levels of alcohol," after slapping some perfunctory dressing on Howie's back, everyone went to bed.

In the morning Brian managed to pull himself out of sleep and knocked on Howie's bedroom door. When there was no response, Brian entered and found his friend unresponsive and breathing shallowly, the bedclothes soaked in blood.

"Brian told me that I had a gray pallor," Howie says. "The color of cement," he kept saying, "and that I was breathing funny."

Brian must have felt the first waves of a rising panic. He called a nurse he once dated and wheedled his way into a house call. When she arrived, the girl took one look at Howie, turned to Brian and said, "You need to get to the hospital. He's in a coma. This guy is dying."

The emergency room doctor immediately took Howie into surgery.

"They said I was in a coma but I heard everything Brian said when he walked into the bedroom. I heard him saying that I looked like the sidewalk on Marshall Street, gray like cement. I remember seeing him, Jimmy, and the nurse in the room. But I saw myself too, on the bed." Howie laughs a little laugh, almost shyly. "It was an out of body experience."

"I was never a believer in stories about people going toward a light and then being pulled back. But I did see the room and the people and myself. It was as if I were looking down at an angle while the nurse kept saying 'He's dying, he's dying.' And I remember saying 'Hey! I can hear you. I can see you!' And being very frustrated. But I also remember that it wasn't so bad, and I was smiling to myself that they all thought I was dying. It was all very calm. Since that day, I have never been afraid of death. Never."

The surgery stabilized Howie and he awoke to a priest by his bedside.

"Jaysus! Howie! Ya might be dyin'! Come on, who tried to kill ya? The Good Lord wants to know!"

Howie grins. "Now, this guy didn't talk like any priest I ever knew."

Maybe he was a Protestant, I think, and then ask, "What kind of priest did he talk like?"

"The kind that's a cop dressed as a priest! They put the vestments on a cop and sent him in there to see what they could find out."

Once again, the era of the Gang Wars had not quite come to a close and if Howie Winter was going to be added to the body count, that only meant that things were heating up again for Boston's cadre of exhausted cops. Better well-informed than sorry.

"What did you say?" I ask Howie.

"I said, very seriously, 'I think it was Ray Gleason.'"

Both Howie and I burst into laughter. Ray Gleason was the Deputy Chief of the Somerville Police Department and "a really good guy." Howie winks. "Obviously not the culprit."

The masquerading holy man threw a half-assed prayer in Howie's direction and quickly departed. Within a few hours, Howie's wound was cleaned, closed and dressed.

"They wanted me to stay, but I had been lucky enough. Better just to get on home."

There were still a few stragglers with scores to settle and happy to ride the tail end of murder with no repercussions except a headline in the local paper that might say "Boston Irish Continue To Exterminate Their Own." Home was still the safest location.

"Too many years of looking over my shoulder. I didn't know who'd tried to kill me. If it was just another customer, or someone...else."

At the Somerville Police Station, Ray Gleason was surprised to discover two plain clothed Boston cops approach his desk, badges in hand.

"Ray Gleason?" the first one asked.

"Boston P.D.," the second said loudly.

Ray looked at the badges. "Wow," he drawled, "All the way in from Boston! What can I help you gentlemen with?"

"Investigatin' an attempted homicide," the second cop boomed. Ray knew the tone. Fucking Boston guys always thought they were FBI.

Both plainclothes guys scanned the room, looking for an audience. "We've come from the hospital seeing Howie Winter. He was stabbed, ya know," said the second.

"Howie is gonna be fine, but the thing is — he's named you as his attacker."

That son-of-a-bitch, thought Ray. In the world of practical jokes, Howie was king. Ray struggled to keep from laughing. A couple of other cops wandered over to see what was unfolding.

"That so?" Ray pointed to the sign on his desk. *Deputy Chief.* "That's somethin', huh? Accusing a Deputy Chief of attempted murder."

"Homicide," said the first. "Technically."

"Ya, right," answered Ray. "Sorry."

The second cop shook his head. "Look this is as uncomfortable for us as it is for you, but what we got was pretty much like a deathbed confession."

Ray acted confused. "You just said Howie was fine."

"Yeah, yeah," the second cop nodded. "But when I talked to him, he *thought* he was on his deathbed. It was a deathbed confession."

"It wouldn't have been a deathbed confession, assuming Howie didn't stab himself," Ray reasoned. "So I'm gonna go on the premise that you're talking about a dying declaration."

The cop's face reddened. "Whatever."

"Why did Howie think he was dying?" Ray asked.

The Boston cops both shifted uncomfortably.

"Uh, well, he sort of assumed it when he saw me," the second cop's voice lowered.

"He thought he was dying because he saw a cop?" Ray shook his head. "Howie has seen a helluva lot of cops in his day, I can't believe the sight of you two would make him break a sweat."

There was silence in the room. After a minute or two of giving the rest of the uniforms in the station a chance to gather around, Ray wagged a finger at the lawmen and grinned.

"Oh no, don't tell me! You didn't actually try and pull the old 'cop dressed up like an Irish priest' gimmick, didja? I mean that went out with handlebar moustaches!"

The station burst into laughter. The Boston cops knew they'd been had. They turned on their heels; bellows and hoots at their backs.

"Wait! Wait! Yoo hoo! Fellas!" Ray called after the quickly retreating cops. "Don't ya even wanna check and see if I have an alibi? The station guys fell apart, hysterical with glee to pull one over on the guys from their self-professed "big city."

Ray sat back in his chair and smiled. Fucking Howie. If his old friend hadn't just been released from the hospital, he'd go over and kick his ass.

Brian was howling for revenge and he and Jimmy beat the bushes, hoping to expose the knife wielder. "Brian was a hothead," Howie says. "He'd have liked to go after this guy, his friends, his relatives, the mechanic who fixed his car — he didn't care."

He shakes his head. "I look at things a little differently. When you allow anyone to push you into an instant response, it generally ends up impacting you instead. Brian wasn't patient enough."

Howie got the identity of his assailant through his own contacts. He received a call from the bar owner bookmaker and Anguilo enforcer "Larry Baione" Zannino. Larry was a tough guy suspected of executing Family enemies and was credited with the quote "We'll kill every one of these Irishmen" when asked about certain guys. He was no one to be fucked with. But he was still very loyal to his friends on the Hill. The last thing he wanted was another war. The supply of soldiers was severely depleted and those left were just starting to get back to business.

"When he called I thought he was just checking on me. Everyone knew I'd been hurt. But the call turned out to be something else."

It was an olive branch offered in hopes of staving off further bloodshed.

"Howie," Larry growled. "One of my guys did it. I can't even say how sorry I am. But I swear to God, he didn't know who the hell you were. These fucking guys are always looking to jump into any beef. This guy is scared shitless now that he knows who he stuck."

Sticking, by the way, was the favorite vehicle for the North End boys. Unlike the gun totin' Irish gangs, they enjoyed the up-close-and-personal act of stabbing and were usually quite proficient at it. This time was an anomaly — a rare failure.

"It was just one of these half-assed wiseguys." Howie grins.

"I heard Larry breathing, waiting for an answer. I felt as he did. Who needs another war? There were barely enough guys left to do business as it was. And really, it was just a little barroom brawl."

"Larry," Howie said. "Don't worry about it. I know he didn't know who I was and I'm OK. I won't mention the guy's name to my crew, and if you do the same, we'll be fine."

Baione heaved a gut-sigh of relief. "Done. And thanks, Howie. I owe ya."

Over in the North End, Larry felt his heartbeat slow back to its normal pace. If the incident in 1961 had been settled with a phone call, sixty odd men would still be alive.

1995. Paramount was filming the Stephen King movie Thinner *in Camden Maine and I was working as a Teamster with a friend of mine, Quinny Sullivan.*

We were standing on set one afternoon, chatting with the locals hired to fill in the background of the scene. One guy was dressed as a thug with slicked back hair, playing a gangster or strong-arm man.

"Where you guys from?" He asked.

"Somerville," I replied.

"Ah," he nodded. "I'm from Charlestown."

We're grown men, one would hope we've put childish border issues behind us.

"I once got in a beef with some guys from Somerville, this was years ago."

I smiled. *"Oh yeah, I remember those days."* We all laughed. It seemed like another lifetime. The extra hitched up his pants.

"Hate to have to say this, but I really took care of business. It was Bunker Hill Day back in the seventies and there was this guy who crossed the line into Charlestown…"

Quinny looked at me and I looked right back. What the fuck were the chances of running into the guy who punched me and stabbed Young Howie twenty years ago on a movie set in a tiny Maine town?

The extra told a tale he'd no doubt fashioned in his mind over the years. Nothing about being made unconscious by a crack in the head from the Somerville guy, but instead a story where he single-handedly dropped a gang of disruptive and disrespectful uninvited thugs with just his trusty switchblade.

"I wiped the street with 'em!" he concluded as the assistant director called the background back to the set. *"Sent them pussies all cryin' back to Slumerville, oh excuse me. **Somerville**. Never forgot it. Of course, things were different back then."*

The primal stirrings that swam upward at the word *"pussies"* slipped away when I thought of Howie slipping into a coma, of Young Howie staggering in pain and of my brother Leo sprawled on the pavement in the projects, his blood seeping away. It wasn't worth it.

I smiled tightly and nodded. *"Yeah, pal. It sure was. Hey, it was nice talkin' to you."*

He swaggered away never realizing the guy who knocked him out was the friendly Teamster he'd been chatting with and the kid he'd almost killed was the son of Howie Winter.

Quinny looked at me. *"Gotta say, Bobby. That was remarkable self control on your part."*

I grinned. *"Sticks and stones, Quinny. Sticks and stones."*

CHAPTER FOURTEEN

Minding Your Own Business
The Pointer Post

MY FATHER IS at his favorite stool down the Pointer Post, chain smoking; his baseball bat next to him, the ice pick on the wall, and the shotgun behind the bar. He's contemplating going down to the Somerville Skating Rink on Somerville Ave. It's a cold November night in 1981 and the boxing club is expecting a lot of spectators.

    Big Bob slowly takes a drag, while Hank Williams bawls from the old time jukebox crammed full of single forty-fives. He scratches lottery tickets. On some days, early morning customers walk into the club and see a large trash barrel filled to the top with scratch tickets from my father's constant assault on the Massachusetts State Lottery Commission.

    He was looking for his financial Mr. Goodbar; the life of not wondering where to borrow the next dollar to keep the bar going and friends safe from that terrible outside beyond the confines of his private VFW club. In his mind, it's Utopia. Howie was away; Sal was in the ground. Where could a Somerville guy now go when he got in trouble with a local or — worse yet — an outsider? Protecting the Post, keeping it alive, was his goal, no matter what the cost. Hence the barrel of dead tickets.

It cost him his family life, but that was the price he was willing to pay to keep himself locked up tight in his own castle, safe from the growing evil polluting the city of Somerville.

Right now the Pointer is empty except for him, everyone else is down the skating rink for the biggest local fight of the year. But Big Bob is holding down the fort at the Pointer Post. He decides to stay right where he is.

The Pointer Post was a private veterans club located on Beacon Street. The building was originally constructed in 1915 as a hen shed. By 1932, the small structure was expanded into a slaughterhouse. As the seventies rolled around, however, it had been remodeled and was a popular club.

He used to hang down the Post drinking and socializing with his friends. The Post was his one steadfast loyalty. When he discovered the men running it were fleecing the place, he tossed them out and began operating the club himself.

The Star Market grocery store located directly across the street had a huge parking lot where overflow Post patrons crookedly parked when they slid into the bar after hours. Much to the chagrin of the market's manager, many times there were still cars parked there the next morning.

My father did the shopping for the Post at the market and occasionally ran into Julia Child loading up her own cart. The famous chef's hit show had sprung from an appearance on WGBH, Boston's PBS channel, and even though she was from California, she lived in Boston and most of the local viewers thought of her as a hometown gal. The old man got pretty friendly with her as he had convinced himself he could cook as good as she. He did make a great tripe, prime rib and sauce. They would stroll the aisles of the market together before the rest of the city woke up. He'd carry her bags to her waiting car and was thrilled each time she kissed him on the cheek with her on-air catch phrase "Bon appétit, Robert!" as she sped off.

The bar had only three rooms; the main room running down the middle with a jukebox crammed full of oldies, a poolroom in the back and the Harley Davidson room where Clem Salvi's wall art was showcased. The Harley room boasted tables and chairs, a Harley video game and wall-to-wall Harley décor. The dimensions are important to illustrate the small space that for many years encompassed the night lives of so many and became my father's sole existence. It was, in its time, a living, breathing entity; a small outpost shut off from the rest of the world with its own set of laws run by an Italian-German dictator.

So many of our collective memories are tied to that three-room bar. The place was packed when that 1986 ground ball went through the legs of beleaguered Bill Buckner in Game 6 of the World Series. Now, after the win in 2004 and the lightening strike of '07, all is forgiven. I wish I could have been with the same crew down the Post when the Sox finally took that Series. There is only one night I can recall when things unraveled, despite my father's watch over the club and patrons, and it almost killed both of us.

To understand the personality of a small town New England watering hole, one must forget all about *Cheers*. The Post wore many hats and there was always some kind of *time* (the local vernacular for any kind of party) going on. There were christenings and birthdays, a bash for St. Patty's Day, a full house the night before Thanksgiving. Name the day, there'd be a party in full swing.

It served as a de facto campaign office for local politicians back when they actually mingled with the masses. From drinking and politics to the natural Yankee progression — athletics, the Post was also headquarters for local sports teams. My father sponsored softball, basketball and Little League teams during the 1980's. During the summer weeknights the club overflowed with players, families and fans.

Back when Boston folks disdainfully referred to our city as "Slumerville", our lack of financial resources was made up twofold by the sheer power of athletics. In any small town, or in depressed areas of larger urban cities, athletics are prized even above education. It's a natural path to follow in a neighborhood where you're required to grow up learning to fight and run with a pack — to move into organized sports. It was also a sure fire ticket out. And if all else fails, as adults we sit around talking about it, like the character in Springsteen's lament, *Glory Days*. Instead, I'm writing about it.

To my amazement, my younger brother Leo was a much better athlete than I. My father was at every football game Leo played in high school. Leo was like Larry Czonka of the Miami Dolphins back in the 80's. He had tree trunk legs and a stocky five foot ten muscular body. The opposing players couldn't tackle him one-on-one and he was surely headed to the pros, but his strength and persistence in the field ended up hurting him.

Back then players were still allowed to go "head hunting" — engaging in helmet-to-helmet assaults. During what would prove to be his last game, the first couple of guys couldn't get Leo down. So the third and fourth started leaving their feet and hitting him in mid flight head to head. After the game, Leo complained of a bad headache. When he got up from the couch for some aspirin, his legs collapsed. We had to carry him down the stairs of our house to meet the paramedics.

I followed the ambulance to the hospital in Quincy, the whole time afraid I may run out of gas. It seems I've spent a good deal of my life chasing ambulances carrying my family members as they speed through the streets toward doctors. To this day if the needle on my truck gauge is close to "E", I always get a picture in my mind of red flashing lights ahead of me and the fear that I won't be able to keep up.

In the emergency room the admitting nurse tersely asked my mother if Leo were on drugs while he lay, semi-conscious, on a stretcher.

My mother became so angry she was shaking. "My son is NOT on drugs, get him into a room and find out what is wrong with him NOW!"

Leo was diagnosed with a cerebral concussion, a bruising of the brain tissue. For young athletes, it is one of the worse concussions because the doctors immediately ban them from all contact sports. Leo was broken hearted, as was the entire family. He was the shining hope for someone in the Martini family to make it big in pro sports. It didn't happen.

Howie, my father and a few other boys from the Hill were always in the bleachers when I played high school football alongside with Howie's sons Gary and Young Howie. The men loved to come see us play (even though I was terrible.) They were parents who wanted to see their sons channel aggression and testosterone toward something more positive than fighting and killing each other. We still fought but we didn't kill each other. Boxing was one of the reasons.

The Somerville Boxing Club was the informal home of the former professional light heavyweight champion of New England Bobby Covino. Bobby was champ from '68 to '70. One of the toughest men to ever stroll the streets of Somerville, and today in his sixties he's still a force to be reckoned with. Bobby and his family lived on the first floor of our family home at 118 Hudson Street in the late 60's. I saw him all over the city growing up; the neighborhood kids were in awe of him.

In the winter of 1981, the boxing club was putting on a show that would consist of eight fights. The guys on the card were all pretty good fighters and some of them went on to fight professionally, like Franco DiOrio, a welterweight with balls of iron. A good and exciting club fighter, but a kid that just couldn't get a break in life. I used to love to watch him box.

Jack DeBennedetto was a heavyweight from Cambridge, undefeated at an awesome 12 and 0. He was fighting an opponent who never had an amateur match in his life and this was a match that was being talked about all across Somerville. It was a kid who after having a couple of hundred street and barroom brawls, decided at the old age of twenty-eight to try and channel his aggression into the ring.

Bobby handpicked the kid after he impulsively jumped into the ring with the former pro and fought three rounds of punching toe to toe only to get hit after the bell rang in the second round. Bobby looked down at the kid and said, "You got balls, but no form. Lesson one, if you wanna box, never put your hand down until you get to your friendly corner, even after the bell rings."

The used car lot was also a good source of boxing information. A customer reported that he saw Covino fighting some Mick from Southie and what a fight it was. The guys dutifully reported the latest local fight news with the details of Covino's Southie sparring partner to me.

I listened patiently and finally said, "One, the kid wasn't from Southie, he's from Somerville. Two, he wasn't just *some* Mick, that was me!"

I'm Italian, Irish, and German, but my facial features are Irish and that's what the customer must have seen; my Irish face and the generally accepted assumption that all Irish came from South Boston.

"Oh Jesus, Bobby!" one of my friends said. "What did ya do that for?"

I shrugged. "I dunno; I'm a pretty good fighter. I thought I'd try boxing."

He shook his head. My friends apparently knew that there was a major difference between street brawling and boxing but were polite enough to keep it to themselves since I obviously didn't.

"Well, ya should have started that a lot earlier in life but I wish ya the best."

They were probably laughing their asses off deep down inside. I didn't care. I wanted to give it a try and I had the advantage of Bobby Covino agreeing to let me take my shot.

I trained with him for four months and sparred with guys who punched my head almost off my shoulders every day. I used to ask Bobby when I would be able to get some hits on them.

"Be patient, kid, it'll come."

At the end of the fourth month, I was visiting Bobby and his wife Greta. There was some news. He told me that the boxing club was putting on a show and asked if I would like to fight. This was a major compliment to a street kid like me; I was over the top excited.

"There's only one drawback, though," he warned. "You're gonna have to fight the New England heavyweight champ with a record of 12 and 0."

I must have already taken too many hits to the head.

"All right, no problem."

Greta was less than enthusiastic. A long time friend of my family, she was also very protective. She knew that in Somerville every male thought he was a tough guy and every tough guy figured his street experience gave him a leg up. What the fuck could the pros possibly know that we didn't?

"You're crazy. You could get hurt, Bobby. I think you should reconsider," she warned. She was wasting her time. My ears had essentially shut down every time anyone suggested that boxing and me were not going to be the perfect match.

The word spread fast in our small burg and my crazy new pseudo career choice generated a lot of talk. This was sure to be an interesting fight and none of the locals, especially guys I had beat the shit out of before, wanted to miss it.

The night of the fight, I was ready. I would win. There was nothing that would throw me off my game. I had trained for this and I...was...ready. I walked into the skating rink to see three thousand spectators. Most of them coming to see me fight in my debut for various reasons. I stood behind Jack DeBennedetto, waiting to get weighed in and I said, "Hey, how's it going?" He had to be as excited as I was! Jack looked back at me like I had killed his mother.

As the first round was about to start, Bobby was in my corner.

"Listen to me now. Jack's been bad mouthing you, calling you a dirty guinea bastard and a fag."

Huh? One guinea's calling me a guinea? Oh, OK, I'm supposed to get all wound up and blood mad. So I tried. Then I looked across the ring.

DeBennedetto was six foot two, nineteen years old and sculptured out of granite muscle on muscle. I winced inside — what the fuck was *I* doing here? The bell rang and I was shoved into the ring. Inside, I was trying to catch my breath; outside I was trying to mount a scary guinea and/or Irish mask of cold steel. I lined up my opponent and was instantly hit with a barrage of left and rights smashing in from both sides.

I was trying to hit him back but his boxing experience was slicing through me, my inexperience was showing tragically. He cracked me in the side of the head so hard I backed up into the corner and my right hand dropped to my side. Jack completely numbed my whole arm with one punch. I charged back in and danced around him until enough time passed for the feeling to come back. I was able to put my right arm back up, offering myself some protection from his nonstop deadly onslaught.

Mercifully, the round ended and I staggered back to my stool, collapsing and panting. Bobby was waiting for me with another pep talk.

"You're doing great, kid! Keep it up!"

"HUH?"

I know I had a completely bewildered look on my face.

"What fucking fight are you watching, Covino? Jack's killing me!!!"

He couldn't argue with that.

"Look, Bobby, when he throws his left jab he drops it and that's when you're going to hit him with an overhand right."

I checked my right arm to make sure it was still attached to my body and would work if called upon. I was now unsure if I even wanted to get back in the ring with that animal.

Round two sounded and I didn't have a chance to balk. I went back in, waiting for the first jab to come my way. It did and I came across with an overhand right. To my own shock (and probably everyone else's) I caught him and knocked him back a couple of feet. Blood ran down his face.

My God, I hit him and I liked it! There might just be a chance I could beat this monster. Jack came at me again and I went after him like a wild animal.

I was pretty full of myself but Round three would be a different story. Jack was pissed by now and came at me in a full barrage of haymaking lefts and rights. I aped him and did the same, because after the last round all things seemed possible. We punched at each other non-stop for the entire three minutes. I could hear an amazing sound rising from the stands. It started slow and then thousand spectators were screaming and yelling "Bobby! Bobby! Bobby!"

The newspaper would repeat it in the next day's issue, a great article about the fight between Jack and myself.

We were so intent on our fists it seemed the round would never end. Finally that bell rang. Jack and I hugged briefly and I started over to my corner.

Bobby Covino was screaming, "You won! Bobby you won the fight!"

My head was going back and forth. It didn't seem possible and nor did I care right then. I was beat up pretty good. Even seeing the screaming crowd full of all the boys from Winter Hill and my friends from Somerville had little effect on me. Jack and I limped back to the middle of the ring and the ref held both of our gloves.

"The winner by decision in the blue corner — Bobby Martini!"

The place went crazy. Jack hugged me with a bewildered look on his face. He really thought he'd beaten me. Truthfully I believe he might have won if the fight had been somewhere other than Somerville. But tonight it wasn't.

I signed a few autographs for some kids. My brother Jimmy hugged and kissed me enthusiastically, even though he himself had been on the receiving end of me more than a time or two. The scene was surreal and hard for me to really appreciate.

My father was nowhere in sight.

I painfully got dressed and started over to the Post for the after party. I had a huge blackening eye and a swollen face. When I walked in, my father looked up from the bar and said tersely, "Go in the back and put a piece of steak over your eye for the swelling."

And that was all he ever said to me about the fight.

I had just beaten the heavyweight champion of New England in my first amateur fight and he sent me for steak.

"OK," I said.

Within moments Covino and the rest of the crew came bursting through the door all talking at once. Every one of them told my old man how great I'd done and gave me more accolades than I deserved. Some tempered their compliments by pronouncing me a pussy for sitting with the steak over my eye, but I didn't care. I could barely move my busted up body.

The old man later told his friends he didn't go to the fight because he didn't want to see me get hit.

I may have believed that then, but I'm a bit wiser now. In many ways, my father felt that his tough guy mantle was slipping and I think it angered him that I was the willing recipient of the newly available title. It was me getting older and him just getting old. Later on, he'd taunt me to come after him, to fight it out — whatever *it* was in his mind. I never hit him back, much as I fucking wanted to.

I became good friends with my nemesis Jack and years later I'd be in his corner at a fight with one huge maniac in Maine. Jack won the Golden Gloves that year along with the New England heavyweight championship. I fought three more times that year and was due to fight Jack in the championship match at Freeport Hall in Dorchester. Then I pulled my neck out sparring at the Somerville Boxing Club.

I was heartbroken.

I would never get to fight again. Bobby Covino came by the day after the cancelled fight and gave me the second place ribbon. His eyes were sad for me. It hurt him that I had gone through all this pain and suffering and now I could only lie on the couch, unable to move due to the neck injury.

I'm a believer that everything is done for a reason. I have eight screws in my neck from past injuries. If I'd tried to fight Jack that day I don't know if I'd be able to walk today.

Hell, I got the chance to do what millions of young guys can only dream about, so I can't complain.

Somerville was a highly competitive town when it came to sports and more competitive when it came to partying after the games. No times were more raucous than the bachelor bashes where hired girls put on quite a show until way past the time the doors should have been locked.

Yet despite the hundreds of long loud party nights, the buddies, brawls and even the women, the clearest memories that still stick in my mind are those of my father, his friends and mine, and me boozing it up, sweating our balls off and singing loudly and off key to all the oldies in that private jukebox.

There were always lines of people waiting on the sidewalk to get in. The cops were rarely called due to his relationship with the department. If they were in evidence, it was generally because they were visiting. In fact, the Post was the place to go if anyone wanted an audience with him. It was also a clandestine meeting spot for attendees in those professions requiring secrecy and discretion.

Howie's incarceration, Sal's murder, the scattering of the original Winter Hill Gang; all the cornerstones that were part of Somerville's foundation were gone. Except for the man at the Pointer Post.

The Boston Globe
May 1, 1980
NEWS IN BRIEF/SOMERVILLE
JOGGER WOUNDED

A 45-year-old Somerville man was shot and wounded yesterday morning while jogging down Beacon St. in Somerville. Robert V. Martini Sr., of 118 Hudson Street, told police he was jogging around 6 a.m. when a 25- to 30-year-old man wearing blue jeans and a denim jacket approached him and asked for money. Martini was shot after he told the man he didn't have any money, Somerville police said. Martini was listed in good condition in Cambridge Hospital yesterday following surgery to remove the bullet.

Not *everything* that you read in the paper about Somerville, Winter Hill, Howie and the rest of us is true. This is a prime example. What was reported was not what really happened at that little non-descript club that functioned as the center of Somerville in the post-Howie era.

I'd been drinking for a couple of days with Brian Halloran when we hit the Post. My father was holding court at the end of the bar. He looked up as we entered and grumbled the same thing he always said. "What the fuck are you doing, coming in here with a strange package on?"

That meant that we had been drinking somewhere else — an insult. The old man wanted everyone to drink in *his* place. It wasn't a matter of money; it was simply for safety. No matter how much his boys drank, if they were in the Post, he could keep them safe from the dangerous and deadly outside world.

He could also keep an eye on what we were up to. He had a sign on the wall, "what you see here, what you hear here, what you do here, leave here." My father was the precursor to "What happens in Vegas." It wasn't exactly true, though. He'd watch everything with an eagle eye, saying nothing, but later on torture my brothers and me with the ugly details of our bad behavior.

Big Bob had one of the longest barred lists in the city. Any minor infraction gained you a place on the list guaranteeing an indeterminate amount of strange loads for an undisclosed period of time. Everyone had been barred at least once, but I was usually at the top of the list.

"I loved your old man, he was a very good guy," Willy Cellata says. "Very charitable, he'd do anything for anybody. He was with you when he had money, and he was also there when you didn't. But the funny thing is that he was the most unbelievable guy when it came to his relationships. One minute, he'd love you, the next…"

"You're barred!" we both say at the exact same time, laughing.

Willy smiles ruefully. "Oh yeah or worse yet — the silent treatment. He'd look right through you and not speak. You had no idea why. But this I gotta say, I miss him."

My father's plumber friend Paul Martins howls with laughter when reminded of the barring process.

"Your old man always talked to me about life and he didn't much care if I agreed with him or not. When I was about to get married, he said 'Paul, don't do it. She's gonna ruin your life.' I told him he was crazy. Bob just shook his head. 'Don't do it, she's always askin' for money.'"

Paul roars as he remembers my father's marital advice. "I listened and then I said, 'Bob, what are you talking about she's always asking for money? You're the only one who asks me for money!'"

He was barred but the old man liked him and wasn't about to lose a good source for extra lottery ticket cash, so the plumber was soon back on the approved list.

My father left every evening at ten and returned at closing before dawn. What he did in between was a mystery. He was seldom at the home he shared with his longtime girlfriend, or at my mother's house; even though she was still his wife, but he returned like Dracula just before the sun rose.

The patrons watched the clock and when the night waned, one of them always announced, "Let's get out of here, he's on his way!" The moveable drunk continued at another location as Bob spent hours cleaning from room to room, listening to music at full volume and smoking.

That night Brian and I were shooting pool, telling the same old war stories and working the room. Part of every evening's activities was to wander from corner to corner, checking out the other patrons and avoiding anyone with who you had a beef.

The regulars were there. Gary O'Brien was tending bar. Old friends Michael McCarthy and Ibby Alewood were tossing back drinks. It was business as usual.

I made my rounds and as I stumbled around the corner, I saw my father arguing with Jimmy Hackett at the bar. I felt the hair on the back of my neck stand up. Jimmy was a dangerous kid. He and a local guy had robbed the Hilltop Steakhouse in Saugus and murdered a security guard for no reason. Hackett also had the attempted murder of a police officer under his belt.

I approached my father and waited a couple of minutes, blearily listening to the argument as anger sawed through alcohol. My temper swam up to the top of all that booze. Who the fuck was Hackett to start shit with *my* father in *his own* place? Finally I shoved myself between them and confronted Hackett. "What the fuck is your problem?"

Hackett turned to me and laughed. "Go fuck yourself."

Or he started to say, "Go fuck yourself" because just as he got the "Fu..." started, I knocked him out. Back then I never let anyone get to that next word, and in Somerville that word was usually "yourself." I always tried to time it so I got them in the middle of "fuck." It makes for a nice punctuation as fist cracks against teeth. I broke Hackett's jaw.

After Hackett hit the floor, his friend Sullivan thought it prudent to depart. Sully was a local tough guy as well, and no one I wanted to mess with unless I had to, so it was a relief when he dragged Hackett away. Unfortunately, my old man wasn't satisfied with my stellar knockout. I'd beat him to the punch, literally. Convinced the guys would be back to settle the score, he grabbed a steak knife and stomped out the door. Brian and I followed, begging him to come back.

"That knife won't do you any good if they bring guns. Let's just get a drink."

An offer of a drink was usually a sure fire way to divert anyone's attention.

"Shut the fuck up!"

And so it went, back and forth for close to an hour. We finally convinced him to come inside as Michael shut and locked the door. Time passed, liquor flowed and the incident was forgotten until someone banged on the door. Without thinking, Michael opened it only to be met with a shotgun to his head wielded by an angry Sully. Hackett darted past his partner; automatic pistol drawn with one thing on his mind. To kill me, my old man, and whoever else got in the way. In his enthusiasm for blood, he inadvertently slammed the door behind him, locking Sully and Michael outside.

My father rushed forward as Hackett aimed and pulled the trigger. He grabbed the barrel, pushing Hackett back. I heard a deafening crack. Big Bob looked down and realized the bullet blasted straight through his hand. Blood spread in a bloom across his front. The room froze and spun for a moment.

The old man took off toward the door that led out to backyard. I ducked behind the bar as I watched my father go faster than I'd seen him move in my life.

Hackett tried to get a shot off at Gary who was hurtling full liquor bottles from behind the bar. He kept yanking the trigger as glassware flew, but my old man had jammed the automatic slider. All Hackett had to do was clear the chamber. Thank God for drug abuse.

All of this was happening in slow motion, even though it was just a matter of minutes. Ibby tackled the fumbling Hackett to the ground. Brian was under the pool table during the entire melee with a pistol in his pocket, seemingly trying to get up. Brian should have gotten up sooner, moved faster, seeing he was the only one in the place armed besides Hackett but it didn't happen.

I was blinded by testosterone, anger, and a surprising lack of self-preservation. I threw myself on top of Hackett, pounding the hell out of him. As we rolled toward the front door Hackett shook me loose and shoved the door open. He heaved himself into the darkness, but I wasn't going to let him get away.

Or maybe I was.

Sully was standing in the entryway, both barrels pointed at my head. I slammed the door.

The blast of both barrels reverberated against the heavy solid oak, one of my father's paranoid defenses against the outside world of strange packages. I was staring right at it, the spot where the spray of bullets should have torn through the wood and into my skull. Behind me, the place was in turmoil. I swayed on my feet, slick with sick sweat, bile swimming up into my mouth, still staring at the door.

"Bobby!" Ibby yelled at me. "Where's your father?"

"Huh?" I grunted.

Where's my father? Where *is* my father? Michael banged on the door, announcing the coast was clear. I yanked it open and the bar emptied as we fanned out looking for the old man. We found him around the corner on the ground. He had jumped the ten-foot fence, shattered his ankle, and was already complaining.

"Don't just stand there like a couple of dumb fucks! Help me!"

"There's my father," I said sluggishly, to no one in particular as I slid down inside myself.

"And there's a fuckin' genius!" He shot back as he shook his head disgustedly. "What's the matter with him?" He jerked a thumb toward me.

Michael bent over him. "You need to stay put for the medics, is there anything I can do for ya?"

My father guffawed. "Let's see, you opened the door and let the prick back in so, no. I'd say you've done enough already."

We waited in silence for the ambulance. As moments ticked by, I smelled the blood soaking my father's clothing. I had a dizzying thought — the little wooden building that had at one time been a slaughterhouse narrowly missed returning to its former self. My vision blurred as I fought against vomit rising and the sirens grew louder. I followed the paramedics as the rest of the patrons wisely scattered.

At the hospital, I tried to follow my father into the operating room, but the nurses kept me out. Through the small window I caught a glimpse of him prone on the table, his face pale, eyes closed, while white-coated men and women worked around him.

It was my fault. I did this. My old man may die, I could have been killed, and seven or eight guys would have gone with me, all because I didn't keep my mouth shut, wouldn't allow my father to handle a situation he probably would more successfully than I.

I was overwhelmed and exhausted from days of drinking and partying and pushing myself closer and closer toward a place I knew I should never go.

All I wanted was to get into that room, to say I was sorry. I must have been raising hell as the next thing I knew I had company. A huge security guard took me by the arm. I twisted around and stared at him with two-day eyes. My first instinct was to knock him out but instead I found myself begging.

"I gotta get in there with my father, he's been shot."

Then I did something very un-Somerville-like. I broke down, bawling against the big man's chest, babbling incoherently about things I've never been able to remember. I was both delirious and disgusted in myself.

The guard treated me with sensitivity and dignity. He hugged me while I cried and helped me into the waiting room, promising to return when there was news.

When I finally walked into the room the next morning, he slowly opened his eyes and stared at me. "Jesus Christ! You look like shit, what happened to ya?"

"The same thing I read in the paper about another guy. I was jogging by the Post and some thug held me up."

He snorted out a laugh and immediately put a hand to his stomach. "Stop it!" He winced. He still had the bullet in his belly.

I sort of hovered over him. "Does it hurt bad?"

He shook his head. "No, it don't hurt at all, because my ankle is killin' me!"

Although he'd been shot, the bullet still in his stomach, the real pain was in his ankle. At 5'8", he weighed around two hundred and sixty pounds. When he vaulted the fence, the middle-aged superhero came down on that ankle, shattering it. He never once complained about the bullet that should have killed him, but God, did he bitch about the ankle! It bothered him up until his death in 1993.

He was unconcerned about sending over someone to protect him. "Aw, don't worry about it."

But I did.

Once I knew my father wasn't going to die — at least not from this — I went down the Somerville Police Department to get some relief. I was sick to my stomach, sure that Hackett and his partner would come back to finish the job. Maybe I didn't go about it in the best way or in the best condition.

I'd been up all night walking in circles, impotent with fury, sick sweat pouring off me. The adrenaline was burning up my nerve endings and my heart was pounding so fast I was sure everyone else could hear it. I pushed past the other cops and right into the chief's office.

Chief Arthur J. Pino wasn't exactly thrilled to see me. He was the acting chief in Somerville at the time. Chief Thomas O'Brien had recently retired and Pino was installed in his place until the civil service exams were scheduled and the city chose a permanent head of the police department. Pino was more concerned with boning up for the test than dealing with the contingent from the Pointer Post.

"Chief, my father is in the hospital. He's all alone, someone tried to kill him."

Pino looked up from his desk and stared at me, expressionless, while I continued with my rant.

He held up a hand to shut me up. "What exactly do you want me to do, Martini?"

I hesitated, fumbling. "What do you mean what do I want you to do? I want you to protect my father, put someone on him at the hospital, you know, in case..." My voice faltered. Was he stupid, this guy?

"You mean in case the guy who asked him for money on the street tracks him all the way down to his hospital bed and tries again?"

I was silent. And surprised. The Somerville cops were friends of my father's, why was Pino acting as if the shooting were no big deal? He knew what had really happened, there weren't many secrets in Somerville. As much as my father was respected, Hackett was feared. He'd shot a cop, for Christ's sake, even though he had managed to elude prosecution. Pino also knew that in this city, there would be no further details forthcoming. If my old man said he was shot on the street, he was shot the street. I wasn't asking for justice, just protection. The Chief knew that as well.

"How about telling me what really happened?"

I could feel rage nipping at the end of those nerves like a fuse and I struggled to keep it down.

"My father was jogging down by the Post and ..."

Pino snorted. "Yeah, yeah, and a thirty year old guy, hmm — how old are you anyway? Late twenties or so? And wearing dungarees — kinda like the ones you got on now — and a denim jacket — shot him. Give it a rest, Martini, you're a fuckin' liar. I ain't putting shit on your old man until someone tells me the truth."

I was sure I could smell smoke somewhere in my mind as I exploded.

"Listen to me, motherfucker! If anything, anything at all, happens to my father while he's in the hospital, it's on you're head. I'm coming after you!"

I don't remember if I was yelling. I couldn't even hear myself. I was deaf with anger, focused on not being able to take care of even one simple thing for my father.

Pino yanked himself up out of the chair so hard it banged against the wall.

"Get the FUCK out of my office right now, Martini! If you ever, ever fuckin' threaten me again, I'll have you locked up for fuckin' ever!"

Maybe he should have arrested me but he didn't bother, as he was preoccupied with events brewing in his own life. But maybe he also could have had just a bit of sympathy.

At any rate, six years later Pino would be in prison and I would have just as much compassion for him as he did for me on that morning.

After that visit I went and found Brian. He was brooding alone at the end of a long dark bar when I stumbled in off the street.

"Bobby," he said. I followed the voice as my eyes adjusted. "You look like shit."

"Thanks a fuckin' lot, I need..."

Brian got up. "Yeah, yeah. I know. I was just waitin' for Hurley. Let's go get them bastards."

John Hurley was a friend of ours from Charlestown. He was heavy into supporting the IRA and every year he dropped off fundraiser tickets for my father to sell. Big Bob didn't give a shit about the IRA, he was more interested in his own small province, but John was his friend, and a childhood pal of Buddy McLean, so he sold the tickets faithfully. John was ready to avenge my father.

That night he picked us up in a hotbox, Irish-armed with plenty of firepower. Brian was next to him. The fourth man asked I not use his name, so I won't. He and I got in the back next to a bag of clothes.

"Who are the clothes for?" I asked.

"You," John said grimly.

The plan was to crawl the local bars until we located Hackett and Sullivan. Once we made them, we'd casually leave. I'd change clothes outside (because you have to have a disguise in Somerville) and go back into the bar alone.

"You take this with you," Brian held up a handgun with the grip taped. "You shoot 'em both, drop the gun and walk out."

I stared at the gun. "You mean like in The..."

"Yeah, yeah," Brian grumbled. "Like the guineas in *The Godfather*, but we did it first."

I wasn't sure if Brian meant we the Irish or we the guys from Somerville. It didn't matter.

"The gun is taped so there's no prints," he finished.

"Ya, OK, Clemenza," John cracked. "We all seen the movie, he's got it."

Brian turned and stared straight at me. "This ain't no movie, Bobby. This is your responsibility. This is your *right*. You gotta make 'em pay for what they did," my brother-in-law insisted.

They had tried to kill my father. I think I was still in shock, shut down.

"OK, Brian."

I was as cold as any screen killer; no way I would fuck up. I just wanted it done. Or thought I did.

We started at one end of the city and worked our way down. I was shaking with fury as we entered the first bar. The crowd was thick and the sight of the four of us parted the alcoholic Red Sea. This was Somerville, again no secrets. All four of us pumped with adrenaline and looking deadly meant something was going to happen. Patrons wouldn't look us in the eye so they'd never have to admit they recognized us and turned their backs quickly so they wouldn't see anything else. It was surreal and morbid when I think about it today. Everyone understood that an individual was about to take a beating or worse, but they simply moved away and kept on drinking.

It was the same everywhere, bar after bar. No Hackett, No Sully, no retribution. We branched out from Somerville into the suburbs and spent a week driving around the state. Brian got leads and like the faithful, we followed, but we never found them.

As a man, I've learned a few things, grown to understand the motivation in adults I didn't recognize when I was young, but I have never been able to reconcile the fact that my own father flew past me in the Post that night after he was shot. I get it. I mean I understand what happened. In a split second, a decision has to be made and fight or flight kicks in. What was he thinking — was he trying to lure Hackett away from the rest of us? I never asked him because he was my father.

And Brian Halloran, my brother-in-law, hiding under the table while holding on to the only other gun in the house, I've always wondered about that as well. Was it calculated, an act on his part to absolve himself after the fact, after what could have been a pre-planned mass murder for hire for some unknown reason? I never asked Brian either. Because I didn't really want to know.

The Boston Globe

April 13, 1980

HIS OWN PISTOL ACCIDENTALLY KILLS\ TAVERN MANAGER

The manager of a popular Boston waterfront tavern was killed yesterday when he dropped his holstered automatic handgun and it accidentally discharged, police said.

Joseph Wagenbach, 42, of 1694 Beacon St., Brookline, was visiting the Veterans of Foreign Wars post on Beacon Street in Somerville at 9:45 a.m. when the accident occurred, police said.

"He went in to drink. He had a few drinks and that's when he went into the men's room," a police spokesman said. "The people heard a muffled sound and then they heard moaning coming from the men's room. When they went in, they saw him bleeding from the leg."

Wagenbach died at 1:55 p.m. following surgery at Cambridge Hospital. Wagenbach, 42, was manager of the Dockside Saloon, 183 State St.

"The holster and gun fell out of his belt. An automatic round was in the chamber and when it hit the deck, the hammer hit," a Somerville detective said. "On this particular automatic — it wasn't a very good one - there wasn't a safety." The bullet traveled through his leg, and stomach and lodged in his heart, police said.

With all the near misses at the Post, one tragic accident sticks in my mind, as it was the result of simple Somerville jackassery gone bad. Brian invited his friend Joe Wagenbach along one night; a nice guy who managed the Dockside outside of Boston's Faneuil Hall.

Joe and Brian were very close, in fact Brian had free run of Joe's Cape Cod home whenever he wanted to take a family vacation.

I had met Joe previously. One night Brian and I were down The Dockside with my childhood friend Michael McInnes. We drank and joked with Joe until early morning. By five a.m. Michael and I had enough and slid out the back door. As we stepped outside, we saw two Boston police officers hovering around my car. This was bad.

I had driven that night. I suddenly remembered our fourth passenger — Brian's forty-five-caliber handgun with the six-inch barrel. It was a huge piece.

"Brian," I said, with one eye on the road and the other on the piece. "What the hell are you gonna do with that? 'Cos I gotta tell ya..."

"I know, I know," Brian muttered. "I wasn't gonna take it in with us."

He might have had it not been for my bringing it up. Brian stashed the gun under my driver's seat as we pulled into the parking lot. Unfortunately for me, he never checked it when he got out. It had slid out from underneath and into plain view.

As Michael and I got closer, one of the cops looked up. In his hand was Brian's big cannon. We both froze, and although we didn't speak, I knew we were both thinking the same thing. Should we run and take our chances or just go forward and see what happened? Both of us knew Brian, therefore we knew that the gun the cop was holding was as hot as...well, a pistol. If they traced it, we'd be in seven kinds of trouble. All I could think was where had the gun been previously and what had it been doing? If Brian had been holding it for any length of time, there was a good chance someone had done something that was now going to land squarely in my lap.

I could say it wasn't mine, I mused in the few seconds it took for us to keep walking. But I wouldn't. I could never tell them whose gun it was. It was the code of our west. After what seemed like an hour I greeted the two officers.

"Hello gentlemen, what's up?"

Both cops looked at me, at the car and then at the gun.

"Is this your car?"

"It is," I agreed.

"Is this your gun?"

"Yes, it is." I was nothing if not amiable. At the same time, I pulled out my gun permit. You have to remember, we'd been inside this bar all night drinking and doing...drinking and now I was talking to two police officers holding what could be a murder weapon they've managed to pull out of my car.

I don't know exactly what I said but it went something like this...

"I just bought this gun today for target practice and I didn't know I was going out. You can see, officers, it's way too big to put inside my pants and I thought I'd hidden it under the seat well enough to keep it out of sight."

Michael was on the other side of the car shitting his pants. I wasn't so well myself. I was doing my best to talk us out of this mess; never in a million years guessing the response I'd get back.

The cop holding the gun glanced at my permit and handed Brian's gun back to me. Neither cop even checked to see if the chamber was loaded.

"OK, there pal, you get yourself back to Somerville and do us a favor, be more careful next time, huh?"

I told the officers thank you very much and Michael and I shakily drove off. After the cops were out of sight, Michael let out a huge sigh.

"What the fuck, how did you pull that off, Bobby?"

Man, I was in just as much shock as he was. "I don't know but at this moment, we have to be two of the luckiest sons-a-bitches God put on the planet."

The next day I saw Brian and as usual, I had to tell him about what he'd almost done. He just laughed and asked for the weapon back, which I was glad to unload. Literally.

He later used that same gun in the attempted robbery of that Boston restaurant by the three stooges, also known as the Gang That Couldn't Rob *Nothing*.

The night Joe tagged along with us, the Post was still hopping by early morning with a dozen or so patrons. The talk turned to debate of individual choices in firearms and my father decided to test the accuracy of each man's gun by the practical method. The old man hung a crude cardboard target on the rug-covered wall and Wagenbach pulled out his weapon.

"What do you guys think? This is a nice looking piece, isn't it?"

He took the first shot and hit the bulls-eye dead center. The noise was deafening. On the other side of the wall was a pizza shop. I don't think my father liked the owner so this exercise may have had a twofold purpose.

My father went next, then Brian and me, and finally everyone took a turn blasting the shredding cardboard. We all turned out to be decent shots. When thirty or so bullets were embedded in the wall, we sat back down and pounded more drinks as the talk turned serious: baseball and women.

We were interrupted by a loud bang from the rear of the club where the men's room was located. Every single guy jumped up; and a dozen weapons reappeared. The door to the head slowly creaked open, Wagenbach behind it. He had a confused look on his face and opened his mouth to say something. He seemed to think better of it and swayed for a second or two. Then he crumpled to the floor.

We rushed over to him and I leaned to feel his pulse. It seemed like it was still going, but I just finished my fiftieth drink of the night and couldn't be sure. Someone ran to call an ambulance.

Joe's gun was next to him. I picked it up and handed it to my father's bookie Jackie.

"Hmm," I noticed. "That *is* a nice lookin' gun."

"Ya," Jackie agreed. "It really does the trick."

"Jack, better take it home and we'll get it back to Joe later."

At least a dozen sets of hands ran across Joe trying to locate a bullet hole. But there was nothing we could see, no entry wound, no blood.

"Maybe it's a heart attack," my old man suggested. "Sit tight, Joe, help will be here in a second."

Gunpowder still hung in the air and as the sirens grew louder, it seemed prudent for the majority of partiers not to be in evidence upon its arrival. When the ambulance hit Beacon, we headed over to my house. We were still going strong that afternoon when I got the call from the Somerville police.

"Is this Bobby Martini? Big Bob's son?"

I cleared my throat. "How can I help you?" I was still drunk but thought I sounded pretty cool.

"I'm calling about Joe Wagenbach."

"He's not here, can I take a message?" was the best I could come up with.

"You don't need to take a message, Bobby. Mr. Wagenbach is dead."

Joe had died at the hospital. The cops knew it was an accident as the bullet had gone through the bottom of his ankle, traveled up his leg and continued hitting organs and bouncing thoughtlessly around inside his torso.

"We figure he unbuckled his pants to use the john and when he did, the gun fell out. It likely went off when the hammer hit the floor. It was a freak accident. But we do need the gun for ballistics, Bobby."

That sounded reasonable. Had I been sober, I might have thought twice about my response. "Sure! I'll get it to you right away. Thanks for calling."

I rang Jackie and had him bring the gun down to the cops. Even in my woozy state, I realized I'd be pushing the envelope by staggering into a station house waving an accidental tool.

If the same incident happened ten years later, I'd be doing time in Walpole.

Back then, though, my father was close with the cops and anything having to do with his children was handled differently than the average guy's. Although I took full advantage of the free passes when I was younger, I'm not so sure it was the best way to handle your kids and their transgressions.

I didn't go to Joe's wake or his funeral. I regret that. He was a great guy who just dropped in for a few laughs.

After the funeral, Brian took my sister Patty down the Cape for a couple of weeks.

"Joe ain't gonna be needing the cottage, ya know, since he's dead."

Brian sure had a way with words.

Nothing lasts forever and the Pointer Post was no exception. It began with the deterioration of my own family. Brian and I never found Hackett and Sullivan that night or any other. They wisely left town, taking off for the steamy tropics of Florida. The boys found semi-gainful employment and a whole new set of criminal partners down South. They headed off to pull a bank job in Saudi Arabia and when the job went bad — the Somerville boys took the fall. They were caught and ended up in a Saudi prison.

While incarcerated, Hackett had one of his eyes stabbed out and Sully ended up in a multitude of violent fights. They did seven years.

Hackett sent a series of letters to the U.S. government asking for their help in gaining release. The correspondence was quite sad to read, Hackett was a borderline illiterate and the majority of his pleas unintelligible.

When their time was up, Hackett arrived home and was immediately jailed for past transgressions. He was found dead in his cell one night. The cause was supposedly bronchitis but perhaps a disgruntled individual from the past finally caught up with him.

I can tell you this, it wasn't me.

Sully found employment after his Saudi bid and is still around. I ran into him at a local gin mill some years later and he told me how fucked up he was that night.

"Believe me, Bobby. I paid my dues for everything I ever done once I was in that prison."

I rarely hold a grudge, and had no doubt what Sully said was true.

"Forget it," I replied. We toasted survival and had a drink together.

My father heard I'd made peace with Sully and barred me from the Pointer Post for about six months. He may not have been speaking to me, but at least he was still alive.

No thanks to Chief Pino. He was convicted in 1986 along with former Metropolitan Police Captain Gerald W. Clemente and others of benefiting from what came to be known as the Police Exam Scam.

A federal grand jury accused them of stealing entrance and promotional civil service exams from a state office and selling or giving them to fellow officers to help them move up the food chain in level and pay scale. The more insidious part of the indictment alleged that the same group also worked to block the promotion of individuals who weren't in bed with them.

U.S. Attorney William Weld was convinced it was part of an overall plan to place key individuals in power positions across the state in an effort to spread control.

"Once you've got your hooks into somebody, if you have a chief and you know he's there because you put him there, then that gives you a lever to use if anything should go wrong in the future."

Clemente, also a player in the 1980 burglary of Depositors Trust Company in Medford, testified that he provided Pino with the captain's exam answers back in 1979 but Pino still failed the test. Then Clemente had to break *back* into the state exam office and change Pino's score. He failed again in 1982 while taking the chief's exam and was replaced, remaining a captain until retiring in 1985. Two years later, in 1987, Pino got four years for mail fraud in the Exam Scam.

The old man held on to that grudge against Sully until his death. I couldn't. My father survived and I hadn't killed anyone. For a time we were very lucky.

But that legendary luck of the Irish is usually just that — urban legend.

CHAPTER FIFTEEN

Funny How Time Slips Away
The End of the Ride

IT WAS A bitterly cold day in the beginning of February 1993. The weather had been brutal and each onslaught of new snow never had a chance to melt due to the frigid conditions. It just layered and settled into a growing mountain. All around Somerville there were banks of white solidified by the severe temperatures.

Parking, a nightmare on any day was now at a premium. Residents shoveled diligently, carving out their own spaces and distinctly marking them. Old beach chairs, trash barrels, and just about anything imaginable stood between white mounds of temporary permanence guarding the locals' parking spaces. If the errant driver, fearless out of desperation, was caught moving these barriers in an effort to pull in, he or she was almost guaranteed a busted window, deep scratches across a new paint job, a flattened tire or even a beating if the "parking attendant" was capable.

I was working on the movie *The Good Son* driving actor Elijah Wood and his mother Debra. We were filming in Beverly, right on the water. Despite the seasonal conditions it was a pleasure working with Elijah. He was twelve or thirteen and already a seasoned performer. And like any kid, he sometimes got bored, tired, or just plain cranky. Much of the film business is waiting around to do your job and it is often challenging for performers to keep themselves at the ready. For the younger ones, it has to be even more difficult. Debbie is a wonderful woman and took great care keeping Elijah on task. She also made sure that Hollywood wasn't going to spoil her child. She made no bones about disciplining her son in front of the Teamster driver, which I also liked.

I can't complain about any of them — the actors. I've driven people like Robin Williams and Meryl Streep and had some of the most fun I've experienced as an adult. And back in 1993, I appreciated driving the Woods daily, talking with Debbie and being with their family.

My own was in the midst of another tragedy, steeling ourselves for an impending loss. My younger brother Joey was suffering through the final stages of AIDS and although we didn't know it then, he'd be dead in less than three weeks. Another brother, Eddie, was twenty-five when he died from the disease seven years earlier. They both contracted it from a girl they shared drugs with in the Mystic Ave projects and were diagnosed with their respective death sentences at the same time.

As I was driving through the snow-blown roads to location, Debbie and I were swapping family stories — the kind of "going to work" chat that makes the time pass. As we did, my mind went back to the summer of 1988. Another brutal season, this the exact opposite — dreadfully hot and, as it turned out, painfully heartbreaking. I was a Metropolitan cop and when my shift ended each day, I got into my truck, cursed my broken air conditioning and picked up my mother. The sweat ran off us as we sat in Boston traffic on the way to the hospital where my brother Eddie was waiting to die. We went every single day.

After dropping my mother off in the evenings, I usually cried the rest of the way home. My brother was wasting toward death from a sickness carried by fucking monkeys. It wasn't even a human disease to start, I thought, and by the end it turned its victims into nothing more than sucked-out shells of bones and pain and horror. The papers were full of idiotic editorials proclaiming that those who got "it" — deserved it. Deserved to have the life sucked from them until they were scarecrows? Because they were men who stayed with each other? Kids who used drugs to beat the fear and depression out of their lives?

I was bullshit angry at everyone. And yet, deep inside the sunken hollowness was still my little brother. I couldn't understand it and gave up trying to figure it out.

During one visit, I talked non-stop, filling up the space between us. As I took a breath, Eddie looked over as if he were going to speak, but instead spat up a big wad of phlegm.

"Bobby," my brother croaked, "Look at what keeps coming out of me, it just won't stop."

I bolted out of the room, crying. It was horrific. As I tried to compose myself, I realized I was afraid, ashamed he may have seen my revulsion. After a while, I returned and stayed with Eddie until he wanted to go to sleep. I was relieved. I *wanted* him to go to sleep. I didn't want to see anything else come up out of him. God forgive me for writing that.

Sometimes my old man and his buddies rode their Harleys up to see him. The old man was taking it harder than any of us because he was always cursing Eddie. My brother was a hellion with both booze and drug problems and fed his habits in such innovative ways it drove Big Bob insane. Eddie was also a character from the day he was born. He was always hustling. If he'd been born later, doctors would have diagnosed him with ADHD. He definitely had it. But in the eighties, my father had his own diagnosis, which he called "being a little shit." He bore a tremendous amount of guilt for that.

Big Bob definitely had reason to complain. One night Eddie took all of the meat out of the freezer and sold it. On another occasion he sold my father's brand new sneakers to a guy on the street. He didn't stop with simple petty theft. Eddie was also an actor. When he needed money, he chose any one of Big Bob's many friends and waited patiently outside the house until the man was surely in bed. Then Eddie slapped on his game face and frantically banged on the victim's door until the sleepy resident opened up.

"It's my father! It's awful! We just rushed him to the hospital! No one knows what's wrong with him! I need money to catch a cab over there right away!"

Time after time, hapless victims fell for Eddie's plaintive request. The next morning my father was awakened by a concerned caller checking on his welfare. The inquiry was followed by the news that nocturnal Eddie had been by. The old man cursed Eddie up and down, wishing him dead a hundred times.

Eddie changed his schemes as the mood hit him and opportunity presented itself. Once, being a good neighbor, he took a man's dog for a walk and immediately sold the canine to a lonely passerby for a nominal fee. I constantly got complaint calls from across the city. Each proved more fantastic than the next and one of my favorites was The Car Loan.

"Bobby, I hate to bother ya, but your brother Eddie borrowed my car and he ain't returned it."

I listened patiently to the caller, nodding to myself and thinking, "Why the hell would you lend Eddie Martini your car?"

"See, Bobby, I really need my car. My wife's been drivin' me to work but she's gettin' pissy."

"OK," I sighed. "How long has he had the car?"

The vehicle's owner thought for a second. "Uh, lessee...I guess about two weeks now..."

"TWO WEEKS? And you're just calling me now? What are you, a fuckin' idiot?"

"Awww, tell ya the truth, I was kinda afraid to call. I didn't want no trouble from your family."

The Martini boys *were* known as a street brawling clan needing no excuse for a fistfight but even I couldn't condone Eddie's two-week joy riding jaunt.

"Don't worry about it. I'll get you your car back."

And I did, all the while Eddie trailing apologetically behind me, "I'm sorry, Bobby, I was gonna return it, I swear, something just came up." Something always came up for Eddie.

At Eddie's wake, my father couldn't even stand by the casket. I stood with my mother and siblings, greeting mourners and accepting condolences from friends and a multitude of Eddie's "benefactors" in his father's place. The old man stayed in the back room by the door. When the mourners asked for him, I directed them to him. Eddie dying really broke his heart. Those things he said in anger, the things we all say from time to time, haunted him.

Joey lasted until a few weeks after this particular day in February. By that time, *The Good Son* had wrapped and I was driving Joe Pesci and Brendan Fraser during a film called *With Honors*.

One afternoon we stopped to eat Italian food in the North End. Brendan ordered wine, pouring me a glass. Teamsters cannot drink during work hours and as we started talking about it, wasn't long before the subject of families came up. I was telling a story about my brother Joey when Brendan held up a hand.

He stopped me in mid-sentence, something very hard to do. I figured I'd unwittingly crossed the line between actors and crew, an infraction that could bring harsh criticism.

"Brendan, I apologize if I..." I started to say, but never finished. The actor interrupted me.

"I need to go see him, your brother."

Brendan was a young guy and the sincere expression on his face touched me. I've never been impressed by actors, producers, directors, or anyone merely because of who they seem to be. Our whole business is based on illusion. And there are a lot of assholes in the entertainment business, just like any other. But occasionally I've been lucky enough to find that someone actually *is* who he or she seemed to be — and then I've been impressed. This kid, Brendan, was one of those people. Years later I read a quote attributed to him. "I believe you have a responsibility to comport yourself in a manner that gives an example to others. As a young man, I prayed for success. Now I pray just to be worthy of it."

I don't know if he really said it, but he definitely lived up to it. He is worthy of it.

The next day, Saturday, Brendan had me pick him up at his hotel and we drove into St. Elizabeth's Hospital. Brendan walked into that room and greeted my little brother like he was an old friend. He had brought along a script and signed it to Joey, with a personal message on the cover. They talked for a while and then finally, I had to get him back to his hotel. It was freezing and Brendan was already exhibiting the kick off to a cold.

"Bobby," he said earnestly as I dropped him off, "you can't tell anyone in production we went out today. They might blame you if I get sick and they have to shut down."

Brendan did get sick and production had to shoot around him for two days. When he returned, I greeted him in front of the producers with, "Hey kid, how you feelin'? Gettin' over that cold?"

He winked at me. "Oh yeah, much better, Bob."

I will never forget that kind act Brendan did for my brother. It lifted Joey's spirits during what proved to be his final weekend.

Monday I was visiting Joey with his wife Sandy. She's an angel, a loyal girl who remained by his side during years of sickness. He lasted five years longer than Eddie because she made sure he followed the strict diet and medical schedule set down for him by the doctors. We stepped into the hall for a moment to discuss future arrangements and by the time we returned, my brother had passed away.

Sandy stared at him for a long agonizing second and then starting gulping at the air. She screamed his name and grabbed at me, crying hysterically. "He can't be dead! We were just talking to him and he was fine! He's not dead!"

I was the older brother and support system for my sister-in-law. I fought the rising panic inside myself as I struggled not to break down in front of Sandy. I pushed her away and walked-ran through the door and out to the closest stairwell. All by myself in a dingy, secluded back hallway I heard the sound of my own sobbing echoing off the walls. I cried until I was hoarse, then wiped my face with my shirt and went back to Sandy. We stayed with my brother for a half hour or so. Then it was done.

Sandy truly loved my brother. She didn't cut and run when he was sick although she could have. She is a more than a good friend; she's family and still celebrates a few holidays a year with us. Sandy never contracted HIV from Joey; for that I am very grateful.

A hospital worker stole the script Brendan signed to my brother and that was sad. Joe Pesci sent a huge spray of flowers to the wake and he signed a photo with the words, "God is good, you be too." Joe was great and I'll never forget him or Brendan, a couple of strangers who turned out to be regular guys.

My father's death came prior to the end of *The Good Son*. The morning Elijah Woods, his mother, and I pulled into the stage area, Elijah jumped out and went off to work. Debbie and I were in the van, still talking when my phone rang. My father had just been rushed to the hospital. It looked like a heart attack.

A black shakiness churned up inside me. I came to realize as I grew older it was anxiety, a word that wasn't in any

Somerville vocabulary. You didn't have it and even if you did, you didn't admit it. Instead it was an annoyance you referred to as a pain in the gut. It had to be physical.

But of course, it wasn't.

"Debbie, I gotta leave, something happened to my father." I bolted to my own car. Debbie literally ran after me, trying to console me but I was deaf. I couldn't think straight. Eddie was gone, Joey right behind him. I don't even remember arriving at the hospital. As I charged through the emergency room waiting area I saw a group of thirty or so outside the double doors of intensive care. Stone-faced tattooed bikers, women with teary faces; it was my father's crew. His friends, and mine.

I grabbed the first uniform I saw. "Where's my father?"

The nurse escorted me through the double doors. The word *intensive* barely describes it. Big Bob was still, lifeless. But this wasn't anything like after the Pointer Post shooting. Machines pumped his chest up and down with that sound a baby makes after taking too much formula; a soft bubbly gurgle. The doctor came in to see me.

"We're waiting for the results to determine how much brain activity is evident."

"Then what?"

"If it's below a certain level, then we would diagnose him as brain dead," he replied patiently.

"And then?" I asked. Why couldn't he just say it all in one sentence?

"We would need a family member to order the withdrawal of the tubes."

"I'm that guy," I replied. "No one but me. I am the guy who will say it. You understand?"

The doctor nodded and turned to leave. I stopped him. "Hey doc, what do *you* think?"

He shrugged noncommittally, "I can't tell you anything until the tests come back."

In my heart, I knew he was dead to us, but my mind was waiting to catch up. Years later, when Howie's son Gary lay in the identical position under the same machines, I knew what was inevitable for my buddy. I knew well the patina of the skin when the brain is checking out and leaving it behind. I would remember this.

My father's friends were still in the hallway, Rat, my father's girlfriend Stevie, Mike D, Clem and his girlfriend Sandy. They all loved my old man. After I told them about my conversation with the doctor, we all sat down, just steps away from the room with the machines, and talked for an eternity about all the good times at the Pointer Post.

Ken "Rat" O'Connell is a Vietnam vet who became a mercenary in Africa after his tour of duty. Shoulder length hair, nose ring, tattoos running across his back, arms and legs, Rat was, and still is, all Marine and proud of it. He is the embodiment of never judging a book by the oft-scary cover.

He also answers comfortably to what could be considered a scary nickname for Somerville, the home of "Never Be A Rat." He explained its origin to me.

"I was born in '47. When I was young, my friends and I wore iridescent clothes, sharkskin jackets with velvet colors, an Elvis thing. My hair was a DA, slicked like a duck's ass, the curl in the front. The clean-cut college kids in town called all of us who dressed like that "the Rats." The more clothes I got, the more names that came along — Uncle Rat, King Rat, and Mr. Rat. The name stuck. It didn't bother me."

He had to have taken grief for it over the years, at least until he reached his full height and reputation. "You walk a line," he says. He knows who he is and that's enough.

"Matter of fact," Rat says, "one of the McLaughlin brothers really gave me shit over it."

"Which one?"

He shrugs. "I dunno. In Jamaica Plain they call him Chop-Chop. He did time for chopping some Chinaman up for too much starch in his shirt. [A story I have been unable to confirm, but have no doubt it is true.] I was in a bar with a bunch of safecracker buddies of mine and they introduced me to him. He even looked like a psycho. The kind of guy that has one drink too many and picks on the kid with the long hair. He says, 'Rat, what the fuck kind of name is Rat? I don't want no rat around me!'"

Rat laughs. "I thought, 'Oh God, here we go.' I wasn't gonna get myself in too much of a fucking problem 'cause I'm definitely out numbered. And you know those kind of fuckers, I don't care who you were, you weren't gonna get out of that bar alive."

Yeah, I do.

"He says, 'It's a nickname, it doesn't mean I rat people out. Actually, it's just the opposite. You don't think for one minute I would tell ya my name is Rat if I was one, do ya?'"

McLaughlin thought for a moment and then agreed. "That kinda makes fucking sense."

Rat rolls his eyes. "You see what kind of idiots they were, that bunch."

My father loved Rat for that and so much more.

The stories went on, but I couldn't. When I get emotionally tired, worn out to the bone, I have to go to sleep. It's a defense mechanism; the same one that hit me after my father visited me with the shotgun. Shut it the fuck down. I can fall asleep in a chair, a waiting room, in the middle of an argument. The fight, the worry or in this case, the waiting would overwhelm me. Shut it down, please.

So after a while I said, "I'm going home. See you in the morning."

I couldn't sit and watch the clock. I went home, lay down and fell right into sleep.

The next morning the Pointer crew was already assembled in the hall when I arrived. The hospital staff brought in more chairs to accommodate the growing crowd. My brothers and sisters were there along with my mother. It was quite a scene. His friends, kids, his wife *and* girlfriend; all in the hall together.

The results hadn't come back but we knew the score. My father had moved on to another place and left his body behind. Rat, Mike D and I moved away from the crowd to a corner.

"What's it gonna be, Bobby?" Rat asked me quietly.

I wasn't quite where I needed to be, but said, "I can't leave him there on machines."

Rat nodded. "He wouldn't want that for the rest of his life."

Mike D agreed. "We know what you gotta do. Everyone does."

"It's OK, Bobby, you do what you need to," Rat encouraged me sadly.

I had to see for myself. For the last time, I walked through those doors. My father hadn't moved. The machines pumped away, artificially supporting the shell of a once great and complicated man. The man who beat me and supported me, humiliated me and protected me, occasionally hated me and always loved me. All of our questions, all of our history would now stay inside me because he couldn't hear me and I didn't have anything more to say anyway. I knew he loved me and that would have to be enough.

The doctor cleared his throat behind me. "We're still waiting on the results."

It didn't matter. I knew the old man was dead. I clenched my fists and struggled to keep calm.

"I don't care. Take my father off the fuckin' machines right now. Now."

He nodded. "Wait here for just a minute." The doctor slipped out and returned shortly with his diagnosis. The brain had been deprived of oxygen too long to ever come back. I nodded. I was back in control and running this show. I had to be, or I would break into pieces.

"Can his friends come in to say goodbye?"

The doctor nodded. I went back and announced the lousy news to all his friends. "Bob's leaving. You can come in and say goodbye before he goes."

I stood by my old man's side as the procession of friends, already mourners, came in one by one, hugged him and told him how much they loved him. Each one left in tears.

As respect dictated, my mother Claire and brother Leo were the last. My mother, even though he lived with another woman, still loved him to death. Literally, as it was about to come any minute. She started crying hard. Leo was crying. It was enough.

"Leo take your mom out of the room. Go home and take care of her."

I didn't realize by my choice of words I was detaching from them and the rest of the family. Another defense mechanism. Disengage. Leo led Mom away.

The room was quiet, except for the suck-swoosh of the mechanical pumping. In a minute or so, I looked at the doctor and gave him the nod. My body gave in and my mind went flat. My hands shook and I clenched them into fists.

Then I watched my father die.

I died for a few moments at the same time, it seemed. Then, I walked out with tears streaming down my face, but at the same time proud I stood by him while his friends said their goodbyes, all the while keeping my composure. He'd be proud I held on to the end before breaking down, he *was* proud I'd made the most difficult decision of my life. I needed it, to feel that he was proud of me.

My old man's wake was enormous. He was laid out in full Harley Davidson regalia — the clothes he loved best. Old friends traveled in to pay their respects. Even the prison guards he'd stayed in touch with through the years after his release attended. Bikers and cops and ex-cons, women and kids; they knew him and loved him for who he was. It was a great thing to see.

The day of his funeral was one of the coldest days in Massachusetts's history and still Mike D, Al, Rangy-Tangy, and six other bikers defiantly escorted the funeral car. By the end of the trip to Mount Auburn Cemetery, there was little feeling left in the bikers' hands, but nothing could have stopped those guys from riding beside my father's casket.

I gave the eulogy and although my father was a difficult man and our relationship more than complicated — it took me only five minutes to write. God probably sent the words to me, I just dictated. The boys said it was pretty good, but I'd have given everything not to had needed to read it at all.

Three weeks later, we buried Joey.

It was a shitty winter. At least the old man passed before he lost another son.

After he died, we met down the Post to decide who would run the club. Ken "Spike" Leva, the Post treasurer was at that meeting. Spike had been my prison guard when I was a guest of the state. Spike's old man hung with my father down the Post years earlier and we found out by accident one night when Spike and I were drinking with the old man.

"Was your father a painter?" he asked Spike recognizing a familiar last name.

"Yeah, he was."

"Well, I'll be damned! You're sittin' in the same seat he used to sit in years ago."

Now it seemed so eerie, Spike in his dead father's old bar seat, and me in mine.

Jerry Vinal was also there. He was the guy Big Bob called in the middle of night to get his poker machines out of the club before the cops arrived. A loyal friend, Jerry was too busy to run a club.

I was working the movies as a Teamster and couldn't take it on. My brother Leo was a cop. We were afraid he'd get in the shit for running a private club. Jerry suggested we let another old pal, Kevin Hannaford, run the place for a while and try to keep it going. I agreed, but now I wish I had taken it over. I was still immature and didn't foresee the possibilities of making a business go.

The torch was passed but the fire eventually went out. The Pointer Post, the once hard rockin' exclusive Somerville haunt for cops and criminals alike ended up losing too much money. Rat finally had to shut it down himself. He gave up the liquor license and put all the Harley paraphernalia in storage.

For some, the Pointer Post had been a home away from home, for my father it was simply home. That once exclusive society, the private world that was ours and ours alone stood empty and silent.

A couple of years after his death, I discovered that in the hours before my father's heart attack, he'd tried to smoke what he thought was a cigarette at the coffee table in the parlor. What to him looked like a smoke was instead a spoon. He was in the midst of having a stroke, but his girlfriend Stevie laughed at him, insisting he go to bed instead of calling an ambulance. I'm not blaming anyone — I wasn't there, but I do feel that with a little more common sense, my father would have lived a little longer.

My father was adamant in his own mind that he could protect his own if he just kept them close and under his watchful eye. The Pointer Post was, for him, like an adult day and night care center. But as much as he wanted to protect us from the outside world, his own compound had its own elements of danger and sometimes he could not protect us or even himself. And maybe that ugly knowledge, that truth he did not want to accept, haunted him.

Toward the end of our writing I finally cornered the guy I wanted to speak with again — Clem Salvi. We were at a neighborhood party and I taped our casual interview. I didn't remember too much of what we talked about until I watched afterward. It was like someone else's home movie.

A bonfire is burning behind Clem and the flicker from the flames surround his salt and pepper hair like a halo. His reading glasses are folded over a gold chain around his neck. He doesn't look very happy. Clem is another typical Yankee. He speaks in short sentences and is very reluctant to talk about the past. I think he feels a certain disloyalty in discussing events that happened so long ago, and with the other players all gone perhaps he feels he holds their secrets for them.

Unlike the other men I've spoken with, he doesn't offer any funny anecdotes or wild tales about the days of the Post, just sits stone-faced and waits for me to ask specific questions.

"Your father always said that he didn't run the Post. 'I'm just the janitor, I'm not in charge,' he'd say." Clem warms up a bit and tells me he and my father used to drink and sing Irish songs.

"We had a lot of good times together."

"What about some of things that happened down there?" I ask.

Clem shakes his head. "Nothing happened down there. There was never any trouble when your father was in charge."

He doesn't want to talk about my father this night. Maybe it's all of the friends in attendance and the cookout, music playing, laughter behind us. I know how he feels. Even after all this time, I expect the old man to be holding court around the fire.

Clem will give me about five more minutes so I ask him to tell me a story, any story, the very last Big Bob story.

"OK," he relents. "Here it is. Your father called me up on a Saturday night and said 'Let's go down the Post.' It was unusual because he avoided that crowd, but this Saturday we went and we had a real good time. We sang and joked around. He hadn't been feeling good the past few weeks."

The old man had high blood pressure and diabetes. His foot still bothered him from the night of the shooting.

"At the end of the night when we headed home, I said, 'I'll see you next week, Bob.' He shook his head and said, 'You might see me but I won't see you.' I just stared. 'What the hell does that mean?'"

Clem was confused but Bob just smiled and slowly walked away. My father died the next week.

Maybe it was the smoke from the bonfire, maybe it was the angle of my camera and the light shining in Clem's face, but as I watched later, I saw what I think were tears in his eyes. I also heard another voice on the tape — my own — say quietly, "Clem, did my old man ever say he thought what happened that night — the night he was shot, did he ever say it was my fault for punching Hackett and getting the whole thing started?"

Clem looked right into the camera and said, "No." Then our interview was over.

I don't know if I would have slaughtered the men who came after my father if we'd been able to find them. I'd like to think that I wouldn't have, that I would have walked away. But with Brian by my side, egging me on, I very easily might have made the wrong decision. It would have been my decision, of course, but it still would have been the wrong one.

For many years, it was too difficult to pass by that wooden door of the Pointer Post, sadly standing closed and silent. It was like a lover you had to leave behind, but still pined for deep down. Eventually it gained some graffiti to showcase the bullet holes from the time someone tried to shoot me.

Recently there was a fire at the Post, destroying virtually the entire inside. I was pissed at first, so bullshit angry that the place where I spent hundreds of nights was completely obliterated. The warm and welcoming smell of stale beer and perfume and cigarette smoke replaced by the singe of charred wood, the walls that boasted photos and bar sayings, now peeled back and raw. My past life in ashes, staring back at me.

But after a while, I felt something loosen up in my chest, something that had been wound tight for a very long time. Like maybe I'd been thinking someday I could walk in that door and it would all be just the way it was. The jukebox playing an old rock and roll tune, my father at his regular seat, the guys back in their places, me swinging a beer and acting like a clown, the girls, the baseball games, the parties. It was still there waiting for me like an old friend.

In some ways, that fire, it took that away from me. Not the memories, I've still got them and I always will. I mean that fantasy that it was all still *there* — that he was *still there* — and as long as I never opened that door, I wouldn't be disappointed.

It made it better for me because now I know, that like my old man, the Post is really gone and there's no getting it back. Sometimes that's what it takes to keep moving forward.

That and the fact that last year I drove over to what remains of the Pointer Post building and took the heavy oak door with the shotgun scars right off its hinges in broad daylight.

CHAPTER SIXTEEN

We're In The Jailhouse Now

JANUARY 1989. I'M a police officer, sitting in a small dingy gray room at the Metropolitan Police headquarters in Boston. Across from me is another cop.

He's trying to keep me out of prison.

I'm trying to focus.

I'm focusing on a sheath of dried paint, peeled backwards from the top of the wall in front of me. It's just hanging there in space. One good yank and it will all disintegrate into shards of chips.

"Here's the deal," the other cop says. "You know and I know that you have information about...lemme say, certain factions you grew up with in Somerville. If you'll just cooperate with us, Bobby, we can make this thing go away. I can pretty much guarantee that you can stay police."

Stay police. Stay police. The one thing I never dreamed I would be was suddenly what I wanted most. I wanted to stay police.

If you've never read Martin Amis, the great fiction writer, give him a try — after you finish reading this book, I mean. He writes cops from the inside guts out. One thing that impressed me was his particular brand of "cop talk." His characters call themselves each "a police." He's right, but amongst ourselves where I worked, we were just "police" — a noun which does not require the grammar's definite article "the" before it. Just "police."

I wanted to stay a cop. I'll admit that I took the test just as a joke, to see if I could pass it. And I did, barely, but because of my disabled vet status I went to the top of the list. So I became a cop. And once I did, I discovered that I really wanted, not only the job, but to do a good job. I let all of my other activities go by the wayside; thousands of dollars owed to me in loans on the street, other "assignments" that although could have been very lucrative, would have put me at the polar opposite of law enforcement. I gave it all up, because I realized I liked being a cop. As old fashioned as it sounds, I liked helping people.

And for a few bucks (well, truth be told, it was more than a few bucks, but it was only money, just the same), I had thrown it all away, and this was my only chance to hang onto it.

I had recently gone through a financially devastating divorce where the Woburn judge awarded my ex-wife virtually everything I made during the week. Without sacrificing my weekend visits with my two young sons, there was no opportunity for extra details and overtime, so when I was sitting alone in my shitty apartment considering the taste of canned cat food, I got a call from an old college friend that — as the cliché' goes — changed the course of my life.

Maybe "derailed" is a better way to put it.

The scheme, stupid as it was, seemed brilliant at the time. This guy I knew, Jose Lee, was in charge of billing in the accounting department at Blue Cross/Blue Shield and figured a way to beat the company out of some cash. He would set up fake accounts with fabricated licenses at banks in the area. Jose would write out checks for $7000, $8000, and more every couple of weeks. Services rendered by various "vendors." I'd deposit the checks into one of our accounts, and take $350 out of the ATM every day. At first I thought I'd just take a couple of bucks, just to get myself back on my feet again. Just do it for a little while. That wasn't what happened. As the country song goes "Once more is never enough."

This went on for months. I can't even calculate or recall what we beat them out of, but it was quite a bit. And for a while I did get back on my feet. Never thought it would end. But it did.

In the end, greediness always gives way to sloppiness. In 1989, Jose issued some checks in the name of an actual company. When the company brought the bogus checks to the attention of the authorities, I was arrested. Worse, I was embarrassed in front of the entire police force. I had made a bad choice in friends and in ethics and now I was going to pay for both.

I have never been one to give someone else up for my mistakes and I wasn't going to let that happen now. After we had both lawyered up, we met for a conference with our respective attorneys. Jose immediately burst into tears. My attorney was Nancy Gertner, now a federal judge and one of the smartest and nicest people I have ever met. John Picardi, ex-deputy Superintendent of the Metropolitan Police had introduced me to her.

*I sat beside her and watched Jose bawling. I may have been embarrassed in front of every single cop I knew but this guy was openly sobbing like someone's grandmother. Well, someone's grandmother who was **not** from Somerville.*

There was only so much of Jose's blubbering I could take until I finally leaned over to Nancy and said, "Let's do this thing. Just put all of the charges on me."

"Bobby," Nancy was whispering back. "You can't be serious!"

My father had even told Jose that the most he would get was a slap on the wrist for his elaborate plan and we could work out a way to pay back the money in question — a figure which was much less than what actually traveled out of the Blue Cross accounting books.

"If Bobby is implicated, they'll do more than throw the book at him, Jose. He's a cop. A cop in prison is very bad business. Don't do this." My old man didn't plead or beg; it wasn't his style. He did, however, state what he believed was fact.

Jose didn't give a shit, he wanted to save his own skin and truth be told, I did the crime as well, so it was payback time. I was going down anyway, might as well go all the way. Even for a cop in prison there was some respect in not rolling over.

Jose was still carrying on. His life was over; he'd never live through it. I gestured toward him and she put her hand over mine to keep from drawing attention to us both. "Nancy, look at him. He ain't a real man. He ain't even capable of admitting his part in this whole scheme."

We both looked on.

"Huh," Nancy snorted. "He sure looks like the mastermind of a crime gang, doesn't he?" Despite the situation, we both had to control our laughter.

"Do it, Nancy," I said. And so she did. I was tagged as the ringleader.

In the court, the little prosecutor, the one I had met before, was drooling over me. He'd tried to nail me to the cross over Billy Barnoski and failed but now he actually had me by the balls for a crime I did commit. It was already ugly and he was demanding ten years in prison. Might as well go for broke.

Nancy managed to get the prosecution, who originally wanted to send me away for ten years, to accept a plea bargain. She argued long and hard, citing my disastrous divorce and subsequent financial situation, and the illness of my brothers as all extenuating circumstances that contributed to my criminality. She was gracious and eloquent and I remain forever grateful to her.

I got two years of weekends at the Billerica House of Corrections. In the end, I only had to do six months of weekends actually in Billerica, and the rest of my sentence as home house arrest Friday, Saturday and Sunday. But that was enough. I think it's easier to do the straight time than to have to go to the prison every weekend.

Home house arrest still required that I check in to Billerica each Friday and then go home to remain until Monday. I had my kids on weekends so I took them with me when I checked in, wanting them to see what I had to go through and what I had lost due to my poor judgment. The only good judgment I did exercise was to keep my mouth shut when push came to shove. And now it had.

I wouldn't be accepting any offers, even though it was costing much more than just my cop job. I told the officer seated across from me in that gray painted room at the Metropolitan Police headquarters that I couldn't help him.

"I'm really sorry, pal. But I got nothing else to say."

He cocked his head to one side and gave me a grim look. "Then you, my friend, are outta here."

And I was off to prison.

On the first day of my sentence I had to report to the Cambridge courthouse and meet a correctional officer. I was then loaded directly into a sheriff's car, without any handcuffs, and brought up to Billerica. As I was brought into the screening room for processing, I recognized the intake officer.

"Jesus, I'm sorry for ya problems, Bobby," he said as I went through.

"Don't worry about it."

I was led into the reception area for the warden, where I realized the receptionist was a girl I knew pretty well. Kathy O'Gorman. She lived downstairs from my mother in the projects. She looked like she was gonna burst into tears.

"Oh God, I am so sorry for your problems, Bobby!"

I smiled and nodded. "Don't worry about it, Kathy."

She directed me to the warden, who I also knew pretty good.

"Jesus, Bobby..."

"Sorry for my troubles?" I interrupted.

"Siddown, smartass, until I figure out what to do with you."

We shot the shit for a while. He did acknowledge the fact that I didn't tell on anyone and that he respected me for it.

"You ain't a rat, that's good. It'll make your time as a cop easier with the population. So, Bobby, where would you like to stay in my prison?" he says, like he's the manager of the Four Seasons Hotel.

I've been to enough hotels to know that a smart guest will always take a recommendation from the concierge.

"I dunno, what's good?"

"Hmmm, let's see..." he flipped through some cards. "Let's try the dorm. Or would you rather go for the infirmary? Take a load off, get some rest, you look exhausted."

I shrugged. "Sounds good." I was exhausted, no doubt. It hadn't fully hit me — what I had done to change the course of the rest of my life. I was still on autopilot.

As soon as I hit the infirmary, it seemed like a good deal. Books, magazines, TV and lying around. Too much, it turned out. It didn't take long for me to hear that there was a guy who was — the best way to say it is "pestering" the younger guys who passed through sickbay. It was the kind of pestering that I couldn't tolerate, no fuckin' way. What consenting people do between each other is fine, but I never could take guys forcing themselves on women and I sure as fuck wouldn't stand by and watch a man forcing himself on other men. Especially the younger guys, kids yanked off the streets on small petty drug beefs who had no fucking idea what they were up against in prison with sick grown men twice their size.

I grabbed the first phone I could get my hands on. "Get me the warden, right now!" I demanded of the voice on the other end.

"Who is this? Bobby?" Kathy asked.

"Yeah, I need him now."

"Where are you exactly?" she asked.

"Infirmary," I was so pissed I could barely get the word past my teeth.

"Uh oh. Hang on."

The next voice I heard was the warden's. "Bobby, what happened? What's wrong? Jesus, you just got here! What did you do?"

"Get me the fuck out of the infirmary!"

"Kathy!" I heard him yell, "Reassign Martini to the dorms."

I tell Howie this story and he laughs, slapping his knee.

"That figures! It sounds just like you, Bobby. The only cop in history to go to prison and be treated like a hotel guest!"

I laugh as well, but it makes me feel a bit embarrassed. I know Howie's experience was quite a bit different. Howie is dressed up for company on this day. Mine. He seems happy that I have come to visit and I feel uncomfortable because of the subject I will bring up.

As I've said, I am not outwardly a very emotional person. I've spent over fifty years keeping my feelings in check and filed away where they cannot hurt me — or anyone else. When you take great pains to avoid getting into situations where you could be affected by something, you learn to avoid them. But writing a book such as this, I can't do Somerville, or Howie or especially the reader, justice, if I don't find out everything I can.

So here's a writing tip — if you think you want to write a book, I suggest either fiction or a historical tale in which everyone is either your own creation or already dead. Don't start with a book that requires you having to interrogate your friends. You will not be very popular by the time you finish. Especially with yourself.

"What do you want to talk about today, Bobby?" Howie looks at me expectantly.

"Howie, I wanted to ask you about the Diesel Tour."

The Diesel Tour, Diesel Therapy, The Bus Rides. Some of the names utilized for a certain fashion of prisoner transit that is — in the area of transport — the ground equivalent of Con Air. There is no comparison between the two when it comes to actually reaching your destination. Call it what you like, but in reality, it is nothing more than state sanctioned torture. If you don't believe me, look it up.

And if you don't believe that it's very fucking hard to ask someone who has taken one of those torturous transfers to describe it for you; look it up again.

His face drops a little and his eyes look out through his glasses at me for a beat. He's looking beyond me and I guess he is thinking about what he said when we began this process.

"Nothing is off limits except for my family. Anything else you want to know, I'll be happy to talk about."

This wasn't one of those things he considered, I'm sure. But Howie's as good as his word, so he leans back into the chair, interlaces his fingers across his lap and we ease into it.

"That time period was positively some of the worst days of my life," he starts.

"In 1982, when the pinball sentence was up, the marshals came and picked me up to start serving my federal time on the horse fixing beef. That's when the bus rides started."

The Diesel Tour. I've heard of it. It's legendary in the con world.

"The Bureau puts you on this pleasure cruise when they see a certain code added to your records. It used to be the letters O.C.," Howie says. "You know, organized crime."

I'd done some research and read a few first hand accounts of prison ground transit from one facility to another (including Eddie Maczenkie's from *My Life As An Enforcer For Whitey Bulger and the Boston Irish Mob*, and he hadn't even had any fucking Diesel Therapy, just heard about it) but as impassioned as the writers were, it seemed pretty hard to believe.

"Believe it," Howie's voice is flat. "I was there. First, they dress you out in the shackles, handcuffed wrists and ankles. Both sets of shackles are connected to chains and those chains," Howie stands up to illustrate, "are hooked to another around your waist."

"Then," he holds his hands out as if still shackled, "they put the black box over your hands."

I must look confused. "The box," Howie says. "You know."

I don't.

"Ah," he nods. "You mean they didn't box you?" I shake my head.

"Luck of the Irish you've got, Bobby. Most cops get boxed." Howie smiles a bit. "The stiffener, they call it. It pushes in between the hands and keeps the chains stiff so you can't bend your wrists." He twists each hand at a ninety-degree angle.

"Does everyone get the box on their hands?"

"No, not everyone," Howie says. "On a bus full of, say, forty guys, there's generally two or three black boxed. Whomever they decide, Bobby."

"You got the box?"

"Every day," he replies simply.

Did they have in custody a very dangerous fifty-two year old of medium build that at any moment would tear his cuffs off and take over the bus in a psychotic rage?

Not hardly. But that's not what boxing is for.

The black box is usually reserved *not* for the most dangerous of the incarcerated, but political prisoners or inmates tagged by the Bureau Of Prisons as requiring special punishment; either crimes against law enforcement or refusal to cooperate with authorities.

"You walk to the bus like this." Howie does the prison shuffle. It's painful to watch. I was spared the chains and shackles and the humiliation that goes along with that part of incarceration.

"I see," is all I can think of to say. "So then, you get on the bus?"

"Yes." He slowly sits back down in his chair.

I am relieved that Howie is sitting again. "OK, so when do they take off the box?"

Howie thinks. "Eight to sixteen, usually, but sometimes more."

"Why eight to sixteen miles?" That doesn't make sense.

He leans forward, shaking his head.

"In eight to sixteen *hours*. When the bus stops and pulls in to some local facility for eight hours, unless they decide to plant you somewhere for a few days or even weeks. Then you get back on the road for as long as they want. Days, weeks, months."

Fuck me. I can't really think of anything to say and Howie sees it. I don't understand. He now takes pity on *me* and doesn't wait for my answer.

"Diesel Therapy is the BOP's medieval way of tormenting certain prisoners," he explains. "You leave one facility for another. Let's say you are leaving Boston and going to your end facility in Kansas. Diesel Therapy takes you on a circuitous route through dozens of states for weeks on end."

So you, as a freshly convicted felon, get on the bus under the guise of being transported to whatever facility where you will begin to serve out your sentence but instead you're hopscotching across the country in a governmental Twilight Zone.

He tells me the basics of each day.

"You start at maybe four every morning, they get you up and chain you."

The first thing veteran bus riders will tell a new addition is that when you kneel down on the bench so your captors can apply the leg shackles, is to try and stretch your feet backward as far as physically possible. It stretches the front tendon so that when you are in an upright position again, there is a small bit of give between human flesh and metal. As your feet begin to swell, you'll need it.

"Then you get on the bus and into your seats."

Seating assignments were designated by the guards, to insure there was no chance of spending the next sixteen hours sitting close to anyone that you might have anything in common with.

The buses had no air conditioning or heat, no matter what the climate or temperature. The only constant was the inmate wardrobe. Short sleeve shirts, pants, and no jackets.

"It was hard to say which was worse. The biting cold was often brutal but at least it kept the human waste almost refrigerated. When conditions were extremely hot, the smell was so bad, you could taste it in your mouth."

"The bathroom, you mean?" I was wondering how they managed that.

"OK, the bathroom. On some buses there is a small closet way in the back. It didn't have a door and it could be used if a guard decided that you couldn't wait until a scheduled stop."

The man hailed as the former one-time head of the biggest non-Italian crime family on the East Coast gingerly describes how one goes about relieving himself on a prison transport bus. The open door policy is the least embarrassing part of the routine.

"It's very difficult as they don't take the box off your hands."

That means if you just cannot wait, if you absolutely cannot hold it and you must take a shit, there's no way to wipe yourself. The consequences of your excrement can also affect the other forty or so guys on the bus.

The toilet was basically a crude seat-with-bucket set up that was not emptied until the end of a sixteen-hour day. Human piss and shit swishes back and forth as the bus maneuvers its way through the United States. If the driver wants to make it worse on you, all he has to do is jam on the brakes while you're balanced on the makeshift throne and everything that has exited from the other men all day long splashes up all over you.

At the end of the day the bus would pull into the cooperating facility for an eight-hour respite. A local lock up where the inmates are herded off the bus and into cells.

"As bad as some of the joints treated their own prisoners, out-of-towners — especially those with notes on their files, got it worse. There were occasions where some guys could get into genpop (general prison population) and have a smoke, walk around, and stretch a bit, before bed. You got bunked where they decided you would."

Many times there were just bare bunks; no sheet, blanket or pillow. Stripped down cells. Sometimes showers, most times not. It was freezing or stifling, but by the end of the day, no one cared.

"It was a treat to have the leg shackles removed and lie down."

Howie was usually stored in solitary confinement in these stopover towns due to his O.C. status and refusal to speak with federal agents.

"The time we pulled into El Reno, Oklahoma everyone on my bus was sick. There were no jackets and the answer to every question was 'Shut the fuck up' and everyone was so ill, for once they all did."

"I was taken directly to the strip search room and I managed to get my clothes off but it was so cold, I couldn't talk. I was standing there with my teeth chattering, naked."

The Hole was underground. "There was one sheet on the two inch, stained mattress. No blanket. I started calling out and then I was yelling. I think I yelled for two hours. Nothing. I was having a hard time walking around my cell and my nose was constantly running. You hate to waste your toilet paper allotment on your nose, so I had to resort to wiping my nose on my arm and the snot crystallized in the cold air. It was disgusting."

The afternoon sun is coming through the window in Howie's living room but we both seem to be cold, our body language gives us away as we both sit with our arms crossed tightly against our bodies. I feel as if I should be asking specific questions or guiding this interview in a direction but I am mesmerized by the story. I try to come up with something.

"What were you thinking?"

Howie pauses. "You know, that's interesting because for a long time I didn't remember what went through my mind during that stay in Oklahoma. Then it did come back to me and I think that I must have had a high fever in that cell."

"Why?"

"I kept thinking that if God came to me and said 'I'll give you your freedom, but you have to live it in hell,' what would I say?"

That's a serious thought for two good Irish Catholic boys like Howie and me.

"What would you say?"

"Put another log on the fire, 'cos here I come!'"

Howie's health deteriorated rapidly during the ten long weeks the government kept him on the bus tour. And no one knew what was happening to him or where he was — not even his attorney.

Diesel Therapy renders its riders incommunicado with not only the outside world, but their own inside world of friends, family and attorneys as well. The purpose of the tour is to not let anything catch up with you. Inmates exist, partially, due to family support. Commissary and telephone accounts are funded by money relatives are allowed to deposit. Soap, cigarettes, candy, chips, and stamps — all of the commissary items a guy may need from the prison store must be paid for from this account. Your account balance never catches up with you while you are bouncing around the country from one facility to another. You can never receive phone calls or mail because family members don't know where you are, you can't call or write your attorney because you have no access to your limited funds. No personal belongings may travel with you; no address books or mementos. Nothing. And no one knows what is happening to you.

"I finally made it to what they called my home prison."

The bus pulled into the United States Penitentiary, Leavenworth, Kansas. The place he was supposed to go from day one. The Hot House.

Maximum security Leavenworth is Big Boy Prison with brutally hardened criminals and guards alike. What has happened inside its walls in the last hundred years is legendary and shocking. It is still called "The Hot House" due to the incredibly high temperatures year-round, despite the recent constantly pumping air conditioning units. Cons vote it the number one worst place to be incarcerated throughout the BOP.

Nevertheless, Howie was relieved to finally arrive.

"I was deliriously happy, it couldn't possibly get too hot for me."

He had to be carried off the bus into the prison, unable to walk due to the months of shackled riding. Sick and feverish, he refused to go to sickbay and instead struggled to settle himself into the community of incarceration as soon as possible. The same reputation that made Howie the object of torture by the Feds served him well as he mainstreamed, finally, into the general population of Leavenworth.

Howie drums his fingers on his knee. "Inside, you had the Detroit blacks, one of the strongest groups in there. You had the D.C. blacks as well; they were big. They had the most blacks from any one area of the country in that prison and they were very well organized. There were the Georgia Boys, all southern rebels. The Aryan Brotherhood," Howie frowns. He doesn't say anything but I get the distinct impression he didn't cotton to that group.

"Then there were the Boston boys, different Latin factions, the Mexican Mafia, the Italian Mafia, the Irish guys..."

I interrupt. "There was a Mexican Mafia, Italian Mafia and then the Irish guys. No Irish Mafia?"

Howie grins a bit. "Come on now, Bobby. Irish guys never have called themselves the Irish Mafia. You ever notice that? You hear about this Irish Gang or that Irish Gang, or in the press it's always 'The Irish Mob' but never Mafia. I don't know why, maybe it has to do with taking an oath."

That's true. You never hear about any Irish *omerta* or oath, pricking of fingers or any induction ceremonies. I guess that's because we the Irish hate to make too many promises and we're not much for shedding blood unless it is absolutely necessary. "So you were just..."

He winks. "Just one of a bunch of Irish guys."

One of Howie's closest friends in Leavenworth was the major Mafia player Russell Bufalino, a man considered by some to be a suspect in the disappearance of Jimmy Hoffa. He was the head of the Bufalino crime family based in Pittston, Pennsylvania and known throughout the country as "The Quiet Don."

Amongst his peers he was considered "old school" — quiet and reserved, never a guy to flash his cash or power around.

"I liked him," Howie says. "We got on well together."

"And Jimmy Hoffa?" I ask, as in "Who did it and where is he, by the way?" I know the answer I'm going to get, but I can't help myself.

Howie waves the subject away dismissively. "Never asked, don't know."

End of story. We are, after all, still Teamsters and some things even we don't want to know.

I can see Bufalino and Howie getting along, as Howie himself is a pretty low-key guy, very reserved. One the hallmarks of his legacy is his propensity for peacemaking.

"I was on the bus with a New York mob guy by the name of Lefty Ruggiero. Lefty was the one that unwittingly brought the undercover cop Donnie Brasco into the mob."

Donnie Brasco, or Joe Pistone, was the FBI agent who infiltrated La Cosa Nostra and his efforts resulted in scores of Mafia convictions.

"Lefty believed Pistone was the real deal, and sort of made him his protégé. Not knowing he was a Fed, of course, but still the mob boys weren't too happy after they found out."

That's an understatement. Lefty was pegged for assassination the very day he was arrested by the FBI and through a sit-down of a different kind; between the FBI and the Mob, the contract on his life was eventually lifted.

"Lefty got twenty years after turning down the chance to become an informant. He ran with me and worked out every once in a while and I thought he was a pretty nice guy. The only problem with Lefty was that he really overplayed his Mob act."

I ask Howie what he means. "Wasn't Lefty a well-known old timer in the ranks of La Cosa Nostra?"

"Yes, he was a made guy, but there is a certain way a classy mob guy acts and Lefty wasn't doing it at Leavenworth."

His reputation was very important to Lefty. In the joint maybe he felt he had to exert a different kind of power. Especially after the embarrassment he had suffered at the hands of the Federal Bureau of Investigation.

"He was kind of looking down on the Boston guys as beneath him and they were starting to get pissed off. There was some of that anyway between the Irish and the Italians. Certain factions were starting to notice and wanted it to stop."

In the small tight knit communities that make up a prison, it is imperative to avoid drawing the undue attention of the administration.

The Boston guys were transfers from Massachusetts' maximum security Walpole State Prison. This particular group of inmates had come specifically from the infamous Cellblock Ten. Known throughout the Northeast as a vicious and dangerous wing, Cellblock Ten was designated as the Departmental Segregation Unit, housing the worst of the worst.

"These guys from Boston were so bad that even Cellblock 10 was done with them. One night Walpole administrators just handcuffed the whole group and shipped them out to Leavenworth."

It takes a unique hardness to survive that block and those who did were not appreciative of Lefty's loftiness. A lot of respected cons at Leavenworth knew the histories of the Massachusetts' transplants and also KNEW they were definitely not taking Lefty's shit for very long.

"One afternoon, I get a visit from Bufalino."

"Howie," Russell began, "I need your help. Is there any possibility you could see your way to speaking to the Boston crew? There's going to be trouble, I think, over this Lefty thing."

Russell held up a hand even before Howie could comment. The situation had to be especially painful for the elderly Italian, as he himself was well known for his tradition of never flaunting his power.

"I know, I know," the old Mafioso continued. "Lefty started this and make no mistake about it, Howie, none of us are too happy with him anyway over this Donnie Brasco thing. But, we don't want to see him get hurt either."

Both men sat in silence for a moment. The "Donnie Brasco Thing" was probably the worst embarrassment in the history of organized crime and many guys wondered how Lefty had been able to suck it up.

The contract on Lefty, however, had been retracted and that meant that even uninvolved parties, no matter what their personal feelings, were to respect the decision. In turn, that meant it was time to circle the wagons.

"I'm new here," Howie replied, "but I'd like to help out if I can. I'll speak to them, but Lefty has got to stop talking to these guys like they're nobodies, Russ. Otherwise, all the talking in the world won't stop it."

"It" was the inevitable violence that follows disrespect like a donkey plodding toward a carrot.

Bufalino nodded in agreement. He knew Howie's reputation as a peacekeeper was like his own. They would have to handle the miscreants quickly.

"So," Howie concludes, "I spoke to the Boston guys, Russell spoke to Lefty and everything calmed down. That was the end of that beef and it never came up again. Once something was settled, it was a badge of honor to keep it settled. And Russell and I became good friends."

Frank Sheeran, long time Teamster and the subject of the book *I Heard You Paint Houses*, is one of the self-proclaimed alleged killers of Jimmy Hoffa and a big Bufalino fan. He absolutely idolizes Russell to author Charles Brandt, likening him to a modern day Al Capone and one of the "two greatest men" he ever met." Sheeran also asserts that Russell was the one who had him do the hit on the other greatest man he ever met — Jimmy Hoffa — and waited patiently while Sheeran did the dirty deed.

In the book, Sheeran reveals a laundry list of all of the other missions he allegedly performed at the behest of Russell and even hints at Bufalino's alleged connection, along with New Orleans mobster Carlos Marcello, Santo Trafficante and Jimmy Hoffa, in the JFK assassination. One of a thousand theories.

Howie grimaces at the topic of Jack Kennedy's murder, like we all do up here.

"One day while we were out in the yard," he says, "I asked Russell how Carlos Marcello was doing and Russell just gave me a disgusted look."

"I don't care how he is," Russell said shortly. The he paused. "That guy, he put a lot of pressure on the Families. But whatever he did, he shouldn't have done. Infamnia."

Infamnia, the Italian expression for great sin, great shame. That much I understood.

"What did he mean?" I ask Howie, I am unable to decipher the rest of this curt code.

Howie lets out a breath. "He meant the pressure from the Administration came down hard on the Mafia, but whoever did kill our President, they shouldn't have done it."

Marcello was questioned by the FBI after the assassination but he was deemed "a tomato salesman and real estate investor" and not the big time mobster the rest of the Mafia knew him to be. The Warren Commission also concluded there was no direct connection between Marcello and nightclub owner Jack Ruby, despite the fact that the two had met previously over a labor dispute Ruby was experiencing. So much for the Warren Commission. And the FBI. Once again at the bottom of their game.

The New Orleans guys were known to act first and ask the permission or agreement from the other Families later. They did what they wanted, when they wanted, and this was also something that didn't sit well with Bufalino the traditionalist.

"I never asked about Carlos again," Howie tells me. "I liked our friendship too much. We used to watch all the ball games and television programs together. He and I always sat in the same spot, on the third row of the benches." He holds a hand up off the ground. "We picked that spot because the view was always the best."

Howie smiles. "Know how I remember that? Well, Russell was older than me, and because he was an older gentlemen I would put out my hand to help him down off the benches and every single time he'd would swipe my hand away and tell me that he didn't need anyone's help." Howie laughs. "It might take him a while to get down, but he refused assistance. And let me tell you, if there were guys behind him waiting, they waited. No one ever said a word."

Bufalino was well respected in Leavenworth by both the cons and the guards.

"He had diabetes but he still loved ice cream. One day a self serve ice cream machine mysteriously showed up in the shop Russell was assigned to," Howie spreads his arms out to full length. "I mean this machine was huge and nobody was allowed to go near it except a chosen few. It was an unspoken rule, and it didn't need to be repeated for everyone to get the picture."

Russell would get his ice cream and then he would point to the few friends he decided could join him in this childhood treat. In essence, Rosario Bufalino, one of the most prominent mobsters of the day, became the Leavenworth Good Humor Man.

"We wanted to get him a hat and a little bell, but no one had the balls to do it," Howie chuckles.

"Did you get some ice cream?"

Howie stares me down. "Are you kidding? Every time! You have any friends like that when you were inside?" he asks.

I shake my head.

"Not that served us ice cream, no."

"What about the cop thing?" he asks, referring to the penchant of cons to stalk former law enforcement guys in prison.

Because I was welcomed as if I were on vacation, and had several friends from the neighborhood already inside, thoughts of anyone wanting to come after me because I was once police didn't enter into my mind. But it was already inside the brain of a dust head weightlifter penned in upstairs.

"Bob, listen," an old Somerville pal confided on my first day. There's a guy already looking to take you out. He's bragging that he's itching to get a cop and he's chosen you. You gotta be careful, buddy."

Great fuckin' news. I'm divorced, disgraced, broke and away from my kids. If that wasn't enough, someone I didn't even know was putting a hit out on me. Who was he? A former stockholder from Blue Cross/Blue Shield? The autopilot was shutting down as the realization of my new home took its place.

Known as a "head case" this pumped up muscle slab was always looking for a fight and was delighted when he heard the news that one of the incoming was a police officer. Fuck it. I hit the gym first thing. I was in great physical shape and one thing I could do in prison was keep my body tuned.

I walked over to the heavy bag and pulled on my gloves. Fuck the guy who wanted to kill me.

I WANTED TO KILL ME!

I'd thrown my whole life away for a few bucks. My old man was bullshit ("You stupid prick!"), insane that I had gone from cop to con seemingly overnight. When I finally did get out of prison, I'd never get back into the Pointer Post — that was for sure. He'd bar me forever. And that was the least of my problems. My life was in shambles. And Jose? That asshole! I started hitting that bag ten feet into the air, both ways for at least fifteen minutes, howling an ungodly stream of expletives the entire time. In my peripheral vision, I saw another guy in the room but I was too far-gone for my mind to acknowledge his presence.

After I finished getting some of my frustration out I was heaving and sweating. Back in the dorm, I tossed my bag on the bed and turned to see my old friend grinning from ear to ear.

"What are you so happy about?" I said as I looked down at myself. I was drenched in sweat. "You ain't gone gay on me, have ya?"

He threw back his head and laughed. "No, Bobby. But you may have a new fan."

"Yeah?" I asked as I peeled off my shirt.

Just what I needed. A potential boyfriend that I'd have to give a beating to now.

"You see anyone in the weight room?"

I pulled off my shoes and shrugged.

"Some guy. But he left. I'm not looking to make any new friends today."

Apparently it was the guy who was gunning for me. He had been waiting in the gym for the cop to show up.

"When he saw you hittin' the bag and howling like a werewolf, he come running up here and says 'Jesus Christ! Stay away from that cop! He's fucking nuts!'"

And that was the last I ever heard of him. By the way, the day after I pled guilty, my ex-friend Jose pled guilty as well. He got a fine and a slap on the wrist, just like my father said he would.

I went to prison.

It was quite a bit later in Leavenworth that Howie Winter discovered he had two un-indicted co-conspirators in the race fixing trial. Two men who never went to jail, nor served time. Two government informants.

James "Whitey Bulger and Stevie "The Rifleman" Flemmi.

The Bureau of Prisons had just about killed Howie trying to force him to talk about the two guys they already had on their own payroll.

I know my mouth is hanging open.

"Jesus Christ, Howie! That's gotta be..." I'm searching for the words and come up with a gut reaction instead..."a kick in the balls!"

Howie smiles. "Yes, it certainly was."

"If you had it to do over?" Keeping his mouth shut about those he knew?

Howie knew the deal. His refusal to roll resulted in swift punishment.

"In reality, as a forty-nine year old guy who had never been arrested, never gone to prison, and in on a non-violent conviction, the norm would have been to send me to a minimum security facility or a work camp. But they didn't and that's the way it was."

He shrugs. He's not bitching and crying "Oh, poor me." He's merely stating the obvious. At any time, Howie could have raised his hand and said "Hey guys, I might have some stories to tell you," which undoubtedly would have landed him in a much better situation.

"Life is made up of a series of choices, Bobby. You make the choice that is right for you and you live with it. So I did. If I had to do over, I'd do the same, although at this age, I don't think I would live through it."

It's time to stop for today. I give Howie the last word.

"Anything else you'd like to say about the Diesel Tour?"

He rubs a hand against his cheek for a moment. Then he says, "I guess you could put down that I am a survivor of federal therapy."

We're at his front door and I pull on my coat. I have one more question.

"Is there anything you'd like to say about the prison system?"

He smiles. "Yeah, I don't ever want to go back."

He holds a hand up in a wave as I walk to my truck.

Later that evening, I'm having a beer when I think of something I want to write. For the purposes of this book, I agreed to something I really didn't want to do. I allowed myself to be interviewed in order to lay out some of the details of my own life as they related to Somerville, Howie and my father. I figured if the individuals I had been interviewing had gone out on an emotional limb to open up their collective pasts to me, the least I could do was respond in kind. The stories I planned to relate in the book turned out much differently than I originally anticipated, because I found myself in many of them — also something I hadn't set out to do. So I agreed to answer some questions, to be fair and I guess, to see how it felt.

It was uncomfortable, to say the least.

One of the questions asked of me was "What was the worst thing that happened to you in prison, other than having to go?"

My answer was "Nothing. It was easy — a good time, didn't have to do no work. It was a joke. I ran the basketball team, the baseball team. I played sports, hit the bag. Nothing bad at all." I can see myself grin as I answered the interviewer.

I look back on that session now as I'm writing and I realize not only was I not being honest, I was being flippant and smug, letting my mouth answer like a jackass when my brain knew better. What I should have answered was, "Nothing. I was lucky. I did six months — weekends only — not in Leavenworth, but in the local prison near my family — and then went to weekend house arrest. I wasn't constantly questioned about my past and made to look like an informer to the other inmates, I wasn't thrown into solitary and forgotten about. I didn't spend solid years away from my children, unable to be at the sickbeds and funerals of buddies and, God forbid, family. No one bothered me or tortured me. I had friends within the prison hierarchy who watched out for me and I came out employed. That's no joke, that's pure fuckin' luck."

Because let's face it, in the prison system, just like in real life, even if you try to stay on the straight and narrow, there but the grace of God go I.

I do thank God every day that I didn't do the time that I could have easily been sentenced to for my crime. I didn't really have to tell you any of this, since you've never seen my interview, but after listening to Howie, and although I couldn't begin to compare my time inside with his, I felt like I had to amend it anyway.

CHAPTER SEVENTEEN

Mother of the Hill, Ellen Brogna

I ASK ELLEN Brogna what she wanted to be when she was a little girl. She looks back at me, poker-faced, and replies, "Oh, I don't know. A mobster's wife?"

My jaw drops. "Really?"

She bursts into laughter, doubling over on the couch in her living room.

"I swear to God, Bobby!" she grins as she catches her breath. "You walked right into that one! Actually, I wanted to become a dancer, saw the beauty in it. I'll tell you a secret. Sometimes when I'm here alone, I push the furniture out of the way, turn on the videos and dance."

"Here" is the home she shares with the man she's been with for thirty-seven years, her husband Howie Winter.

The women of Somerville are key pieces in the puzzle of the sociological make up of the men. They come from slightly different, yet startlingly similar situations and each one found a different place inside to perch in order to survive. Some remain sheltered by choice, like Annemarie Sperlinga, others eyes wide shut, seeing but not believing until it was all over, like my sister Patty, and then there's Ellen. Eyes open, seeing and recording it all, Ellen is the Mother Historian of all things Winter Hill.

Yet despite the contrasting emotional paths the women have chosen, still one thread weaves strongly through each of them, binding them together; the need to survive. In the world of survivors, Ellen is probably queen. And a very complicated one.

To start off, Ellen Brogna Winter is really just Ellen Brogna.

"I always liked my name, why should I change it just because I got married?" she asks no one in particular. She points at my notes to make sure I write what she's saying. "It's Ellen Brogna."

Got it.

Ellen, in her fifties, reminds me of the actress Anne Bancroft. She's lively and animated. Well spoken, she's not above using the local vernacular of profanity to punctuate, yet is at the same time thoughtful in her responses. She wants to be sure I get the facts correct and has had her problems with several books in which writers have used her name.

"I don't care if they write about me but get it *right!*" She is exasperated after years correcting what has been written and being misrepresented by people who don't know her. "Especially that writer in Boston," she says. "You know who I mean!"

I do but I'm not mentioning his name, so he may be disappointed there is actually a published book about Winter Hill and Howie Winter that doesn't include him. If you see him flipping through these pages in the local bookstore, tell him not to bother.

He offended her on a personal level, it seems. "Do you know what he called me during Howie's trial? 'The Ice Princess'!" The interview hasn't even started and she's already up off the couch. Obviously, the writer never spent anytime with Ellen. Ice Princess is definitely NOT what she is.

"Can you imagine how that feels?"

I can. There's also a book on the shelves that portrays me negatively and inaccurately, but what can you do? Beating the shit out of someone (which I briefly considered) or sucking it up (which I did in the end), are the choices. Simply hope anyone reading that which presents you erroneously is either someone who knows you for who you really are — good and bad — or someone who doesn't give a shit anyway.

"He also called me," she takes up a mocking tone, 'the ever loyal Mrs. Winter', what's that supposed to mean?"

I'm not sure. Loyalty in Somerville is never considered an insult. It must be a Boston thing.

"Fuck him," I say. "Here's a good place to start. Tell me some things about you." Howie takes this off-camera opportunity to sneak a look at the newspaper. He is so used to the camera and me by now and figures that with Ellen in the room, we will have forgotten all about him.

Ellen sits back. "I had to get that out of my system first." But that's not all she was doing. I'll write it just as she tells it to me.

"My mother was Irish and English, born in Cambridge. She was also," she pauses for effect, "I think maybe a little bit Jewish. My father was Italian from Chelsea. He was a chef — good thing since he had twelve kids." A big family, even by Irish-Italian Catholic Somerville standards.

"My childhood was sheer madness! I never remember a time where there weren't at least sixteen people living in our house. My parents also raised my two younger cousins."

"How did your father support that family?" I ask.

"He worked two or three jobs at a time. But my parents never turned anyone away. If someone needed a place to sleep, they'd make it happen. A girlfriend of mine got pregnant and moved in. If it had been me, I'd have gotten thrown out because he was an old-school guinea!"

"How big was the house?"

Ellen's family home was her grandparents' house as well. Many of the homes when we were growing up were two or three family structures, sort of the precursor to the condo, but on a much lower economic scale. Called double or triple-deckers, it wasn't unusual to have three generations of one family living in separate self-contained floors under the same roof.

"Seven rooms and every room was a bedroom! Sometimes even the china cabinet had a little bassinet on it!"

I get a vision of an infant snoozing among the cherished pieces of family china everyone had and no one ever used. It might even be one of my own memories, although the Martini's nine couldn't hold a candle to the Brogna's count. Back then, the Irish and Italians were fully practicing Catholics, birth control was a fantasy and with so little money, fighting and fucking pretty much covered the entertainment for any family. The more kids that came along, the further each of the older ones became distanced from the parents as the nuclear family expanded to its own huge universe.

"If you were a kid that needed a lot of love or attention, you were disappointed. Love was food, clothes, and a place to sleep. For me, it was enough."

Even the kitchen sink was a bathtub. Ellen was ten and still soaking in the kitchen. "Can you imagine? Three of us shared bathwater — the number of kids my mother decided a full sink could clean."

Meals were done in shifts and consisted of what was available.

"My father brought food home from the restaurant. Then there was the government food and my mother's relatives paid a small room and board. That helped out."

The food was rationed to ensure that the people bringing in the money to buy it were granted priority status. "At dinner time, the grown ups ate first. We sat at the kids' table and waited."

She cultivated another trait prevalent in children of large families. "I was very independent. I had my own goals. At that time, no one attended school regularly if they could get away with it. As soon as you were old enough, you wanted to work. School wasn't encouraged like it is now."

Ellen's mother had her hands full. It was impossible to keep track of everyone or to clothe all of the children in suitable school attire.

"If the older kids got up before you, there wasn't anything left to wear, and I was seven in the pecking order," Ellen says wryly. "But in the second grade, after I repeated a year, I said, 'I'm never gonna do this again.' And I didn't. I passed all my siblings in elementary school, went on and graduated. It was a big deal, most girls were desperate to get immediately married to get out of the house."

Ellen explains, "Girls didn't get their own apartments then. At least if you got married, and you were lucky, the husband's family might have a lower head count. But we were all too young."

Something else was evolving in her life. The ugly symptoms of severe illness began to manifest themselves. As a teenager, she began to break out in red rashes across her body. She was vomiting regularly and shaking uncontrollably. "The doctor ran test after test. He couldn't find anything."

The physician couldn't locate the cause because it was in Ellen's own home. "There were so many fights. My mother's family were all alcoholics. And my brothers? Whatever they wanted, they got — the girls had to work. And I had to shovel snow to contribute while my brothers got cases of beer and pints of Chivas from the household money? No way."

The screaming fights shattered decibels. "My mother was deadly afraid of my older brother Jimmy. He was a bad drunk and had to be pacified. His girlfriend lived with us and she was a whack job. I'd be shaking, hiding behind the parlor chair. One day I broke out in a rash and couldn't breathe."

The doctor caught on to what was afflicting the fourteen year old. She was on her way to a full-blown ulcer and suffering from anxiety disorder. The constant warfare didn't have any impact on the rest of the family but Ellen was pushing it deep down inside.

"I was too analytical, always wanting to know the answer when I didn't understand why things were happening, especially at home. I couldn't accept why my mother wouldn't fix the situation."

"Did you always speak your mind?" I ask. "Because you have ever since I've known you."

She throws back her head and laughs. "Yes, I did, but it was much harder back then. I was very shy and didn't interact with a good portion of the family because they were always drunk. Fear is something I carry with me to this day. But you build walls and you learn to deal."

We are all professional wall builders. I'm one myself. I don't even think it's a conscious choice. The booze, the crime, the violence comes out and the walls automatically go up to protect childhood as much as possible. Once they're up, they rarely come down for the rest of your life.

Yet breaking up a family for any reason other than financial was simply not done. Her symptoms eventually lessened, but anxiety has been her constant companion throughout the subsequent decades.

"It's always right around the corner, but I managed to keep it together, keep going to school."

"And you eventually did get married," I remind her.

"It took eighteen years to make up my mind. But I didn't do it to escape. I did it because I wanted to. So, Bobby," she smacks her palm on her lap, "let's get to what you came for."

The history of Ellen and Howie.

"When I was fourteen, I began to pass by the corner where Howie, Sal and their buddies hung out every day. As I got older, I started to take a second look."

"I knew who she was," Howie muses from behind the sports page. "She caught my eye. But she was way too young for me."

"I'll tell it, Howie!" She interrupts. "Yes, I was seventeen and he was forty-two but why wouldn't I be attracted to this quiet, reserved man?"

Howie also introduced Ellen to something seldom experienced— it was called, she learned — fun.

"He was charming. Every girl in the city wanted to jump into the car and have a ball with us. It wasn't scary; it didn't trigger anxiety. I was having fun and felt safe. There was no argument with my parents when I finally left. It was like, 'Take her — she's got to get out of this life.'"

Howie was married to Sissy at that time, but Ellen had no idea.

"I'm certainly not an idiot. I knew he had kids but he lived alone and never mentioned a wife."

Even on the small close-knit Winter Hill, things are not always what they seem. The marital status of the guys on the corners was never discussed. What men did in the street was separate from their home lives and had been for generations. Howie was indeed married but hadn't lived with his wife for years. He supported her and his children, but they lived apart.

"When did you find out?"

"Not until 1977 when he was in jail on the pinball arrest. I was on my way over when Charlie stopped me."

Howie's son-in-law was adamant. "Ellen," he said firmly, "you cannot visit. It's family only."

Ellen was nonplussed. "That's OK, just tell them I'm one of his girls and I'll slip in with everyone else." She flashes me a grin, "I was about as old as his kids were."

"That's not going to work," Charlie sighed. "His wife will be there."

"His *what?*"

"I guess you had to know sometime. Howie is still married."

Ellen shrugs. "What could I do? I was already almost seven years into it by then. And with everything else that was going on, it became a non-issue."

Another non-issue was the subject of children. It sprung from choice and ended by necessity. She winces slightly. "I'd seen enough in my own family to know I didn't want that kind of life. I didn't feel the motherly impulse to have my own children. It's weird because now I can't keep kids away from me."

It isn't weird if you know Ellen. Like many of us, she has a hardened exterior, sort of a brilliant disguise, yet she is the neighborhood magnet for anyone needing assistance, advice or a babysitter.

"I've been hurt over the years because of it. It seems like I've spent so much of my life protecting Howie that the maternal instinct is second nature to me. So when I got pregnant in 1973, I made the decision to terminate. Then came a time when I thought I did want a child. It almost killed me."

In 1981 Howie was incarcerated at Shirley Prison preparing to begin his federal sentence for horse fixing. Ellen was suffering through a bad pregnancy. Constantly ill, she was sicker than the usual nausea associated with the first trimester. "I tried to hang on but it was too much of a strain."

In her fourth month, she lost eleven pounds. Her doctor confirmed there was no longer any heartbeat coming from the baby. He gently informed Ellen her body would most likely protect itself by miscarrying naturally within a few days. Her body, however, did not cooperate and she deteriorated.

"I was admitted to the hospital with such a high level of toxicity in my blood, I was slowly being poisoned. They had to go in and take the baby."

After the operation, she got worse and the doctor feared she might not recover. Her widowed father hovered over her, hoping for the best, but it was time Howie be told he must prepare for the worst.

"The doctor called the prison administration and they actually brought Howie to the phone."

Howie has been reading the paper across the room and pretty much ignoring Ellen and I.

"Howie," I interrupt him, "what were you thinking at that time?" As the words jump out of my mouth, I wince. Like Ellen, I'm known for my bluntness and sometimes my thoughts escape before I can catch them.

He puts his paper down. "Oh, it was terrible. They thought she was going to die."

When a priest was called in to administer the Last Rites, Howie wrangled a visit to the hospital under armed guard. "But she didn't even know I was there. I thought it was the end," Howie says slowly.

The woman he loved would die; he would go away to a federal penitentiary. That was his future.

It was the only occasion that Ellen can remember in which the Feds did not try to make a deal with Howie in order to improve his situation.

"They knew who I was, even back then," she says of law enforcement. They'd get to know — and *hear* — her much more as the years went by, but for now, she was recognized as his steady companion.

"Often they tried to use his children as a vehicle to get him to cooperate, as if he could lessen any perceived embarrassment of his family. But that time, they didn't dare make an offer."

Perhaps Ellen's impending death was too raw even for them. But she slowly recovered and Howie went away.

"With regard to kids, I'll say this. I never felt cheated because I didn't give birth. It just wasn't my fate." But she has spent her lifetime with a man who has his own component of sons and daughters.

"What's your relationship with Howie's children?"

My deal with Howie is that he has afforded me complete access to anything I need, I can ask any questions whatsoever; the only subject that is closed completely is his family. My deal with Ellen is different, however. There is nothing I can't ask, but whether she chooses to answer is up to her. She can also throw me out of the house.

Ellen does address the issue and not without a touch of bitterness.

"They don't exist to me. That's how I've learned to deal with it. Except, of course, for Gary."

There's a slight hitch in her voice. "I loved his son Gary and I miss him terribly."

Howie's often told me Gary and Ellen were true soul mates. They delighted in each other's company and spent many happy times together, bringing along Gary's current girlfriend of the moment. His death devastated not only his father and his siblings, but his stepmother as well.

"I was very close to him. The girls [Howie's daughters], I believe, have always blamed me because their father was not with their mother, even though they'd been separated long before we'd ever met. Over the years things never changed."

She gives me a "what are you gonna do?" look. "Not that it didn't hurt, it did. But Gary and I? He was one hundred and ten per cent here for me when his father was arrested. He never pushed me aside for anyone. There was only one incident between us."

Howie was facing years in jail and even Gary lashed out in anger and frustration at the protracted sentence his father received.

"What are you gonna have for the rest of *your* life, Ellen? At least my mother has her children."

Ellen stared at him. "I knew he regretted it right away, but I gave it right back anyway. 'Then maybe your mother should divorce your father and she can be the one on the run.' It was just frustration."

I've seen Ellen angry before, more than once, but this is the first time when I have felt she was close to tears. "I really loved Gary and I miss him every day," she finishes.

I know. I do too.

I ask Ellen to describe her marriage. She complains, good-naturedly, that I'm making her feel as if she's playing Twenty Questions. "We'd been together for years and marriage is just a piece of paper to me but I didn't have a good feeling about the future. So I said, 'What are you doing next Friday night? I think it's about time we did this.'"

She had what might be called a premonition. Perhaps it was fear that history could repeat itself, or worse yet, be rewritten. With Winter Hill teeming with rumors about investigations, informants and a body count that didn't exactly rival the Gang Wars, but was enough to merit headlines, there was no guarantee that someone from the past with a grudge could suddenly appear out of the shadows.

"I'd been through the hard times when he was away. I kept our lives going. But I knew who he was. Maybe someday he'd go to jail again, or God forbid pass away, and I'd have no rights to the life we'd built together. So after eighteen years I figured we should do it. And we did."

I want to talk about prison life for those on the outside. When my old man was in jail for taking the Fifth, it was like a medal of honor to my brothers and me. He refused to inform on his friends and chose to go away. It *was* difficult for my mother, as she needed his financial support as well as whatever parenting he felt like contributing. But the old man lived with his girlfriend, so any pain my mother suffered was lessened during his incarceration. She had the solace at least he wasn't with another woman.

For Ellen, it had to be a much more difficult emotionally. She actually was the girlfriend with no guarantee of future security. "It becomes a way of life. You're a prisoner in your own world; slave to the telephone, the mailbox, the flight that's going to take you wherever 'there' is at the time. And you don't even consciously make that decision."

She'd been with him for almost a decade. Neither of them realized when he was arrested in 1977 that not only would he be convicted, but that he'd go from state prison after his parole directly into the federal system.

But from 1980 to 1981 Howie was living in a prison cottage at Shirley in close proximity to Ellen. Her existence revolved around their visits. "I went every weekday from ten in the morning 'til ten at night. That was my world for the two years he was there."

They fashioned a routine in the little cottage that was gradually accepted as their normalcy. Ellen convinced herself that it wasn't that bad. And it wasn't, in comparison to what was to follow.

"In October of 81' they sent him to Concord. In January, he started moving and was finally sent on his bus trip to Leavenworth."

Ellen was living close to her family. She laughs uproariously at my assumption that she was well taken care of emotionally.

"Bobby, what's wrong with you? Haven't you been paying attention? They needed *me* to take care of them. My father had five children at home. I think he liked the thought I'd move in and take care of everyone. I did for the first year."

Ellen still had the house she and Howie had been living in. She may have been devastated by recent events — the loss of her mother, unborn child, and now — by proxy — her common law husband — but she began sharpening her self-preservation skills.

"When the IRS took it. I bought another one at auction. A different home seized from Howie."

The irony isn't lost on me. Having to buy one's own property back at auction.

The letters, the calls and the occasional visits made Ellen's world even smaller. I wonder what the holidays were like. I prepare myself for an earful. Generally she is much more animated and quick to jab her points home. But today, she's made a special effort to remain introspective. There is only so long, however, Ellen will be patient. Instead of taking my head off, she throws hers back, laughs and claps her hands delightedly.

"Holidays? The best! I never had that growing up — those big Christmases with piles of presents. Howie made sure each one was like Chuck E. Cheese for a kid who'd never had pizza! I wanted luggage, perfume, everything! You know, like when you were growing up — those little things you always wanted but couldn't have?"

Very well. And now that I could have them, they don't seem very important to me. I'm just lucky to still be around. But I know what she means.

"I'll tell you a great story, in case any women read your book, they'll love this!" she exclaims.

Good. I'm kinda low on the women stuff, I can tell.

"My friend Joanne and I had gone to visit Howie. She got a three-carat diamond from a boyfriend the week before and we spent the next five days just staring at it. We're sitting in the visiting area and Howie is admiring the ring. Then suddenly he says 'OK, Joanne, you can take it off now.' She pulls the ring off and hands it to Howie who gives it to *me*! I couldn't believe it! Even the guard nearly fell over!"

Their overseer actually left his post for a closer look. "My God, that is one beautiful ring!" he exclaimed. She's right; it IS a great story for the chicks. But Ellen being Ellen barely recovered from the shock when her mind began churning. "I took it to a whole different realm," she admits. "Does he want me to marry him? He isn't even fucking divorced! But I figured it could only get better."

Meaning?

"He was sharp. This was 1979. He knew what time he had ahead of him. He said to himself, 'Let me reel her in good now.'"

Now it's my turn to mock-scold her. "Way to suck out all of the romance, Ellen!"

She shrugs. "You want romance, watch Lifetime, I thought you were here for the truth."

From behind his paper, I hear Howie make a "Hmmp!" sound. He's voted on the side of romance.

"Was there ever a time when you considered divorcing him?"

Not a moment of hesitation. "No. When we got married it was only a year and a half later he was rearrested. I knew he was going down for the count. But I had those choices to make before [his arrests]."

"Weren't you on the run for a while?" I ask innocently even though she knows I'm full of shit.

The Feds were looking to force Ellen to testify in the horse fixing trial and brought her in frequently to question her. She had nothing to say, ("What the hell did I know about horses?"), but the inherent fear of being served and having others assume she must be the bearer of information was more than enough to put any non-witness in jeopardy.

She was told although the court deemed her a "link in the chain of events"; she would not be protected with any sort of immunity. The trial was imminent, and no one prepared her for what her presence inside the courtroom could mean to her personally once she was outside. It soon became evident.

Each time Ellen was dragged into court Stevie Flemmi and Whitey Bulger confronted her attorney, demanding to know what she'd said. Johnny Martorano knocked on the window of her car as she was pulling out of her driveway. "What are you going to say, Ellen?"

"I said I was going to let my principles guide me," which is Somerville for "I really don't know anything but I'm going to say even less."

"Apparently," Ellen finishes dryly. "He didn't understand my answer." Martorano also paid her attorney a visit. Things began to get ugly all around. Then Howie told her the most ugly truth.

"I want you to do what you think is best. But I can't protect you from them out there," she points out a window. "I knew what he was saying. It wasn't the attorneys and Feds I needed to worry about."

Ellen was never served. "They couldn't find me. They went to my father's house looking for *Ellen*. Now, my dad was an old time guinea who swore up and down he didn't have a daughter named Ellen and to get the fuck off of his porch."

The old man wasn't lying. When he'd had his seventh child baptized, he used the name Helen. "Who knows why?" Ellen muses. "But he never even called me Ellen, not once."

We both get a laugh out of the father of twelve swearing to Feds he had no daughter by that name. They must have thought he had so many kids, he'd forgotten her!

"I put everything in storage and went away for four months. It was a scary realization. Suddenly, you became deathly afraid of people you'd known for years, you'd eaten dinner with, laughed and cried with. The truth was that..."

She doesn't say any more. But I know. The truth was that no matter how many jokes or dinners, triumphs or tragedies you had shared, you were always one step — or one subpoena — away from disappearing forever. Some of us up here are loyal and some of us are expendable. And sometimes, no matter how shocking it is to discover — we are both.

"It was a difficult time and it only made the anxiety even worse."

I've got several friends who suffer differing degrees of anxiety and depression. I never have, yet I see how painful it can be. "Have you ever taken any medication for the anxiety?"

She dismisses the idea. "It wouldn't have done any good, Bobby, and I never wanted to take anything that distorted my thinking," she says earnestly. "Suddenly I was afraid of the people around me. I didn't want medicine that left me at a disadvantage. Just figured I'd work it through. And I did. But that isn't what keeps me up at night anymore. It's fear," she tells me honestly.

"Aging and what comes with it, being in a relationship in which age starts to have an impact. I pray we go together because that's how we spent our lives. I don't like the thought that I'm going to be here without Howie."

Now we're winding down. I have a better picture of who Ellen is, and maybe she does too.

"What are you most proud of?"

This one comes easily. "I always tried to do righteous things and stood by everything I believed in. I always will. I like myself."

"Last question, describe your whole life in one word."

"Fucked up," she shoots back at me, laughing again.

"That's two words, Ellen."

She smirks, "You walked right into that one, Martini."

Again. Now you see why there are so few interviews with women in this book. They get me every time. "Ellen, let's close by going back to the beginning. You always wanted to be a dancer?"

She smiles. "I didn't get that, but I got so much in this life and one thing I never dreamed I'd have."

"What is that? Not the luggage, the jewelry, the perfume," I tease her.

She smiles and lightly touches her chest. "A sense of center peace."

I shake my head. "Center peace?"

"No commotion, nobody beating up someone else, no police at the house and drunks falling in at every hour of the night. No more prisons or steel bars. Just me and Howie and it's nice and peaceful."

Does she have any regrets?

"One. That we didn't have more 'outside' time together. Fifteen years was spent with other people in a big room or behind locked doors. I would've liked to enjoy him more."

A lifetime on the Winter Hill merry-go-round, years wasted, time lost. We make our decisions, by action or association, and pay accordingly, although we are always surprised when the bill comes. Ellen's was expensive, as was her husband's. Maybe she's right. Maybe a shot of Welbutrin or Paxil still ain't enough to take away the fear of always being one step ahead of nothingness. I really don't know.

It's getting late, maybe later than I think. "Ellen, what's your best memory?"

"First," she replies, "my most painful memory is my mother's death — and my father's pain after. That really sticks out in my mind. For a good memory, here's the best. I went to visit Howie after he was arrested in '92. I was talking to Gary on the phone as I was waiting. When I'm nervous I talk, talk, talk. Gerry Farina [Howie's codefendant] had already made bond. I was telling Gary I was so happy for Gerry's wife. At the same time, Gary was saying that Howie made bond, but I didn't hear him."

Gary finally managed to get the news across.

"I dropped the phone! I was jumping up and down, guards looking at me like I was nuts! To see him walk out! I remember saying to myself, 'we've got another shot.'"

If I live another fifty years, I'll never forget the look on Ellen's face as she answered me. It's more than hopeful and for a second, it reminds me no matter how little time may be left, some of us still get lucky enough to get one more shot.

After packing up my camera and notebooks, I walk to my truck in the light that film camera guys call magic hour. When the sky is not yet dark, but saturated with color and shadowed highlights. Behind me, Ellen calls out.

"Hey Bobby, come back and talk anytime!"

I turn to see her and Howie framed in the doorway. He waves, I wave back. I'm struck by the fact that they act as if I'd been a welcomed guest and not the man dissecting their lives and writing their secrets. The only piece missing from this greeting card picture of the Brogna-Winter family is my old friend Gary. As soon as I can find my voice, I call back. "You can count on it."

CHAPTER EIGHTEEN

Disorganized Crime: the Drug Beef, the Snatch, the Raid, and Charming Billy

The Boston Herald
May 18, 1993
EX-SOMERVILLE MOB BOSS PLEADS
GUILTY TO TRAFFICKING IN COCAINE
By Andrea Estes

Howard "Howie" Winter, who once ruled an organized crime gang with a power rivaling the Mafia's, went to jail yesterday for trafficking in cocaine. In a move that surprised prosecutors, Winter, 63, of Millbury pleaded guilty and was sentenced immediately to a mandatory 10-year term in federal prison.

Winter admitted arranging the delivery of six kilograms of cocaine to a friend who was secretly cooperating with the federal Drug Enforcement Administration, the Massachusetts State Police and the U.S Department of Labor's Office of Labor Racketeering. The gangster reportedly refused to cooperate after his arrest when urged to turn informant on his former Somerville-based Winter Hill gang associates, James J. "Whitey" Bulger and Stephen "The Rifleman" Flemmi.

"Want to know what REALLY happened? Well, here's *exactly* what happened," Ellen begins. "It was January 5th in 1992."

We're in front of JT's Corner Store in Millbury, almost fourteen years after her husband was picked up by law enforcement on a cocaine beef. It's November, the New England chill just starting to settle in, but it has no effect on Ellen. At a trim fifty-something, Ellen is animated as she speaks; legs planted firmly apart, her right hand pointing around the parking lot. The wind whips her shoulder length brown-shot-with-gray hair around her face and she waves a Styrofoam cup as she acts out the story. Ellen has a presence about her, from her looks (like she might be the road manager for The Stones), and the way she dresses (stylish black pants, blue ball jacket, over-sized sunglasses) down to her shotgun manner of communicating ("Are you listening to me, Bobby?") and I know she's a force to be reckoned with. Howie stands off to the side, grinning. There's no stopping Ellen once she gets going.

"It was about 7:30 in the morning. We pulled in right about here," Ellen points to a spot. "I was driving and I waited outside. Howie went in to get the newspapers and then we were going to breakfast."

Ralph Spring is working the register at JT's just as he was in 1992. JT's is a typical small town store; variety stores they used to be called and in fact, we still refer to them that way. A pleasant middle-aged guy with glasses, he greets Howie with a big smile. I ask him about the morning the Feds visited. Ralph moves to the register.

"I was standing here, Mr. Winters came in like he does just about every Sunday."

Here's some more Massachusetts trivia. We're notorious for changing words and names. Just try and convince anyone up north that "irregardless" isn't a word. It's impossible. I've also noticed that many people, including guys Howie has known for decades, refer to him as "Winters" instead of "Winter."

Through the course of my research, I've also seen the incorrect spelling in newspapers and court transcripts. And, I admit, after reviewing my own interviews, I've done it too on occasion. It's not disrespect; it's just the way it is.

Howie is standing on the other side of the counter.

"So, Ralph, was Howie where he is now?"

Ralph, like Ellen, acts out the story for me. We are our own reality show crew.

"He'd bought the papers and was headed for the door when it swung open and Mr. Winters stepped aside to let three gentlemen in. But they didn't come any further. One of them said, 'We'd like to talk to you.' So I started right over, to see if I could help Howie out."

Ralph is not a huge guy and he was alone. No weapon, not even a baseball bat. Three guys come strolling in for what could have been a hit, yet Ralph moved forward without a second thought. "I wanted to help Howie, just in case." He assumes I know what "what" could have been.

"One of them brought out a badge fast, held it up in the air over his head."

The agent was probably as apprehensive about the storekeeper as Ralph was of him. Law enforcement was aware of Howie's status within the neighborhood and it was crucial they identify themselves quickly.

"I stopped. I realized they were cops of some kind. They talked quietly for a few moments and they all went outside."

It happens that fast. The Feds. Just like the Mob. Except that the Mob kills you right then and there. The Feds take you away and you may or not come back.

Outside JT's, Ellen picks the story back up. "I noticed a white van next to us. Howie came out and tossed the papers into the passenger seat and immediately said, 'Don't get out of the car.'"

Ellen twists her body around to show me what happened next. "I turned toward my window and there's two men with badges.

"'Ellen,' one said to me. 'Go home. Don't leave the house. Don't contact anyone until we call.' But I wasn't leaving until they answered me. 'Where's Howie and what the hell is going on?'"

"We've got him," one informed Ellen. "Please just go home."

She shrugs. "They had him. As they pulled away, I saw Howie in the van. I had no idea what they meant when they tried to order me not to call anyone. Why shouldn't I call our lawyer?"

I nod. "So Ellen, you went home and waited for a call, right?" I can't help myself.

Ellen bursts out laughing. "Yeah, right, Bob! That's exactly what I did! Bullshit! I drove home as fast as I could, called Gary and said 'Get your ass over here right now. They've got your father.'"

The temperature gets the best of us. We retire to the Winters' comfortable living room. Jackets off, heat on, Howie's papers and hot coffee on the table, we return to the story.

I smile as Howie eases down into his comfortable chair; he looks like a grandfather. Ellen is across the room, perched on the couch, a rocket at the launch pad. The last time I was here, she was subdued and introspective. Talking about herself was very difficult, but now all of that anxiety is gone because she's back to what she has done for almost forty years — fiercely looking out for Howie Winter.

"You were arrested that morning?" I ask Howie.

"Not exactly," he tells me. "I wasn't even read my rights until ten or so hours later."

"Did they take you to jail?"

Howie shakes his head. "No, to a suite at The Sheraton in Framingham." A hotel suite? This is definitely not like my own experience of being hauled in.

Ellen wants the story told as it happened. "Let me get back to where I was. I called Gary, like I told you. I was afraid, Bobby."

Afraid of the Feds?

Ellen makes a kind but pointedly "get a clue" expression. "I didn't know *who* took him. At first — yes — I thought they were cops or agents because of the badges. But as I thought about it, I began to feel scared in a different way. Badges, big deal. Howie was *gone.* That could have meant a lot of different things."

I know what she's saying and those "different things" hang silently between all three of us. I think of Ray Liotta in the nighttime arrest scene of *Goodfellas* where he tells the audience that if it had been a Mob hit instead of just the Feds, he would have been dead before he realized what was happening. That may be true for the Italians, but the Irish are big on kidnapping, torturing and then finally killing you. Nothing is easy for us.

"Then Howie called!" she says. "About thirty minutes after they took him."

"Ellen," Howie said calmly. "Go into work, don't deviate from your routine. I'll call you there."

She was working at a club just up the street from their house and her usual Sunday routine after breakfast would be to go in, ready the day drawer for business and calculate the receipts.

"He sounded calm." Howie smiles at me as if to say, "Yes I AM the one who stays calm."

"Did you ask where he was?" She shakes her head. We Somerville folk know that the telephone is not always our friend, especially if it suddenly becomes a party line without our knowledge.

"I called Gary back and told him to meet me at work. Then I called Howie's lawyer Albie Cullen and told him what had happened. I put on my jacket and went up the street."

Once they were together, Ellen and Gary fearfully waited for the phone to ring. The chilling statement, "We have him" could belie many alternatives.

"Finally, it rang. It was a guy who identified himself as a federal agent. 'You need to come to The Sheraton [in Framingham] Come now, come alone, don't tell anyone where you're going.'"

"What did you say?" I ask.

"I said "Baffangu you!"   She makes the universal punctuation; the palm of one hand slapped into the bend of the other elbow.

Baffangu is the American pronunciation for the famous Italian phrase actually spelled "Vaffanculo", and impolitely translated can mean "Fuck you" or "Go take it in the ass", depending on the mood of the speaker. Thanks to the movies, however, even the Irish know that its most popular translation is pretty much "Go fuck yourself."

Way to start off a conversation with the Feds, Ellen. "That's what you said to the agent?

"That is exactly what I said. Gary was next to me and I said out loud so the agent can hear me, 'Gary, you can't come with me, you'll have to stay here.' I'm torturing this guy on the phone even more."

Howie's voice returned to the line. "Ellen, do what they say, it's all right. Tell the day manager at the club to get three thousand dollars ready, just in case." Howie was anticipating bail.

"I walked into the lobby and one of the men from that morning greeted me. 'Ellen,' I'm Bill Chase.' I recognized his name, he was the one they put on the women, because he's charming." She pauses and grins. "And he is. But here's how I knew about Bill Chase. Someone told me."

She pauses and looks over at Howie, who we catch reading the paper. "Can I say how I knew?"

Howie nods and waves his hand, sure, fine. "Say whatever you want."

She leans closer. "I knew because Stevie Flemmi told me. *Years* before, but I didn't even think back then — how the hell would he know [the assignments of a federal agent]?"

I'm not following her. She shakes her head.

"How the hell would Stevie have known a federal agent so well that he could say to me, 'be careful because he's the one they use to question the women.' Stevie knew all of the players."

"It didn't register until years later, when they were all pulled in. I realized that Stevie had tipped his hand [as an informant] to me and I never realized it."

Bill Chase eventually felt Ellen's wrath. Years later, she phoned him. "Bill, you son of a bitch! You were trying to get information about us all along." But Ellen being Ellen, she also had to tell Bill what Stevie had said, how he almost blew his cover.

"And I said, 'you were pretty charming!' I had to say that too, because he really was."

Back to the lobby. "So here I am with Bill Chase. He had black hair, handsome, nice shoes. He looked like he should have been wearing Armani, like a Hollywood movie detective. Now, me? This was years ago, so I'm wearing heels." From what little I know about women's shoes, I'm guessing her hand gestures are creating a set of four to five inch spiked heels in the air.

"I'm lookin' like Park and LaGrange (a corner known for the working ladies that hung there) with the blue heels, blue stockings, blue pants and a tiny halter top thing." She covers her breasts to demonstrate. "I swear!" She holds up a hand in oath. "I was...well, I was *dressed*."

Ah, the days when women *really* dressed. Chase led Ellen to the elevator and pressed the button. "I was so nervous, I was shaking. Bill thought there was something wrong with me."

She points at Howie. "He knows." The paper comes down. Howie nods. The paper goes back up.

"My blood pressure drops sometimes. I felt like I was going to faint." Ellen pantomimes going into a swoon. "Anyway, we get off the elevator into a huge suite. There's Howie. Not dead. Not in cuffs. Just sitting on a couch with his arms folded."

"You had to be so relieved."

Ellen gives me the evil eye. "I was gonna kill him!"

There were others in the room. "Four guys in all — Bill Chase, Tom Duffy [state trooper], DEA Agent Dan Doherty, Assistant U.S. Attorney George Vien."

One of them told Ellen they'd have to go through her pocketbook. Ellen's anxiety dissipated as blunt bravado took precedence over angst and what the future might hold.

"I said, 'Go ahead you sons-of-bitches!' I sat down across from Duffy and asked, 'What is he here for?'"

There was a bit of shifting and an uncomfortable pause.

"The thing of it is, Ellen," Duffy said. "He's got himself in a little problem."

"They just didn't want to say," Ellen was astonished. "They dragged me down and didn't want to say what's going on. Howie, stalling, had told them, 'I'm not gonna say a word without my wife here.' So they had to bring me down, but now they didn't know what to do with me."

"Ellen," Tom started again. "Did you talk to anybody?"

"Yes," Ellen replied. The trooper slammed a hand against his thigh and yelled, "Son of a bitch!"

"I got right back in his face and said, 'What the fuck! Did you think I was going through this alone? You hauled my husband's ass away. I called his son! I said 'Howie, what is going on here?" The agents intimated to Howie that perhaps he should be the one to clue Ellen in on the situation.

Howie shrugged and replied, "I got myself in a little jam."

The agents tried to pacify her with coffee and sandwiches, but Ellen wasn't having any, her anger rising. "I don't want your coffee, I don't want your food. Get away from me!'" She strode into the bathroom and slammed the door shut.

Four big guys clustered outside the bathroom, anticipating what Ellen and her badass stilettos might do next. Howie wisely stayed on the couch. Ellen's mind was whirring. If somebody's done something and Howie's involved, why he isn't in custody? There's only one reason — they must be pressuring him to flip. Otherwise he'd be in a cell by now. She had figured it out.

Howie's newspaper comes down. He hasn't missed a word.

"That's what they do, Bobby," he patiently explains, "when they want you to become an informant — what they call a "government witness" — in exchange for some relief. They yank you off the street and into seclusion." It's crucial to snatch the candidate early in the day, without any witnesses. "They want to get you in, make a deal and put you right back on the street so no one knows they've gotten to you. Otherwise, somebody might figure it out."

In the bathroom Ellen knew the game was on. "I finally came out." The agents parted outside the door. "Thanks," she sniffled, as she emerged, a perfect portrait of scared, confused wife.

"May I please have some time with my husband?" she asked shakily. The agents left the room.

"The minute they shut that door, I pointed a finger at Howie and said, "What is going on?"

"Here's the deal," Howie confided to his wife. "They've got some wiretaps, some video..."

"For what?" Ellen demanded.

"From a confidential informant..."

Ellen was unraveling. "Who the hell are you talking about?"

"I don't know," Howie continued patiently. "It's confidential."

"Bullshit!" Ellen concluded. Her husband nodded. But there wasn't much they could do about and there were other friends involved.

By the time the agents returned, the Winters sat silently. The Feds had their own announcement. "Ellen, if Howie gave you any information concerning anything that happened in this room, we've told him we'll pick you up for conspiracy and obstruction of justice."

She makes that dismissive face my daughter makes when she says "Yeah whatever, Dad." It infuriates the shit out of me, so I can imagine what it did to the boys with the badges.

Then the hammering began in earnest. "They were at him," Ellen says. "To get him to roll. It didn't faze him."

Howie finally spoke up. "Ellen, what do you want?"

Five pairs of eyes turned to the one woman dressed for a night on the town. Ellen shrugged. "You're a grown man. Let your conscience be your guide, whatever you can live with. You can either become a rat or you will go away for a long fucking time. *But this I will tell you...*"

Uh oh. Today, across the room, Howie's newspaper goes back up.

"If the shoe was on another's guy's foot, you'd be going fucking down!!!"

The agents were quick to join in after realizing that Ellen's diatribe wasn't aimed at them, and instead directed toward a different criminal element. "She's right, Howie! She's right!" They all chimed in.

"They were like a chorus, all repeating each other," Ellen laughs. "So then I turned on them."

"I said, 'What does Howie get out of this?' I knew they must want some kind of information, probably about Stevie and Whitey. And I knew Howie made his decision long before I'd arrived. It was just time to see how far they'd go to get what they wanted. So I said 'Is he gonna get immunity?'"

The men were indignant. "No, but it would make a real difference in where he serves his time."

"What difference? If this rat, whoever he is, gets to go free, and he," Ellen points to the man behind the paper, "...gets nothing, well, that would be how I made *my* decision."

Howie had nothing more to say. That was it.

"The party," says Ellen, "was over. Nobody was so fucking charming anymore!"

The men began putting on their jackets and Ellen moved into efficient wife mode.

"I said 'Howie give me your jewelry and the stuff in your pockets.' I knew he had his numbers there, but they were on to me. 'No, we'll take that! [The items].' I told them, 'give me the fucking jewelry at least.' And they did."

Ellen had no idea where they were taking her husband or when she'd see him again. As the group emptied out into the hallway, Bill Chase sided up to Ellen.

"Would you like me to drive you home?" The charm was back on.

Ellen snorts with laughter at her own response. "'Ya?' I said. 'And who's gonna drive MY car home? I'll get myself home.' The last thing I wanted was Chase in my house when I had business to do."

At home, Gary and his girlfriend Nancy were waiting in the kitchen. Ellen dropped into a chair, bitching. "That son of a bitch! He did it to me again! Gary, I need two things..." She grabbed a pen and began scribbling frantically on a piece of paper. "One, give me that bottle of wine! Then..."

Ellen knew she couldn't leave the house without being followed. With Howie refusing to roll, the word would soon be out on the street that he was locked up.

She shoved the piece of paper at Gary. "And two, you gotta go! I can't leave. Try the Moose Club, try anywhere you have to, pass this off to whoever you can...NOW!"

Gary took one look at Ellen's scrawled message and ran out the door.

"The dumb ass, he took *my* car! Way to *not* get followed! 'I was yelling 'What's the matter, you don't got gas?' But [the Feds] must have assumed he was just running an errand. And he was."

Howie's son started at the Moose Club and put the word out. Then he barreled over to Howie's buddy Kenny Schiavo's and banged on the door. Kenny's son opened up and Gary handed him the note.

"Read this, fast!"

The kid read the note, jumped in his own car and screeched off to find his father. In the meantime, Gary went off to pass the word further, hoping to find Gerry Farina. The note he took with him was short and directly to the point. It said:

D.E.A., FEDS HAVE HOWIE! LOOKING FOR GERRY FARINA, KENNY SCHIAVO.

In Somerville terms, it meant it was time to take a lengthy and immediate vacation via The Jimmy Flynn Plan. This was far worse for these guys because unlike Flynn, they *knew* that they had been involved in something and if they got caught, there was going to be hell to pay.

Young Kenny flagged his father down as he was coming off Route 93.

"What's the matter? What's wrong?" The father exclaimed.

The kid gulped in some air and said simply "Dad, don't go home!"

The old man got the message immediately and didn't stop for the finite details. "Good enough for me!" He waved goodbye and got back on the highway. It would be a year and a half before the law caught up with him, about the average time period for a Somerville Vacation. The Feds missed him by minutes, but not Farina. The word came too late and he was picked up that afternoon.

Howie shrugs. "I had played for time. The longer I stalled, the better chance people would know I'd been picked up."

"So," I say, "that would give them [Kenny and Gerry] a chance to get away?"

Howie is non-committal. "Well, at least they could get prepared for what was coming." It also lessened law enforcement's chances of keeping their own activities under wraps.

Ellen spoke to Howie's lawyer and found out Howie would be arraigned the following morning. She showered, drank an entire bottle of wine, and fell into bed. Suddenly, there was loud pounding.

"Bam! Bam! The front door, the back door, lights shining in the windows. I jumped out of bed naked. I could barely get my robe on and I said, 'Geez! What the fuck NOW???' I called Gary. 'Get back over here!' He was saying 'Oh God! NOW what happened?'"

It was a raid on her home.

"As I come down the stairs, a big guy pushes me into a chair, four more right behind. He yells in my face, 'Is anyone else in the house?'"

"I'm naked under my robe, it's the middle of the night. My husband is in jail. I said, 'If you can find anyone, tell me. Otherwise, I'm going back to bed.'"

The cop turned on her, yelling. "You sit right back down!"

"Oh no, I don't think so!" Ellen yelled right back. "I didn't do anything! You better call a fucking ambulance or arrest me because I'm gonna get dressed and I'm gone!"

I have a fleeting fantasy of a police raid on a house in which the occupants would be Ellen and my sister Patty. I bet there weren't enough cops in Somerville to be able to handle that kind of search. They'd have to bring in more guys from Boston.

"Bobby! Pay attention!" Ellen commands. "There's more banging. Gary — I had forgotten I called him! As soon as they recognized Howie's son, the cops turned on him."

"He can't come in here now." The lawmen were adamant. So was Ellen. Done with the orders, she snapped right back. "He doesn't stay, I don't stay!"

The five cops began their search as Gary and Nancy pushed their way into the house.

"It's a police raid and Gary brings a date! God, I loved that kid!" Ellen smiles. She doesn't say anything for a minute and we both sit there. The newspaper wavers a bit across the room. Ellen claps her hands together to jumpstart herself.

"They even went through Nancy's purse. Lipstick, tampons, falling out. She's bitching and they're telling her to shut up. Gary's rolling his eyes. I go upstairs to see what the second story guys are up to."

The actual search began politely enough. "They were carefully moving things, I wasn't trying to make it harder. But honestly Bobby, there was nothing in our house. No drugs, no paraphernalia, maybe two hundred dollars in my grocery fund. As things progressed, I think they got pissed."

Room after room, as nothing was found the searching turned to ransacking.

The raid party tromped down into the cellar, pulled all of the clothes and furs out of a cedar chest and tossed it all to the floor. Nothing. They ripped out a wall. Nothing. Christmas decorations in the attic were brought down to the living room, searched — nothing — and then dropped down into the cellar on top of the growing mound of personal belongings.

The officer upstairs in the bedroom went about his business quietly and efficiently. "I wish I remembered his name," Ellen says. "He was a complete gentleman. He did what he had to without tearing things up and was very courteous." The rest of the men engaged in wanton tossing with seemingly no direction other than to cause household mayhem.

Maybe you're saying to yourself, "Howie Winter was arrested, they had to search the house." If police have a warrant, they have every right to search. But as a former cop, I know there's a way to search a house, and a way to torture people as you search their house when you don't find a goddamn thing. It's a way to add injury to insult.

The search went on for two and a half hours. Ellen left the house and came back to more of her belongings littering the floor. Finally, up in her bedroom, she tripped over a huge pile of her own jumbled clothing torn from the closet. As she tried to keep her balance, she slapped a hand up against a dimmer switch so hard part of the wall caved in with a loud crunch.

Things wrapped up very quickly after that. The dejected cops trudged out of the house and its inhabitants surveyed the damage. Photographs and memories spanning two lifetimes were mixed in with kitchenware and food. But there was also a court date the next morning so Howie's wife had to prioritize. Ellen tells me she began bellowing about what to wear to court.

We both laugh loudly and newspaper rustles; a signal that this isn't supposed to be a party. It is, after all, the only interview Ellen and Howie have granted since this event — and on tape, no less. We get the message.

"I was in full-blown anxiety. Howie's room and desk were perfect, but everything else was a mess from the attic to the dining room. A glass jar of maraschino cherries in the closet was broken open just for spite, left dripping all over the clothes and into my good shoes. Their informant told them there was something here and when they didn't find it, they got pissed."

"The informant," I hint, "must not have known Howie all that well."

"He knew him well enough to cause all of this, but our house was clean, always."

I take my chance. "So who was it, Ellen, the informant?"

She holds up a hand. "I'm getting to it. Gerry's wife told me at her house they ripped all of her underwear drawers apart, closets, and cabinets. She even found clothes in the dishwasher! The dishwasher, Bob, can you believe it?"

The court convened at seven the next morning. As Ellen and Gary sat waiting under the watchful eyes of her former Fed friends, Howie was being readied for his court appearance with even fewer friends around him. "They had me in a cell at the state police and as we walked outside, there must have been forty to fifty newspaper reporters and cameras waiting."

"It's very calculating," Howie says. "They put me in a car with two cars ahead and two behind, a convoy to the Federal Building. All the lights flashing on the cop cars."

Like John Gotti.

Howie laughs. "Exactly. So people will ask 'Who is that? Who've they got?' It sticks in the mind of any potential jurors. It's a smart way of influencing anyone who might end up in the jury pool."

To the dismay of the media, it was over quickly. Howie entered the courtroom and, according to reports, greeted Vien as if they hadn't shared a suite at The Sheraton twenty-four hours earlier ("Hi, George, How are you?"), and shook hands with the two prosecutors. "Winter's handshakes," the Telegram reporter wrote, "suggested fighters touching gloves at the start of a boxing match."

It's a great turn of phrase, but he hasn't been called "The Gentleman Gangster" for nothing.

Howie was arraigned on charges of cocaine trafficking, kissed Ellen goodbye and was turned over to await a bail hearing. Outside of the U.S. Magistrate's courtroom, there was an inordinate amount of chest puffing in front of the press.

When asked why Howie had been arrested on a Sunday, U.S. Attorney Wayne Budd was quick to answer. "There comes a time," he intoned, "as you're pressing ahead with these matters when it's appropriate to strike and we determined that yesterday was a very good time to do so."

Sure, an early Sunday morning when most businesses are closed and the streets are empty is the best time to whisk a guy off the street to try and flip him. No mention was made of invitation to rat and "go back to your normal life" that had been extended when rest of the city was at Mass.

I ask Howie what the Feds discussed while they were holed up at The Sheraton in the hours before Ellen arrived.

Howie carefully folds his newspaper and sets it on a small side table, adjusts his glasses.

"'We've got the goods on you, Howie.' They tried to talk me into becoming a witness, to tell them some stories. And if I did, they would let me go home."

"Which people?" I ask.

Howie rotates a hand, indicating more than a few. "Frankie Salemme, Flemmi, Bulger...that crew." He pauses for a moment as if wondering if he should go on. "Also a dear friend of mine, Kenny Schiavo. What they were really interested in was ties to federal law enforcement. They wanted me to tell stories about police officers I'd known all of my life."

We know a lot of the same cops, I am interested in names the Feds mentioned, but Howie shakes his head.

"I didn't have anything to say. I have to tell you, I never, ever...did anything wrong with any of those guys. Nor did they [do anything illegal]." Howie punctuates his words with the side of his left hand smacking forcefully into the palm of his right.

"I know good cops, good people." Howie is almost wistful that the Feds had questions about the local cops. "There are people who helped me in because we were friends, out of kindness, not ever for financial gain. Never."

Howie has a history as a man respectful of local cops — men and women who may have been on different sides on occasion but shared his commitment for a safe, crime-free neighborhood. Howie was remanded to federal custody two days later. The charge was cocaine distribution, a crime that could potentially yield a two million dollar fine and a forty-year prison sentence. He was sentenced to a ten year bid in May of 1993.

"Who turned you in?"

Howie smiles that tight little smile he uses when he's pissed. "A federal informant named David White. Just a guy who asked me for a favor," Howie tells me. "For the Big Dig."

CHAPTER NINETEEN

Lawyers, Guns and Money:
The Season of Winter's Discontent

THE ENTIRE COUNTRY has heard of Massachusetts' famous Big Dig. The most expensive highway project in U.S, history kicked off in 1985 and wasn't completed until 2006 and at a cost of somewhere around twelve billion dollars over budget.

On the other side, it was viewed as a virtual cash cow for any vendor with anything available to contribute for a price to a project that was sure to last at least a decade.

"Howie," White implored, "Willya talk to Billy? I want to get my trucks on the Dig."

William "Billy" McCarthy was the president of the International Brotherhood of Teamsters Local 25, the same level position once held by the probably-late Jimmy Hoffa.

White told Howie that he had formed a company and had even convinced a prominent politician to be president of the company.

"I told him all right, I'd think about speaking to Billy," Howie is emphatic. "But everything had to be on the up and up.

Over at Local 25 they were running everything strictly legitimate."

The Feds had their eye on Local 25 and the organization was making a major effort to insure that that the shadow that seems to follow that particular arm of organized labor would be diminished, if not eradicated.

White had been in trouble in the past, but all he wanted was a leg up in the legit world. "He assured me that he just wanted to get back on his feet. So I figured I'd give the kid a break."

Howie's seal of approval was the "break" White needed to launch his new endeavor. And he launched with a vengeance. According to Howie, White forged his new president's name on a note to purchase twenty Mack trailers and twenty dump trucks to the tune of one million dollars. The money was rolling in, there was more than enough to cover the payments on the loan, had White decided to do that instead of pocketing the profits.

White took himself to the next level and attempted to strong-arm several companies on the Dig to use more of his trucks.

"The Feds caught up with him and he rolled right over."

He landed squarely on top of Howie — as did the accusation of trafficking in cocaine.

But first, White showed up at Howie's house. "He seemed pretty agitated," Howie says. "I wasn't privy to what was going on with the trucking and I sure as hell had no idea that he was in bed with the law."

Howie goes on, "'Howie,' White says. 'I think you and I are in trouble with the trucking business.'"

Howie holds up a hand. "I said 'Hold it, Dave. I haven't done anything. I haven't seen dime one from this whole thing.' Again, I should have seen it coming, but I didn't."

But White wouldn't let up. He said to Howie, "Well, I'm in trouble, I need to make some money fast."

Howie was plagued by friends needing to make money fast. Kenny Schiavo was a childhood friend who had also fallen on hard times. "Kenny and I had been truck drivers together when we were young guys. He was the one of the nicest guys I ever knew."

Kenny was a professional gambler and not very successful. "He brought me with him on a couple of sit downs where he owed huge amounts of money to bookmakers I knew. He was deep in debt and having hard times at home. Kenny had seven or eight kids at this point; he and his wife were splitting up. He was really in a bind."

No one understands that more than I do. It's an ugly, desperate feeling, as if you are trapped into a corner with no way out. There always is a way out, of course, but sometimes we can't seem to see it.

"And," Howie says after a moment or two. "Kenny was dealing drugs." He shakes his head in dismay. Perhaps he's looking back at Sal and how in the end, it was drugs that brought about Sal's death.

"Kenny wanted a way out of debt and wanted to unload some larger amounts of coke. 'Howie, do you know anyone?'"

Howie was in the process of building some fifty or so duplexes in the Worcester area and didn't want to screw it up, even for a friend. "I never had involvement in the drug trade and I didn't want to start," Howie says sadly. "I hated like hell to turn the kid down, he was really jammed, but the drug business wasn't for me. I hoped that Kenny would find someone to help him do whatever he needed to."

And then there was White on Howie's doorstep, needing to make some money the fast way. "Howie," White said. "Do you know anyone who could supply me with some coke? I got a big customer base that would take it right off my hands."

"It was that simple. Stuck in the middle of two friends, one on each side needing to get out of his respective hole. I thought about it for a long time."

Just a couple of days earlier the only thing Howie had on his mind was building duplexes and going on to a very prosperous living — legitimately. The issue was the one many of us in Somerville wrestle with and suffer from — that loyalty thing. Born into it, right or wrong, and it stays in our blood. You don't turn your back on a friend, even if you put yourself out on a limb. It's not an excuse; don't get me wrong. The other thing we don't do is make excuses for what we choose to do.

"I was torn. Then I made the phone call that changed the course of my life. I called Dave and told him I might be able to help him."

Kenny was ecstatic when Howie told him he might have a channel to move his merchandise. Howie told White that the terms of the deal were immovable; White was never to meet the supplier. In this way, Howie figured he could keep Kenny out of further trouble. Although White eventually testified that Schiavo was on hand at the exchanges, Howie flatly and angrily denies it.

"Bullshit. They can say anything they want about me. I don't care, but White never — not once — met Kenny. I was the go-between to make sure it never happened. I wanted Kenny to get out of debt, not into more trouble. White never even set eyes on Kenny, I don't care what the fuck he testified to."

White, wired for four months by the Feds, was given $27,000 in marked bills for the payoff at a prearranged meeting the August prior to Howie's arrest. After the deal, Kenny spent some marked bills and the indictments began flying.

"How much was your end?" I ask Howie, as there was never any evidence presented that he had possession of marked bills.

Howie sighs. "Five hundred bucks. That was for expenses, meaning the risk."

Five hundred bucks on a twenty-seven thousand dollar deal?

"It was more or less a friendship thing. I really didn't need the money."

He was in the process of making hundreds of thousands legally and he put his life on the line for nothing.

Once again, Howie was in jail and Ellen was alone. "Well, I wasn't completely alone. Gary was here with me. After all the talk on the street about Howie being taken to The Sheraton, everybody was calling. I mean, everybody."

The Somerville Telegraph. Our version of every small town's quickest way of spreading the news — talk, talk, talk. And there was plenty of it. Most everyone knew that Howie was headed off to another degree at government college during which he would undoubtedly study in silence, but there were still a few itchy trigger fingers wondering if he had made a deal and if any names had been mentioned.

"So, " Ellen sighs, "two days went by with the phone ringing off the hook. Everybody in town had called at least once. But George Kaufman called and kept calling."

"Ellen. Listen. You gotta come down. I gotta tell you something from the other guy."

The other guy was Stevie Flemmi.

I don't find too many things scary, but for Ellen to be summoned to see Stevie "The Rifleman" Flemmi while Howie was incarcerated gives me that creeping feeling you get when you walk out of the blistering sun into freezing cold air conditioning. The look on my face must give me away.

Ellen blows out a breath. "Bobby, I always knew Stevie to be my friend. I know what they say about him now. I know what turned out to be true, but in my personal experience with Stevie was friendship. George, I figured, was calling me down because no one was about to talk on the phone."

Gary drove Ellen to the meeting. "We pulled into the garage lot and suddenly a guy came toward us, real fast and reached for the door handle on the back driver's side door. Stevie jumped in my car and started talking right away."

"This is unbelievable, Ellen! You gotta talk this guy out of Cullen. He needs to go with Richie Egbert. He's got to dump Albie."

Albie Cullen was Howie's lawyer, and a good one. He had been Sal's attorney during the pinball trial and was also a friend. But Richard Egbert was *Stevie and Whitey's* lawyer.

Ellen shakes her head. "I said 'Stevie, right now whoever pays for a good defense and gets him the justice he needs is the guy who's his lawyer!'"

Stevie tried a different tact. "What happened, Ellen?"

"I'm not liking this. So I kept it very loose, told him we didn't have all the details. 'But I just found out this guy Dave White has pretty much screwed my life up. Howie is probably going in the can."

Stevie immediately commiserated. "You know, I tipped Howie that the guy was no fucking good."

Ellen was incredulous. "I can't imagine Howie doing business with a guy that he was told was a rat. White was involved in our life. We were all set. We owned the house, everything. We refinanced, we bought trucks, and now we are screwed."

Stevie patted her hand sympathetically. "It's a fuckin' shame. But don't you worry, honey. We're gonna do a fundraiser, everything is gonna be all right."

Fundraiser. When the community gets together and has a bake sale or carnival to benefit some poor sick kid. That wasn't what Stevie was talking about, of course. There wasn't going to be a fair in the town square with a big banner proclaiming "The Howie Winter Legal Defense Fund Charity Event." This was his way of saying that "the boys" would actually be picking up the tab for the attorney — who in this case just happened to be their attorney as well.

"It's for the best, Ellen," Stevie insisted. "You're the only one who can convince him this is the way to go."

Sure it was for the best. Richard Egbert was the man for Howie as far as his former employees were concerned. They wanted to pay for it. It was worth it, no matter what the bill. After all, it would be a private secure pipeline to anything that was going on with — or coming out of — Howie Winter.

"Look, Stevie," Ellen said, "I'll tell Howie but whatever he says, goes." Stevie kissed Ellen on the cheek and got out. Ellen shrugs. "I didn't realize it but the wheels were already in motion. The next day Gary went to Egbert's office. Just to see what he said, if he would see Gary, to find out what was going on."

Egbert was very enthusiastic. (So much so, Ellen says, that when Gary returned, he reported to his stepmother that it seemed a set up).

"You know, Gary..." Egbert began, "I'm not technically your father's lawyer yet, but I'd like to take it on."

"I'll see what my father says," Gary replied. But there seemed little choice in the matter for the Winters. It appeared to Ellen and Gary that a new attorney was a foregone conclusion.

That evening, Ellen spoke to Howie by phone and detailed the events, as Howie was soon due to appear in court for his bail hearing.

This was a difficult situation for Ellen and Howie. Albie Cullen was a friend, but the fact was the couple could not afford to mount the funds for the kind of defense the present case warranted. Egbert was also a solid attorney. Howie was silent for a few seconds. Then he asked, "What about Albie? He's gonna be in the courtroom for the bail hearing."

"Howie, I don't know what to say. I guess you're just gonna have to tell him."

The morning of the hearing, Ellen ran into Albie Cullen in the hallway of the courtroom. "This is the freaky thing," she says. "I didn't say a word about what had happened, but Albie seemed strange. He wasn't too keen on trying to get Howie bail."

As soon as the court was called to order, Ellen heard Attorney Cullen ask to address the judge. "He said something like 'Your Honor, I want to discharge myself from the case. Mr. Winter informed me he doesn't have the ability to pay. So someone else is going to step in.' That was the way to get Richard in."

During a break in the proceedings, Ellen was sitting in the hallway of the court with Albie. "I had to know. I said to him 'Albie, I don't understand what just happened.'"

Albie looked Ellen straight in the eyes and replied, "I'm not the type of guy *they* pay, Ellen. Let's just leave it at that."

Ellen is pensive, not her usual animated self as she talks. "I didn't understand then, I only knew they wanted Howie to use their attorney and they'd pay for the defense. Now as I am older it's pretty clear. Richard Egbert was their guy and Albie was someone that," she pauses, shakes her head. "Albie was someone who was not their guy."

"They? Whitey?" I ask.

"I'm sure," she replies. "Stevie and Whitey were a team. I only spoke to Stevie, but Whitey, why wouldn't he be involved? However," Ellen says, "I did have my day with Stevie." In a conversation after the change in attorneys, Ellen sought Flemmi out.

"Stevie, whatever Howie did, it seemed to cause a chain reaction. Howie's the one going to trial but this seems to be all about you and Whitey."

She didn't stop there. "I also told him that at The Sheraton they wanted Howie to have a conversation about you and Whitey. I told my husband that you gotta believe if the shoe was on the other foot, they'd make sure you'd fucking *hang*."

Ellen has balls. She had no hesitation in calling out The Rifleman to his face when she felt she was right.

"Jesus Christ, Ellen! What did he do?" I ask,

She grins. "He burst out laughing. What the fuck did I care? I said it! I was mad and my husband was the one at the end of a rope."

On January 27 a bail hearing was held for Howie during which a series of tapes secretly recorded by the "confidential informant" were heard. The content of the tapes is a matter of public record, as is Egbert's cross examination of Dan Doherty and Egbert's establishing that the tape also included the informant attempting to convince Howie to sign a deal for a movie.

Howie Winter was granted a $500,000 bail.

"Gerry Farina," Ellen says, "got $250,000 because the judge said Gerry Farina couldn't fight his way out of a paper bag. That's a terrible thing to say. Howie came home, but they called every night to verify he was in the house. He always was."

Howie laughs out loud. "This very nice fellow would either call or Ellen would call him. They'd talk for a few minutes about the weather or the Sox. Then I'd get on the phone, 'Howie, you there?' and I'd say, 'Yes, I'm here,' and he'd go back to speaking with Ellen."

On May 17, 1993, Howie pled guilty and, along with Gennaro "Gerry" Farina, received a ten-year prison sentence. The media was rife with rumors there must have been some kind of deal for Winter.

"There wasn't any deal," Howie grumbles. "What kind of deal is ten years? Richard was sure I wouldn't get a day over a nickel and so I pled guilty, but when we arrived in court — bam — ten years."

"The newspaper quoted me as saying 'That's life," Ellen says. "And it very well could have been a life sentence for a sixty-three year old man, but we were lucky."

Prosecutor Fred Wyshak pushed for a thirty-year sentence for what in the end was six kilos of cocaine. Winter was a career criminal, he insisted, and should be put away for the mandatory sentence for a defendant with two or more convictions involving violence or drugs. Judge Edward Harrington refused to accept the contention that the horse fixing conviction involved violence and the sentence stood at ten years.

Howie served eighty-five percent of his sentence. Kenny Schiavo was eventually caught.

"He came back into his own neighborhood because he missed his kids," Ellen says. "They picked him up eating a donut and drinking a cup of coffee."

During Kenny's trial, Howie was subpoenaed as a witness against him, refused to testify, and was rewarded with an extra six months for criminal contempt.

Howie explains, "They wanted that contempt charge to hurt. I did my sentence, then the six months. No halfway house, not one day. Another way of screwing you." The Feds were still steaming that Howie would once again be a free man, it seemed.

"The judge said," Ellen intones, "Mr. Winter, I'm not doing this out of vindictiveness, but to teach you a lesson.'"

Six months into Howie's sentence, Ellen got a visit from her old friends, the Feds.

"It was because of the wiretap. They had up to one year after they began tapping your phones to actually inform you that they had been doing so."

Tom Duffy and Dan Doherty dropped by with the paperwork. This was their first visit since Howie had been gone, but she had spoken to them on several occasions on the phone. "At that time, I had one of those jokey messages on my answering machine. It was a Jamaican voice. They said to me, 'You know, Ellen it was cute in the beginning but after a while it kinda got old.'"

"So why the hell did you keep listening?" She retorted.

Ellen laughs out loud. "Bobby, I think they just kept calling and coming by because they liked to hear me swear!"

They knocked on the door and she opened up with a special greeting for them.

"Hey guys! Come on in!" She spread her arms wide. "Take a look around. You'll notice that this house could fit four times inside of the rat's house. So let me ask you, who's the real drug dealer?"

Ellen took the notification of the wiretap and checked the date. "'Oh geez,' I said to myself. I started thinking back over everything I could have said during that time, I was horrified!"

Ellen was not horrified wondering if she had inadvertently given the government information about criminal activities. She hadn't. It was more of an embarrassment factor.

"I was running Pudgy's [strip club]. I talked to strippers all day long. Some of them were good girls and some of them...weren't. There was a fair amount of trash talking, it was part of the job."

The Feds were privy to all of her conversations, many of the variety that each of us would prefer strangers not listen to and none that had to do with her husband.

"It was embarrassing, what else can I say? No wonder they wanted to keep listening!"

The fifty-three year old Kenny Schiavo was finally arrested in March of 1993 and convicted of drug trafficking and conspiracy in December of 1994.

"He died," Howie says sadly, "I think it was cancer of the blood. They took him from Ray Brook in New York where he was serving his time to the Mayo Clinic in Minnesota. They sent him back to prison with a clean bill of health. They never let him know he was dying and they never treated him."

It takes a lot for Howie to say what he wants to, but eventually he does.

"As far as I'm concerned, they killed him. When Kenny's time was up, after eleven years, I believe, he was taken from the prison hospital to another hospital and finally to his aunt's. He passed away soon after his release. I don't have any regrets that I tried to help him. I wish things had turned out differently."

David White? What happened to him? Nothing.

Ellen and David's wife Wendy were, at one time, good friends. Ellen even babysat for the White children. As the women's lives began to unravel, things twisted. Ellen called Wendy and outright asked her why she didn't tell Ellen that the Feds had been in the White's home.

"She told me that Dave said he was cooperating with the Feds, but it wasn't about anyone she knew. It's like she was living in a dark room, couldn't see anything."

And yet the women stayed in touch. Wendy wanted to testify against her husband, according to Ellen, but David was threatening her. "Do what you have to do, Wendy," Ellen advised.

The next call Ellen got was Richard Egbert. She must not give Wendy any advice; the Feds were saying she was intimidating a witness.

"Intimidating a witness by telling a friend to do what you have to?" Ellen explodes. "We were still babysitting their kids!" Ellen explodes. "Despite what her husband had done, she was a friend. I watched her kids in my house while Howie was out on bail!"

Howie liked the White children, as did Ellen. It didn't bother him to have them around.

In 1995 Bill Chase doled out a backhanded compliment. When he was made Police Chief in the town of Worcester, the local paper reported that at his swearing in ceremony, he had some special words for the incarcerated Winter. "I want to give a sincere thank you to all of the people who have helped me along the way. I am very pleased at being selected as police chief here, and I want especially to thank someone who cannot be here — Howie Winter."

It was Chase's involvement in putting Howie away that propelled him toward future success.

And the attorneys? Albie Cullen had his day, if you read between the lines. In 1996, one year prior to Stevie Flemmi admitting he had been a government informant since 1965,

Richard Egbert told The Boston Globe that he would never represent a client who cooperates with law enforcement. "Egbert says he tells his clients he does not want to, in effect, represent a government agent. If they want to cooperate, 'they should get other counsel, not me,' he said. "I have deep-seated beliefs in this area, and I can't overcome them.'"

In the same article Albert Cullen said, "That while a lot of lawyers say they will not represent a cooperating witness, they do so." One the few "stand up guys" he represented, he said was Howie Winter.

The same man who refused to testify for the prosecution even when ordered to do so under a grant of immunity.

CHAPTER TWENTY

The King of the Hill Today

THE MORNING OF the last interview I take special care shaving and dressing, even though I'm wearing my usual jeans and sweatshirt. It seems like a formal occasion. I feel a bit sad. I'll see Howie again, certainly, but from now on we'll be a couple of guys hanging out and not two men dredging up lifetimes, attempting to figure how we got here. It should be a relief, but it doesn't feel that way.

Howie opens his front door as I get out of my truck. He smiles and ushers me into the kitchen for coffee. On the table are the Dutch Masters cigar boxes. The lids open, the photos waiting patiently.

As Howie brings the cups to the table he says, "Well this is it, eh?"

I nod. "We're pretty close to being done."

We sit and he says, "I left off at the drug beef, I believe." And then he tells me the rest.

Howie and Gennaro "Gerry" Farina pled guilty. Although prosecutor Fred Wyshak argued for thirty years, calling Howie a "career criminal" with two previous convictions involving violence, U.S. District Judge Edward Harrington rejected his request. Even though this was Howie's third strike, the race fixing conviction was not classified as a violent crime. The men were sentenced to ten years.

"Gerry and I were shipped to Lewisburg."

There was no excruciating bus ride across the country. The friends were sent straight to maximum-security Lewisburg Penitentiary in Pennsylvania. The facility had a reputation snapping at the heels of Leavenworth after its infamous 1995 riot resulting in the transfer of over four hundred prisoners. Gotti, Hoffa, John Wojtowicz (real life counterpart to Al Pacino's hapless bank robber in *Dog Day Afternoon*), Goodfella Henry Hill and again, Whitey Bulger, all called it home for a time.

"It housed the most violent offenders on the East coast," Howie says, "rapists, murderers; not guys convicted of a couple of kilos of coke. I wasn't about to take it, relive another Leavenworth. The Feds hoped I'd be at Lewisburg for my entire sentence and I believe that's why I got there so quickly."

Even though Howie hadn't done business on Winter Hill for over a decade and the newspapers now referred to him as the "former gangster", he was sent to the facility that housed so many organized crime figures that its G block is commonly referred to as "Mafia Row."

"It's not that the company was bad," he's quick to add. "There were plenty of Boston guys, the Philly crew once run by Anthony Bruno, [the mobster Fat Tony Ciulla claimed financed his bankroll and was eventually assassinated by rung climbing underlings]. I just wouldn't take it — the status of a maximum security inmate."

Incarcerated once more, Howie was looking ahead to yet another new start. "I was trying to shake the organized crime label and besides," he smiles, "anyone who was at my last trial probably walked away thinking I was a major player in *disorganized* crime."

Howie met with the prison counselor. "I told him Gerry and I were given the wrong classification and if he didn't reclassify us, we were going to sue him personally. Legal threats weren't what I wanted to do but they gave us no choice. I'd have done my whole bid in Lewisburg."

He was somewhat successful and within a few months he and Gerry were sent to medium security Ray Brook in New York. "We should have been in minimal security but at least we were out of maximum. I fought the Ray Brook officials for a couple of years until they sent me to the minimum-security prison Schuylkill in Pennsylvania."

Prosecutor Wyshak was a frequent visitor. There was still pressure for Howie to flip on his former Marshall Motors underlings. Howie has little patience when relating Wyshak's performances in front of the other inmates. "They'd send a guard to remove me from general population. Just sitting in a room with Wyshak, neither of us speaking for hours."

The Feds held little hope Howie would talk so when the time allotted for the "interview" ran out, Wyshak personally escorted Howie back to his cell and began his show.

The prosecutor would pat his charge affectionately on the back and loudly announce, "Thanks for the info Howie! Good stuff, good stuff!"

"Thankfully, most cons knew the routine," Howie says, "and had been through the same bullshit themselves but it could have put me in real danger."

The administration took it one step further.

"Right after those visits, two guards usually appeared at my cell," Howie sighs. "I was so used to what was coming, it was boring after so many years of being fucked with. We'd all been at this since the late 70's. I think even the prosecutors were tired of playing the same old game."

Administration announced there were, once again, death threats against him. Howie was to be sent to the Hole for his own safety. "I told them I'd sign a release exonerating them from anything that might happen, but they weren't having it. They [the Feds] wanted the inference I had talked. No matter how many times we did the same old dance, they never gave up."

Kenny Schiavo was eventually convicted and sent to the same facility, even sharing a cell with John Gotti Junior for a while.

"There was a time," Howie tells me, "when it seemed like half of Charlestown was inside with me. Tommy Doherty was there. He is a standup guy, a former cop and never once opened his mouth. He was in the same boat because he refused to give the Feds what they wanted — more names."

Things could have been tougher for Tommy. A bad cop thrown in with a bunch of cons is the equivalent of tossing bloody meat into a lion cage — every animal wants to tear off a piece. Howie made sure his fellow inmates knew part of the reason Tom was in was his refusal to indict others in his own crimes.

"When Tom arrived I brought him to all the cellblocks and introduced him as a friend of mine." That was all the other convicts had to hear. Tom was never bothered. Tom and Kenny became good friends as Kenny's health began to deteriorate. After a multitude of complaints Kenny was granted a medical exam.

"The doctors told him he was perfectly healthy. We all knew Kenny was ill, but the Bureau didn't want to help him until it was too late. Once you're in their system, you're just a number and the sooner they can delete that number the better."

Kenny was diagnosed with cancer and sent to a hospital in Minnesota where, Howie insists, "they said he was cured and sent back to Ray Brook."

When Kenny returned, he appeared worse than ever. He was finally transferred to Fort Devens in Massachusetts. After a while he couldn't walk and ended up in the hospital. He died a week or so after his release.

"The BOP killed Kenny. They did it to him and his family. What the BOP forgets is that every man in their custody has someone that loves him on the outside."

I hate to disagree but I don't think they forget so much as they don't give a fuck.

Here's a quick lecture about families from an ex-con to any who may be considering the glamorous life of crime. When you're convicted and head off to prison, your entire family ends up doing emotional time right alongside you. Collect phone calls with an operator informing a son he is receiving a phone call from a prisoner father is debilitating. Sending an incarcerated child funds for a prison commissary account knowing it slashes the budget for the rest of the kids is a painful choice to make. Grade school is transformed from a learning experience with playground recesses into a stomach-churning sentence for the taunted children who have a parent who is "away." The worry of neighbors and coworkers whispering innuendos just out of earshot makes simple daily living its own sentence. Every single crime has scores of victims. Just a little unappetizing food for thought.

Ricky Sperlinga was at New York's Otisville for his own drug beef. If a Boston boy has to be incarcerated, Otisville is a good location; families can visit and return home the same day. When Ricky discovered Howie was at Ray Brook, he managed to get himself transferred even though he had it made where he was. I think to be near Howie was to be close to a link with his murdered father.

Howie nods, "He wanted to be with me." Howie was not glad to see Ricky in the system but welcomed his friend's son into the fold.

"He was the talk of the prison. He'd hit bag for four or five hours a day. He was relentless, definitely not a guy to be fucked with. And what a hockey player! We had great games at Ray Brook."

A book about Somerville can't help but end with one more sports story. Street hockey was very popular at Ray Brook. The heavy concentration of Boston boys made sure of it. Charlestown is known as a hockey puck of a town and a little barrier like prison isn't enough to squelch the sport.

The Charlestown Fidler brothers were legends around the circle of ice dwellers. "As a matter of fact my son Gary and one of the Fidler boys both got thrown out of Boston College together, I believe for defecating on a poor bystander's car windshield," Howie muses.

"Howie, I want to get back to the hockey games. You played in prison?"

"Well," Howie smiles shyly. "I was like the team doctor. If someone got hit in the eye with a puck, I'd get some Scotch tape and anything that was clean to tape the up wound. No one wanted medical attention because the guards would immediately stop the game."

Sal's son, the one his sister called "The Messiah", was the peacemaker.

"The whole goal was to keep the game going, you know how we are about sports. If two guys got into a beef, Ricky stepped in to cool everyone down. Generally he managed to keep it what it was supposed to be — a friendly game between guys doing time. He was pretty good like that."

When Howie was finally sent to Schuylkill, "I went alone. Gerry was let out early on one of his appeals. I got a job at the laundry and I was pretty happy there. I got myself in trouble though," he admits. Howie was warned not to give out extra blankets but as with his homeless valets in the old days, he found it hard to refuse. "Guys would come in and tell me they were freezing so I gave each an extra blanket."

A prisoner was caught with an extra cover and Howie went down. "They didn't have any proof but I was punished for Blanket-Gate by being sent from job to job."

Howie also began to have health problems. "I had a hernia for over a year. It kept opening up, I had trouble walking, and the pain was unbearable. But I didn't exist to the prison doctors."

It was a physician in another facility that eventually diagnosed and treated Howie's condition.

"In 1999, I had to go to court in Providence. The Feds shipped me to a local joint [jail] up there. I was in so much pain I finally had to see a doctor. I was sent to the hospital and they repaired my hernia."

The aftercare left more to be desired. There are no narcotics in jail — legally anyway, no matter what the level of pain. "I chewed aspirin, but at least the hernia was fixed."

While he was in Rhode Island, Howie ran into Whitey's former associate Kevin Weeks, the lookout for Bulger when he executed my brother-in-law Brian Halloran.

"I'd never met Kevin before that I could recall. I know he's written he used to come up the Hill but I don't remember him. Whitey never brought any Southie guys with him. But I did talk to him in prison. It was just made public that Whitey had been informing for the FBI all those years."

Incarceration could have been uncomfortable for Weeks and Howie wanted to put the younger man at ease.

"No one here is going to hold you responsible because Whitey turned out to be an informant," Howie said to Weeks. "Just because he's a rat doesn't mean people will think of you as one. Two weeks later, Weeks ended up telling the government everything he knew and he had his reasons."

Like Johnny Martorano before him, Weeks was shocked to discover Whitey was not the man — or friend — he had appeared to be throughout the years.

In 1997, the Boston arm of the FBI was forced by a judge to admit what The Boston Globe had been trying to reveal since 1988 and had been going on for decades — Whitey Bulger and Stevie Flemmi were FBI informants.

Despite the rumors kicking around the Hill for almost a decade, Howie couldn't believe what he and the rest of Boston were reading.

"I really was the only one up the Hill that liked those guys, even though I never trusted Whitey. I felt differently about Stevie," Howie is more uncomfortable with the subject of Flemmi.

"Stevie I liked the most. So did Ellen, she and Stevie were friends. He was always a gentleman with her. I couldn't fathom it. I couldn't believe he'd been in bed with the Feds for decades."

Howie removes his glasses and rubs his eyes. "Then it came out, the things he had done. And the two girls."

He's referring to Flemmi's ex-lover Debra Davis and Deborah Hussey, the daughter of another girlfriend. Their deaths were so heinous there isn't a stomach that doesn't roll at the mention of their names, mine included. Howie's face belies his own nausea. The business up Winter Hill, no matter what it was, never had anything to do with women during the time of Buddy, Howie and Sal.

Howie never saw it coming — Flemmi's betrayal of Winter Hill.

"I was in shock. Stevie had done a lot of things for a lot of people, especially the North End. In a million years I never would have suspected him. It broke my heart more than a little. That just goes to show you how naïve I'd been."

Stevie did not inform on his colleagues because his heart couldn't live with a moral outrage of beating in step with the law. He didn't turn to the government for protection against outside influences bearing down on him with threats against his home and hearth. Stevie Flemmi didn't even rat on his friends to save his own life – until he was finally arrested. The Rifleman and his pal Bulger spent decades setting up those closest to them and then tattling on the same guys in hopes of fulfilling the self-serving prophecy of taking over the city without fear of any interference. They plotted to elevate the art of violence and murder in a new regime.

In the end it backfired, but by then dozens of lives were ruined and scores of bodies floated in their wake.

In July of 2002, Howie was released from prison, and in his seventh decade once again returned home to Ellen and to start over. He'd lost pretty much everything, including his youngest son, but he still had his dignity, his integrity and the few bucks he'd managed to squirrel away.

"So," Howie says, "I just picked up where I'd left off. I like building things and I've been back at it ever since."

He begins to return the photographs to their respective cigar boxes. I want to know what Howie thinks about his old crew, now that it's all over. So I ask him to add a few words to the names I bring up.

Sal Sperlinga? Howie blinks. "I still miss him every day."

Buddy McLean? That name makes Howie smile. "Oh, Buddy was the best. We grew up together. I always wished we could have grown old together."

"Howie, what about Whitey Bulger?"

He sighs. "Very devious; a master of putting a twist on things."

A question comes to mind that's been bothering not only myself, but also all the Somerville faithful over the years. "Howie, everything I read about Bulger links him with the Winter Hill Gang. But he wasn't one of you, isn't that right?"

Howie leans his elbows on the table. "Bobby, the media, the papers, they can write whatever they want. But it wasn't until I was away that Whitey and Stevie moved in. That much is true. Let me tell you how it went. In 1972 Donald Killeen was murdered. He ran the rackets in Southie and his crew had been in a beef with the Mullen Gang."

In typical Irish style, Killeen's brother had won a fight with one of the Mullen boys by biting the tip of his nose off. Just like after Salisbury, the two gangs went to war.

"After Killeen was dead, Whitey was next in line to take over Southie. But since the Mullen crew vowed revenge, he was also next in line for assassination. He was actually hiding out when he came to see me. Whitey was scared; he knew he didn't have a crew big enough to survive. He wanted my help."

A sit-down between the two gangs was arranged and Howie negotiated a binding truce to keep Bulger alive.

"After that, I offered Whitey use of my bookmaking office and he was at the garage almost daily. I couldn't get rid of him. But his booking business in Southie grew and we all profited by it."

The rest of the story I've told. Sal didn't think much of Bulger and his lieutenant Flemmi and after he and Howie were jailed, Whitey was banned from Marshall Motors.

"Everything he touched, Whitey poisoned. We didn't want his poison in our city. He was putting too much heat on us and was told to get the fuck out of Somerville. He moved to the Lancaster Street garage in Boston. So what do I think of Whitey Bulger? I saved his life and he repaid all of us by marrying the Feds and slaughtering women. That's what I think of Whitey Bulger. But a member of *my* Winter Hill Gang?"

Howie closes the cigar box in front of him. "No."

"Do you think he'll ever be caught?"

Howie thinks for a moment. "I don't know. He's a very clever man, that's for sure. Hey, did I ever tell you about the cat Stevie gave me?"

I shake my head. If he wants to tell me a story about a cat, I'm game.

"One afternoon Stevie and Jimmy Martorano were waiting at the garage when I got back from lunch. They looked like a couple of schoolboys with a secret. The rest of the guys looked as if they'd been wrestling. Everyone was covered with sweat."

"What are you fellas up to?" Howie asked as he headed to his office. Stevie ran ahead, blocking his way.

"Hold on, we have a surprise for ya, Howie!" Stevie said as Jimmy rushed into the office. After a great deal of rustling and a small crash, the door opened and Jimmy exited, a leash in his hand. At the end of the leash was a full grown mountain lion.

"What the fuck is that??" Howie jumped back.

"A mountain lion." The big cat yawned and plopped down. Stevie leaned and scratched its belly.

"I know *that*!" Howie snapped. "I meant what the fuck is it doing here?"

The boys looked hurt. "It's a present for you, Howie. We know you like cats."

Howie laughs. "Sure, I like cats. I like elephants but I wouldn't have one as a pet. This was back when rich people could buy exotic animals for pets. It was a popular practice, although barbaric, because they'd buy wild creatures and get bored with them. Soon the animal got sent to the pound. But Stevie assured me this one was trained."

Moments before Howie arrived, the "trained" cat had escaped from its cage and some of Boston's best criminal minds had been chasing it around the garage trying to get it back inside.

"What did you do?" I ask.

Howie shrugs. "What could I do?" He looked down at the cat busy licking his heavy coat. The cat looked up, his amber eyes studying Howie.

The cat, Stevie and Jimmy looked expectantly at him. "I couldn't disappoint them and I did like cats. And the look on Stevie's face! He looked so," Howie pauses, "happy."

"I walked the damn thing down the street to our apartment. Ellen almost had a heart attack when we came through the door but once the big cat curled up on the rug, that was that."

For a while the two humans and the mountain lion cohabited very well. "The first couple of weeks things went fine," Howie remembers. "When I sat at the kitchen table, the cat would put both of its paws on my shoulders from behind and rest there. I'd walk it down the street so it could relieve itself. Back then you didn't have to carry a bag to pick up the droppings but I'll bet I contributed to that law being passed! What came out of that cat was worse than anything I'd ever seen at a horse stable."

Ellen and Howie fed the cougar the finest meat the butcher had to offer. "You don't give an animal like that ordinary cat food," he explains. "You want to keep it happy and not hungry."

But living with the newly crowned king of the Somerville jungle was a short-lived truce.

"One afternoon I got a frantic call from Ellen yelling for me to get the fuck home. The cat had positioned itself across the top of the refrigerator and wouldn't come down."

No amount of coaxing would move the enormous feline and as the hours went by, the lion began to get nasty, baring its fangs and growling at Howie.

"He refused to budge. Ellen locked herself in the bedroom and said she wasn't coming out until the cat was gone. Finally I called Animal Rescue and they sent a little lady over." Howie roars as he tells me the woman wore gloves that ran the length of her arms to her shoulders. She quickly corralled the cat and Howie watched the rescue truck drive away.

"It was a relief, the cat needed to be where it was supervised, had some room to exercise and couldn't hurt anyone. But I missed it when it was gone. I think if I'd gotten it when it was a baby, things could have been different. I'd have trained it so it listened and it would have been a much better cat." Howie smiles a small smile. "So that's the story about the cat."

But he and I both know that he wasn't talking about the mountain lion at all.

Howie grins wide at the name Alex Rocco, the former Bobo Petricone. He's a great Somerville success story and even though Howie is a friend, he's also a fan.

"Alex...Bobo...did very well. He won an Emmy and he's a great character actor. We stay in touch at least once a month. Alex is a great, great guy."

Bobby Martini Senior? "Bobby was wonderful, a loyal friend. He'd give you anything he had."

I want to keep that thought in my heart. My list is complete but Howie's isn't.

"What about Bobby Junior?" he asks playfully.

I'm uncomfortable — always — with the subject of me but I tell him to go ahead.

"Bobby Junior, God bless him. He's had a very heavy cross to bear all his life and it's amazing he survived the way he has. I think he's so outgoing and funny all the time because of the tragedies in his life. He doesn't want to look at any bad side of anything."

Funny, I never think about that cross. It's the luck of my draw. Despite the fact that I am a grown man, I feel my face grow hot. Maybe if I wasn't Bobby Junior, I might cry. Instead I clear my throat.

"Do you ever see any of the guys from the old days?" I ask.

Howie shakes his head. "Most of my friends are gone now. The best friends I have are Gary's friends, like you." He smiles. "You're a pretty great bunch of guys."

There is quiet between us as we wait, two fathers, each who suffered the loss of a child, each for the other to speak. Gary was my best friend and the light in father's eyes.

Yet despite that I also suffered the unimaginable horror of losing my eldest son Rob, at the very least, I was there to see my boy to his final rest. When Gary died, Howie was not allowed that privilege. The thought makes my chest ache like something is cracking inside. It is a familiar feeling since my son died.

Howie breaks the silence first. "It was devastating. My son passed away when I had less than a year to go but the Bureau would not allow me to pay my respects."

It is common practice for the BOP to grant permission for an inmate to attend the funeral of a child under guard but Howie was embroiled in the dispute with them to have his security level lowered.

His voice tightens. "They outright refused me. And that was the end of it." Howie will not say anything further. I don't blame him. It hurts. I know.

I've been damn lucky to live as many years as I have, and between growing up in Somerville and working in movies, I've collected good friends along the way. Some are here in town, others scattered across the world. Also, sadly, a great number have passed on. I miss them, but Gary? Gary's passing out of my life was so profoundly painful; it's difficult for me — even today. With all of the friends who remain, there is still a lonely empty spot inside my heart for Gary, right behind the one for my son.

"What's a typical day for you now, Howie?" I ask the man who once reigned on the Hill.

"I like to work on my projects, read and go to lunch with my friends. Have a glass of wine once in a while. I bet that sounds kind of boring compared to the old days, but it's a good life."

"Are you happy?" I ask.

Howie is thoughtful. "I am. It's been a long road I traveled and I survived."

Howie closes the lid on the last cigar box. The Dutch boys stare back in silence. I am reluctant to say anything because the book is done and some small part of me wants it to stay here in the kitchen, to keep the memories coming, to keep my past alive. A rare instance, I need a little push to keep moving.

"So Bobby," Howie says as he slides away from the table, "You want to go have lunch?"

Yeah. I do.

EPILOGUE

IN JANUARY OF 2008, Howie Winter sold the Marshall Street Garage to a Pentecostal Church headed by an African-American preacher devoted to "uplifting and winning the lost at any cost."

The church has no plans to renovate the area located underneath the trap door.

Once the house of worship gets up and running, the preacher has extended an invitation to former Winter Hill Gang members to stop by any time to talk about their experiences and regrets.

To date, he has had no takers, not even from the FBI.

AFTERWORD

SO NOW YOU know we finished the book. One last note about writing.

We didn't read books about the Winter Hill Gang when we started. We didn't need to and I wasn't really interested. Until I got a call from a friend who suggested I pick up a copy of *Legends of Winter Hill: Cops, Con Men, and Joe McCain, the Last Real Detective* by local writer Jay Atkinson. My buddy suggested I read it as I was mentioned in it.

Mr. Atkinson called me a "dirty cop" and a "thug', strongly suggesting that I got my cop job because of my father's influence with his pals at Teamsters Local 25. That pissed me off. If you've read this far, you know me better than Jay Atkinson, so you know what I did. A dirty cop implies something much different than insurance fraud. I was never dirty on the job. As for implied "thugginess"? A thug would have tracked the writer down and beaten the daylights out him. A gentleman merely responds in writing, as I will do now.

Mr. Atkinson, my brother Leo never told you we came from a "crossroads" household, a meeting place for gangsters as you quoted him. Our father was never a "union boss"; he was a

Teamster grunt who drove trucks and eventually became a mechanic. Nor did he train boxers — another embellishment.

One crucial lesson I learned was after reading Washington Post editor Ben Bradlee's autobiography. In essence, the lesson was "write the truth." Mr. Atkinson, Leo never, ever told you that Whitey Bulger set foot in our family home, never mind "often congregated." Shame on you, you've got Big Bob spinning in his grave.

And finally, when you penned the phrase "gangsters like Sal Sperlinga and Howie Winter and Whitey Bulger" — comparing two men to a serial killer, you may have sold a few books, but you proved to those of us who have known all three that you don't know what the fuck you're talking about. In your quest to glorify McCain, you neglected facts. There were only a few legends on The Hill and I don't feel you depicted any of them. That being said, your other book *City Of Amber* was really quite good.

My brother Leo was befriended and then screwed by his sergeant and supposed good friend Joe McCain Jr. and it didn't surprise me much. I'm a firm believer the fruit doesn't fall far from the tree. In Joe's case, his father turned on the actual friends that got him into the police business and was forever banned from enjoying the camaraderie he had as a young man growing up in Somerville. It has been alleged that Joe Jr. convinced the city to suspend Leo for a while so Joe could force the mayor to make him a lieutenant. It was only rumor but it is something that is talked about quite a bit around town.

Leo and I stood on the sidewalk, watching the St. Paddy's Day parade come up the street. I asked my brother what he thought about being misquoted and our family misrepresented. "Leo, the least we should do is write the guy a letter. Let him know we don't appreciate what he wrote. It wasn't right."

Leo waited a long minute, watching the marching band step by, instruments gleaming in the afternoon sun, his face serious. He took a pull off his beer and handed it to me. Then a grin spread across his face.

"Aww Bobby, I don't really give a fuck, do you?"

Leo's smile was a little kid's. He reminded me of Joey; and of Eddie, and of my own sons. Mischievous to cover a certain amount of pain; it is also our birthright.

I grinned right back at him. "Naw, I really don't."

"Besides," my little brother said, "You set it straight when you write your own book." He pointed at me. "You promised to tell the truth, didn't ya? You be sure to say I'm good lookin'. You got that?"

"Leo," I answered, "you're a good lookin' man." We burst out laughing and finished the beer.

Maybe Leo was right. It didn't matter. We Martinis know who we are. But it smarted just the same. If you're going to tell even a small part of my story — at least get it the fuck right. I didn't want to do the same without backing it up with facts. We took great pains to follow each story and court case back to its roots. I couldn't have done it without willing participants.

My parents are gone from this world, but I still thank them for putting up with the pain and aggravation we all caused them. I wish my father lived long enough to see it lain out across these pages and wonder what he would have said after reading it.

To my partner, EK, thank you very, very much. You're a great writer and teacher.

I also want to thank the many people that welcomed me into their homes and afforded us countless hours of questions about what could only have been personal pain and loss.

My sister Patty relived the bleak days after her husband's murder for me. As of this writing, she awaits the court's decision of how much money the Feds have to pay for assisting Whitey in Brian's slaughter. Annemarie and Bobby McCarthy let me come back to see them time and again, checking facts and opening old wounds. On May 21 of 2010, the couple suffered any parent's greatest nightmare and Annemarie's heart broke once again. Their beautiful daughter Keri lost her brave fight against cancer. Still, the McCarthys go on.

Ellen Brogna is one of the strongest women I know and her help with dates and details was immeasurable, her friendship invaluable.

I would also like to thank the following; Lisa Martini (for her patience), Joseph and Madeline, Rat O'Connell, Mark Sullivan, Brian Leahy, Tommy Leahy, Bobby O'Neil, Tom Doherty, Louie Ferrara, Eddie Accamondo, John Baino, Vinny Ciampi, Tom Cullen, Russell Bufalino, Charlie Demetri, Jimmy Demetri, Ibby Alewood, Neil Rooney, Bob & Lee Cargiano, Dave Deveney, Bob Racicot, Vinny Fabio, Paul Moran, Kate Mattes, Ed Begley Jr. and many more. Thank you especially to those there for me when I lost Rob. The end of 2008 was sweetly bitter — I received the unbelievable news our book was to be published and it came crashing down a month later when my son died. Thank you to all who helped me out of 2008 and into 2009. I won't forget your support and kindness. I miss you Rob and love you always.

As for me, EK, I wish I could thank everyone who pushed me to keep writing; I am trusting you know who you are. Thank you, Reno for being very patient with Mom. I wouldn't trade you for the world. Thanks to all of the girls in the production office who proofed us. My sister Michele who spent long hours doing legal research and my nieces who let me read aloud to them to see how it sounded, despite the fact it wasn't available on iTunes. My sisters Gale and Dina who always thought I was a best seller. My patient parents, Chet & Margo. The very patient capo di tutti capos, Terry Miller. Kellie JoTackett, Simi Wein, Chick & Rosie Bernhard, Lizzie Elwell, Burt Reynolds, Stephanie Lundy, Allison Millican and Alison Troy, Jeffrey Donovan, Gabrielle Anwar, Emily Sherman, Sarah Arvanities, Mitch & Amy

Reeves, Melanie Grefe, Artie Malesci, Donnie Abbatiello & Donnie Perron, Christina Lesch — all supportive — always.

Thanks to my close friends Gus Bailey, Jack Taylor, Inspector Brant, Hank Chinaski, Shane MacGowan, Frances Farmer, Harriet M. Welsch, and the inimitable Eddie Hart from Scituate.

Ellen Brogna, thank you for spending time with an "outsider." Your edits and fact checks were more than helpful and you, along with Patty, never hesitated for a moment when it came to telling me the truth about your life, Howie and Brian's lives and life in general. You chicks taught me much.

We both want to thank our loyal transcriber, Margaux Susi, who spent long hours deciphering what it means to "pahk your cah in Havahd Yahd." God bless her! The eyes of Kathy and John Oberteuffer. Thank you, Ken Bruen.

And finally, thank you Bobby. For letting me into Somerville, allowing me the opportunity to work with you, breathing life into the ghosts of the past, never worrying about the cost we all pay for living and reliving that darkness on the edge of town. You're a brave guy. Keep passing the open windows.

Now we'll steal something from Stephen King and hope he doesn't mind. In his most recent book (yes, Bobby has become a fan — with all of those words in such special order, how could he not?) King did something that made an impression on both of us. He thanked the reader. It made perfect sense. If not for the reader, all the hours of interviews, painful stories, and carefully arranged words would mean nothing. We didn't just hope to write the story. We really wanted you to read it.

And now that we're finally done, all that is left to say is…not bad for a fifty-six year old Teamster and a movie chick, right? Thanks for reading us.

Bobby Martini & Elayne Keratsis, 2008

The Winter Hill Guys at Blinstrub's in the 1960's. Left: Howie Winter.
Ernie "The Greek", Aniello Squillante, Bob Martini Sr., Carlo Gianelli,
Eddie Coleman. Right: "Tony Blue" Agostino, Younger MacDonald,
unknown, Sal Sperlinga, Dick McGinlly, Raymond Grande.

Me, in elementary school in 1960.

I could have been a contender...if I'd started ten years earlier.

James "Buddy" McLean and his son Jimmy in the 1950's
during happier times.

The dynamite found under Buddy's car in 1961,
the fuse that lit the Irish Gang Wars.

Buddy McLean's car, moments after his assassination
in October of 1965.

The Sperlinga family at Disney in the 1970's.
From the left: Sal, his son Ricky, family friend "The Geezer"
and son-in-law Bobby McCarthy.

Sal with his beloved granddaughters Tara and Keri in the 1970's.
The family suffered another tragedy when Keri passed away
from cancer in 2010.

The gentlemen of Leavenworth 1984. Ed Dunn, Howie Winter, Russell Bufalino, Carl "Tuffy" DeLuna, Tino "The Greek" Fiumara.

Brian Halloran, my brother Jimmy and my sister Patty, Brian's wife in 1978. Brian was murdered after his life, and his relationship with Whitey Bulger began to unravel.

My mother and me when I was a cop at my brother Leo's police swearing-in ceremony in Somerville in the 1980s.

Ellen Brogna and Howie at the christening of Kenny Schiavo's son Nicholas in 1989. Kenny eventually died after being refused adequate medical care in prison.

Big Bob at *his* post in The Pointer Post during his reign in the 1990's.

My mother and her brood at Joey's wedding in the 1990's. Karen, Leo, me, Patty, Jimmy and Joey. My brother Eddie was already gone by then. Joey would follow in a couple of years.

Leo, Big Bob and me, having a good time
at The Pointer Post in the 1990's.

My sister Patty and our dad in the 1980's.
He wasn't thrilled when she married his friend Brian Halloran.

The front door of The Pointer Post that saved our lives in 1980, it still has the bullet holes to prove it.

At the time of Gary's death (from complications of diabetes), Howie was incarcerated and was refused permission to attend the funeral.

Me today, still raising hell, with my friends Hollywood stuntmen Chick Bernhard and Artie Malesci. These guys do for money what I used to do for fun. Well, the fighting part anyway.

Howie Winter and Me today.
A couple of Somerville survivors.